BOYS BE™

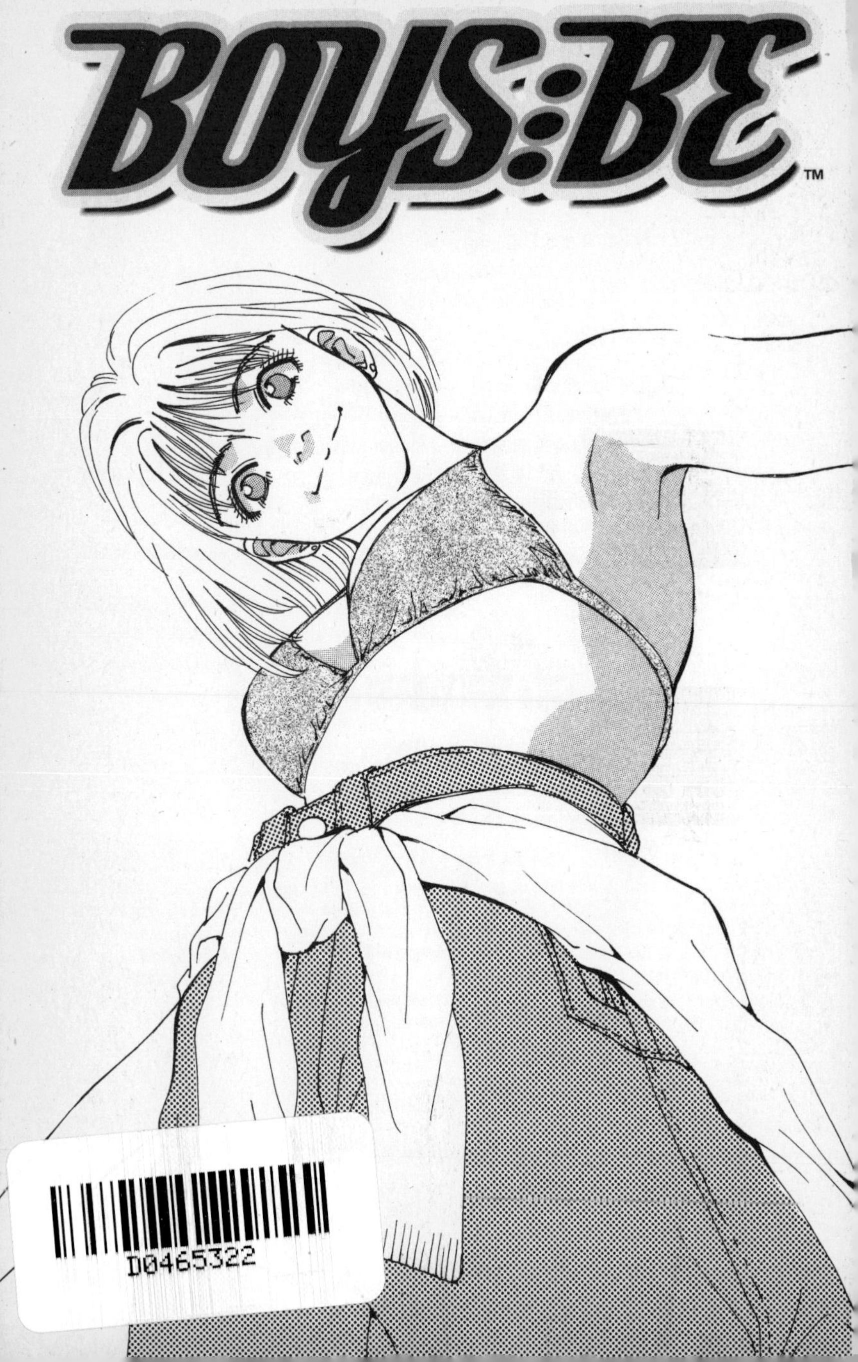

BOYS BE Second Season Vol. 1
Written by Masahiro Itabashi
Illustrated by Hiroyuki Tamakoshi

Translation - Katherine Schilling
Retouch and Lettering - Vicente Rivera Jr.
Production Artist - Yoohae Yang
Cover Design - Gary Shum

Editor - Jake Forbes
Digital Imaging Manager - Chris Buford
Pre-Press Manager - Antonio DePietro
Production Managers - Jennifer Miller and Mutsumi Miyazaki
Art Director - Matt Alford
Managing Editor - Jill Freshney
VP of Production - Ron Klamert
President and C.O.O. - John Parker
Publisher and C.E.O. - Stuart Levy

A 🐾 TOKYOPOP® Manga

TOKYOPOP Inc.
5900 Wilshire Blvd. Suite 2000
Los Angeles, CA 90036

E-mail: info@TOKYOPOP.com
Come visit us online at www.TOKYOPOP.com

ISBN: 1-59532-099-7

First TOKYOPOP printing: November 2004
10 9 8 7 6 5 4 3 2 1
Printed in the USA

BOYS BE Second Season
Vol.1

Writer
Masahiro Itabashi

Artist
Hiroyuki Tamakoshi

HAMBURG // LONDON // LOS ANGELES // TOKYO

CONTENTS

REPORT 1 Love, Piercings and Judo (Beginning)......5

REPORT 2 Love, Piercings and Judo (Middle).........29

REPORT 3 Love, Piercings and Judo (End)............53

REPORT 4 High Heel Complex.................................77

REPORT 5 Forbidden Cosplay.............................101

REPORT 6 Climax! Wanting Love Syndrome...........125

REPORT 7 A Toast to a Regrettable Night.............149

REPORT 8 Steamy, Dangerous Night.....................173

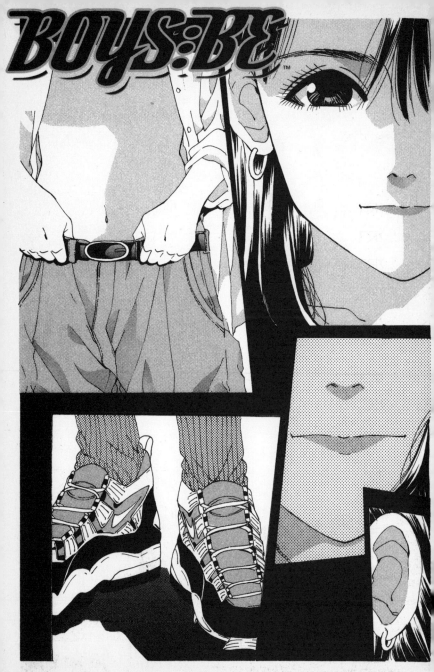

REPORT 1 Love, Piercings and Judo (Beginning)

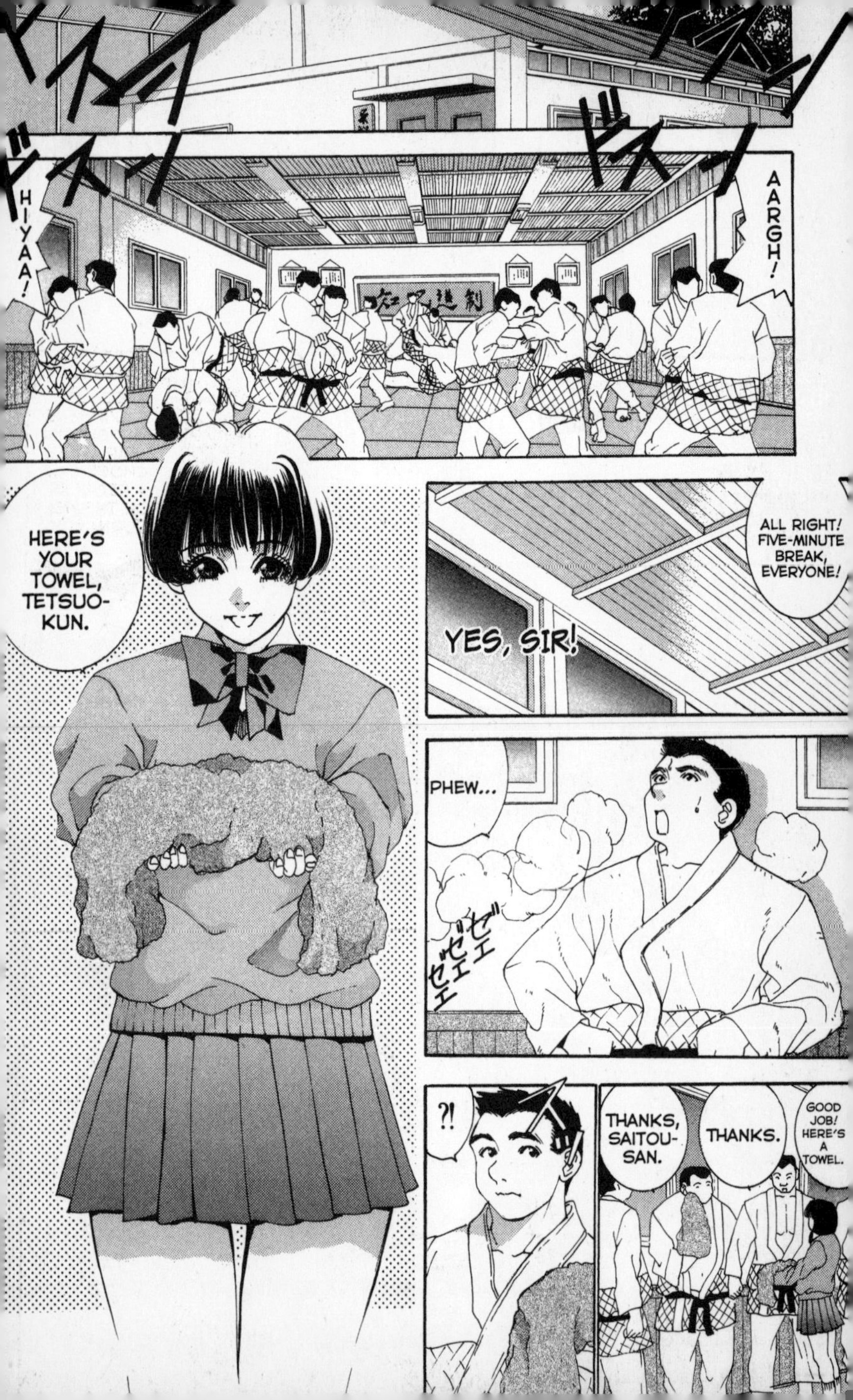
AARGH!
HIYAA!
ALL RIGHT! FIVE-MINUTE BREAK, EVERYONE!
YES, SIR!
PHEW...
GOOD JOB! HERE'S A TOWEL.
THANKS.
THANKS, SAITOU-SAN.
?!
HERE'S YOUR TOWEL, TETSUO-KUN.

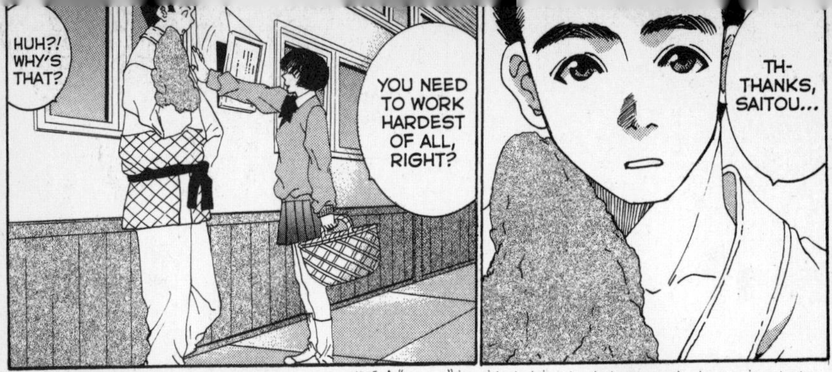
TH- THANKS, SAITOU...
YOU NEED TO WORK HARDEST OF ALL, RIGHT?
HUH?! WHY'S THAT?

NOTE: A "manager" is a girl who brings towels, keeps records, cleans equipment, etc.

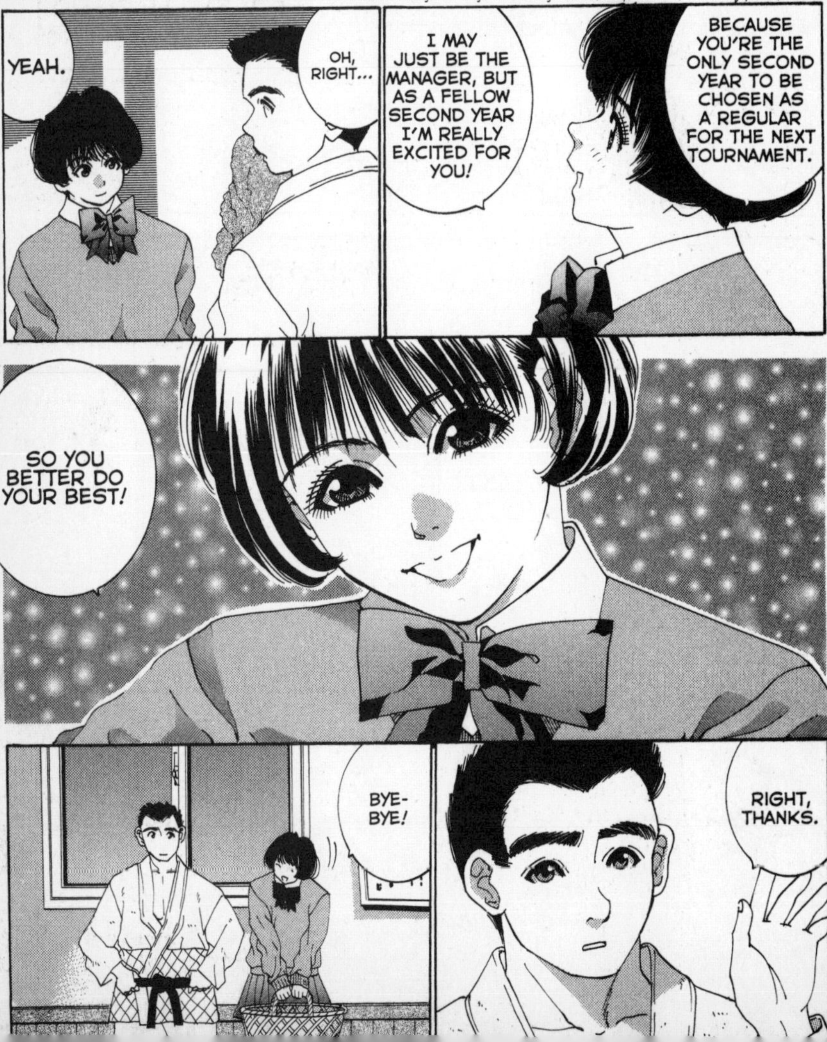
BECAUSE YOU'RE THE ONLY SECOND YEAR TO BE CHOSEN AS A REGULAR FOR THE NEXT TOURNAMENT.
I MAY JUST BE THE MANAGER, BUT AS A FELLOW SECOND YEAR I'M REALLY EXCITED FOR YOU!
OH, RIGHT...
YEAH.
SO YOU BETTER DO YOUR BEST!
RIGHT, THANKS.
BYE-BYE!

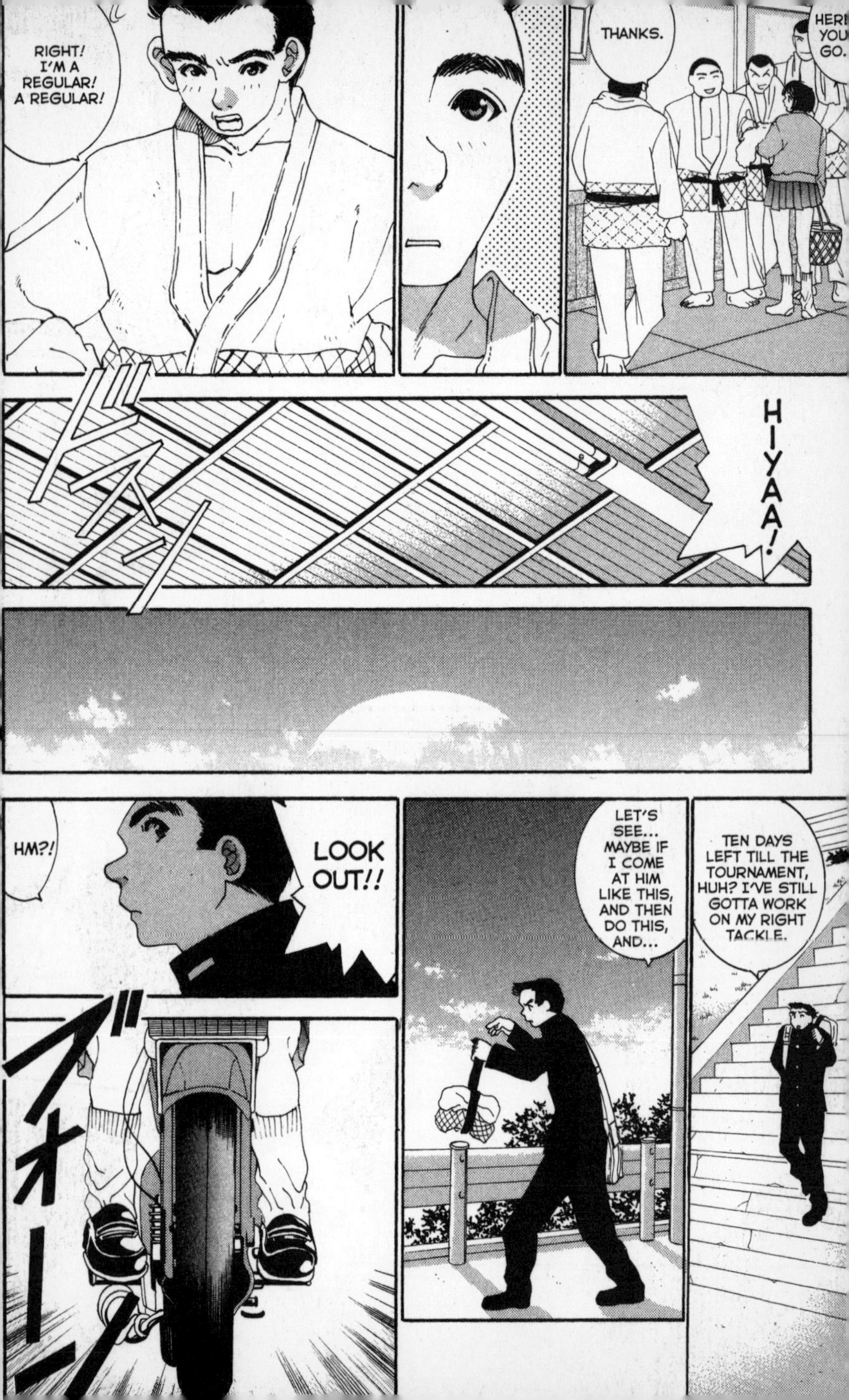
HERE YOU GO.
THANKS.
RIGHT! I'M A REGULAR! A REGULAR!
HIYAA!
TEN DAYS LEFT TILL THE TOURNAMENT, HUH? I'VE STILL GOTTA WORK ON MY RIGHT TACKLE.
LET'S SEE... MAYBE IF I COME AT HIM LIKE THIS, AND THEN DO THIS, AND...
LOOK OUT!!
HM?!

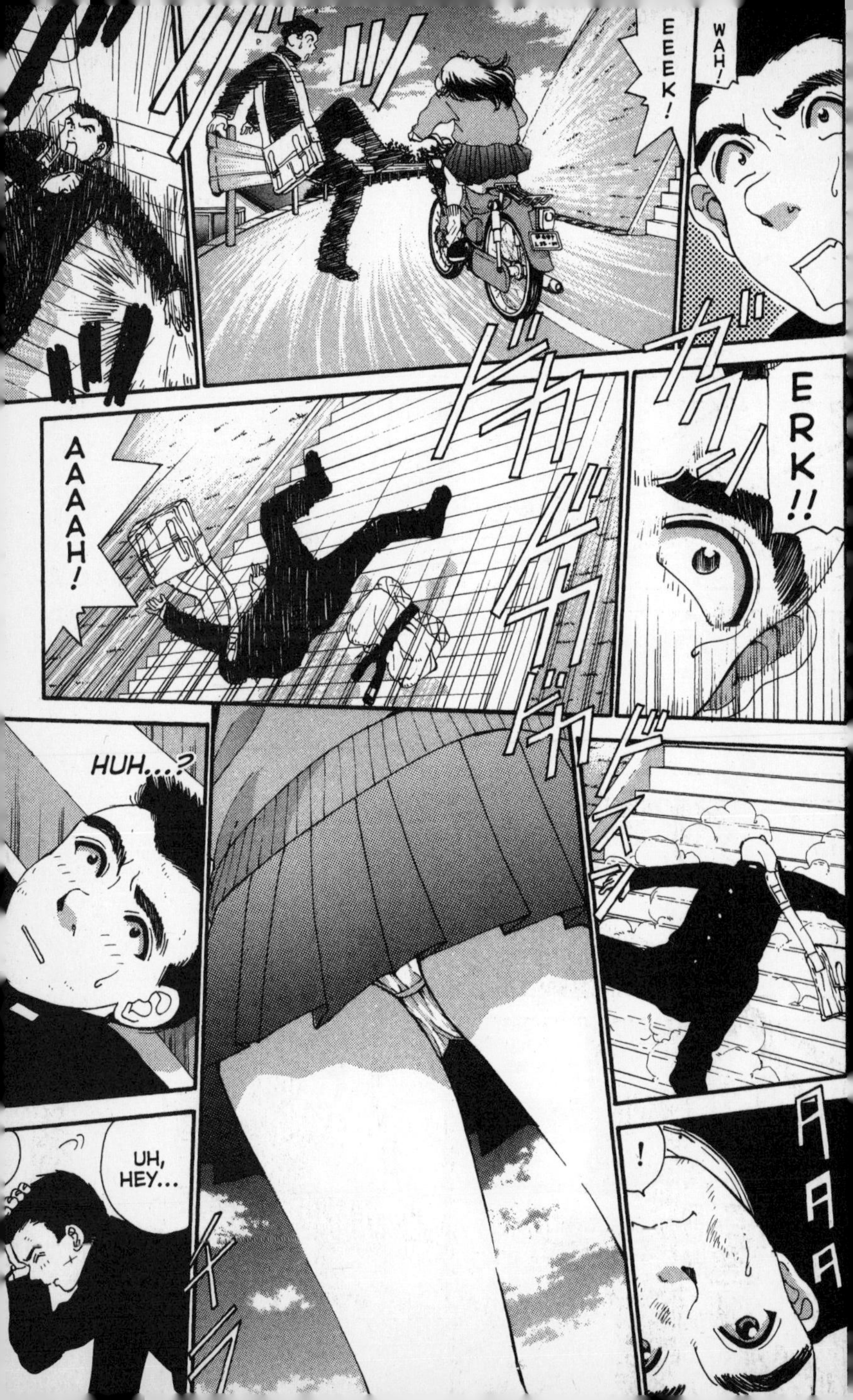
WAH!
EEEK!
ERK!!
AAAAAH!
!
AAAA
HUH...?
UH, HEY...

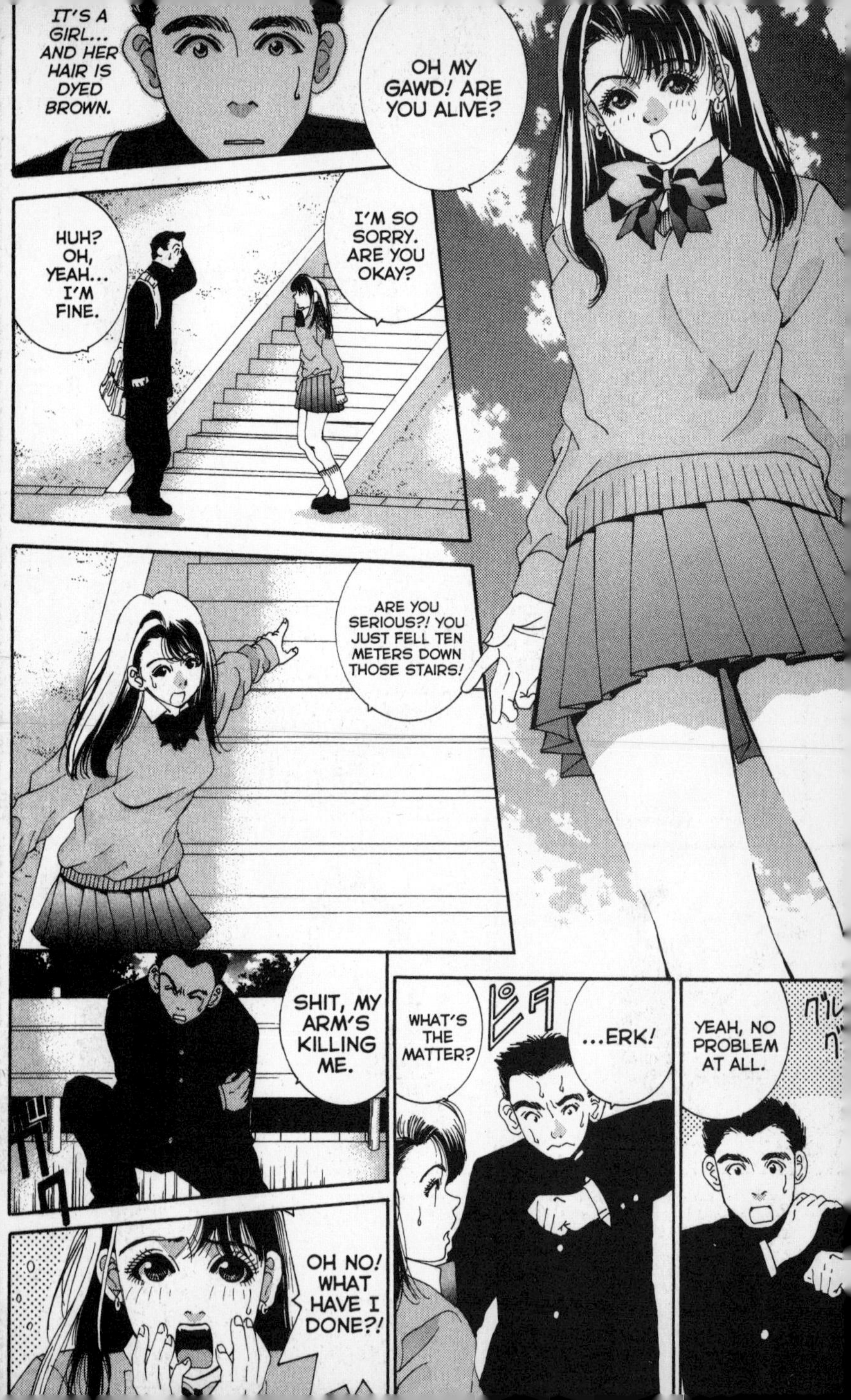
OH MY GAWD! ARE YOU ALIVE?
IT'S A GIRL... AND HER HAIR IS DYED BROWN.
I'M SO SORRY. ARE YOU OKAY?
HUH? OH, YEAH... I'M FINE.
ARE YOU SERIOUS?! YOU JUST FELL TEN METERS DOWN THOSE STAIRS!
YEAH, NO PROBLEM AT ALL.
...ERK!
ピタ
WHAT'S THE MATTER?
SHIT, MY ARM'S KILLING ME.
OH NO! WHAT HAVE I DONE?!

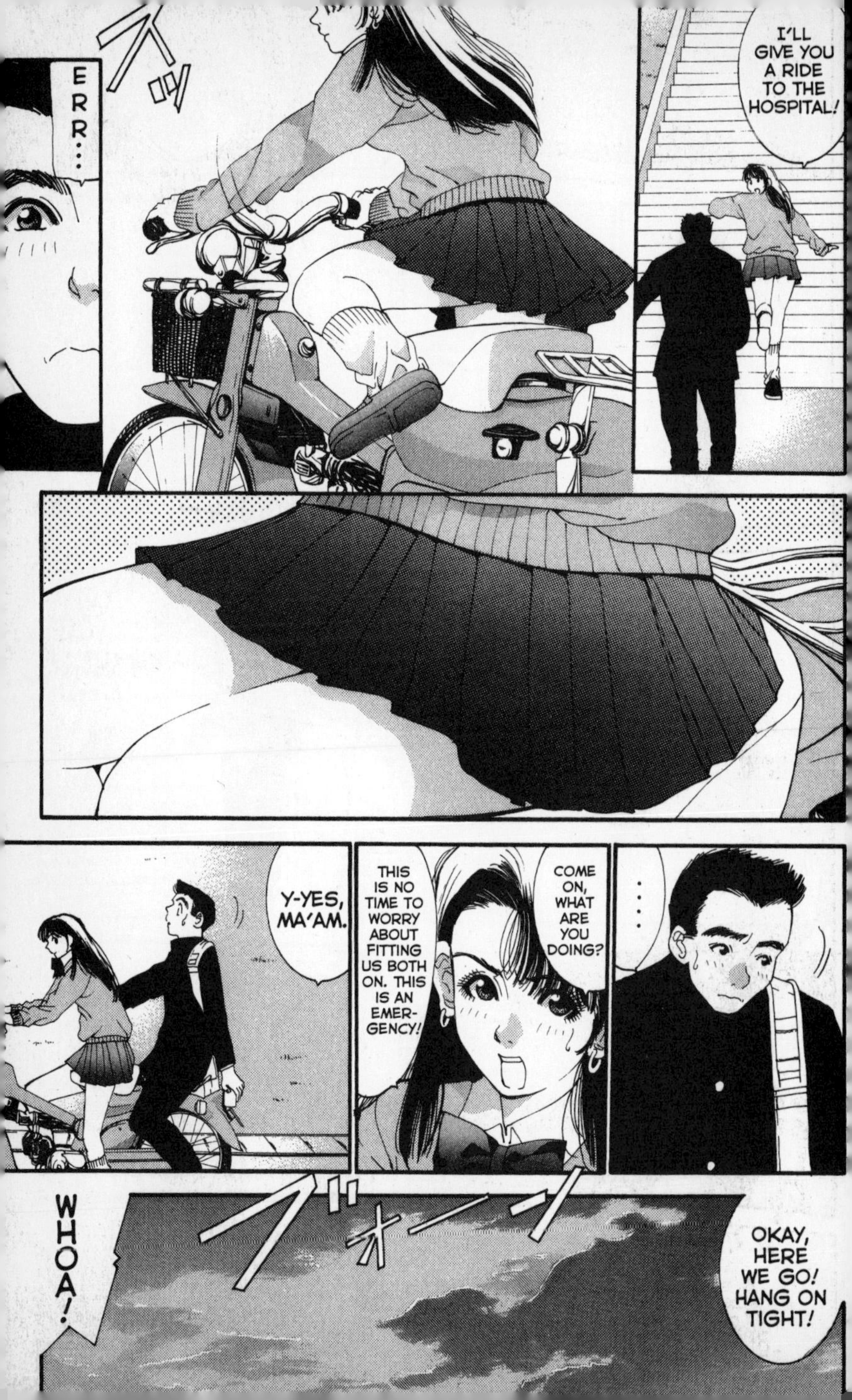
I'LL GIVE YOU A RIDE TO THE HOSPITAL!
ERR...
....
COME ON, WHAT ARE YOU DOING?
THIS IS NO TIME TO WORRY ABOUT FITTING US BOTH ON. THIS IS AN EMER-GENCY!
Y-YES, MA'AM.
OKAY, HERE WE GO! HANG ON TIGHT!
WHOA!

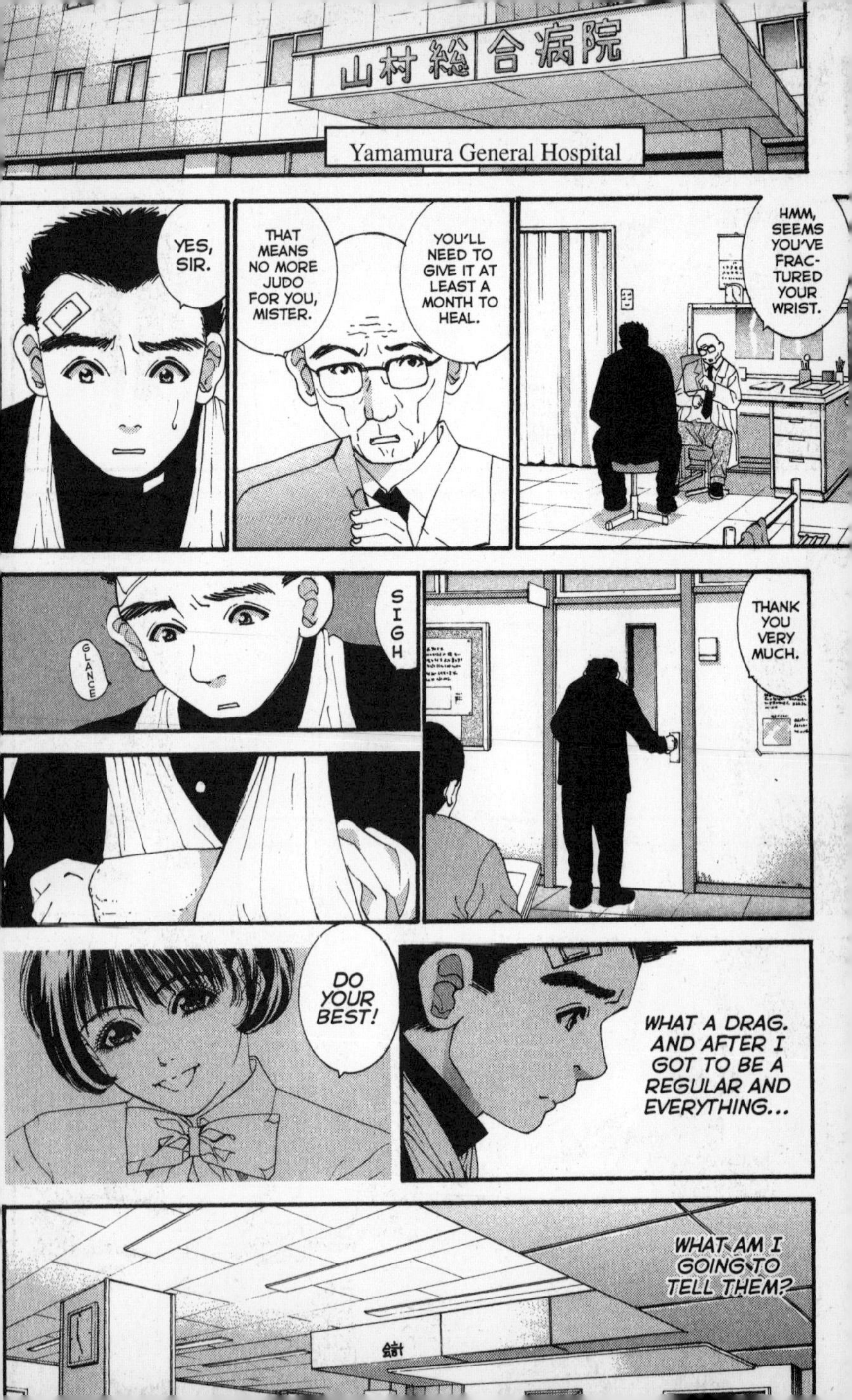
山村総合病院
Yamamura General Hospital
HMM, SEEMS YOU'VE FRAC- TURED YOUR WRIST.
YOU'LL NEED TO GIVE IT AT LEAST A MONTH TO HEAL.
THAT MEANS NO MORE JUDO FOR YOU, MISTER.
YES, SIR.
THANK YOU VERY MUCH.
SIGH
GLANCE
WHAT A DRAG. AND AFTER I GOT TO BE A REGULAR AND EVERYTHING...
DO YOUR BEST!
WHAT AM I GOING TO TELL THEM?

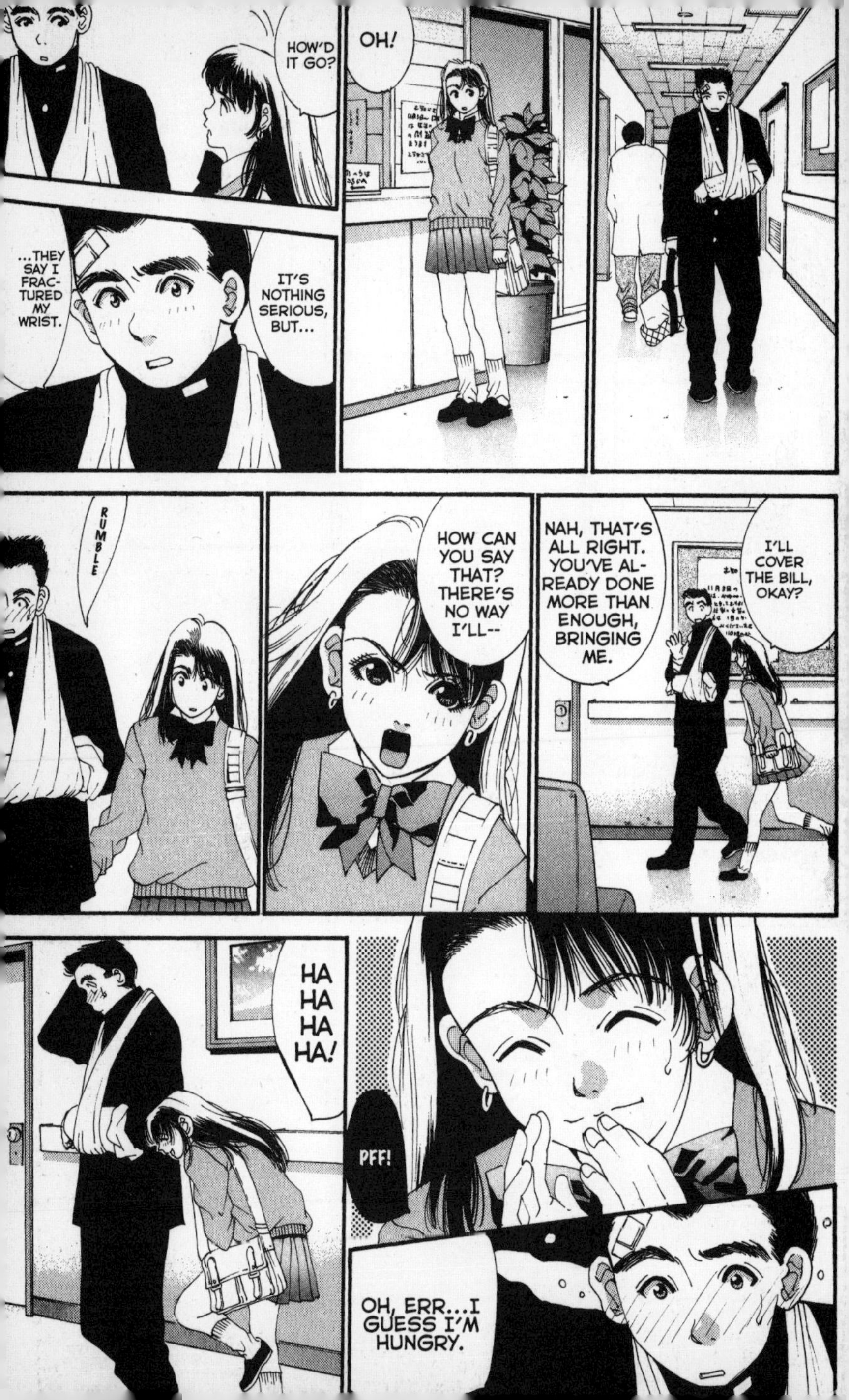
OH!
HOW'D IT GO?
IT'S NOTHING SERIOUS, BUT...
...THEY SAY I FRAC-TURED MY WRIST.
I'LL COVER THE BILL, OKAY?
NAH, THAT'S ALL RIGHT. YOU'VE AL-READY DONE MORE THAN ENOUGH, BRINGING ME.
HOW CAN YOU SAY THAT? THERE'S NO WAY I'LL--
RUMBLE
PFF!
OH, ERR...I GUESS I'M HUNGRY.
HA HA HA HA!

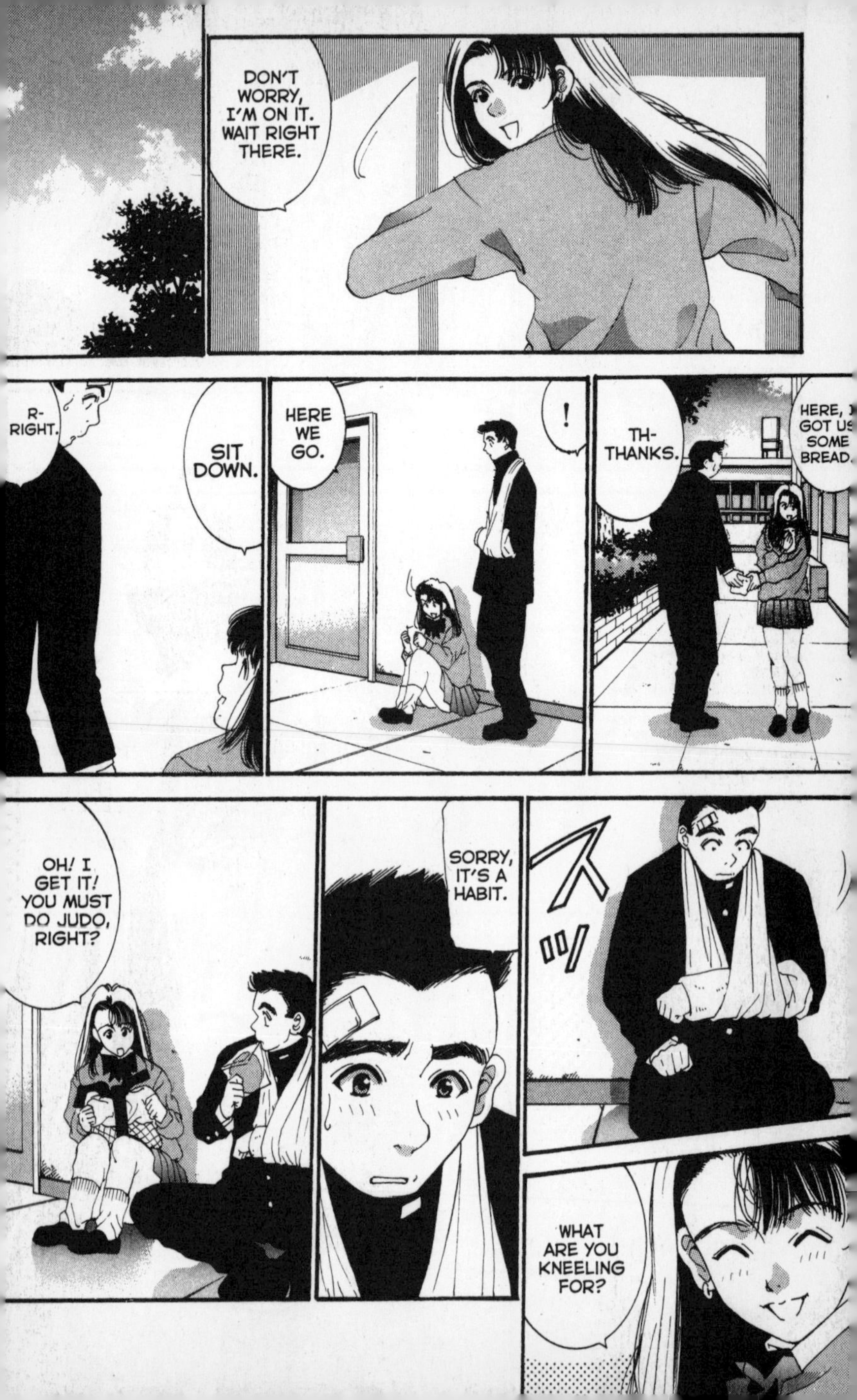
DON'T WORRY, I'M ON IT. WAIT RIGHT THERE.
HERE, I GOT US SOME BREAD.
TH- THANKS.
!
HERE WE GO.
SIT DOWN.
R- RIGHT.
WHAT ARE YOU KNEELING FOR?
SORRY, IT'S A HABIT.
OH! I GET IT! YOU MUST DO JUDO, RIGHT?

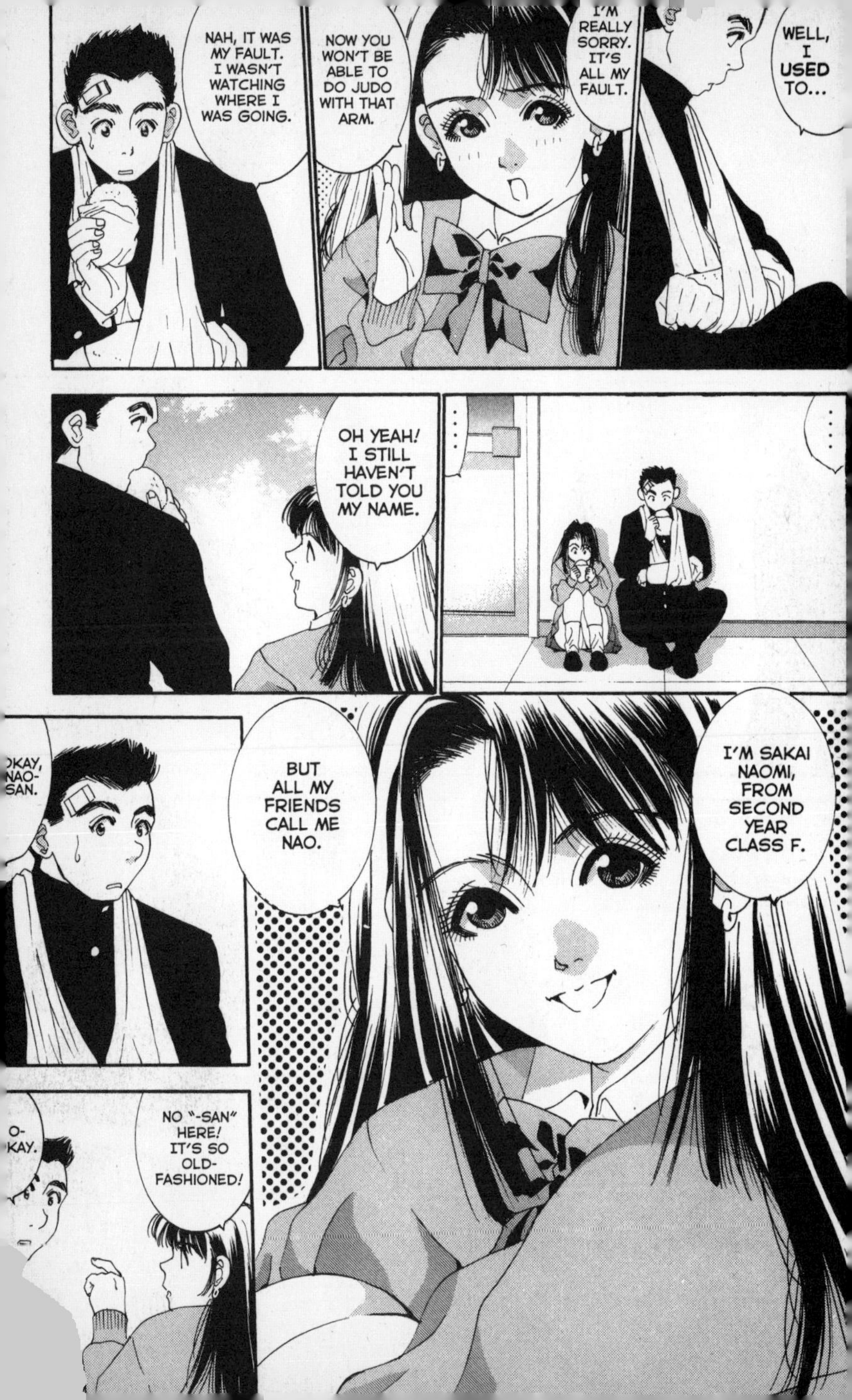

WELL, I USED TO...
I'M REALLY SORRY. IT'S ALL MY FAULT.
NOW YOU WON'T BE ABLE TO DO JUDO WITH THAT ARM.
NAH, IT WAS MY FAULT. I WASN'T WATCHING WHERE I WAS GOING.
....
....
OH YEAH! I STILL HAVEN'T TOLD YOU MY NAME.
I'M SAKAI NAOMI, FROM SECOND YEAR CLASS F.
BUT ALL MY FRIENDS CALL ME NAO.
OKAY, NAO-SAN.
NO "-SAN" HERE! IT'S SO OLD-FASHIONED!
O-KAY.

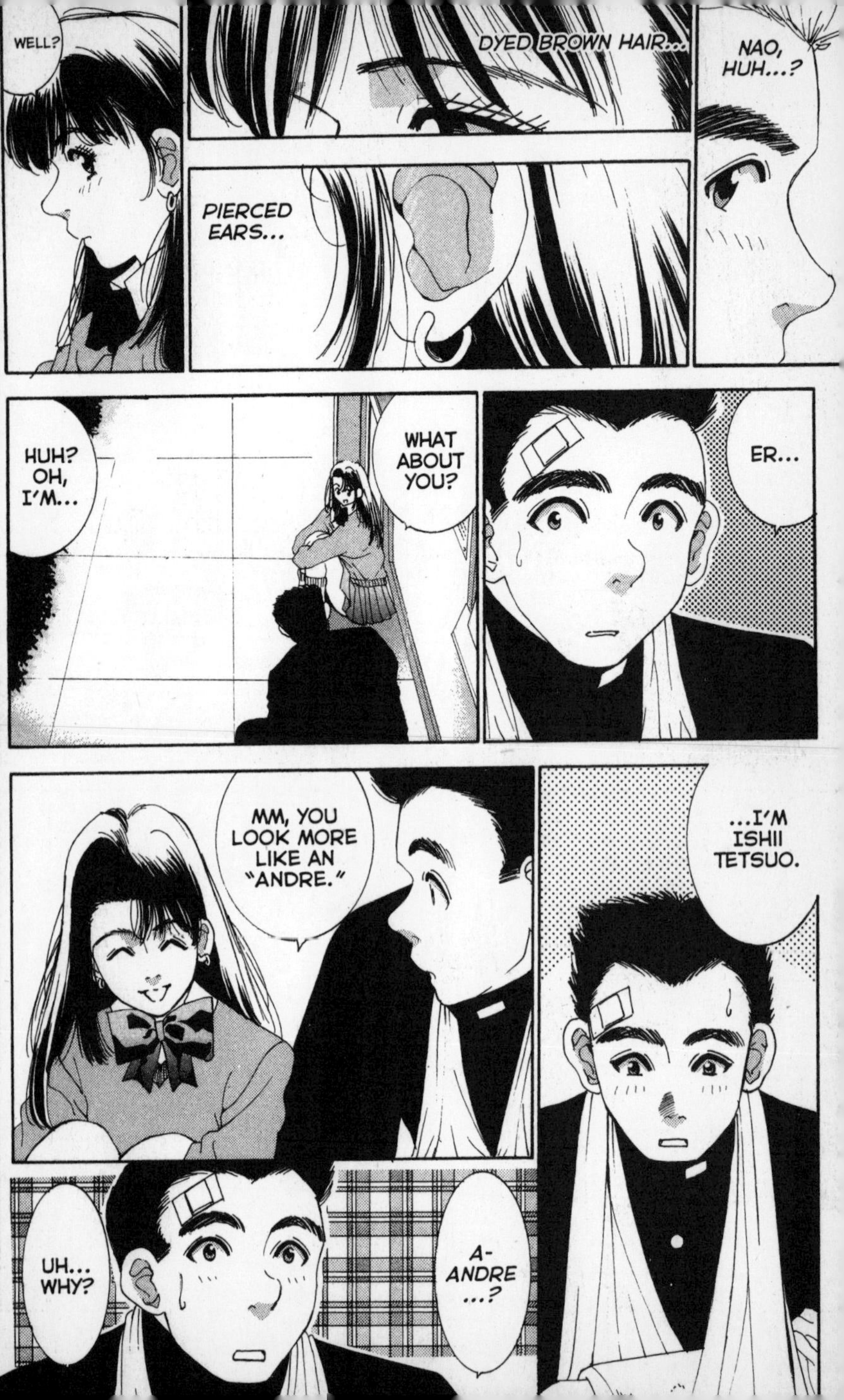
NAO, HUH...?
DYED BROWN HAIR...
PIERCED EARS...
WELL?
ER...
WHAT ABOUT YOU?
HUH? OH, I'M...
...I'M ISHII TETSUO.
MM, YOU LOOK MORE LIKE AN "ANDRE."
A-ANDRE...?
UH... WHY?

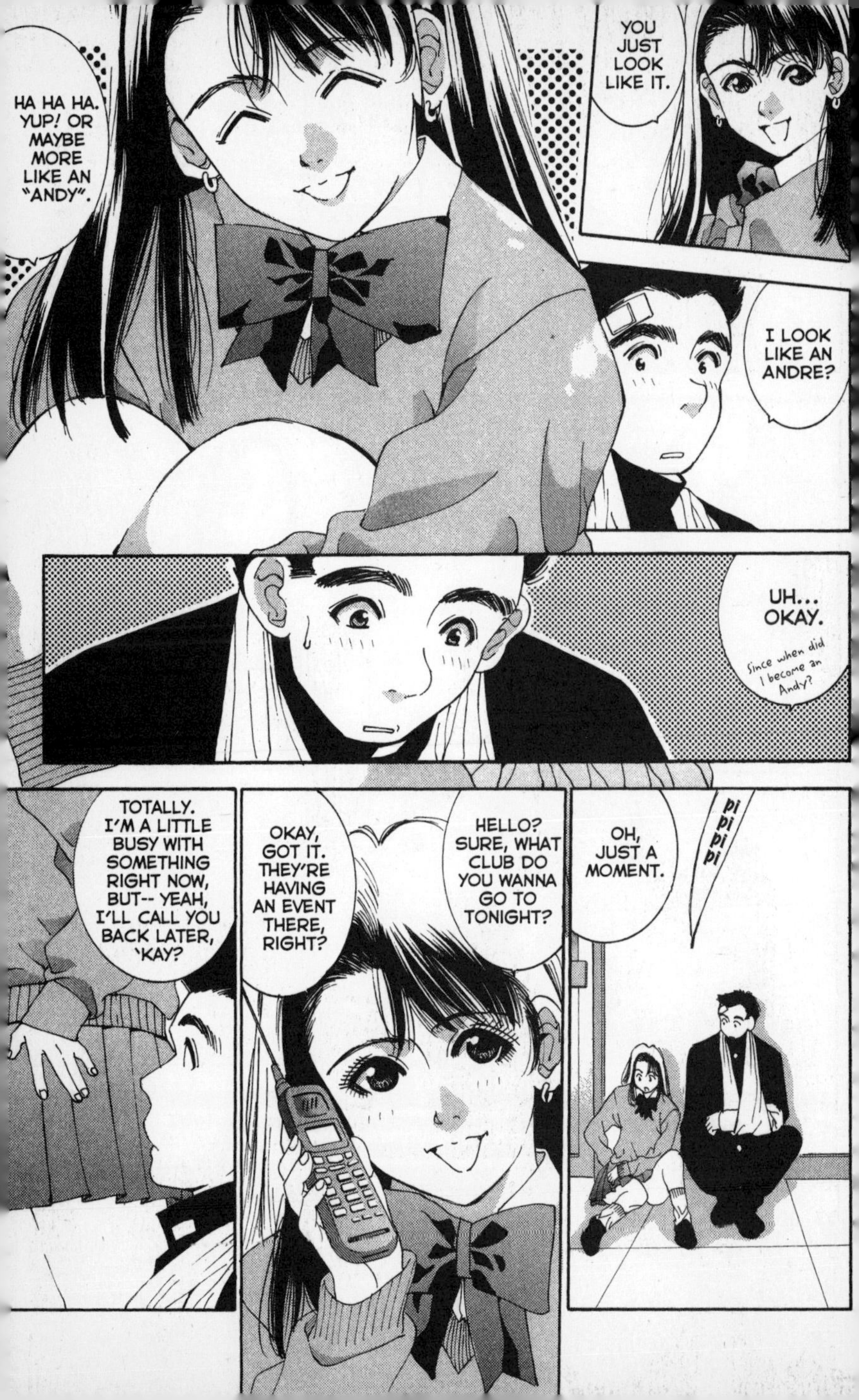
YOU JUST LOOK LIKE IT.
I LOOK LIKE AN ANDRE?
HA HA HA. YUP! OR MAYBE MORE LIKE AN "ANDY".
UH... OKAY.
Since when did I become an Andy?
pi pi pi pi
OH, JUST A MOMENT.
HELLO? SURE, WHAT CLUB DO YOU WANNA GO TO TONIGHT?
OKAY, GOT IT. THEY'RE HAVING AN EVENT THERE, RIGHT?
TOTALLY. I'M A LITTLE BUSY WITH SOMETHING RIGHT NOW, BUT-- YEAH, I'LL CALL YOU BACK LATER, 'KAY?

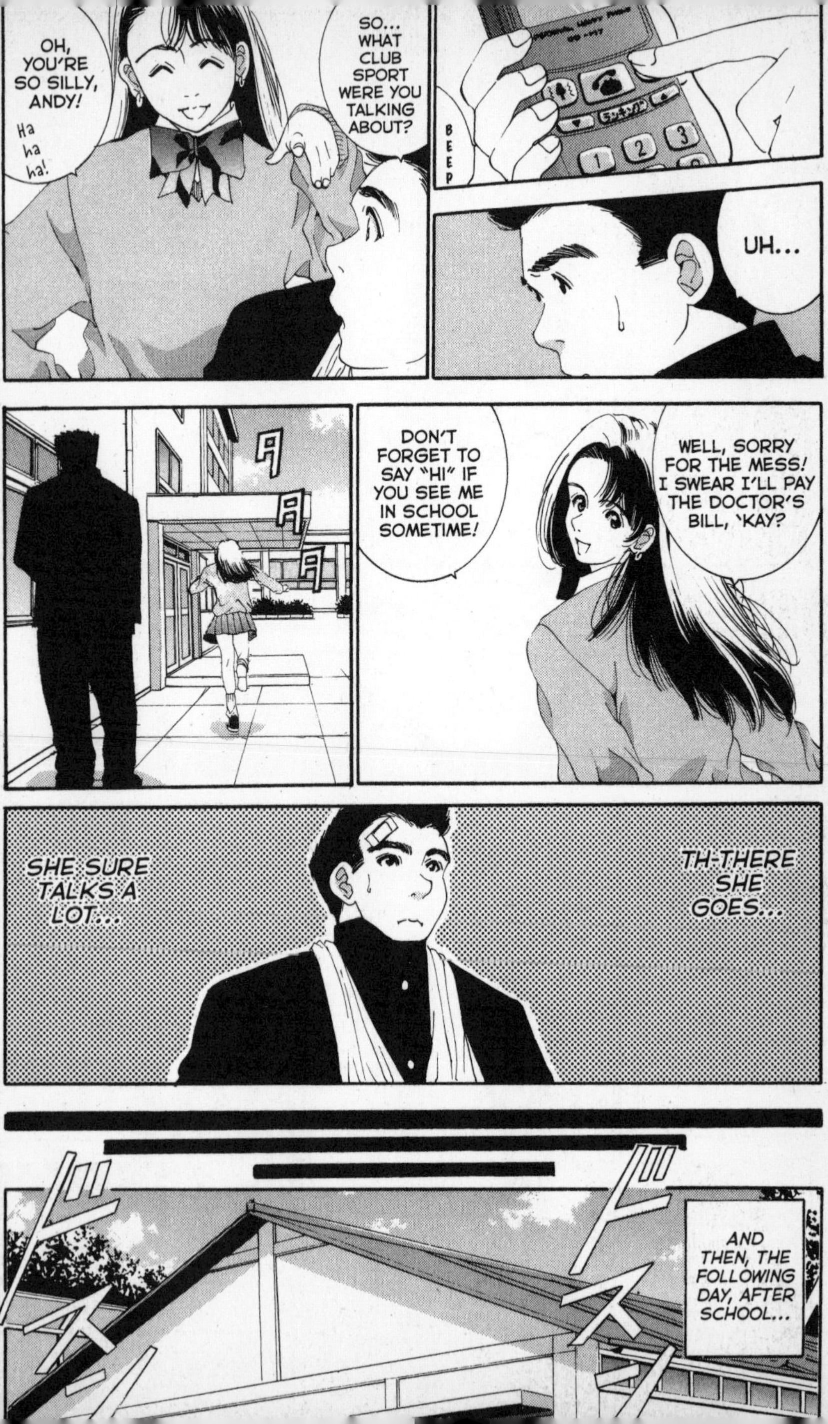
BEEP
UH...
SO... WHAT CLUB SPORT WERE YOU TALKING ABOUT?
OH, YOU'RE SO SILLY, ANDY!
Ha ha ha!
WELL, SORRY FOR THE MESS! I SWEAR I'LL PAY THE DOCTOR'S BILL, 'KAY?
DON'T FORGET TO SAY "HI" IF YOU SEE ME IN SCHOOL SOMETIME!
TH-THERE SHE GOES...
SHE SURE TALKS A LOT...
AND THEN, THE FOLLOWING DAY, AFTER SCHOOL...

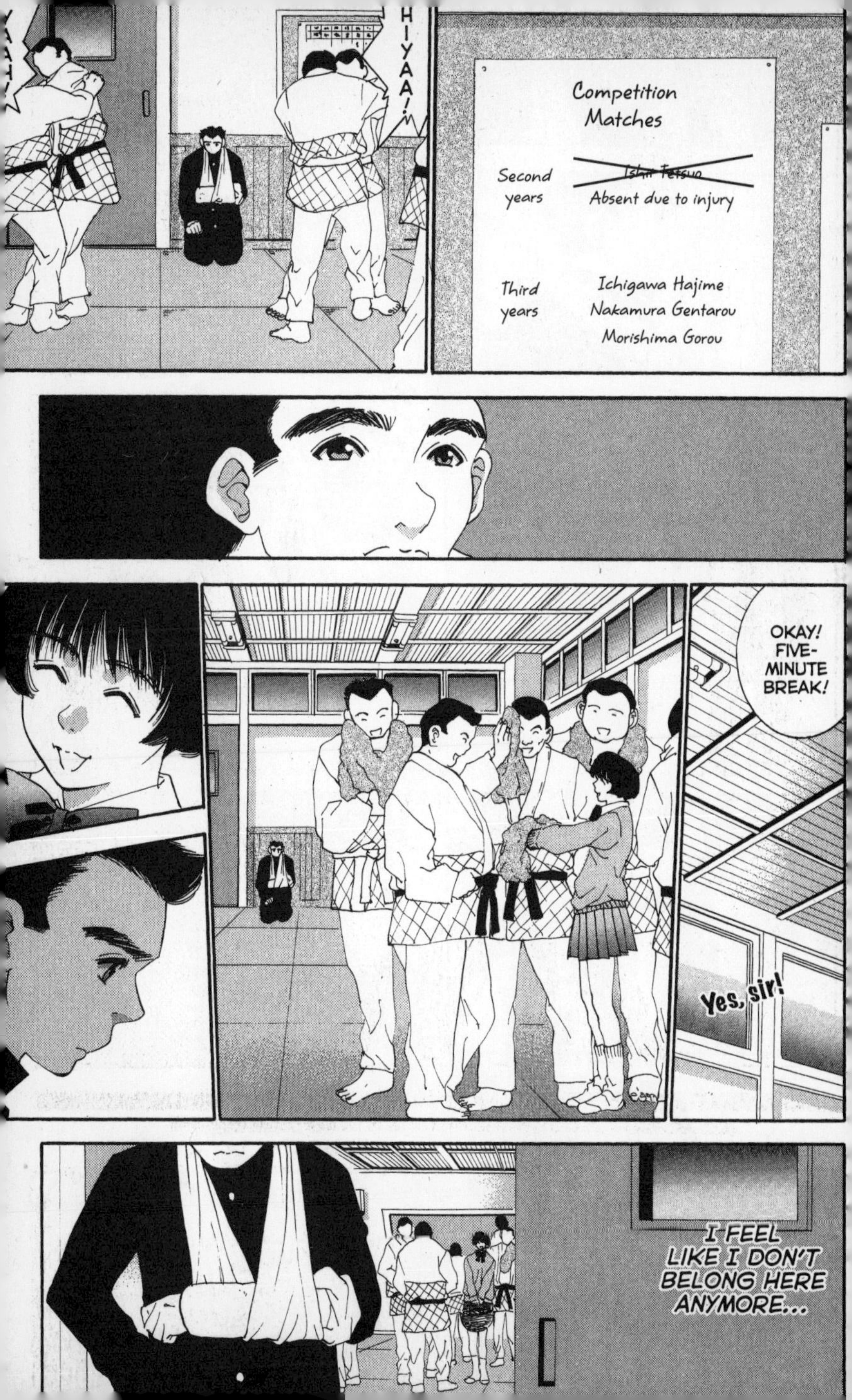
Competition Matches
Second years
~~Ishii Tetsuo~~
Absent due to injury
Third years
Ichigawa Hajime
Nakamura Gentarou
Morishima Gorou
HIYAAA!
OKAY! FIVE-MINUTE BREAK!
Yes, sir!
I FEEL LIKE I DON'T BELONG HERE ANYMORE...

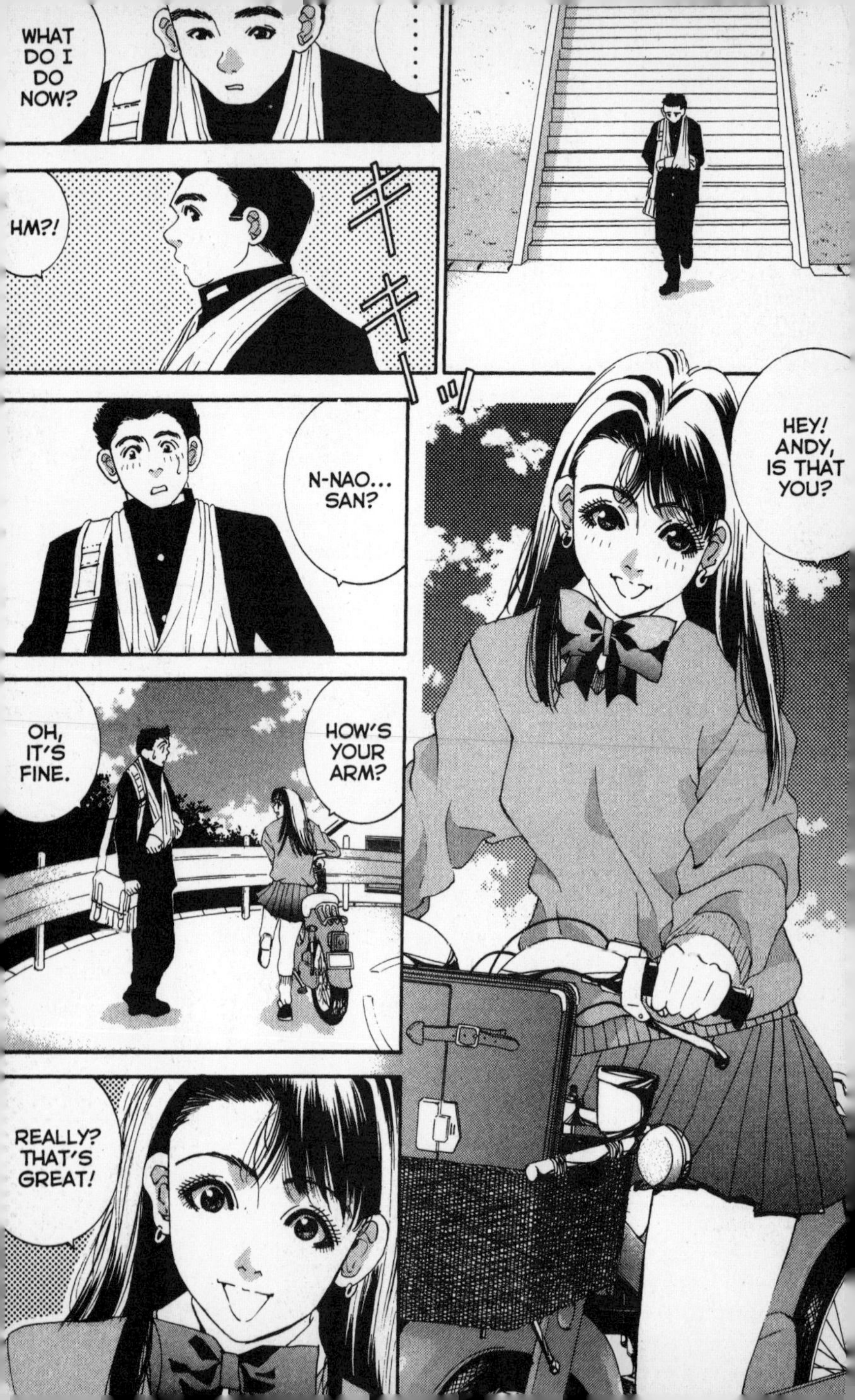
.....
WHAT DO I DO NOW?
キキーッ
HM?!
HEY! ANDY, IS THAT YOU?
N-NAO... SAN?
HOW'S YOUR ARM?
OH, IT'S FINE.
REALLY? THAT'S GREAT!

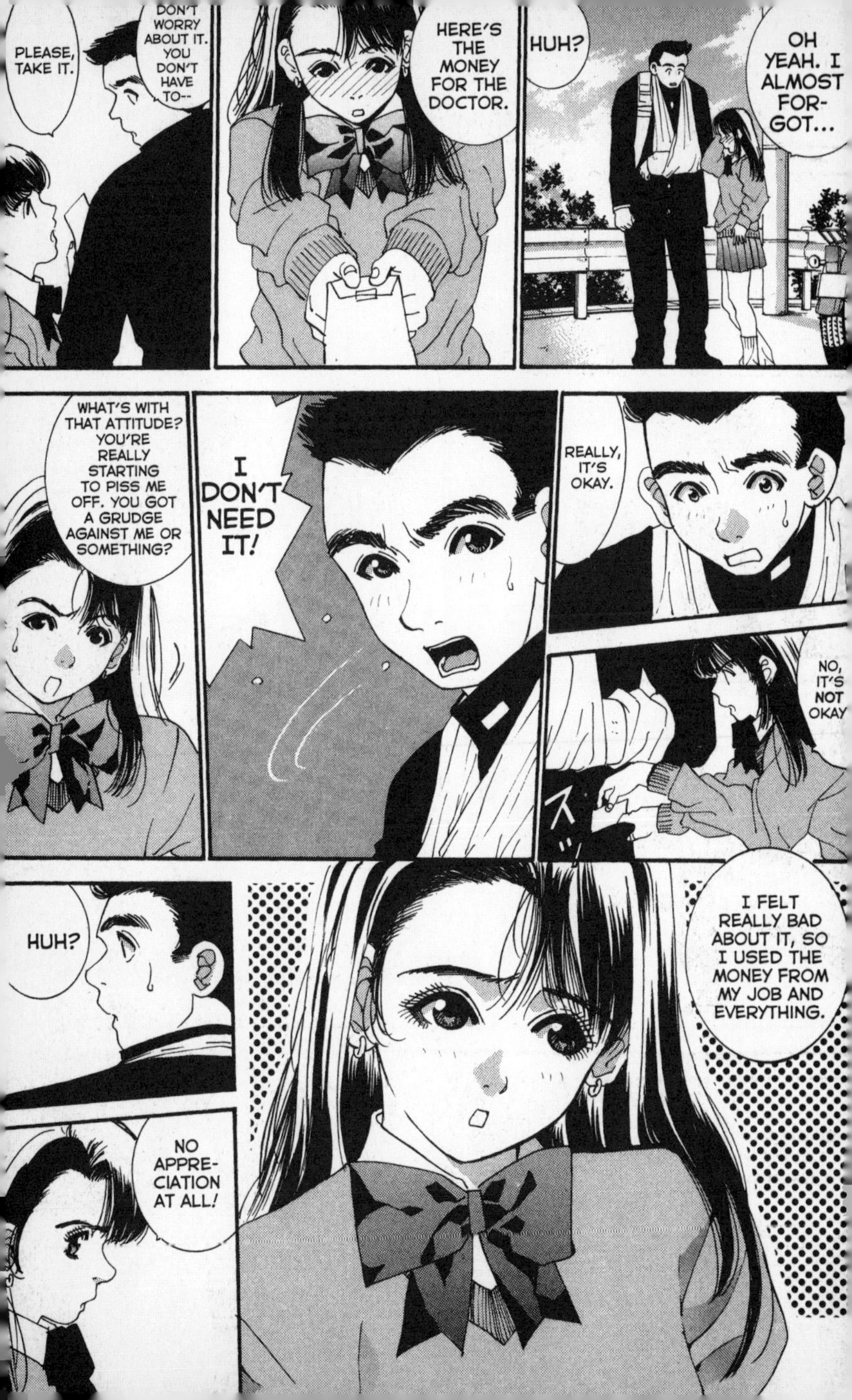
OH YEAH. I ALMOST FOR-GOT...
HUH?
HERE'S THE MONEY FOR THE DOCTOR.
DON'T WORRY ABOUT IT. YOU DON'T HAVE TO--
PLEASE, TAKE IT.
REALLY, IT'S OKAY.
NO, IT'S NOT OKAY
I DON'T NEED IT!
WHAT'S WITH THAT ATTITUDE? YOU'RE REALLY STARTING TO PISS ME OFF. YOU GOT A GRUDGE AGAINST ME OR SOMETHING?
I FELT REALLY BAD ABOUT IT, SO I USED THE MONEY FROM MY JOB AND EVERYTHING.
HUH?
NO APPRE-CIATION AT ALL!

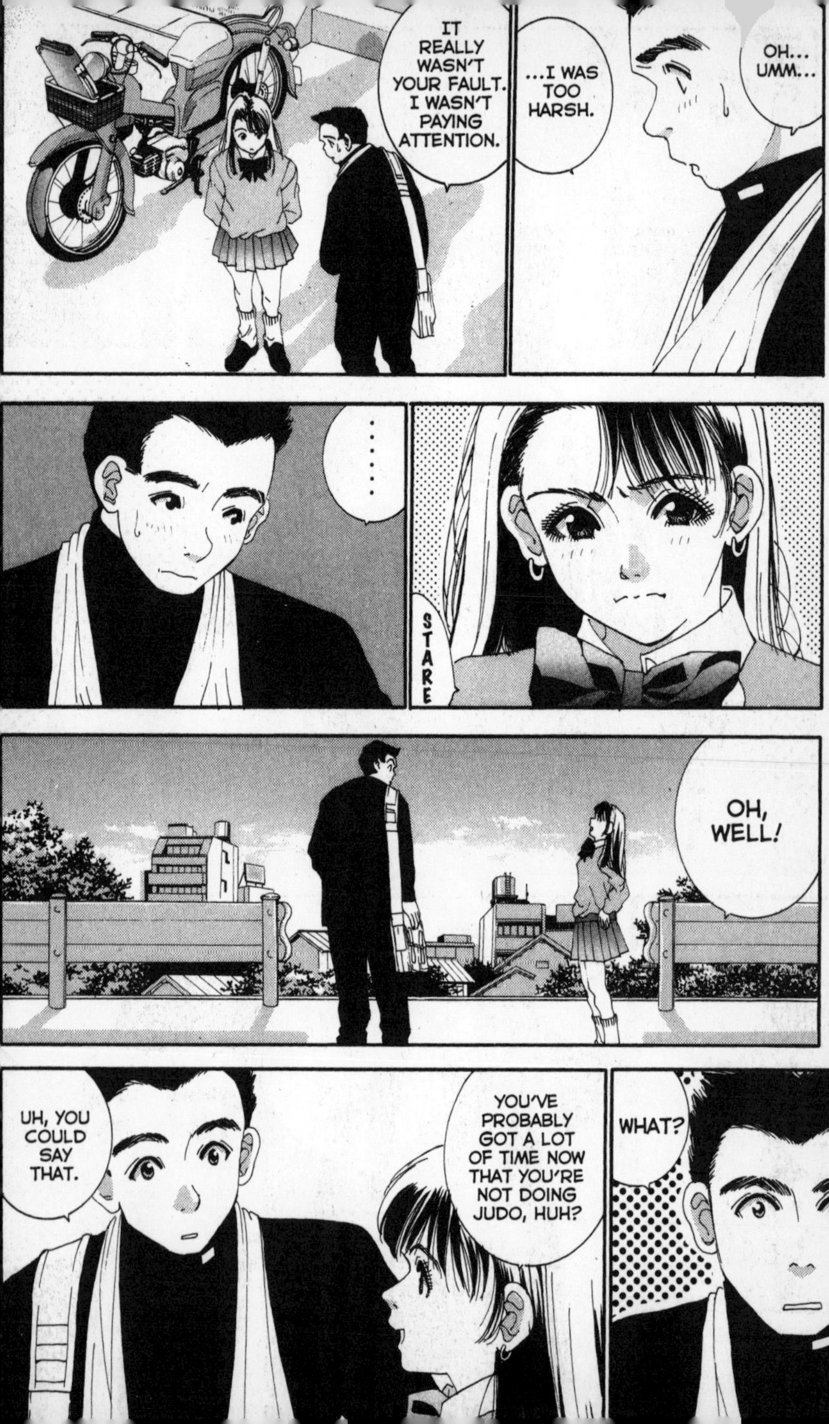
OH... UMM...
...I WAS TOO HARSH.
IT REALLY WASN'T YOUR FAULT. I WASN'T PAYING ATTENTION.
STARE
......
OH, WELL!
WHAT?
YOU'VE PROBABLY GOT A LOT OF TIME NOW THAT YOU'RE NOT DOING JUDO, HUH?
UH, YOU COULD SAY THAT.

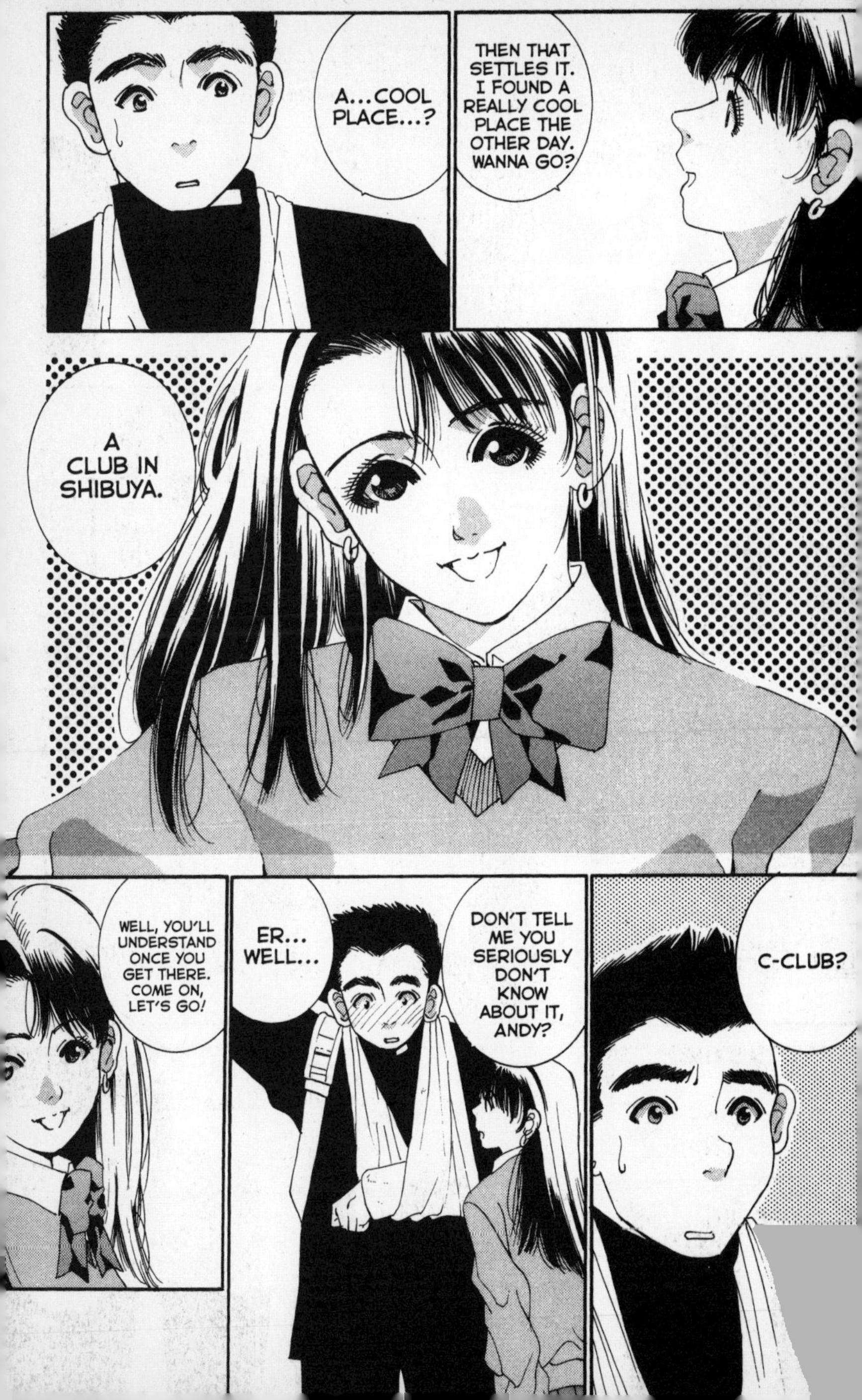
THEN THAT SETTLES IT. I FOUND A REALLY COOL PLACE THE OTHER DAY. WANNA GO?
A...COOL PLACE...?
A CLUB IN SHIBUYA.
C-CLUB?
DON'T TELL ME YOU SERIOUSLY DON'T KNOW ABOUT IT, ANDY?
ER... WELL...
WELL, YOU'LL UNDERSTAND ONCE YOU GET THERE. COME ON, LET'S GO!

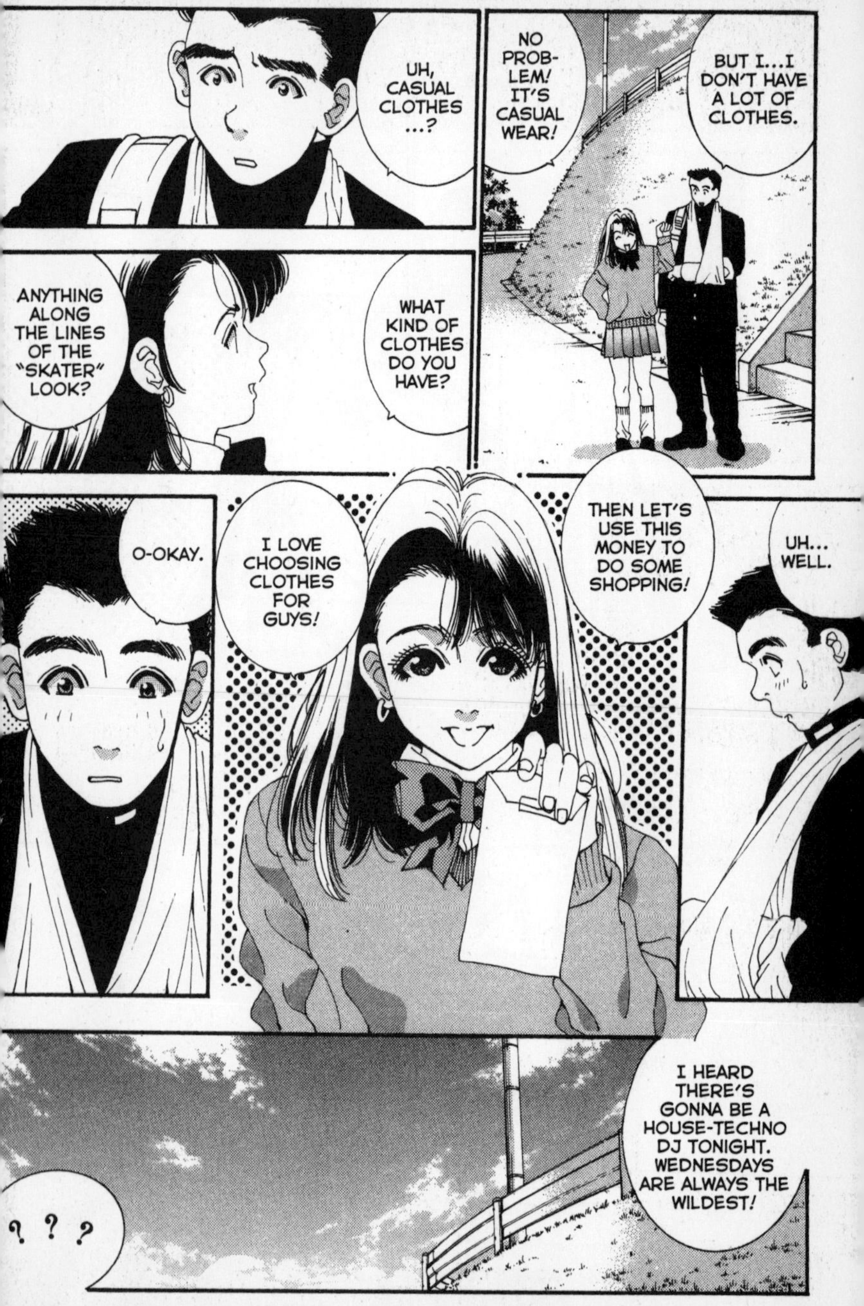
BUT I...I DON'T HAVE A LOT OF CLOTHES.
NO PROB-LEM! IT'S CASUAL WEAR!
UH, CASUAL CLOTHES ...?
WHAT KIND OF CLOTHES DO YOU HAVE?
ANYTHING ALONG THE LINES OF THE "SKATER" LOOK?
UH... WELL.
THEN LET'S USE THIS MONEY TO DO SOME SHOPPING!
I LOVE CHOOSING CLOTHES FOR GUYS!
O-OKAY.
I HEARD THERE'S GONNA BE A HOUSE-TECHNO DJ TONIGHT. WEDNESDAYS ARE ALWAYS THE WILDEST!
? ? ?

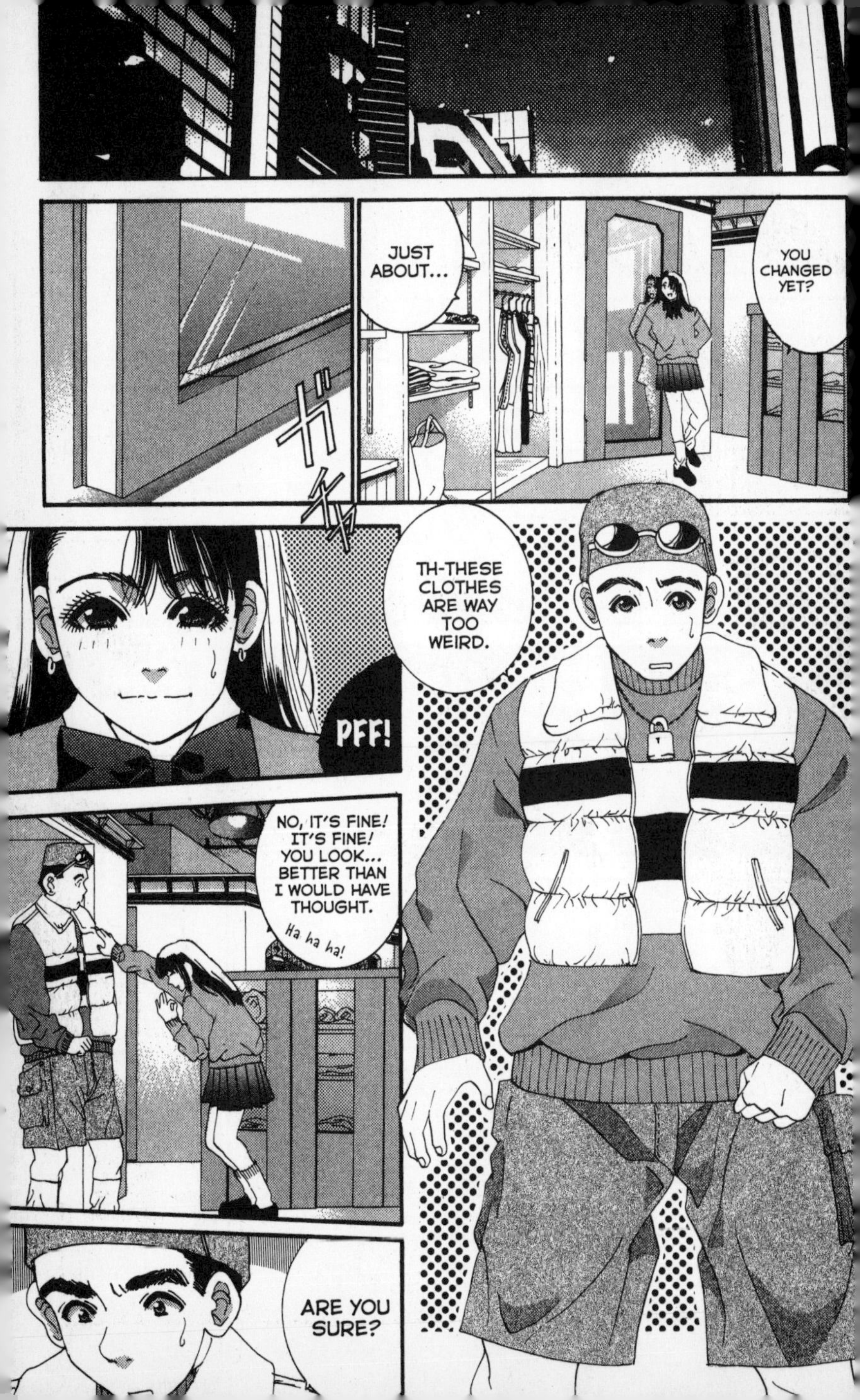
YOU CHANGED YET?
JUST ABOUT...
TH-THESE CLOTHES ARE WAY TOO WEIRD.
PFF!
NO, IT'S FINE! IT'S FINE! YOU LOOK... BETTER THAN I WOULD HAVE THOUGHT.
Ha ha ha!
ARE YOU SURE?

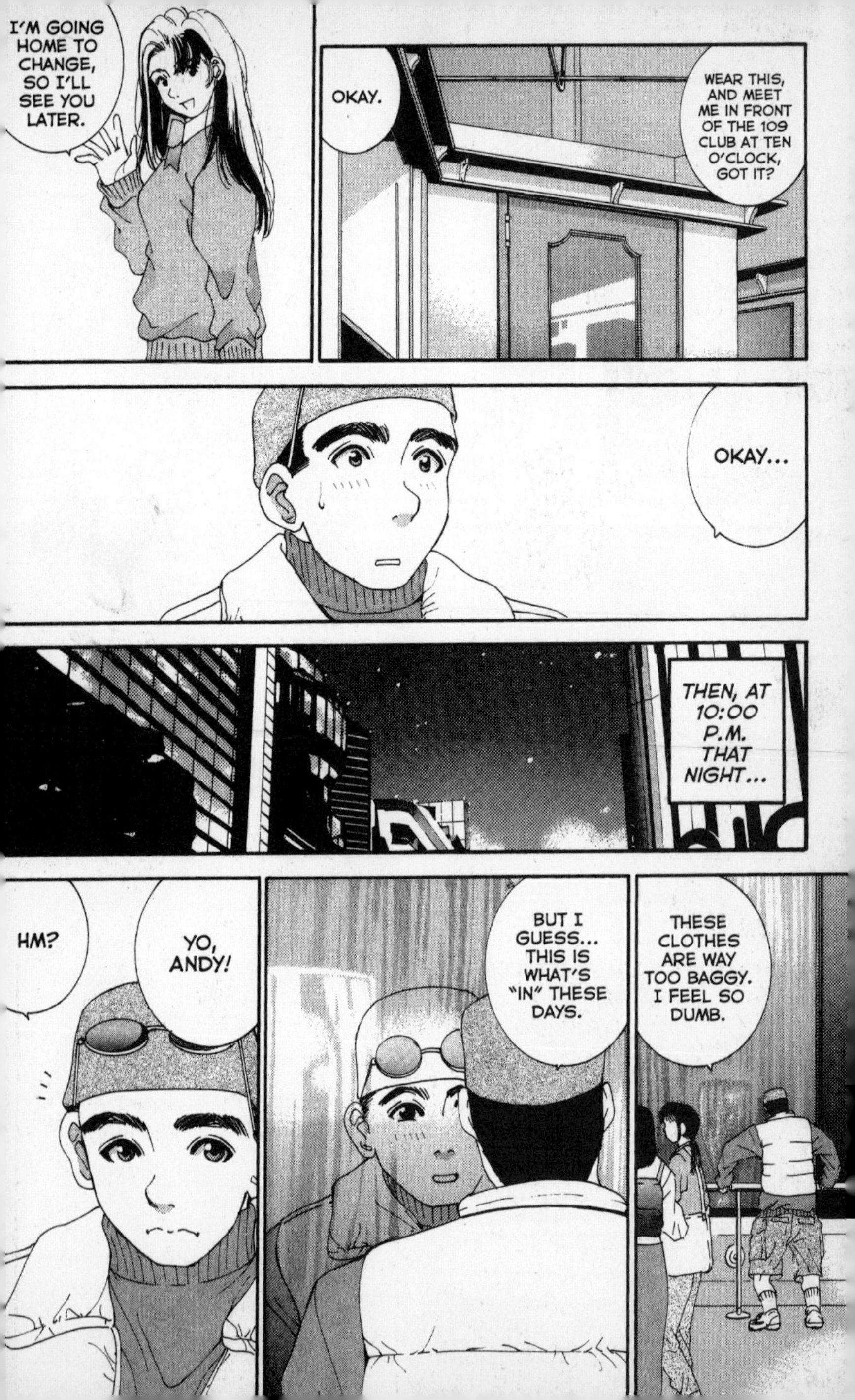
WEAR THIS, AND MEET ME IN FRONT OF THE 109 CLUB AT TEN O'CLOCK, GOT IT?
OKAY.
I'M GOING HOME TO CHANGE, SO I'LL SEE YOU LATER.
OKAY...
THEN, AT 10:00 P.M. THAT NIGHT...
THESE CLOTHES ARE WAY TOO BAGGY. I FEEL SO DUMB.
BUT I GUESS... THIS IS WHAT'S "IN" THESE DAYS.
YO, ANDY!
HM?

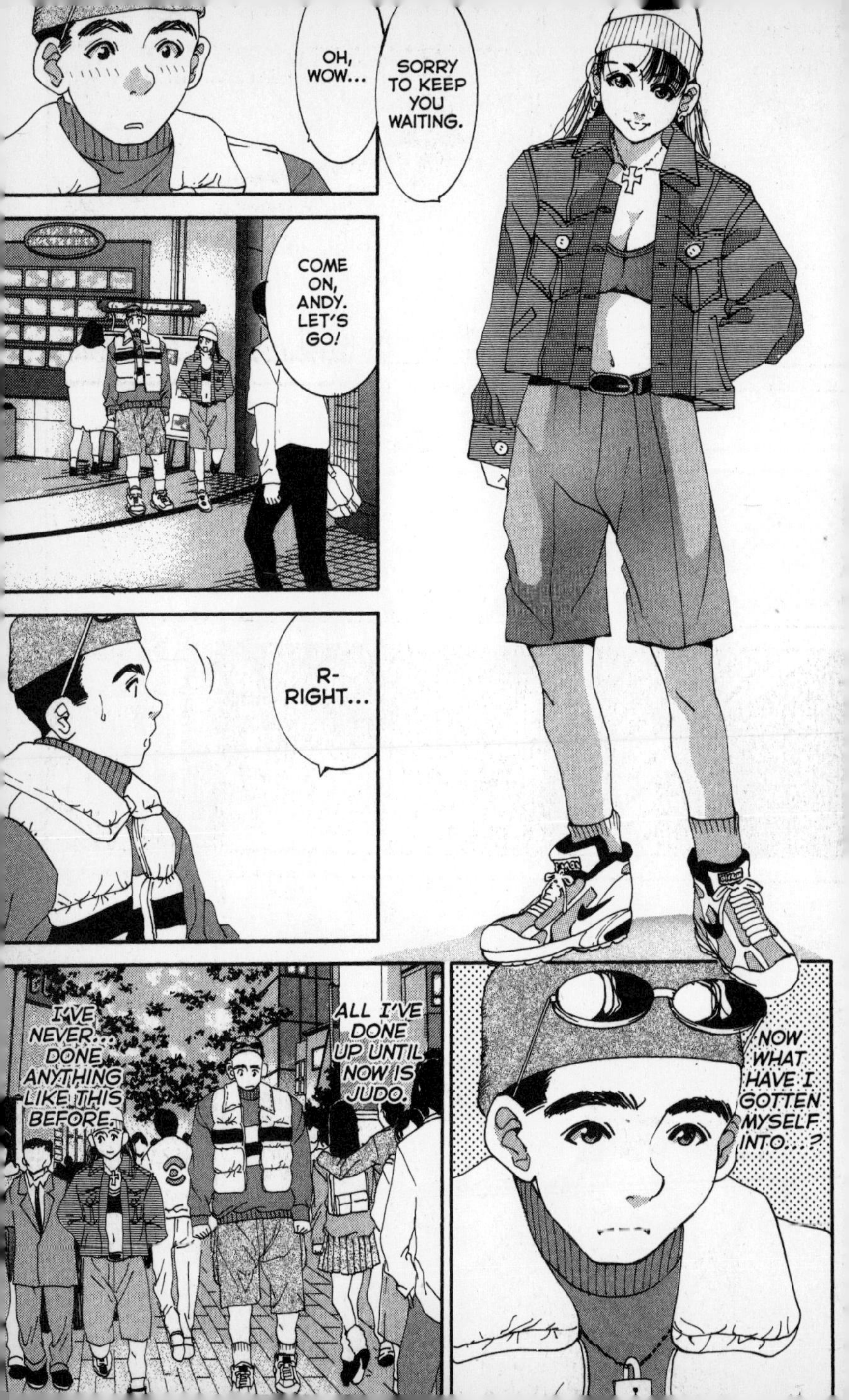
SORRY TO KEEP YOU WAITING.
OH, WOW...
COME ON, ANDY. LET'S GO!
R- RIGHT...
NOW WHAT HAVE I GOTTEN MYSELF INTO...?
ALL I'VE DONE UP UNTIL NOW IS JUDO.
I'VE NEVER... DONE ANYTHING LIKE THIS BEFORE.

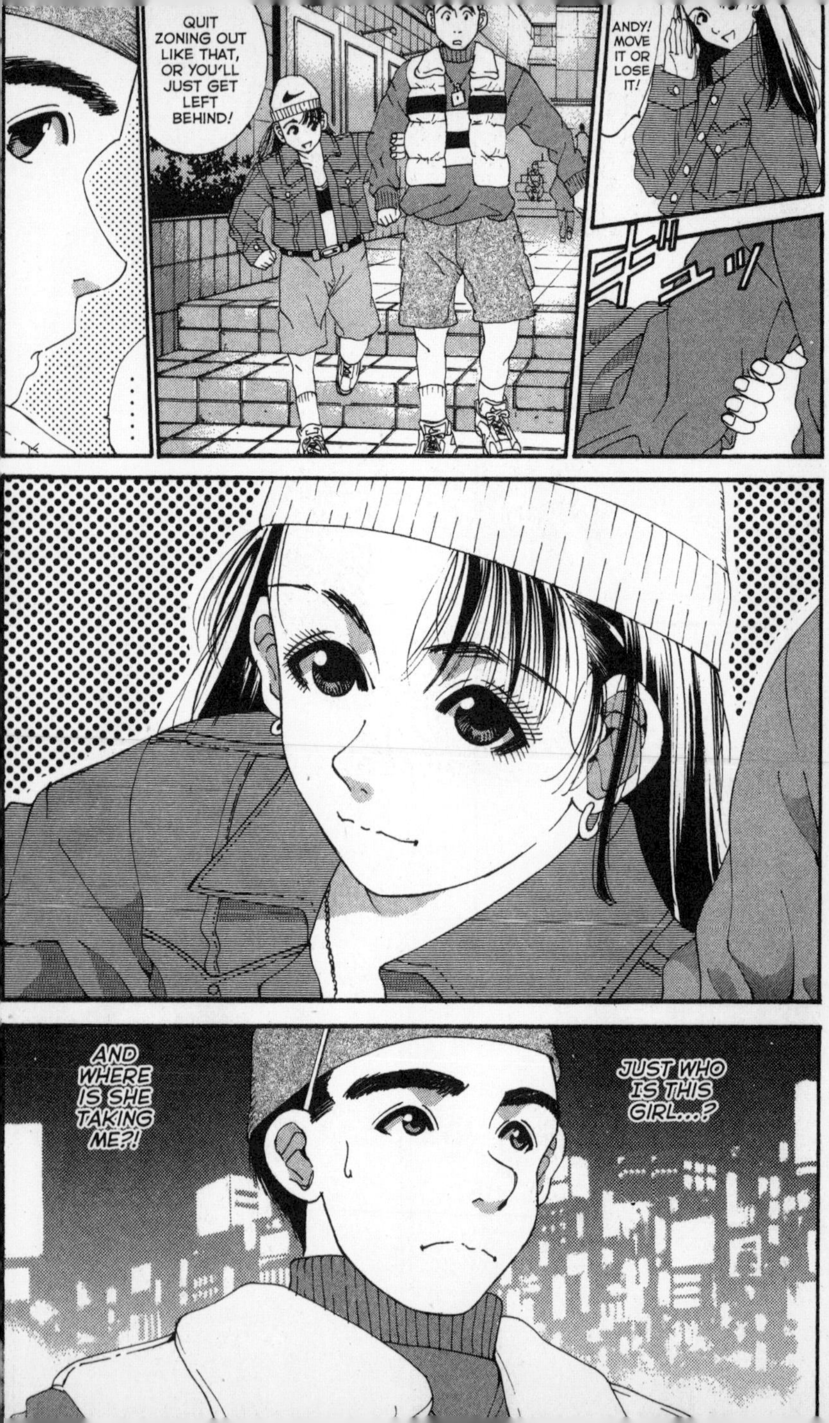
ANDY! MOVE IT OR LOSE IT!
キュッ
QUIT ZONING OUT LIKE THAT, OR YOU'LL JUST GET LEFT BEHIND!
.....
JUST WHO IS THIS GIRL...?
AND WHERE IS SHE TAKING ME?!

BOYS:BE™

REPORT 2 Love, Piercings and Judo (Middle)

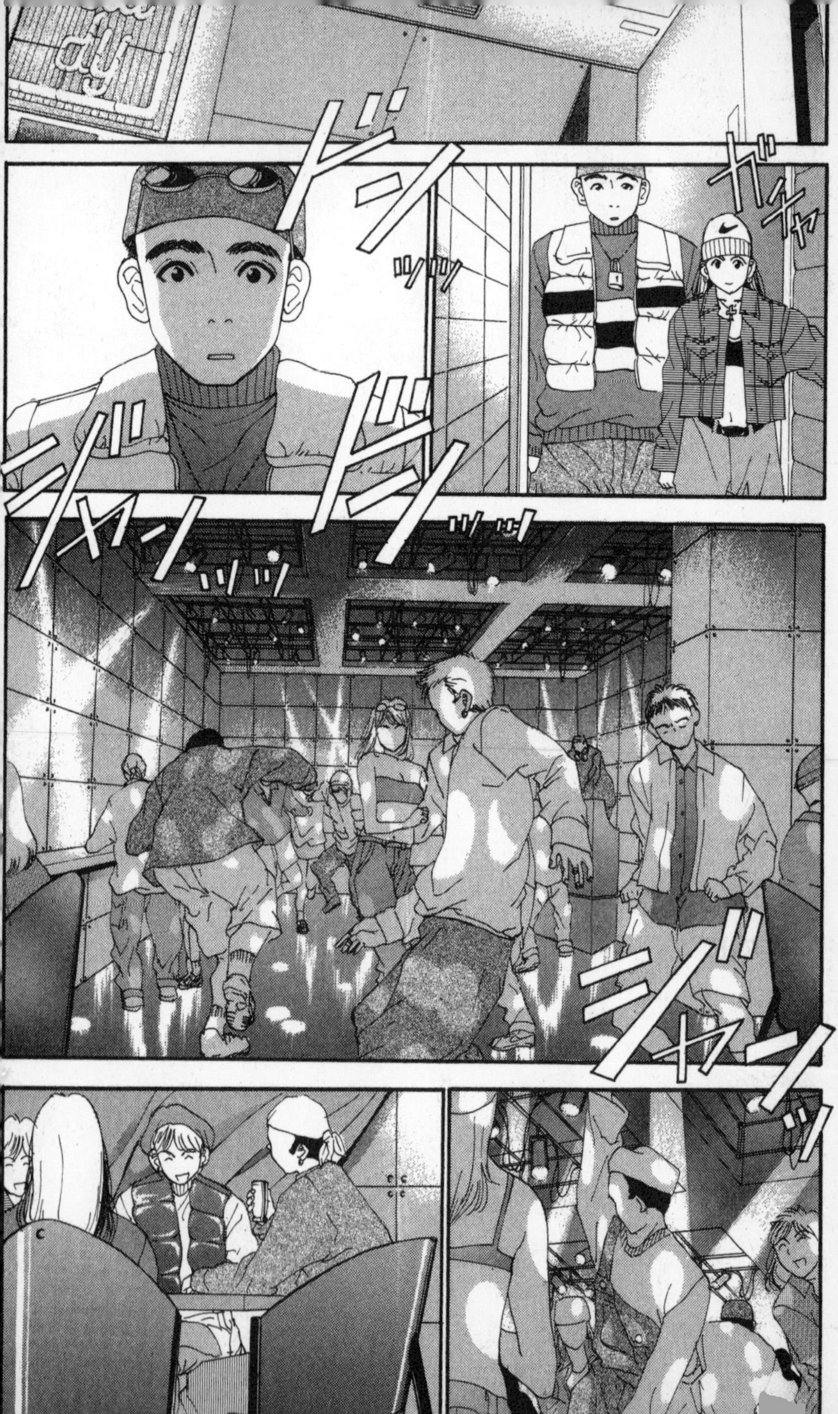
ガチャ
ドーン
ジャーン
ドン
ジャーン

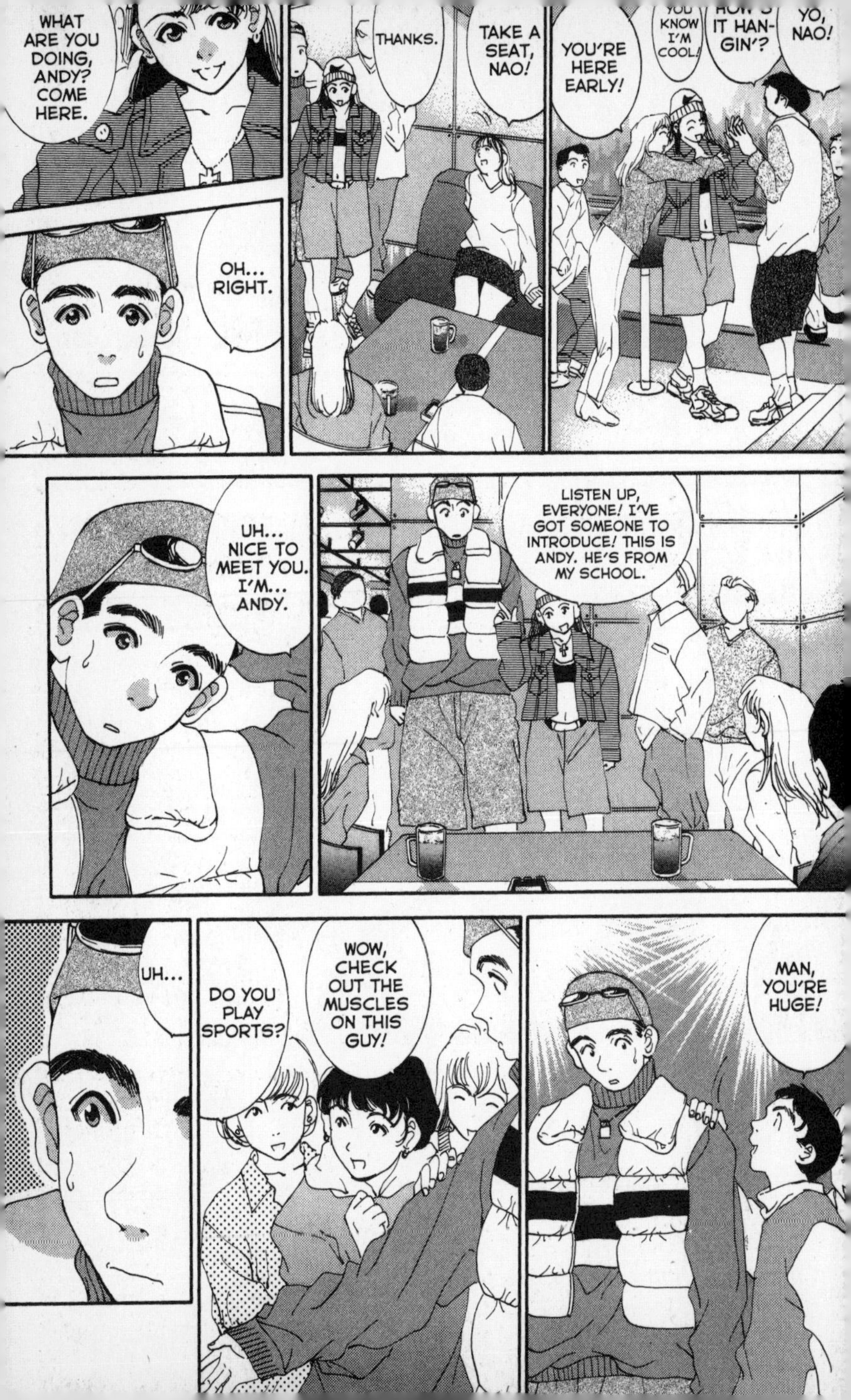
YO, NAO!
HOW'S IT HAN-GIN'?
YOU KNOW I'M COOL!
YOU'RE HERE EARLY!
TAKE A SEAT, NAO!
THANKS.
WHAT ARE YOU DOING, ANDY? COME HERE.
OH... RIGHT.
LISTEN UP, EVERYONE! I'VE GOT SOMEONE TO INTRODUCE! THIS IS ANDY. HE'S FROM MY SCHOOL.
UH... NICE TO MEET YOU. I'M... ANDY.
MAN, YOU'RE HUGE!
WOW, CHECK OUT THE MUSCLES ON THIS GUY!
DO YOU PLAY SPORTS?
UH...

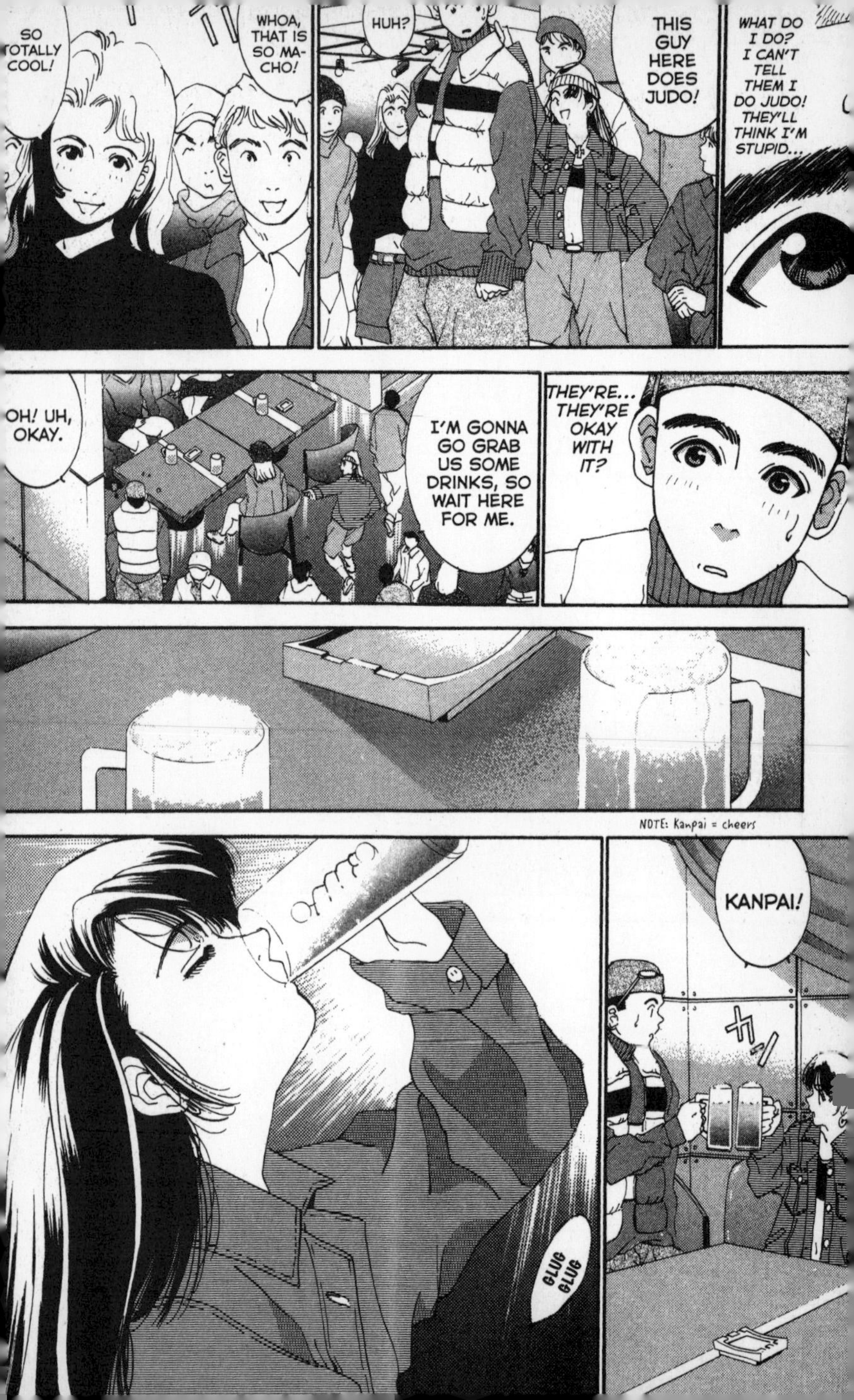
WHAT DO I DO? I CAN'T TELL THEM I DO JUDO! THEY'LL THINK I'M STUPID...
THIS GUY HERE DOES JUDO!
HUH?
WHOA, THAT IS SO MA-CHO!
SO TOTALLY COOL!
THEY'RE... THEY'RE OKAY WITH IT?
I'M GONNA GO GRAB US SOME DRINKS, SO WAIT HERE FOR ME.
OH! UH, OKAY.
NOTE: Kanpai = cheers
KANPAI!
GLUG GLUG

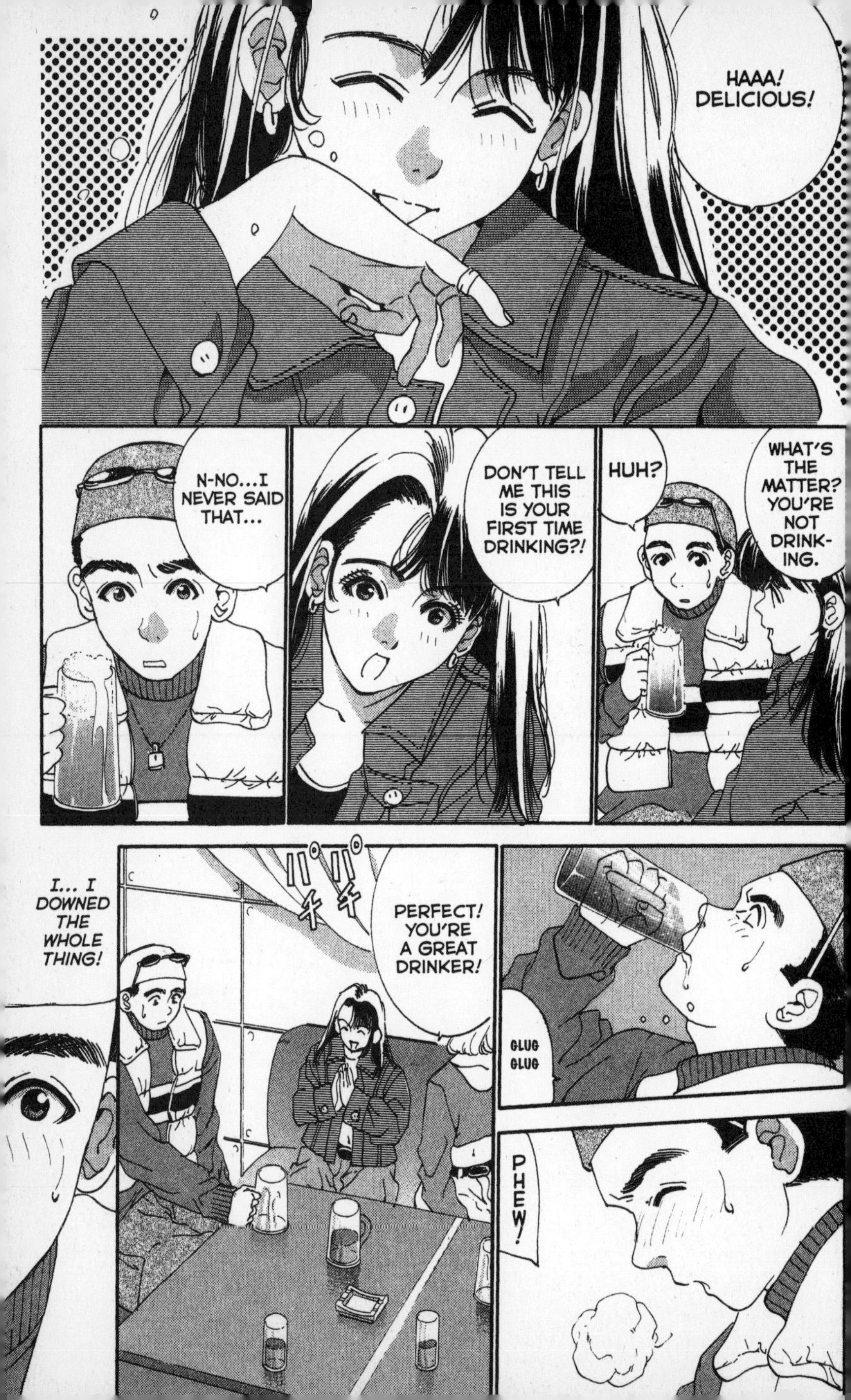
HAAA! DELICIOUS!
WHAT'S THE MATTER? YOU'RE NOT DRINK-ING.
HUH?
DON'T TELL ME THIS IS YOUR FIRST TIME DRINKING?!
N-NO...I NEVER SAID THAT...
GLUG GLUG
PHEW!
パチ パチ
PERFECT! YOU'RE A GREAT DRINKER!
I... I DOWNED THE WHOLE THING!

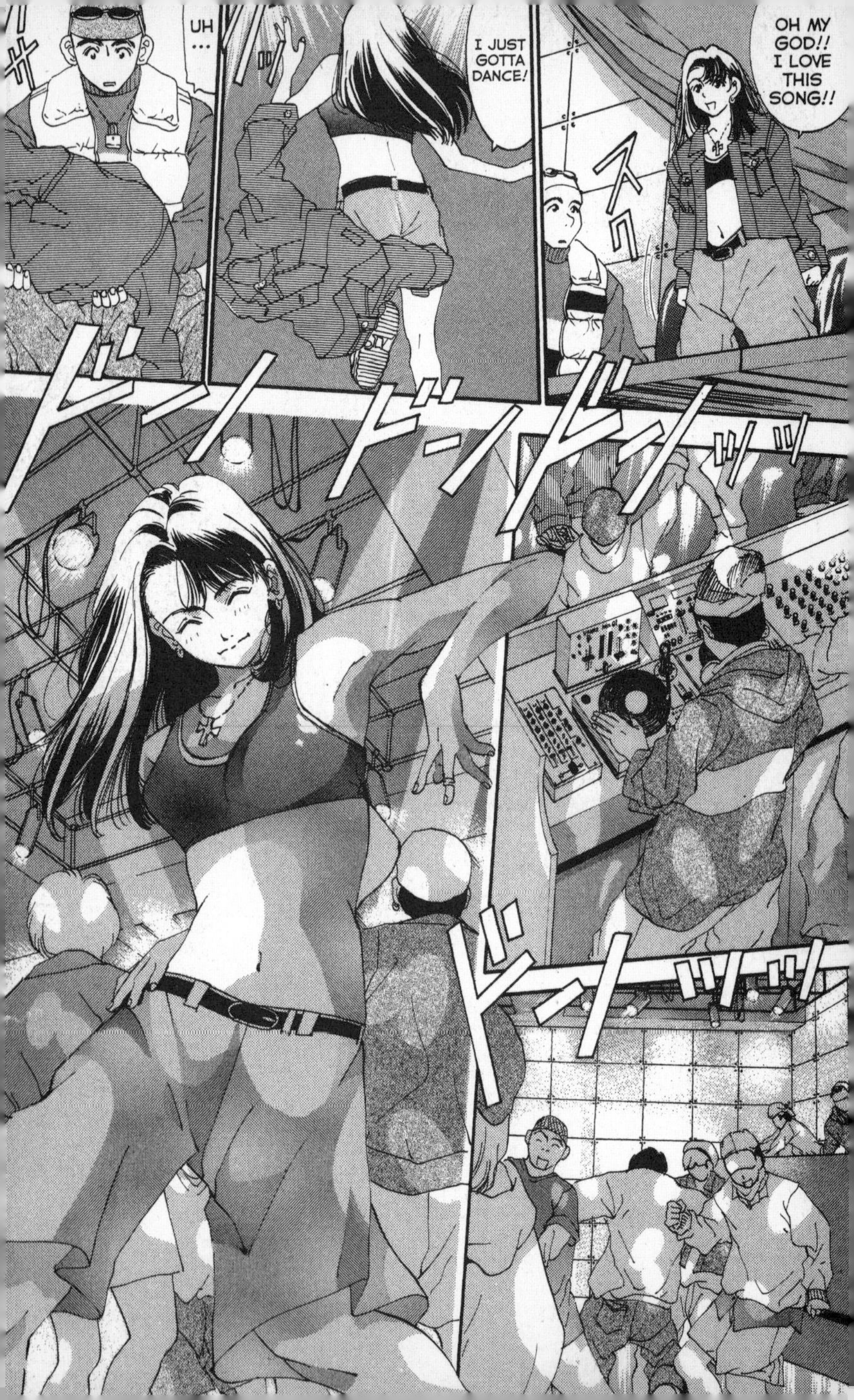
OH MY GOD!! I LOVE THIS SONG!!
I JUST GOTTA DANCE!
UH ...

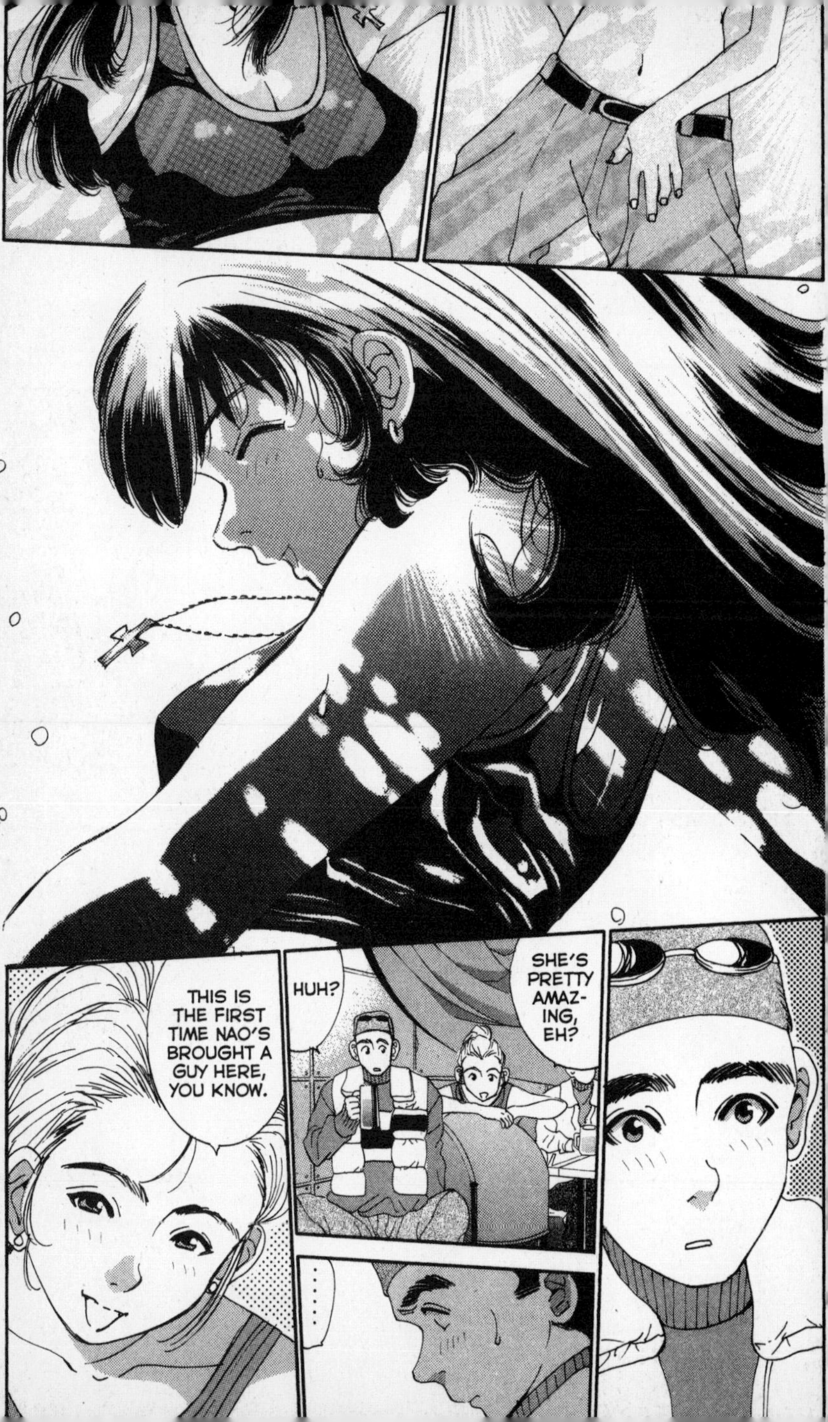
SHE'S PRETTY AMAZING, EH?
HUH?
......
THIS IS THE FIRST TIME NAO'S BROUGHT A GUY HERE, YOU KNOW.

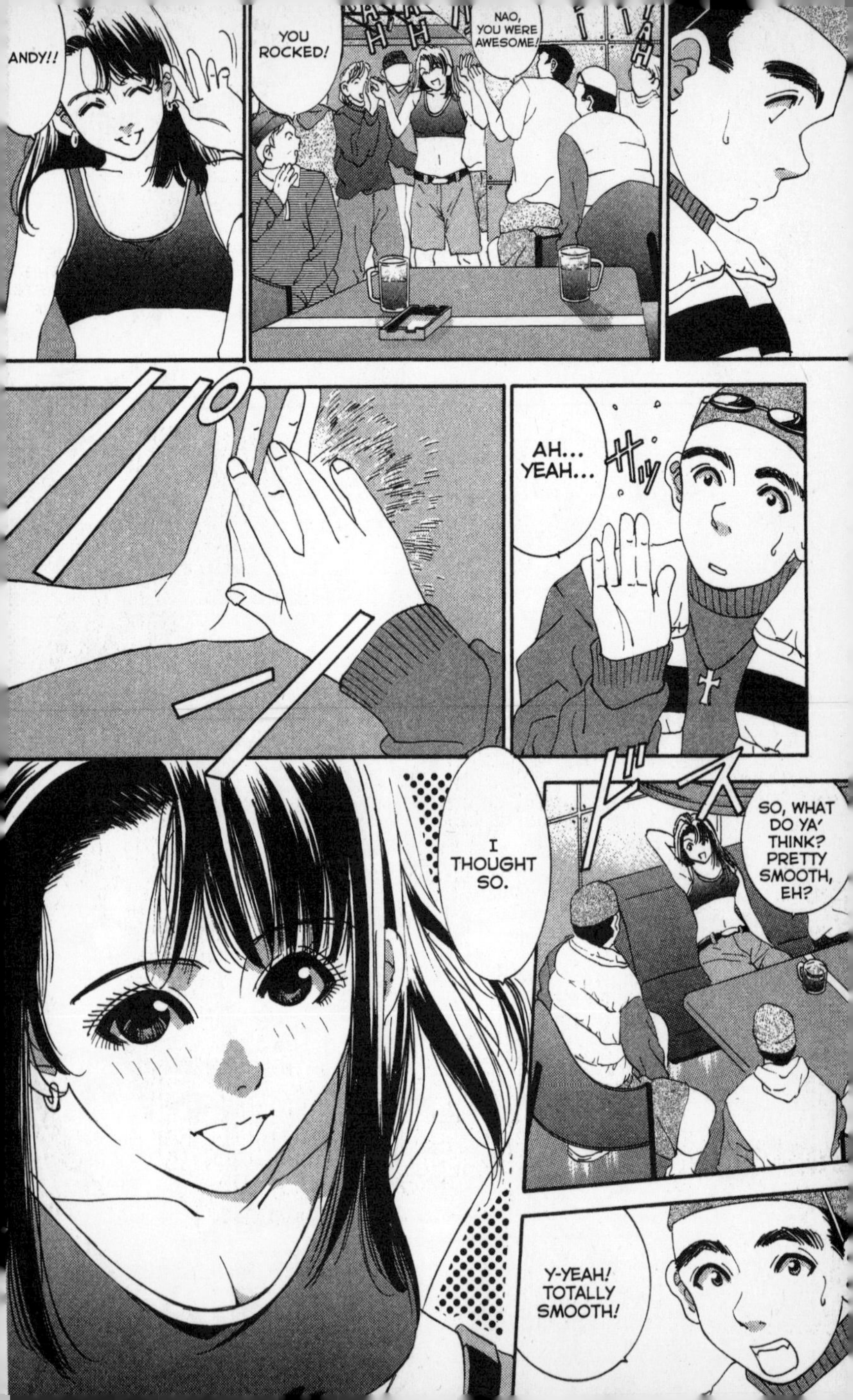
NAO, YOU WERE AWESOME!
YOU ROCKED!
ANDY!!
AH... YEAH...
SO, WHAT DO YA' THINK? PRETTY SMOOTH, EH?
Y-YEAH! TOTALLY SMOOTH!
I THOUGHT SO.

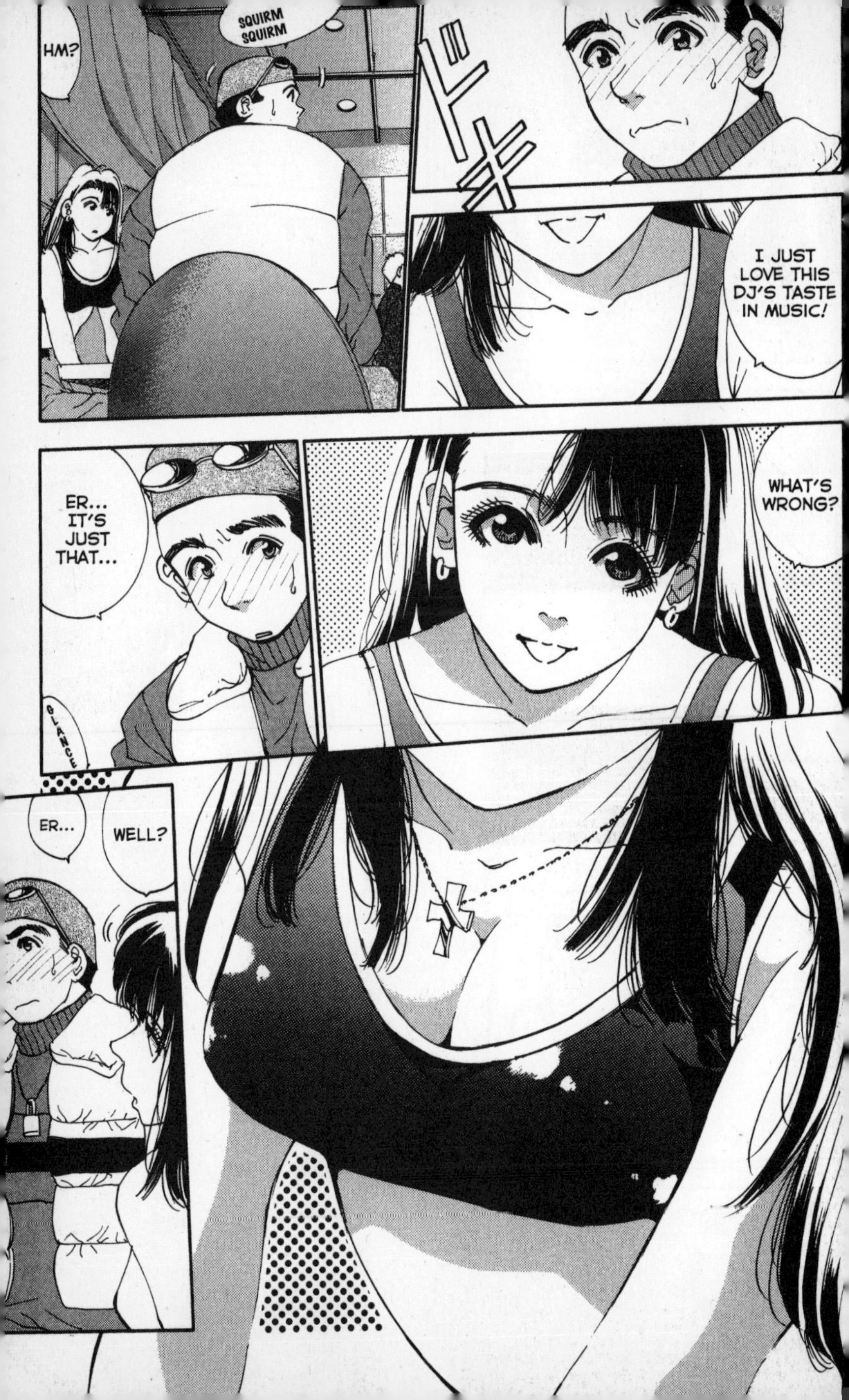
ドキ
I JUST LOVE THIS DJ'S TASTE IN MUSIC!
SQUIRM SQUIRM
HM?
WHAT'S WRONG?
ER... IT'S JUST THAT...
GLANCE
WELL?
ER...

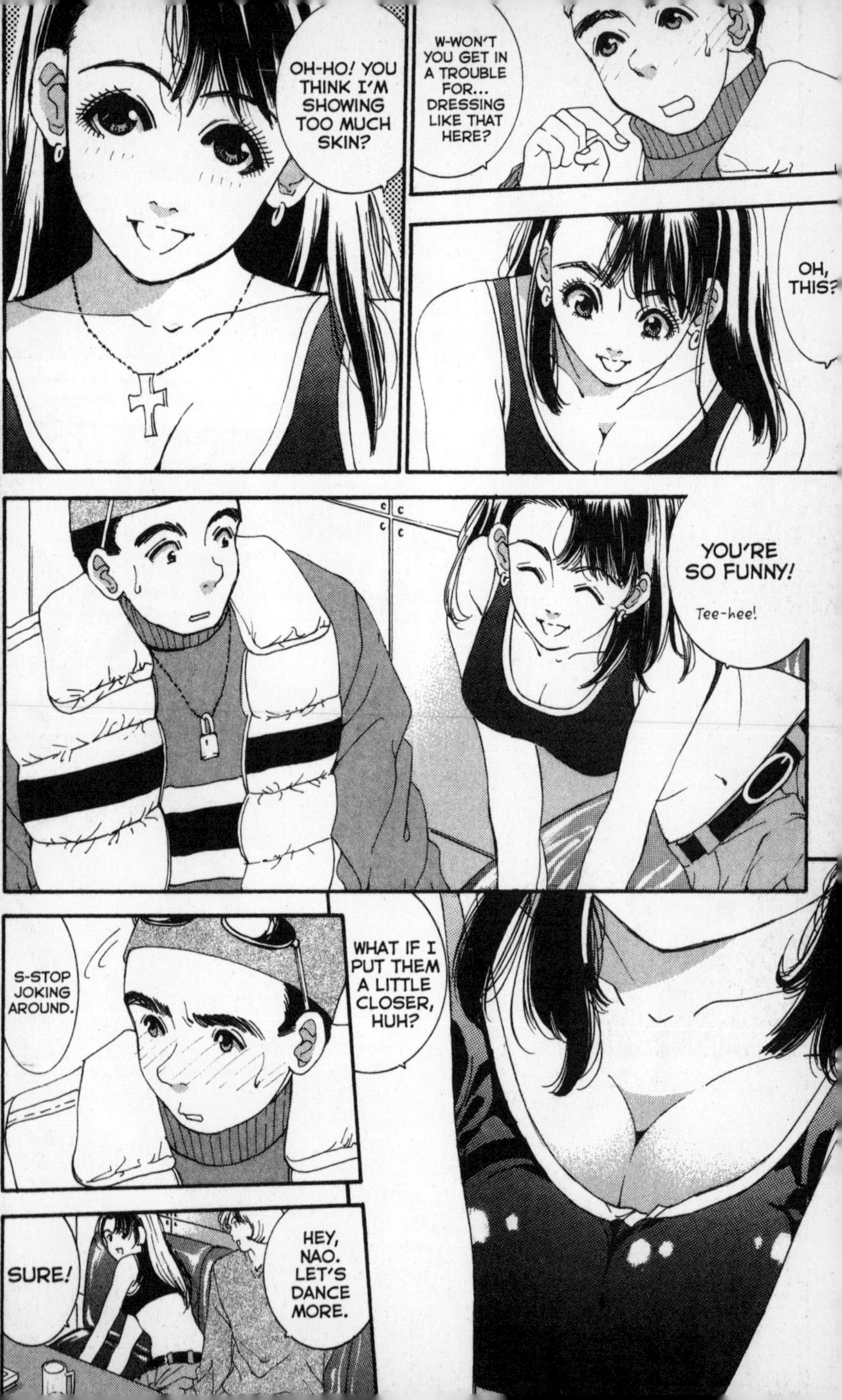
W-WON'T YOU GET IN A TROUBLE FOR... DRESSING LIKE THAT HERE?
OH, THIS?
OH-HO! YOU THINK I'M SHOWING TOO MUCH SKIN?
YOU'RE SO FUNNY!
Tee-hee!
WHAT IF I PUT THEM A LITTLE CLOSER, HUH?
S-STOP JOKING AROUND.
HEY, NAO. LET'S DANCE MORE.
SURE!

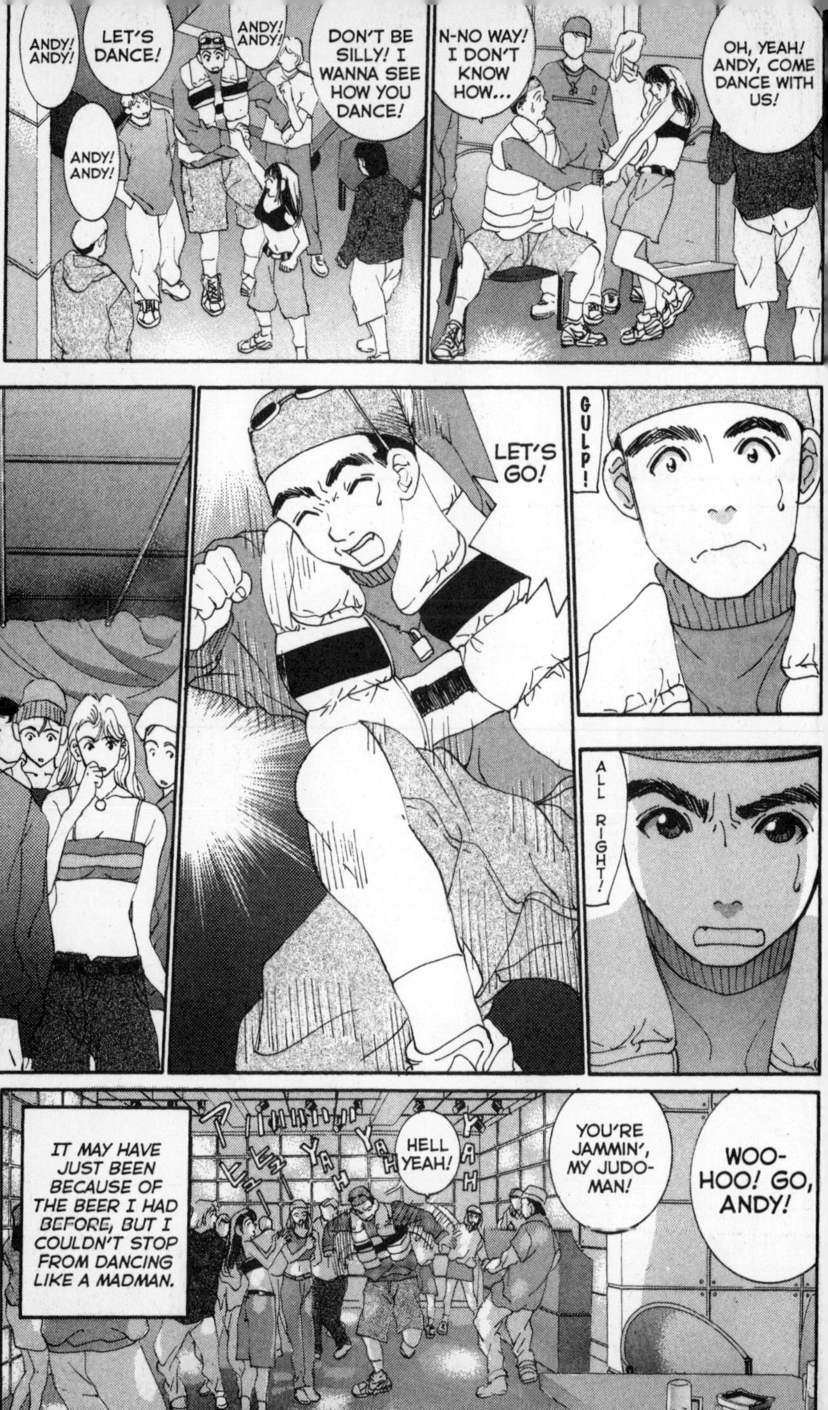
OH, YEAH! ANDY, COME DANCE WITH US!
N-NO WAY! I DON'T KNOW HOW...
DON'T BE SILLY! I WANNA SEE HOW YOU DANCE!
ANDY! ANDY!
LET'S DANCE!
ANDY! ANDY!
ANDY! ANDY!
GULP!
ALL RIGHT!
LET'S GO!
WOO-HOO! GO, ANDY!
YOU'RE JAMMIN', MY JUDO-MAN!
HELL YEAH!
IT MAY HAVE JUST BEEN BECAUSE OF THE BEER I HAD BEFORE, BUT I COULDN'T STOP FROM DANCING LIKE A MADMAN.

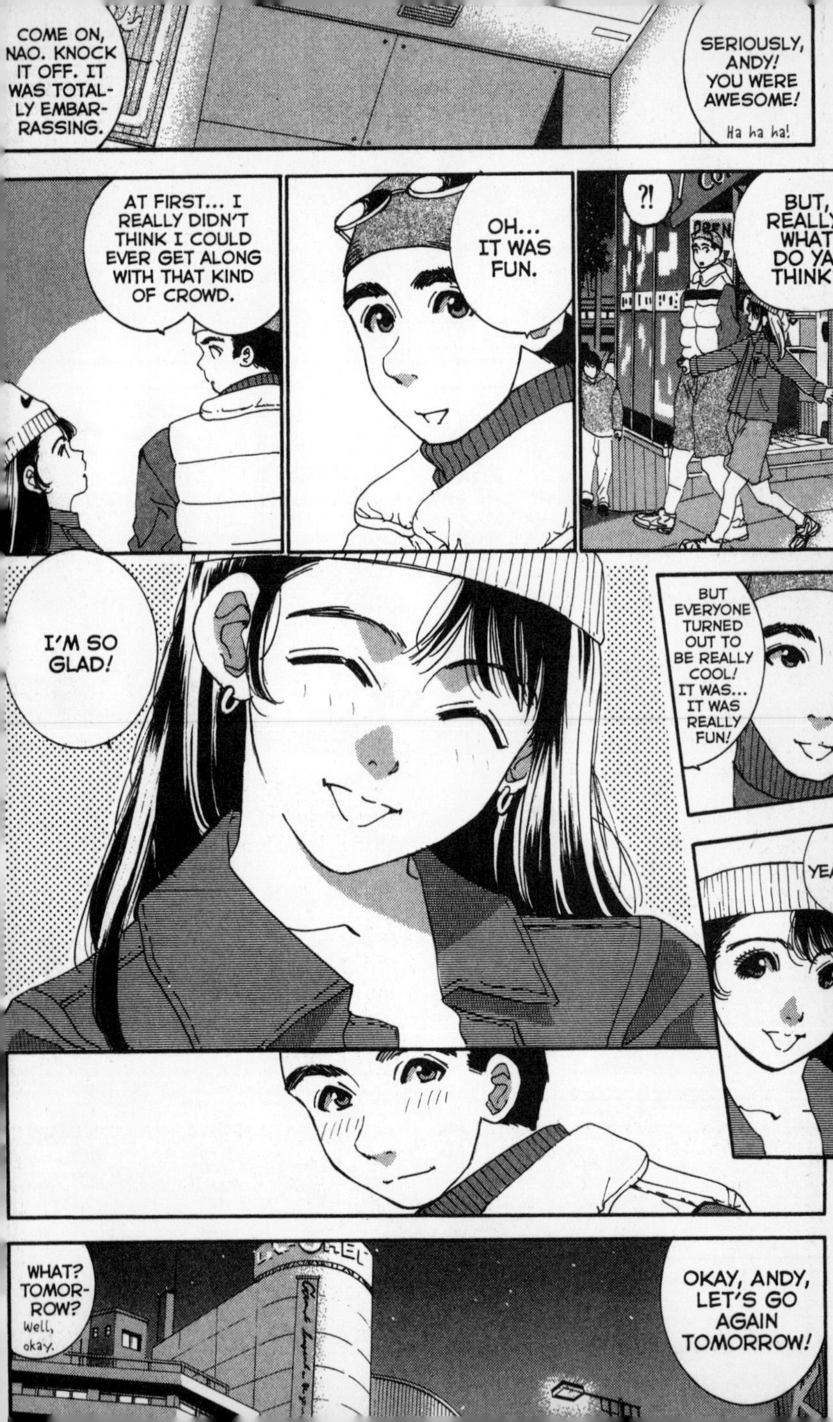
SERIOUSLY, ANDY! YOU WERE AWESOME!
Ha ha ha!
COME ON, NAO. KNOCK IT OFF. IT WAS TOTALLY EMBARRASSING.
BUT, REALLY. WHAT DO YA' THINK?
?!
OH... IT WAS FUN.
AT FIRST... I REALLY DIDN'T THINK I COULD EVER GET ALONG WITH THAT KIND OF CROWD.
BUT EVERYONE TURNED OUT TO BE REALLY COOL! IT WAS... IT WAS REALLY FUN!
YEAH?
I'M SO GLAD!
OKAY, ANDY, LET'S GO AGAIN TOMORROW!
WHAT? TOMORROW?
Well, okay.

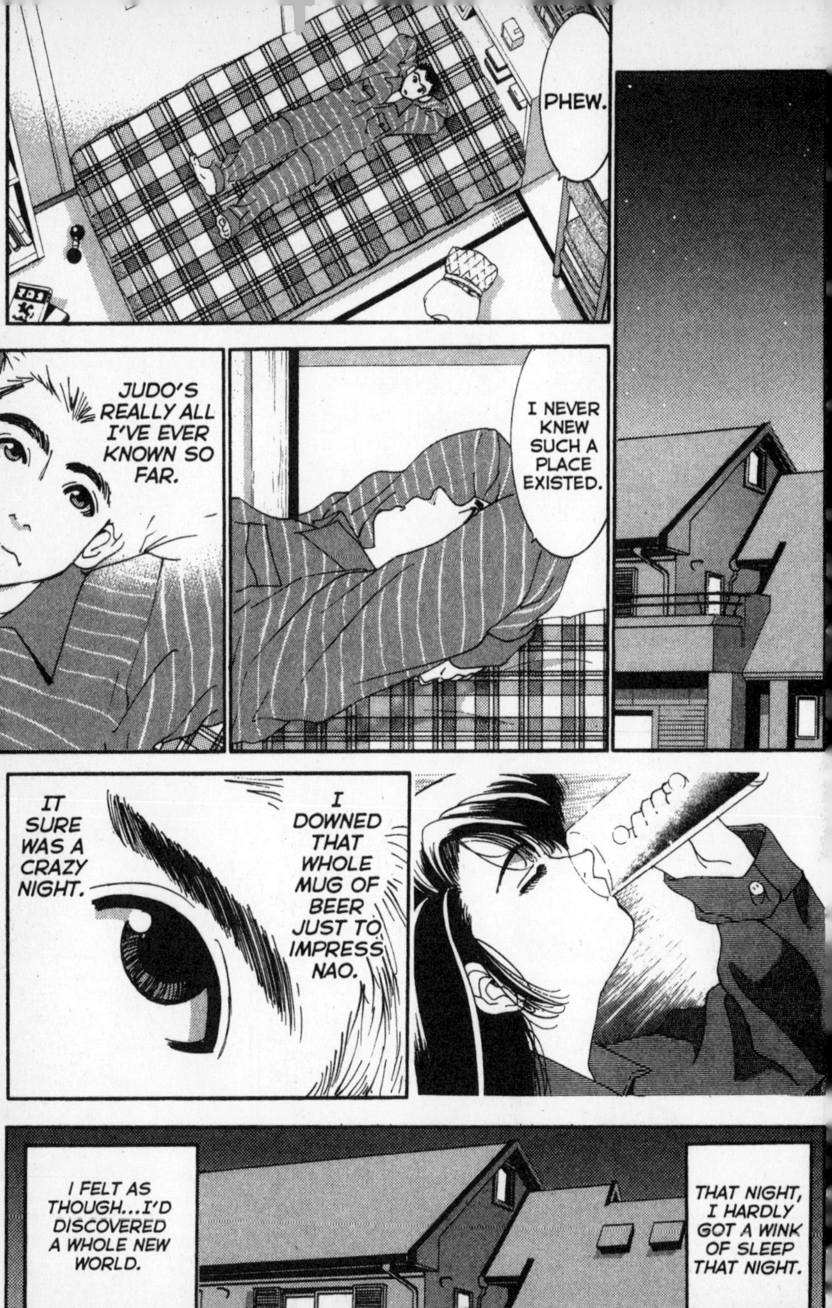
PHEW.
I NEVER KNEW SUCH A PLACE EXISTED.
JUDO'S REALLY ALL I'VE EVER KNOWN SO FAR.
I DOWNED THAT WHOLE MUG OF BEER JUST TO IMPRESS NAO.
IT SURE WAS A CRAZY NIGHT.
THAT NIGHT, I HARDLY GOT A WINK OF SLEEP THAT NIGHT.
I FELT AS THOUGH...I'D DISCOVERED A WHOLE NEW WORLD.

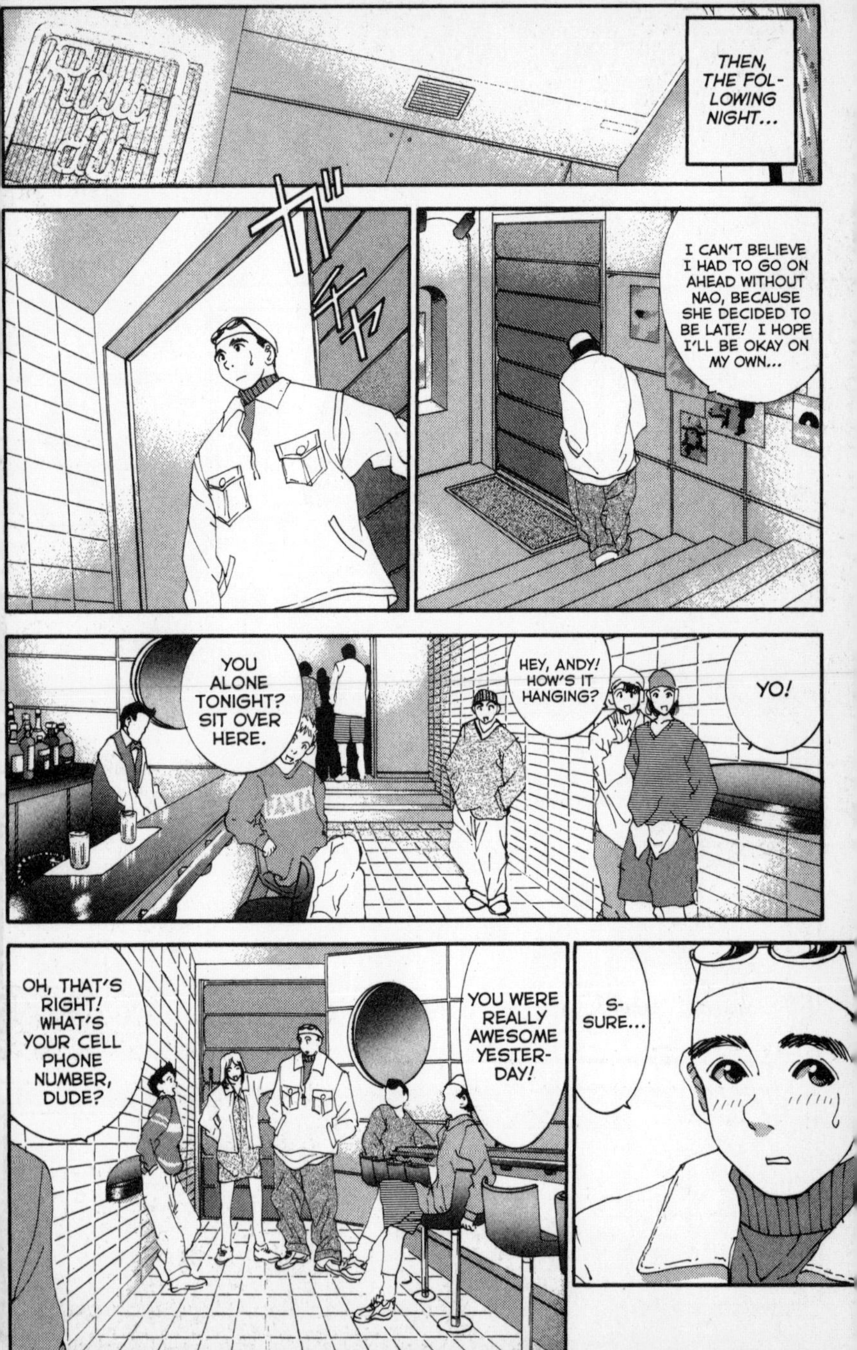
THEN, THE FOL- LOWING NIGHT...
I CAN'T BELIEVE I HAD TO GO ON AHEAD WITHOUT NAO, BECAUSE SHE DECIDED TO BE LATE! I HOPE I'LL BE OKAY ON MY OWN...
ガチャ
YO!
HEY, ANDY! HOW'S IT HANGING?
YOU ALONE TONIGHT? SIT OVER HERE.
S- SURE...
YOU WERE REALLY AWESOME YESTER- DAY!
OH, THAT'S RIGHT! WHAT'S YOUR CELL PHONE NUMBER, DUDE?

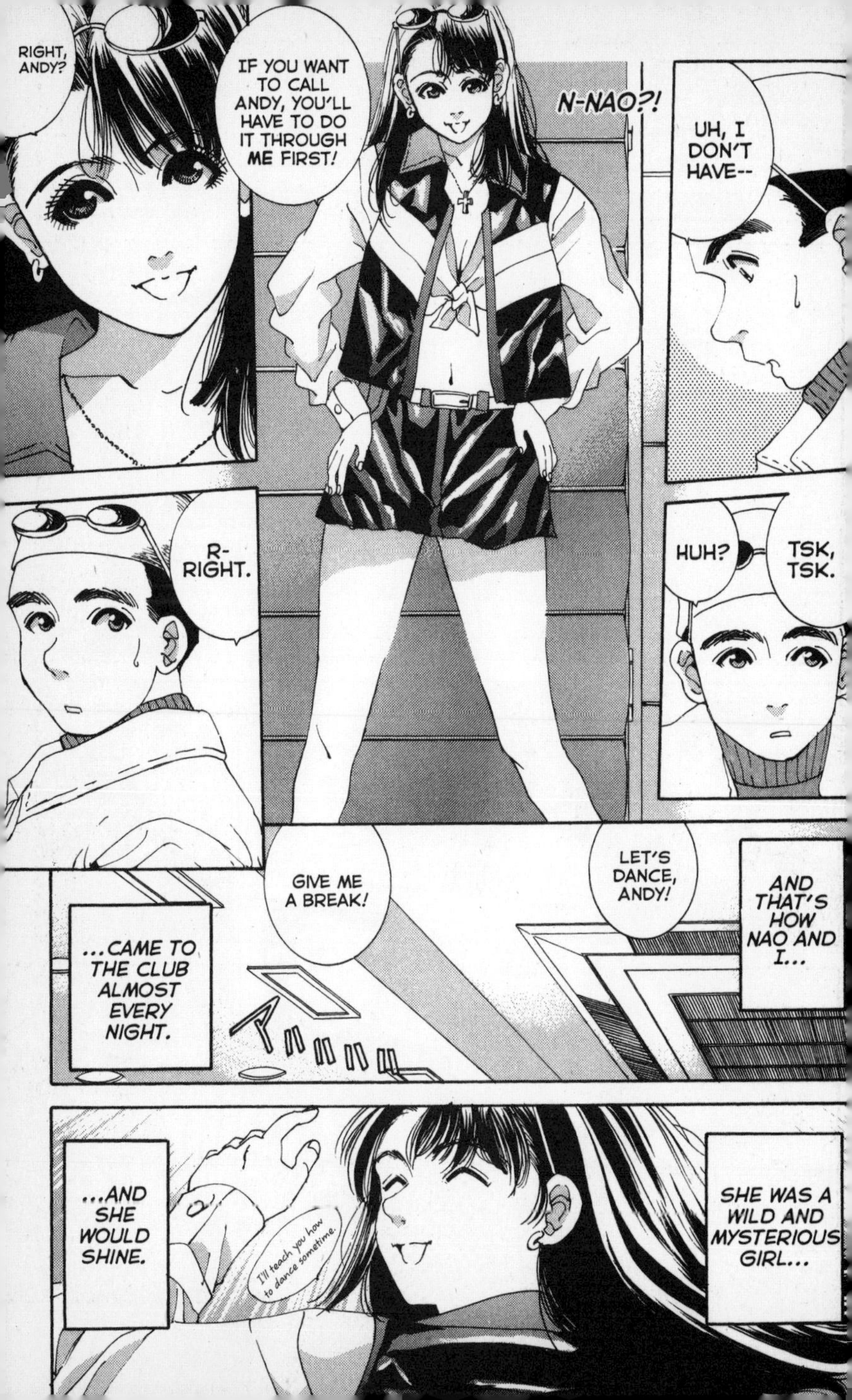
UH, I DON'T HAVE--
TSK, TSK.
HUH?
N-NAO?!
IF YOU WANT TO CALL ANDY, YOU'LL HAVE TO DO IT THROUGH ME FIRST!
RIGHT, ANDY?
R-RIGHT.
AND THAT'S HOW NAO AND I...
LET'S DANCE, ANDY!
GIVE ME A BREAK!
...CAME TO THE CLUB ALMOST EVERY NIGHT.
SHE WAS A WILD AND MYSTERIOUS GIRL...
I'll teach you how to dance sometime.
...AND SHE WOULD SHINE.

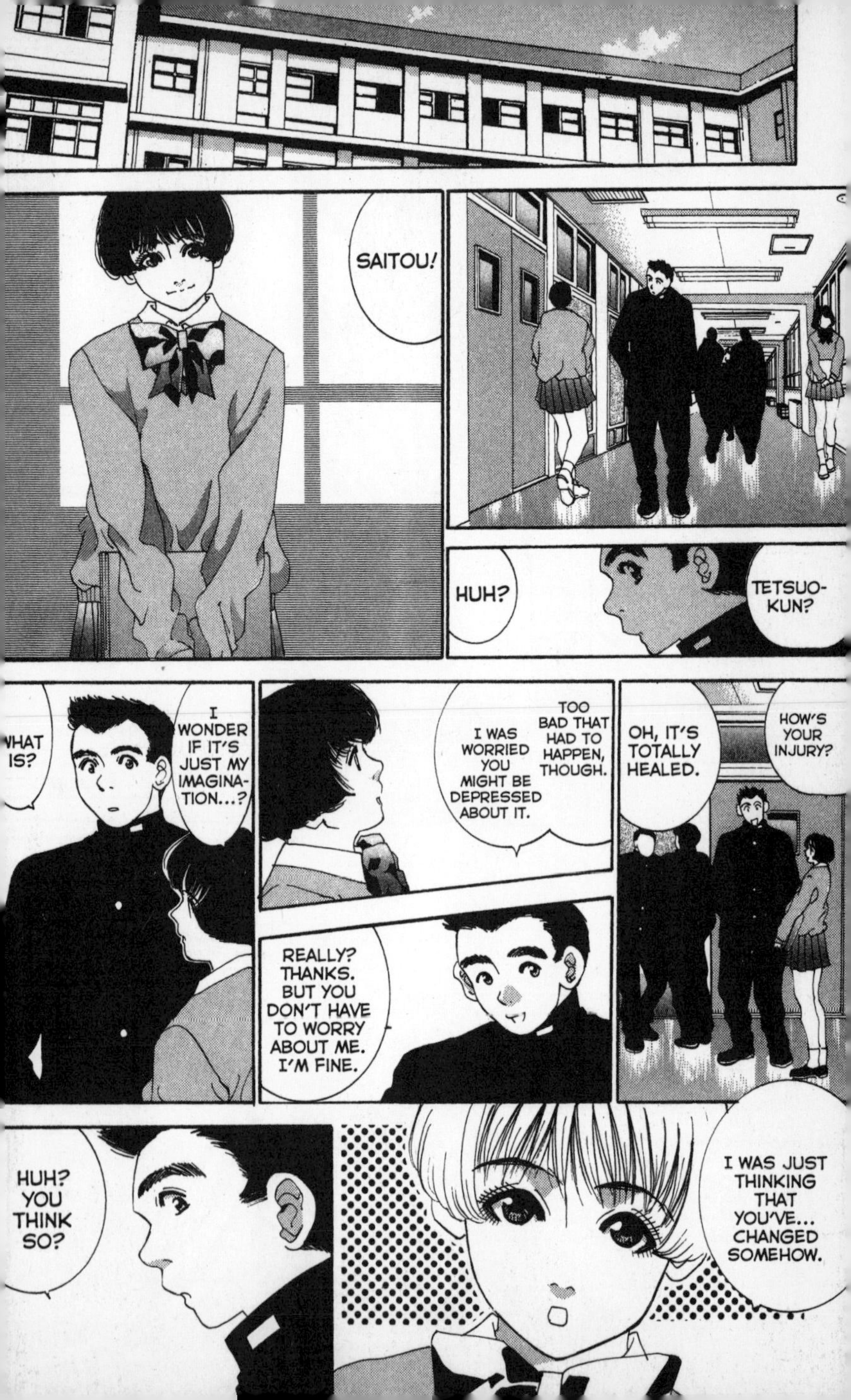
TETSUO-KUN?
HUH?
SAITOU!
HOW'S YOUR INJURY?
OH, IT'S TOTALLY HEALED.
TOO BAD THAT HAD TO HAPPEN, THOUGH.
I WAS WORRIED YOU MIGHT BE DEPRESSED ABOUT IT.
REALLY? THANKS. BUT YOU DON'T HAVE TO WORRY ABOUT ME. I'M FINE.
I WONDER IF IT'S JUST MY IMAGINATION...?
WHAT IS?
I WAS JUST THINKING THAT YOU'VE... CHANGED SOMEHOW.
HUH? YOU THINK SO?

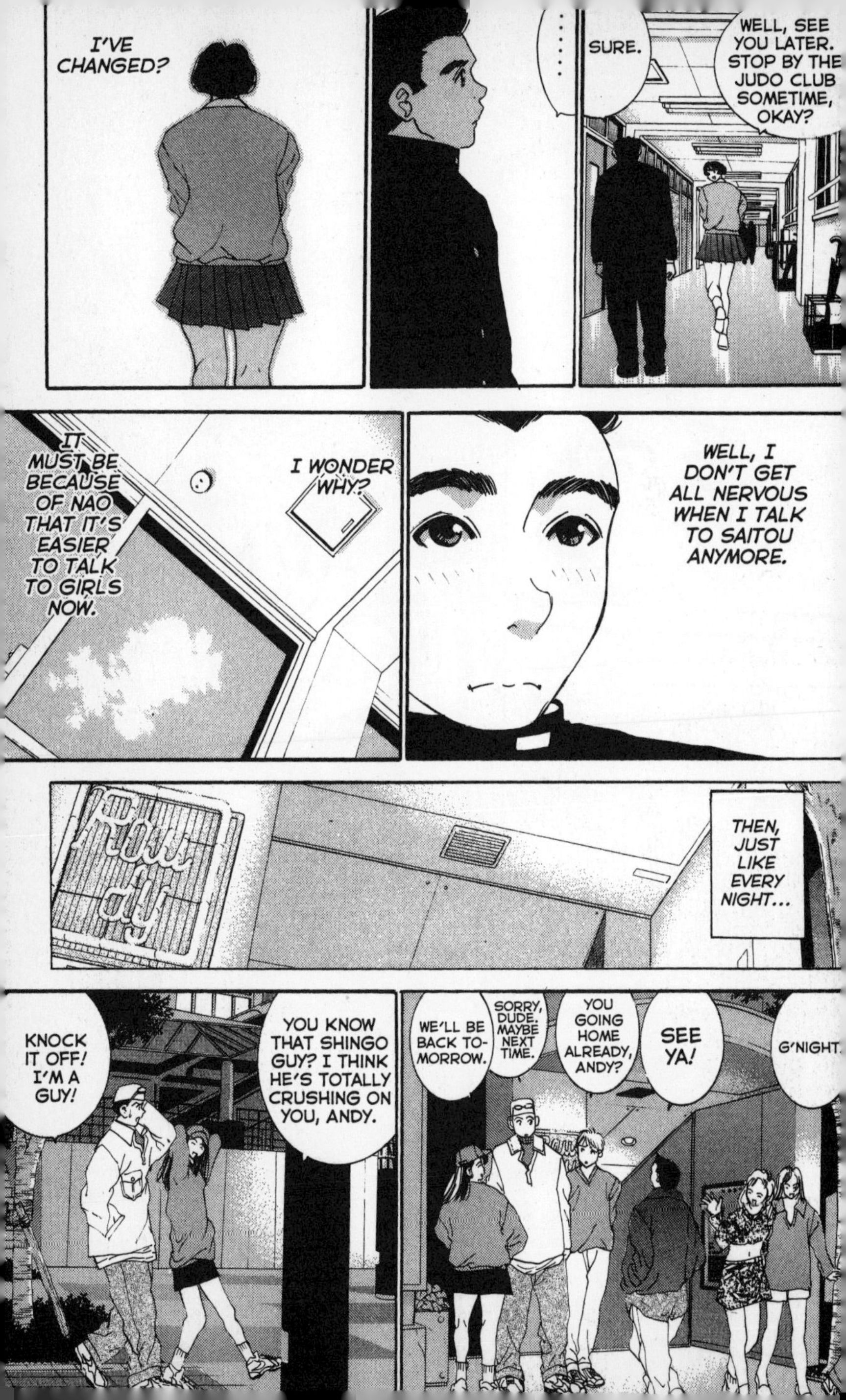

WELL, SEE YOU LATER. STOP BY THE JUDO CLUB SOMETIME, OKAY?
SURE.
......
I'VE CHANGED?
WELL, I DON'T GET ALL NERVOUS WHEN I TALK TO SAITOU ANYMORE.
I WONDER WHY?
IT MUST BE BECAUSE OF NAO THAT IT'S EASIER TO TALK TO GIRLS NOW.
THEN, JUST LIKE EVERY NIGHT...
G'NIGHT.
SEE YA!
YOU GOING HOME ALREADY, ANDY?
SORRY, DUDE. MAYBE NEXT TIME.
WE'LL BE BACK TO-MORROW.
YOU KNOW THAT SHINGO GUY? I THINK HE'S TOTALLY CRUSHING ON YOU, ANDY.
KNOCK IT OFF! I'M A GUY!

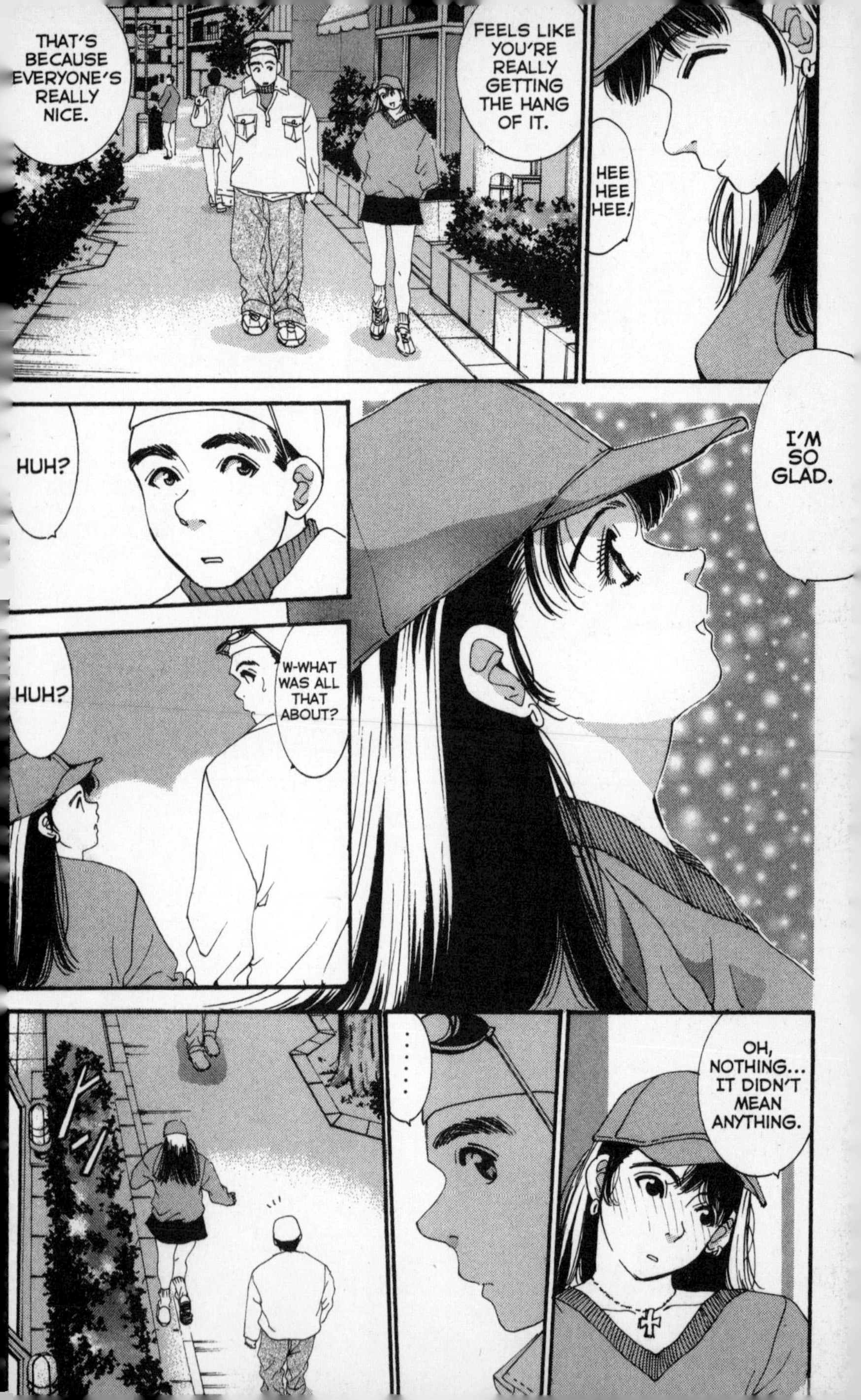
FEELS LIKE YOU'RE REALLY GETTING THE HANG OF IT.
THAT'S BECAUSE EVERYONE'S REALLY NICE.
HEE HEE HEE!
I'M SO GLAD.
HUH?
W-WHAT WAS ALL THAT ABOUT?
HUH?
OH, NOTHING... IT DIDN'T MEAN ANYTHING.
......

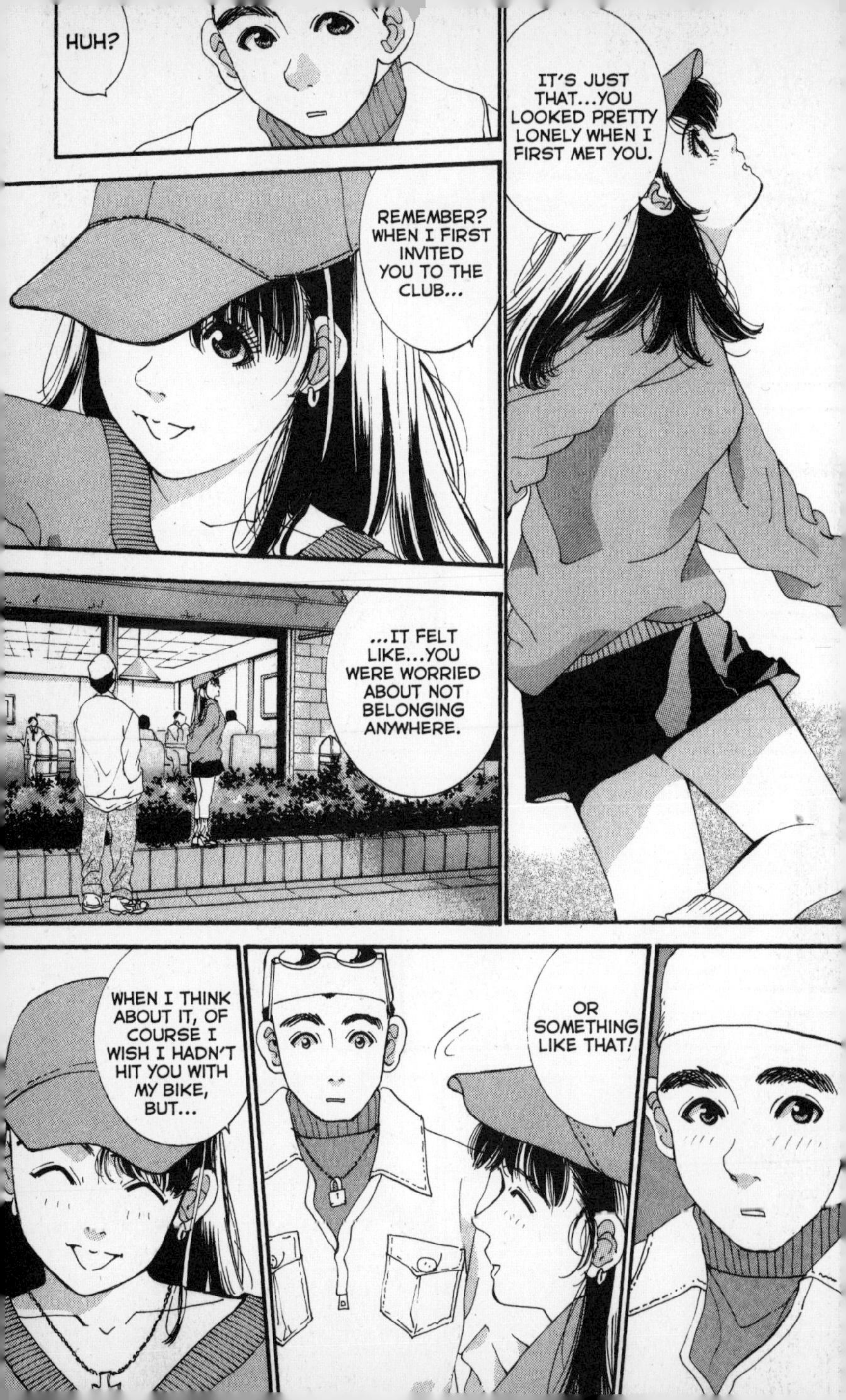
IT'S JUST THAT...YOU LOOKED PRETTY LONELY WHEN I FIRST MET YOU.
HUH?
REMEMBER? WHEN I FIRST INVITED YOU TO THE CLUB...
...IT FELT LIKE...YOU WERE WORRIED ABOUT NOT BELONGING ANYWHERE.
OR SOMETHING LIKE THAT!
WHEN I THINK ABOUT IT, OF COURSE I WISH I HADN'T HIT YOU WITH MY BIKE, BUT...

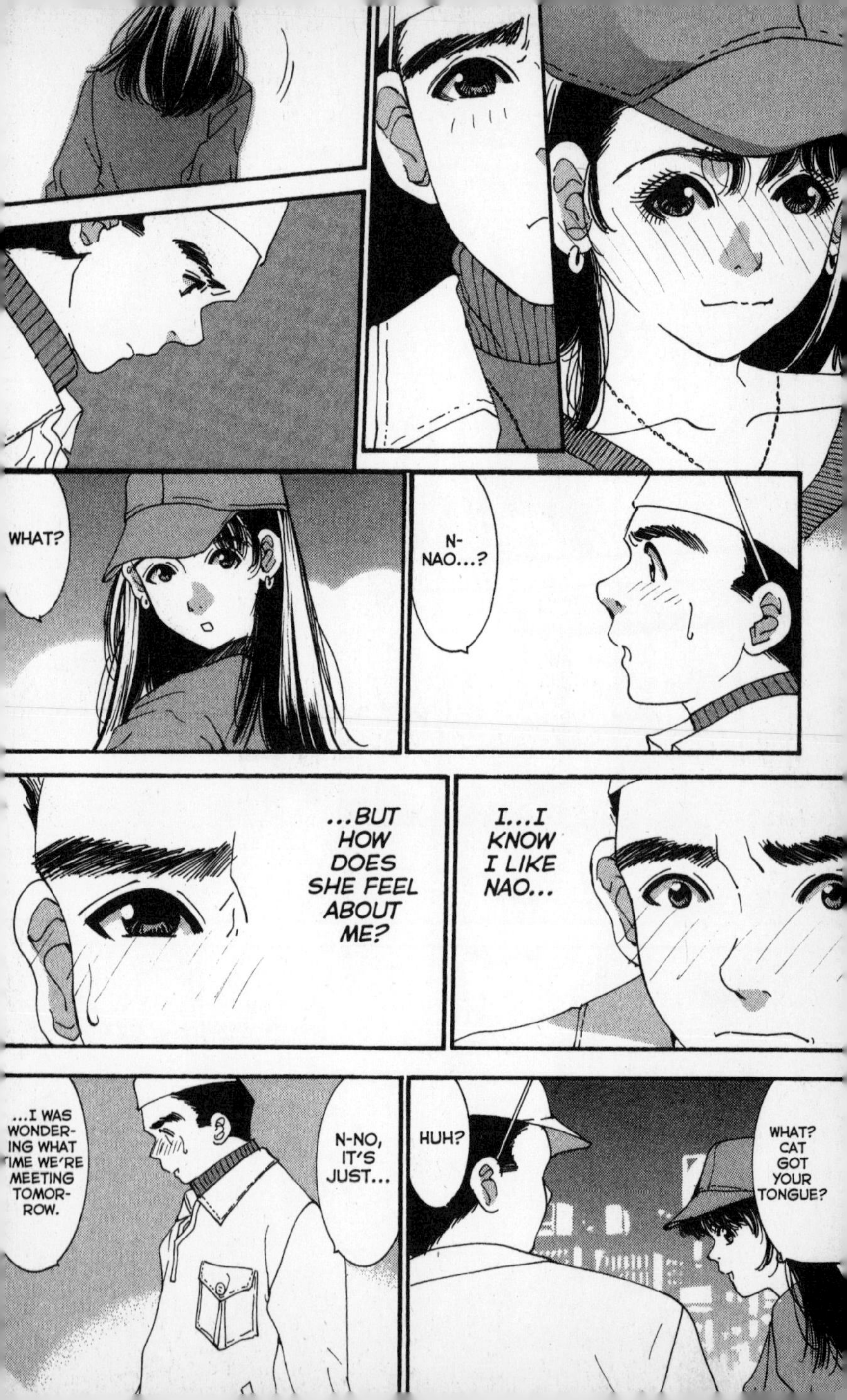
N- NAO...?
WHAT?
I...I KNOW I LIKE NAO...
...BUT HOW DOES SHE FEEL ABOUT ME?
WHAT? CAT GOT YOUR TONGUE?
HUH?
N-NO, IT'S JUST...
...I WAS WONDERING WHAT TIME WE'RE MEETING TOMORROW.

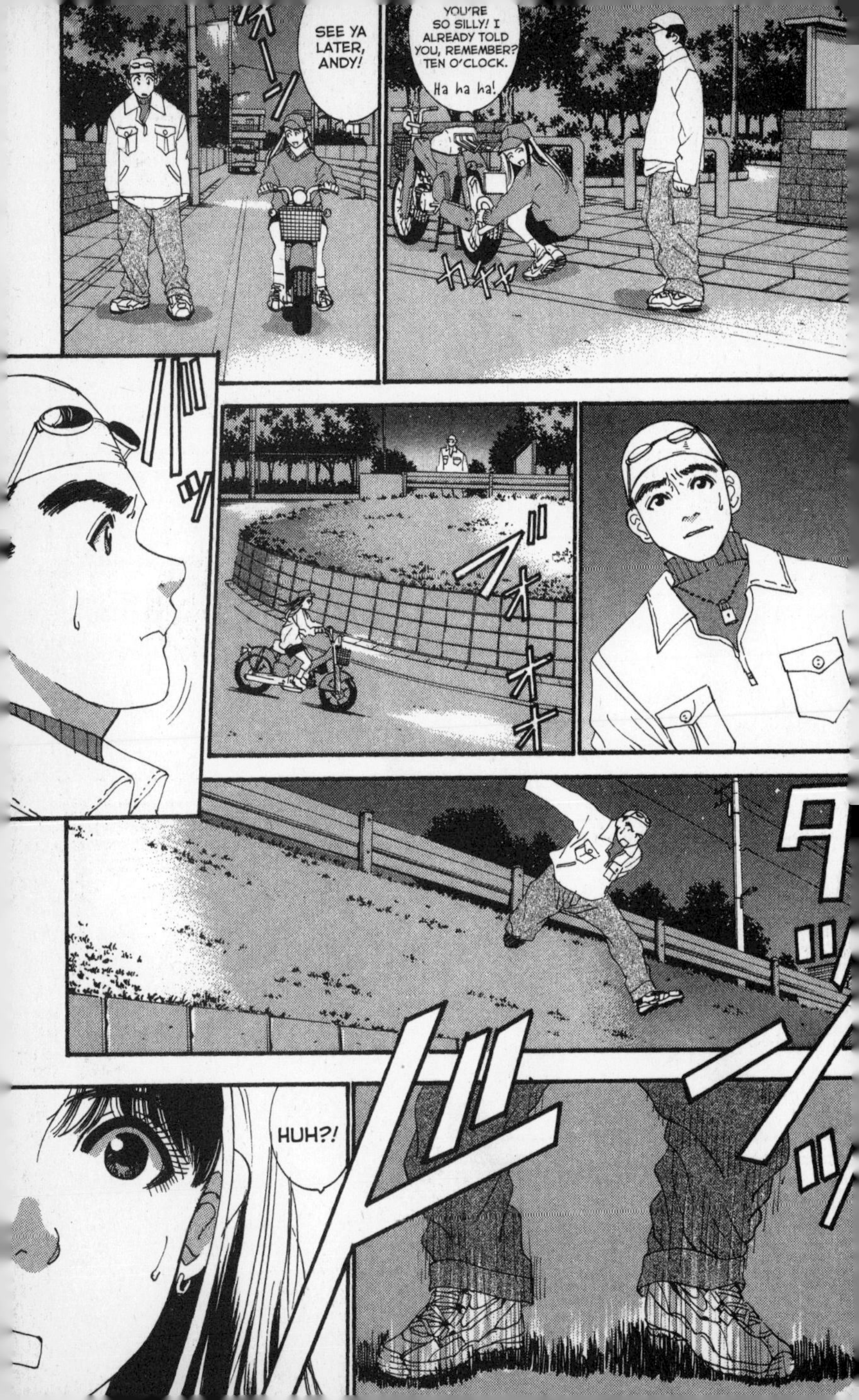
YOU'RE SO SILLY! I ALREADY TOLD YOU, REMEMBER? TEN O'CLOCK.
Ha ha ha!
SEE YA LATER, ANDY!
HUH?!

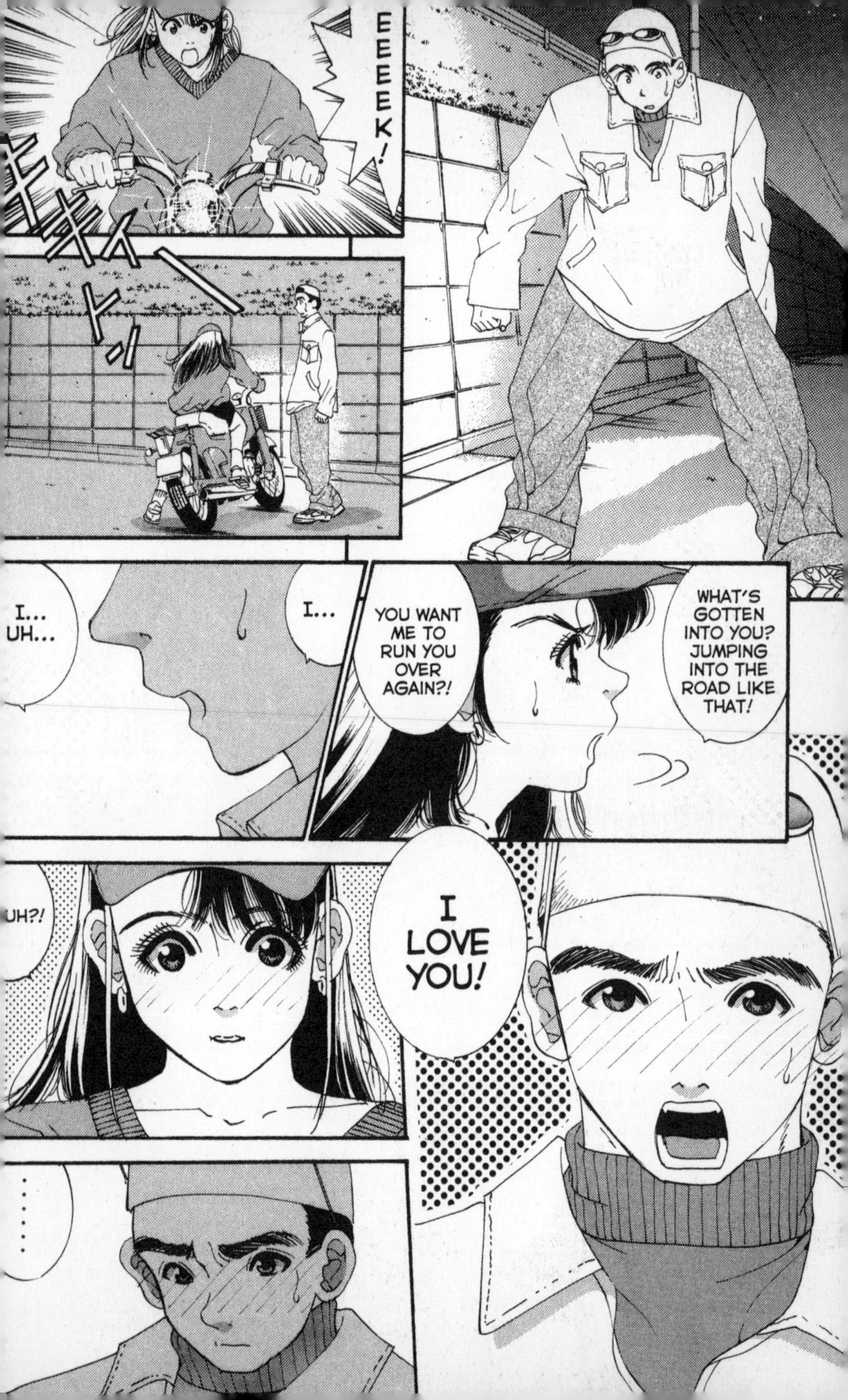
EEEEK!
WHAT'S GOTTEN INTO YOU? JUMPING INTO THE ROAD LIKE THAT!
YOU WANT ME TO RUN YOU OVER AGAIN?!
I...
I... UH...
I LOVE YOU!
UH?!
......

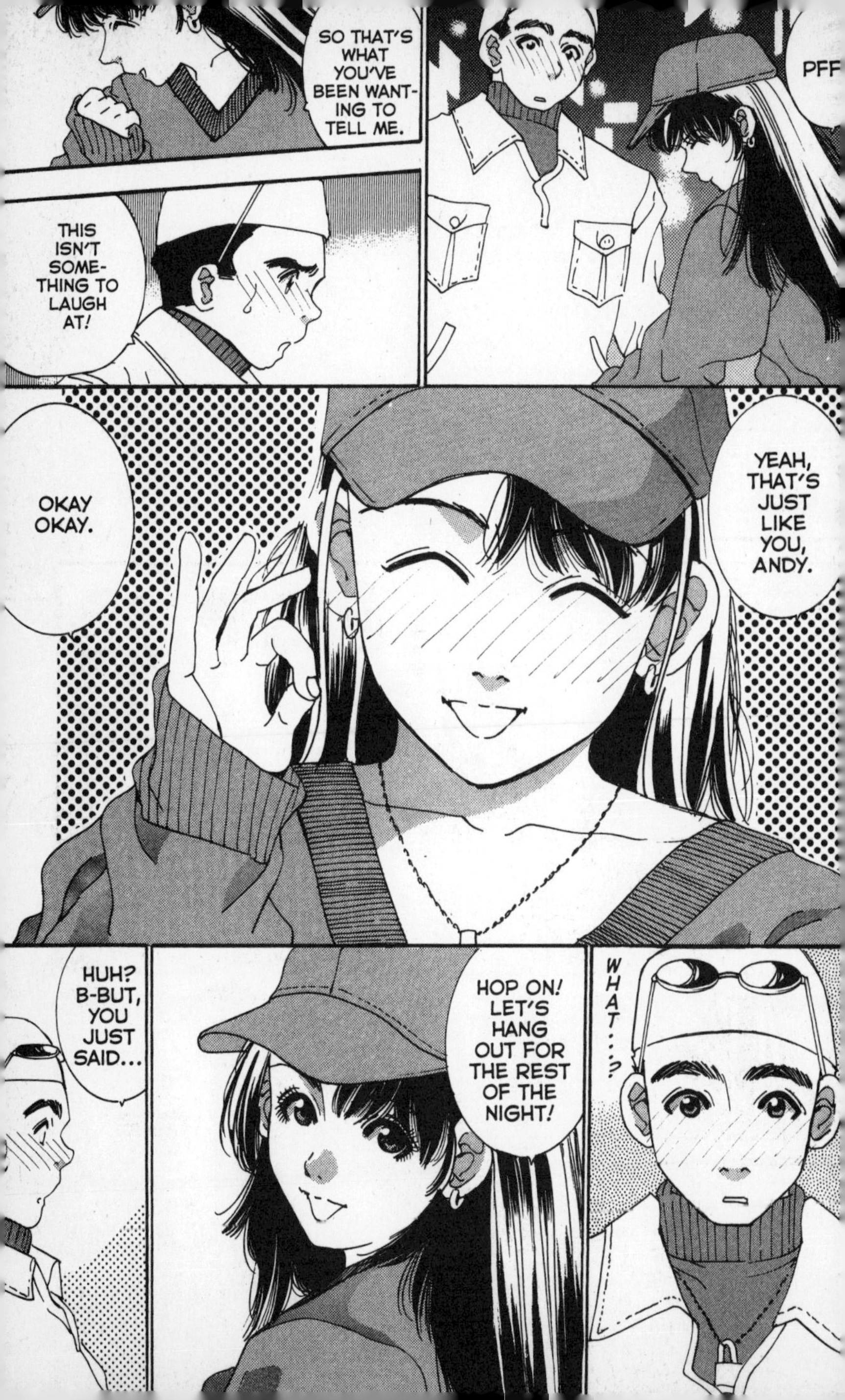
PFF
SO THAT'S WHAT YOU'VE BEEN WANTING TO TELL ME.
THIS ISN'T SOMETHING TO LAUGH AT!
YEAH, THAT'S JUST LIKE YOU, ANDY.
OKAY OKAY.
WHAT...?
HOP ON! LET'S HANG OUT FOR THE REST OF THE NIGHT!
HUH? B-BUT, YOU JUST SAID...

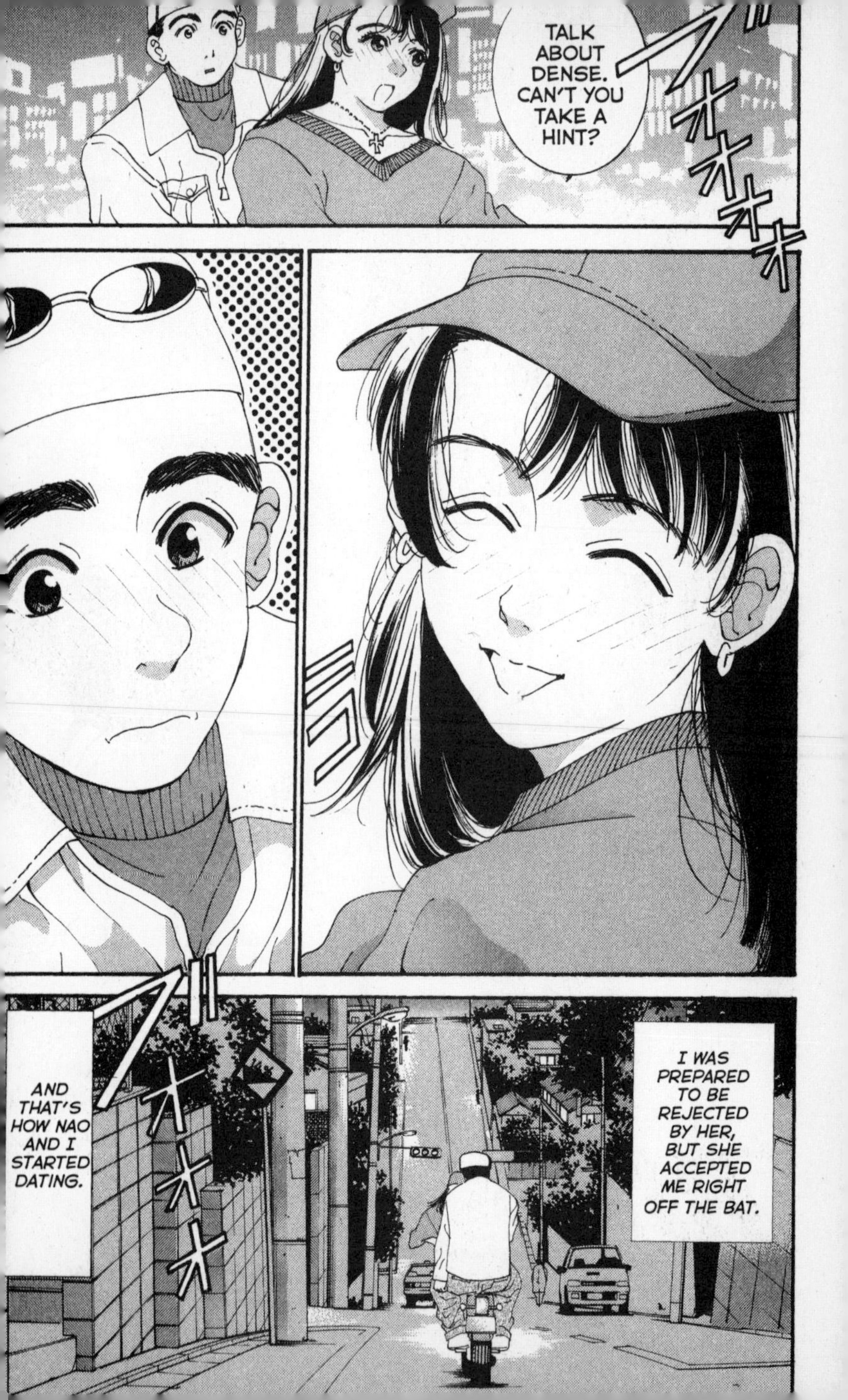
TALK ABOUT DENSE. CAN'T YOU TAKE A HINT?
I WAS PREPARED TO BE REJECTED BY HER, BUT SHE ACCEPTED ME RIGHT OFF THE BAT.
AND THAT'S HOW NAO AND I STARTED DATING.

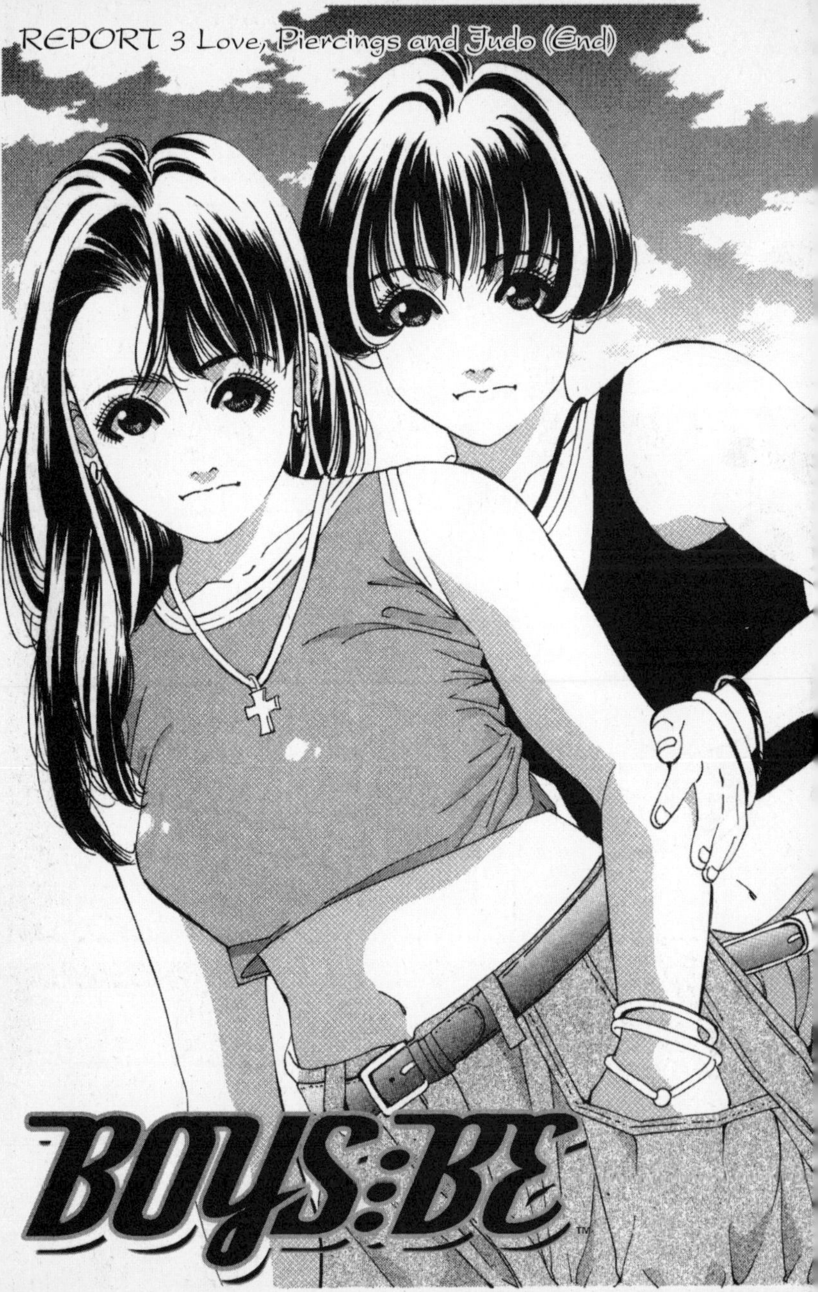
REPORT 3 Love, Piercings and Judo (End)
BOYS BE

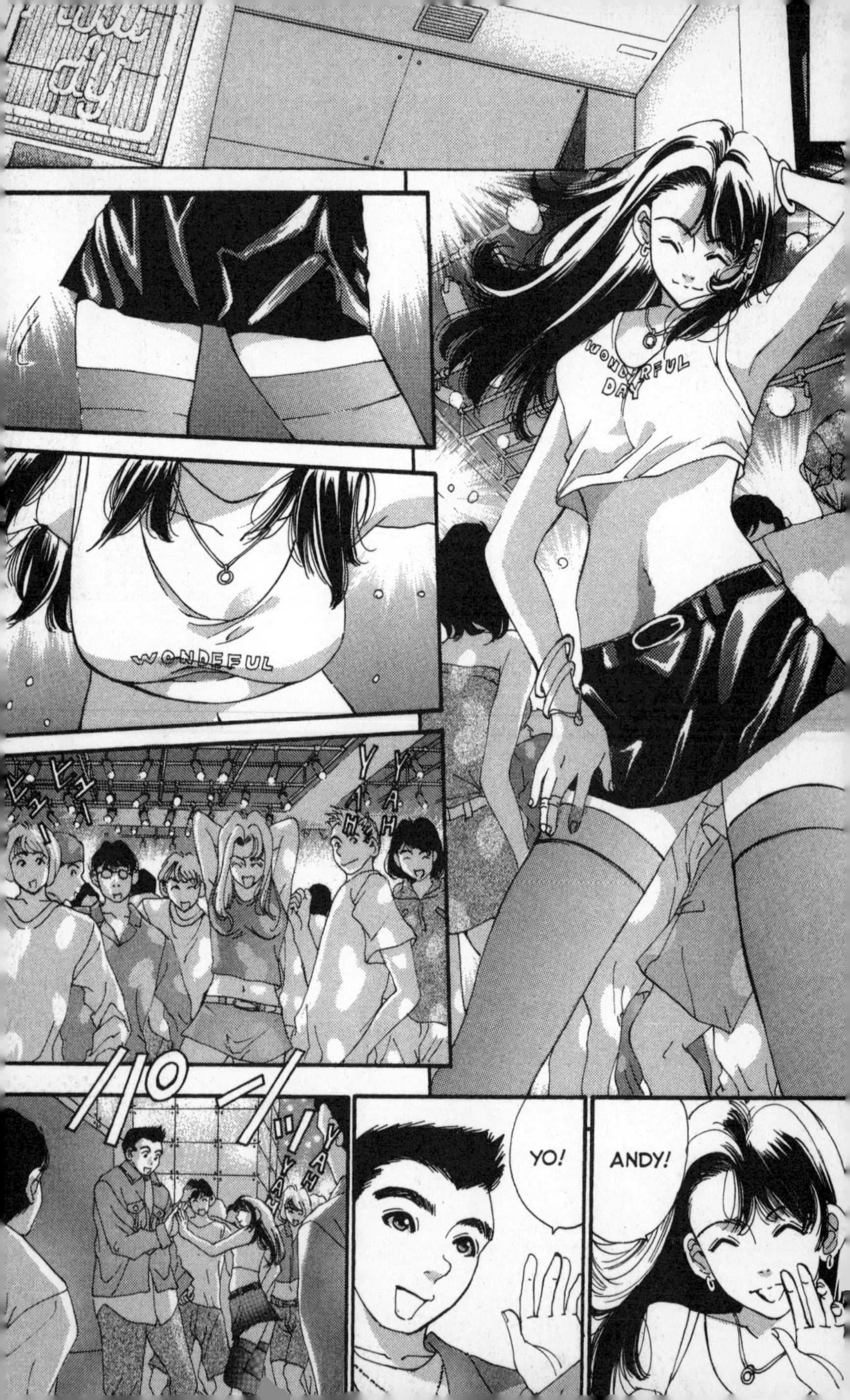
WONDERFUL DAY
WONDEFUL
ヒューヒュー
YAH
ANDY!
YO!
YAH

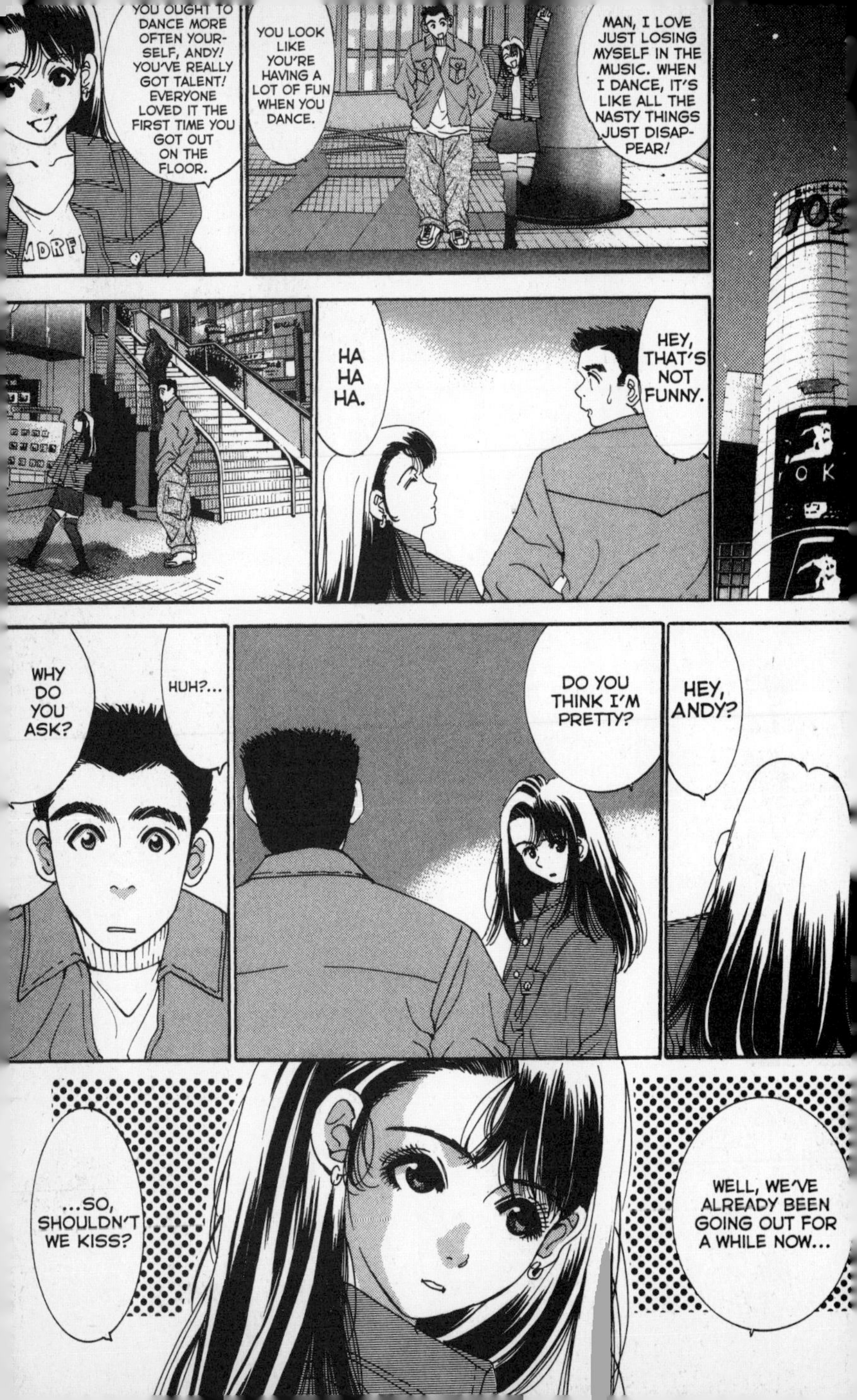
MAN, I LOVE JUST LOSING MYSELF IN THE MUSIC. WHEN I DANCE, IT'S LIKE ALL THE NASTY THINGS JUST DISAP-PEAR!
YOU LOOK LIKE YOU'RE HAVING A LOT OF FUN WHEN YOU DANCE.
YOU OUGHT TO DANCE MORE OFTEN YOUR-SELF, ANDY! YOU'VE REALLY GOT TALENT! EVERYONE LOVED IT THE FIRST TIME YOU GOT OUT ON THE FLOOR.
HEY, THAT'S NOT FUNNY.
HA HA HA.
HEY, ANDY?
DO YOU THINK I'M PRETTY?
HUH?...
WHY DO YOU ASK?
WELL, WE'VE ALREADY BEEN GOING OUT FOR A WHILE NOW...
...SO, SHOULDN'T WE KISS?

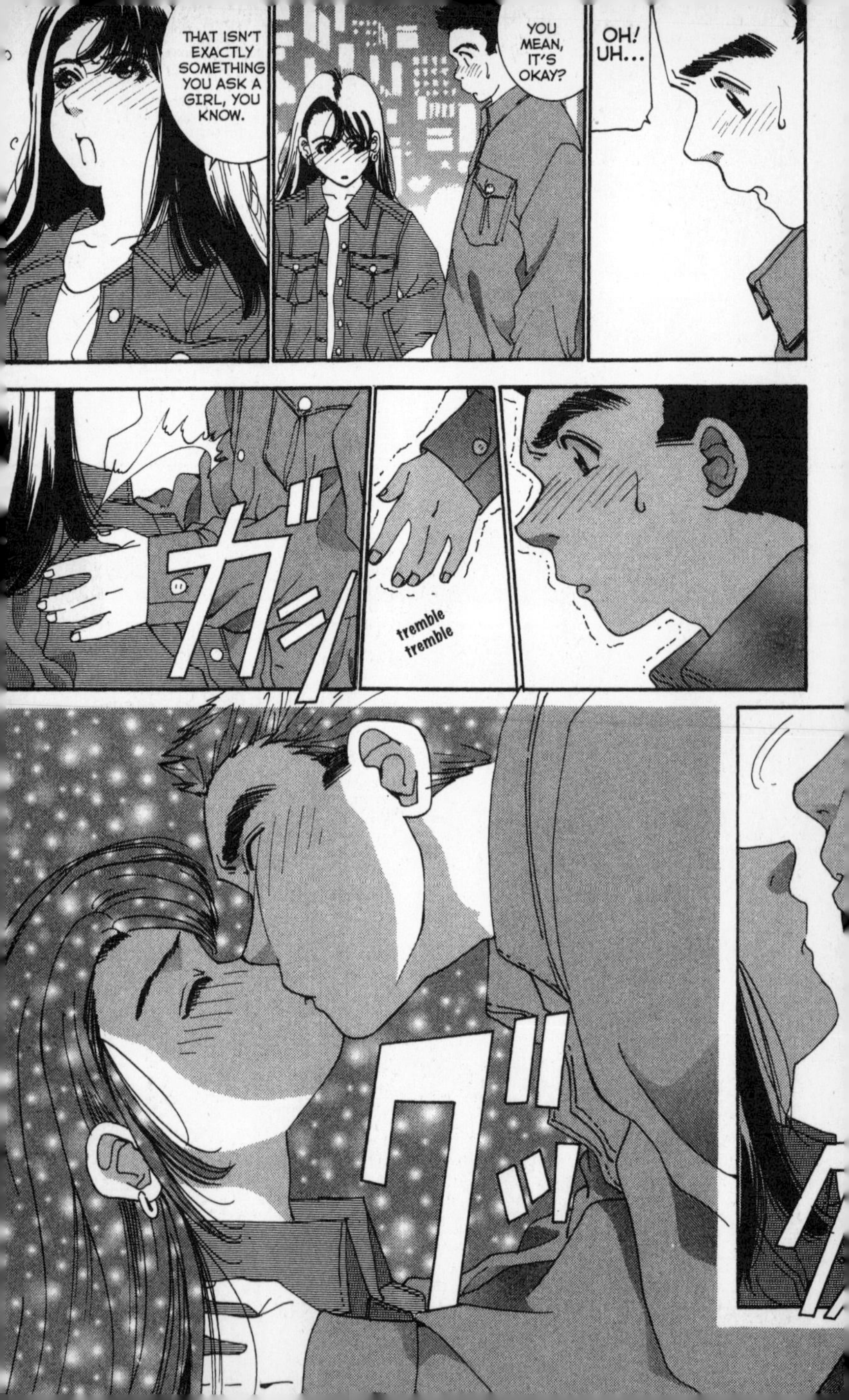
OH! UH...
YOU MEAN, IT'S OKAY?
THAT ISN'T EXACTLY SOMETHING YOU ASK A GIRL, YOU KNOW.
tremble tremble
ガシ
グッ

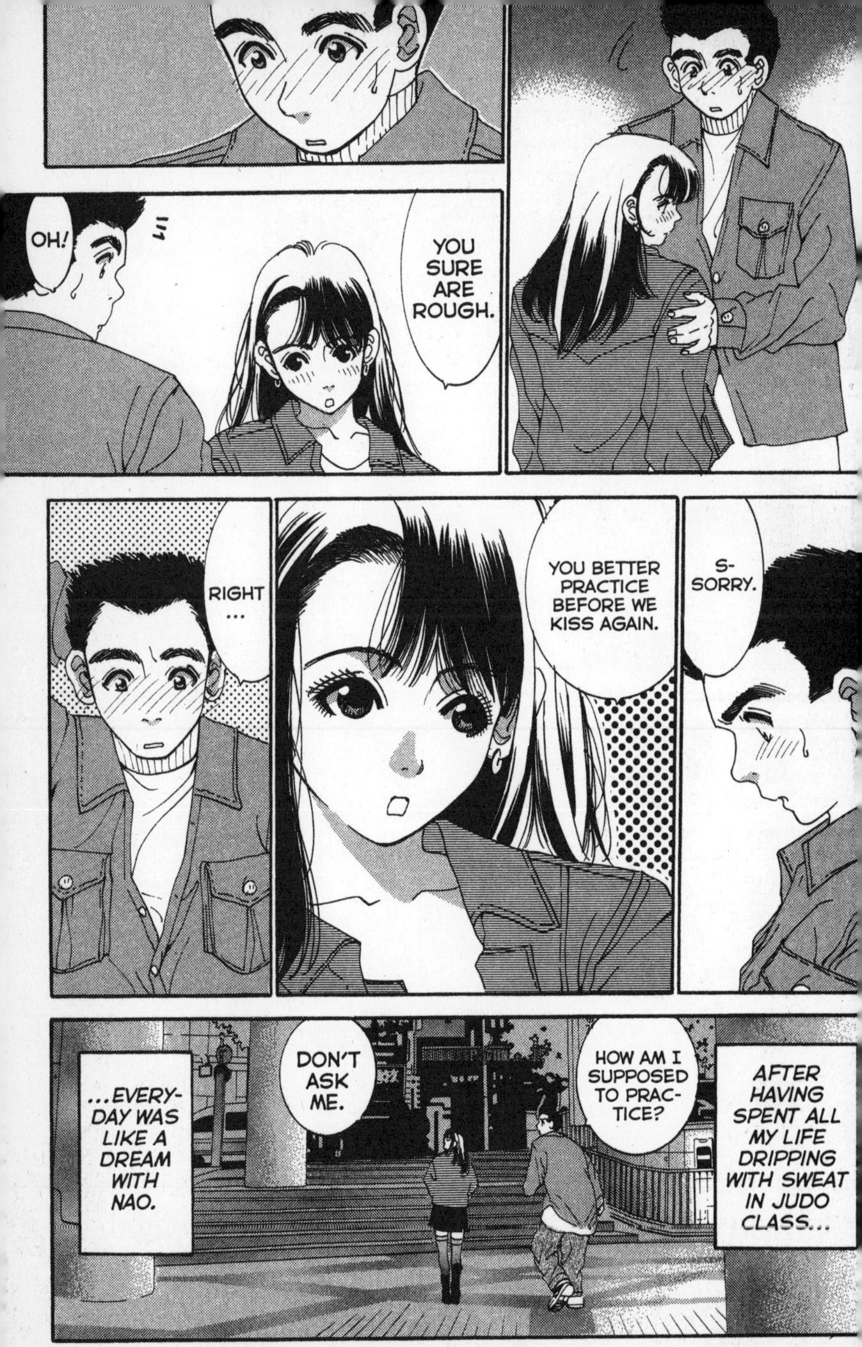
YOU SURE ARE ROUGH.
OH!
S-SORRY.
YOU BETTER PRACTICE BEFORE WE KISS AGAIN.
RIGHT ...
AFTER HAVING SPENT ALL MY LIFE DRIPPING WITH SWEAT IN JUDO CLASS...
HOW AM I SUPPOSED TO PRAC-TICE?
DON'T ASK ME.
...EVERY-DAY WAS LIKE A DREAM WITH NAO.

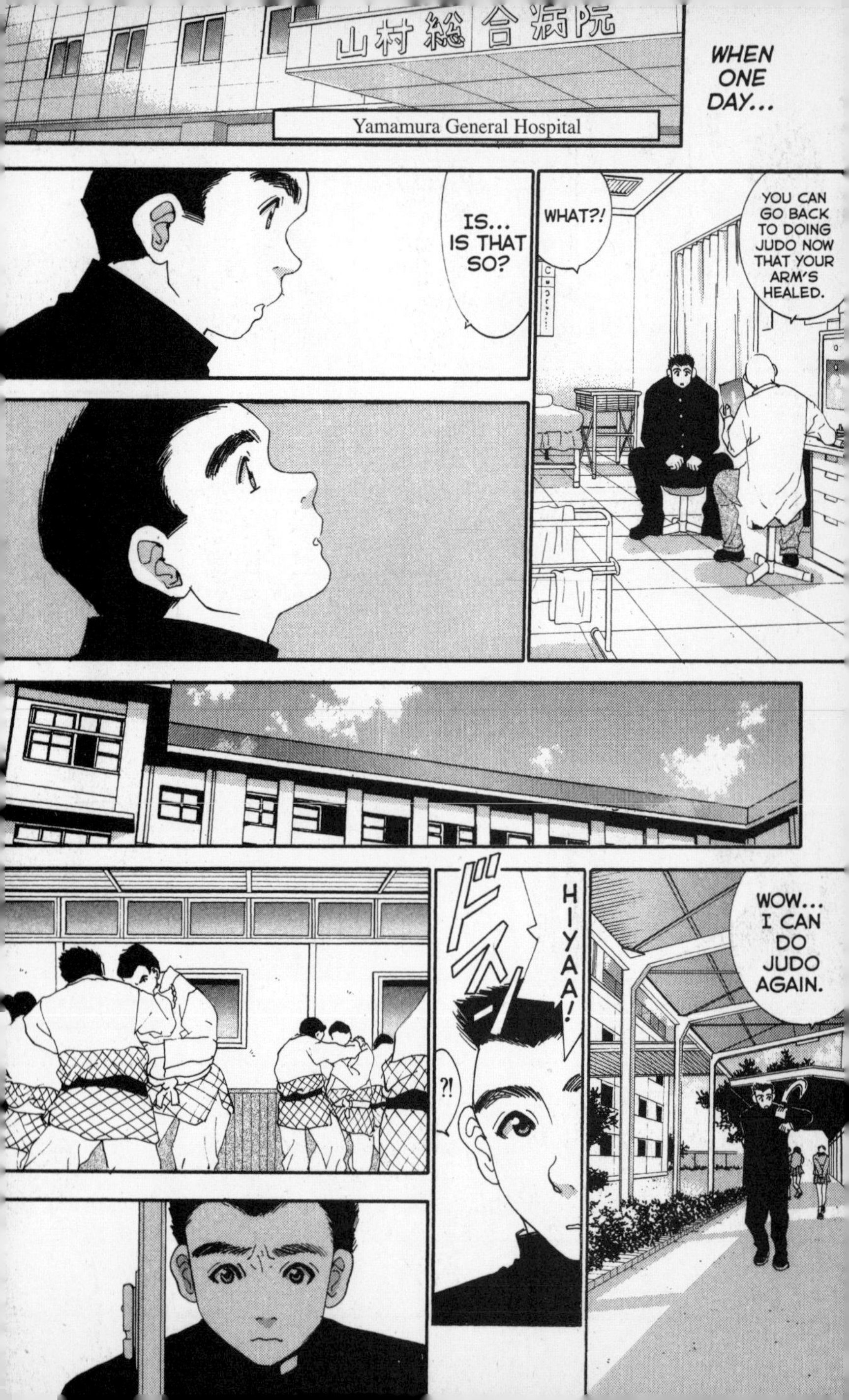
WHEN ONE DAY...
山村総合病院
Yamamura General Hospital
YOU CAN GO BACK TO DOING JUDO NOW THAT YOUR ARM'S HEALED.
WHAT?!
IS... IS THAT SO?
WOW... I CAN DO JUDO AGAIN.
ドス
HIYAAA!
?!

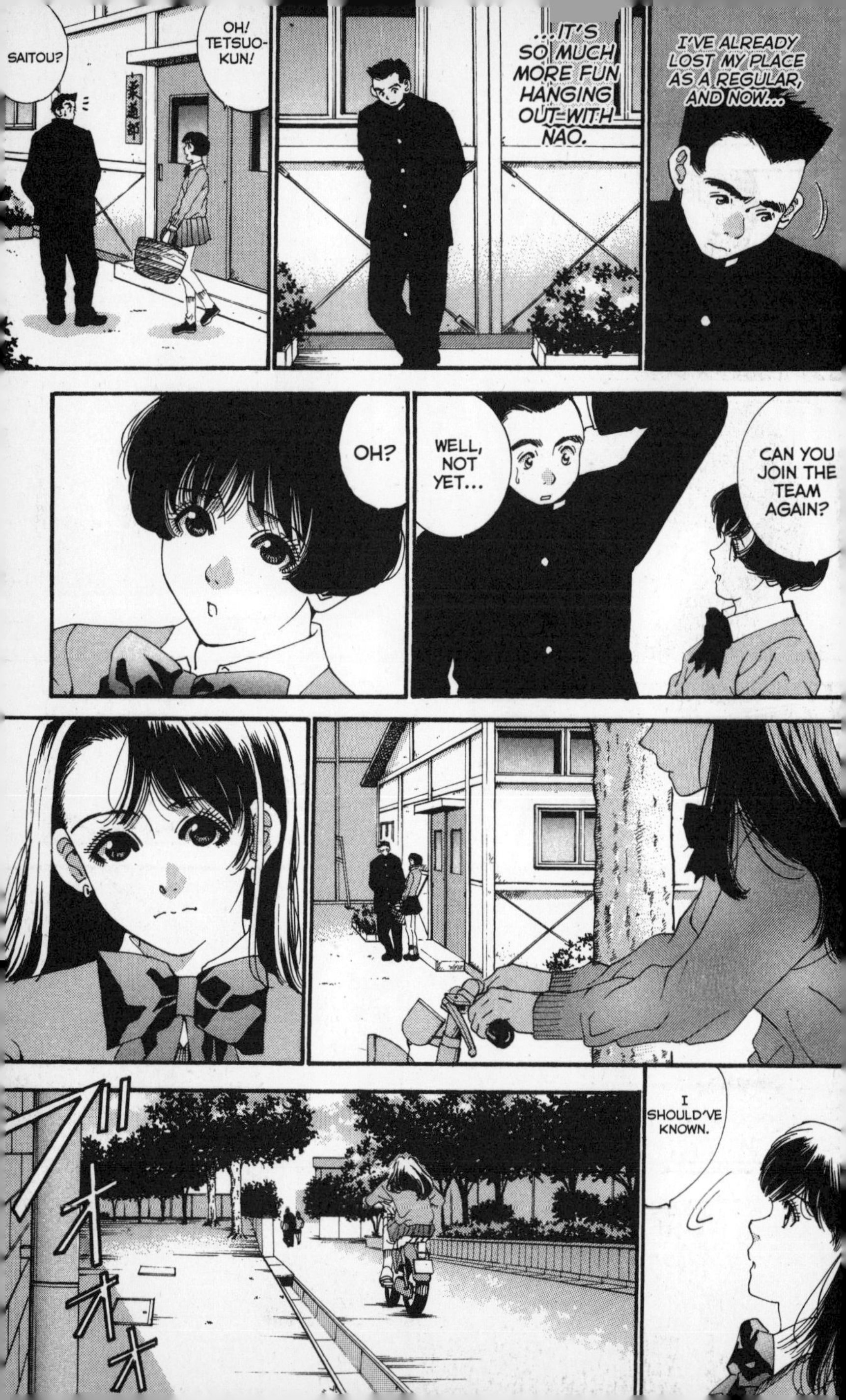
I'VE ALREADY LOST MY PLACE AS A REGULAR, AND NOW...
...IT'S SO MUCH MORE FUN HANGING OUT WITH NAO.
OH! TETSUO-KUN!
SAITOU?
CAN YOU JOIN THE TEAM AGAIN?
WELL, NOT YET...
OH?
I SHOULD'VE KNOWN.
ブオオオオ

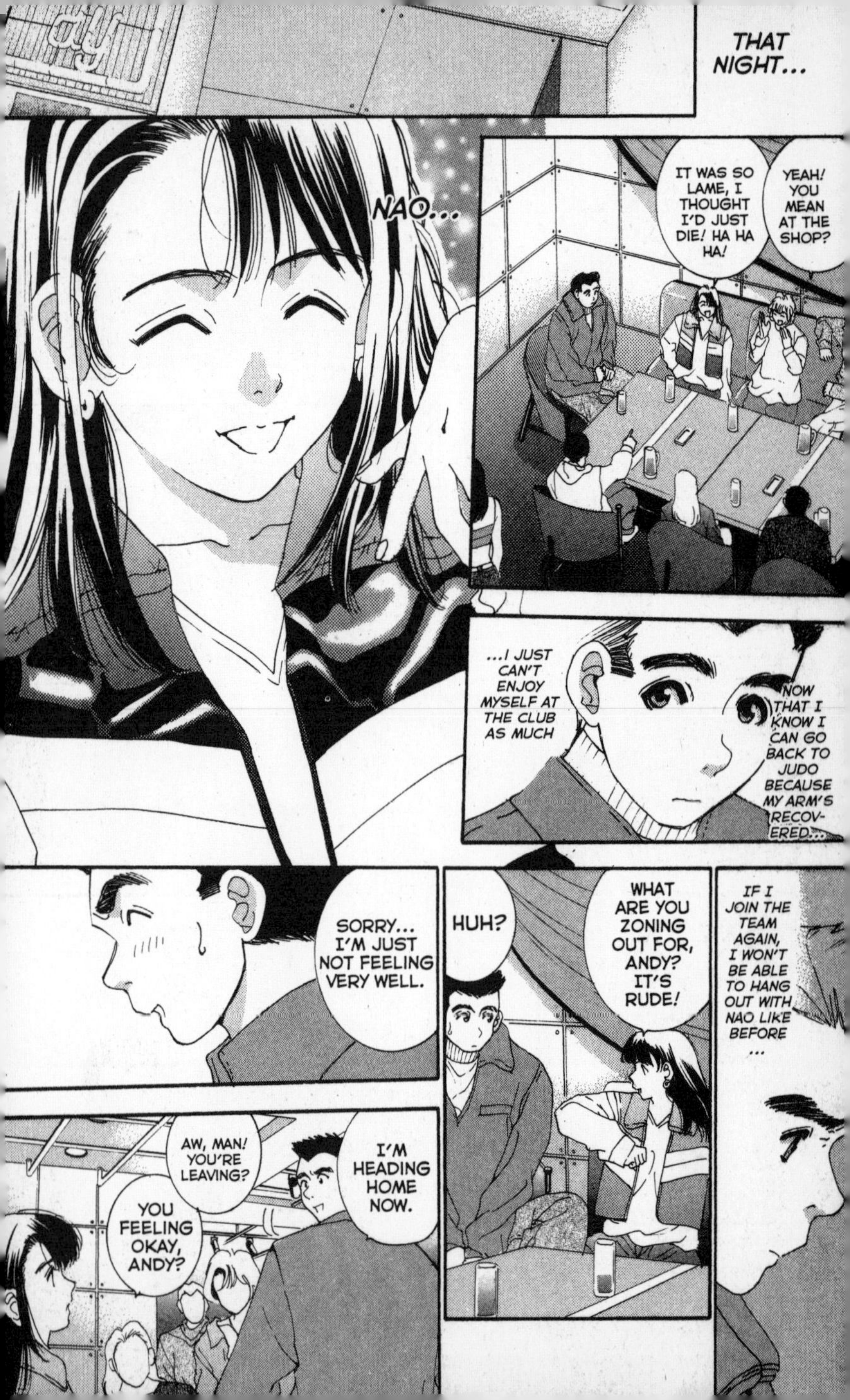
THAT NIGHT...
YEAH! YOU MEAN AT THE SHOP?
IT WAS SO LAME, I THOUGHT I'D JUST DIE! HA HA HA!
NOW THAT I KNOW I CAN GO BACK TO JUDO BECAUSE MY ARM'S RECOVERED...
...I JUST CAN'T ENJOY MYSELF AT THE CLUB AS MUCH
NAO...
IF I JOIN THE TEAM AGAIN, I WON'T BE ABLE TO HANG OUT WITH NAO LIKE BEFORE...
WHAT ARE YOU ZONING OUT FOR, ANDY? IT'S RUDE!
HUH?
SORRY... I'M JUST NOT FEELING VERY WELL.
I'M HEADING HOME NOW.
AW, MAN! YOU'RE LEAVING?
YOU FEELING OKAY, ANDY?

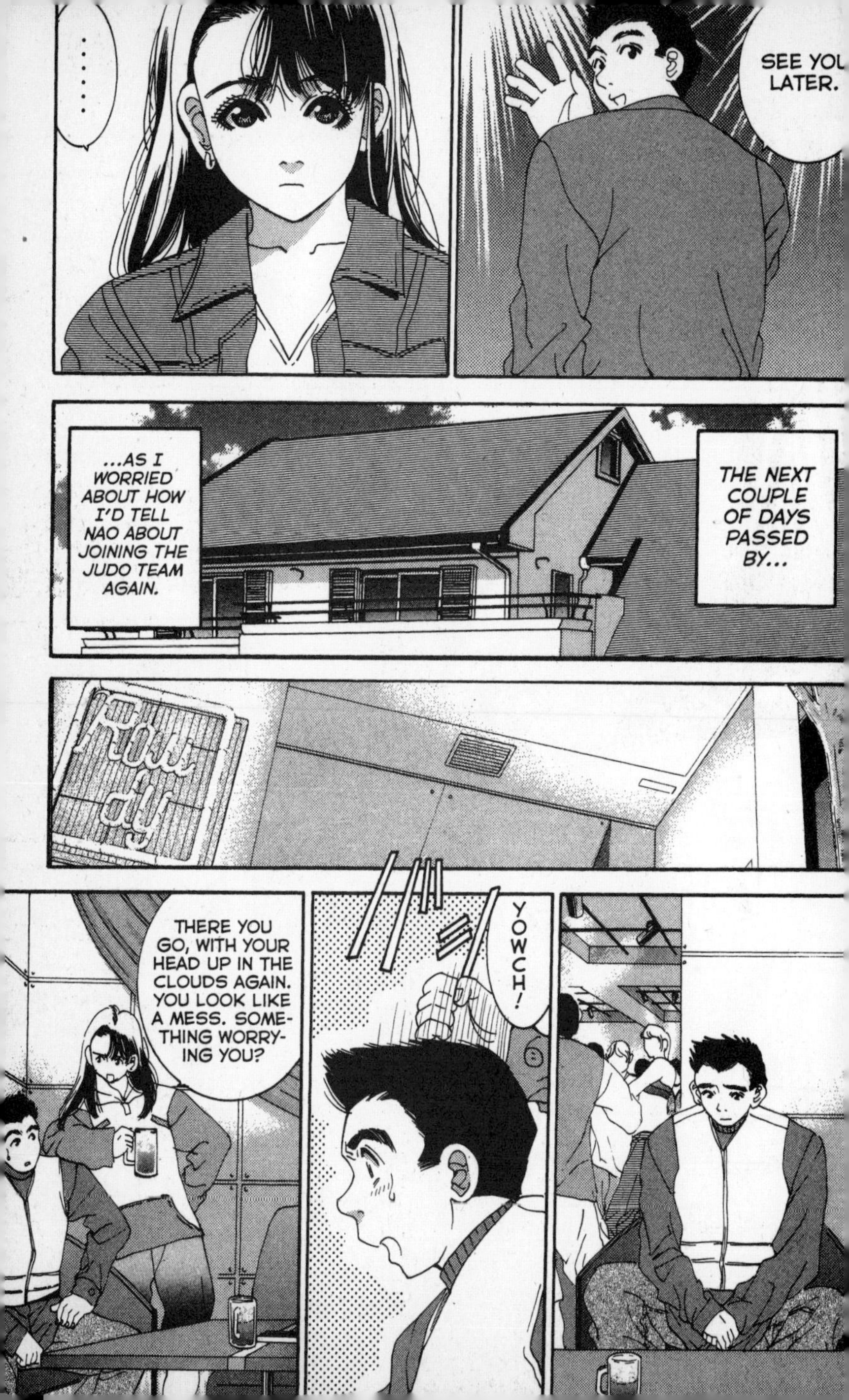
SEE YOU LATER.
......
THE NEXT COUPLE OF DAYS PASSED BY...
...AS I WORRIED ABOUT HOW I'D TELL NAO ABOUT JOINING THE JUDO TEAM AGAIN.
YOWCH!
THERE YOU GO, WITH YOUR HEAD UP IN THE CLOUDS AGAIN. YOU LOOK LIKE A MESS. SOMETHING WORRYING YOU?

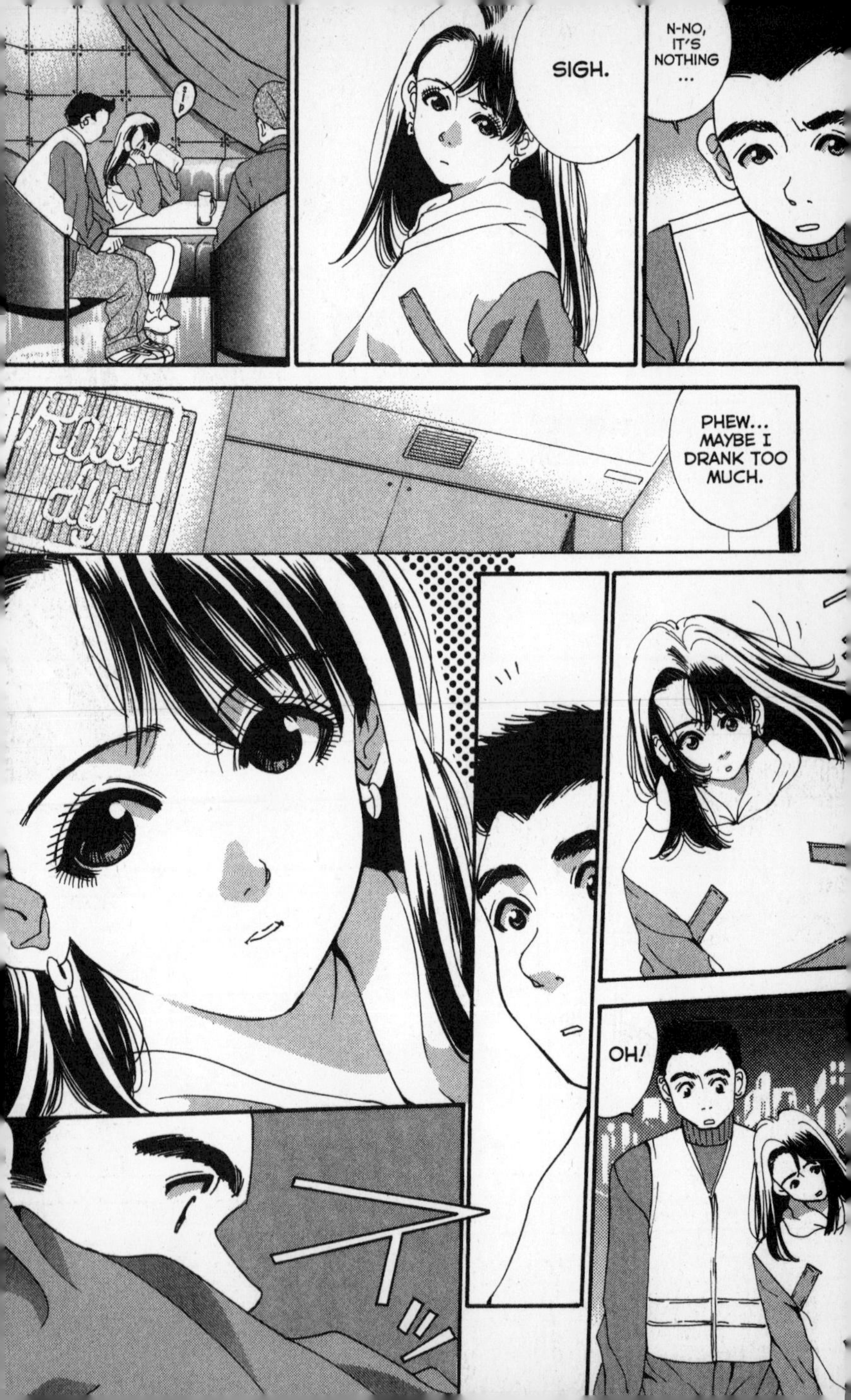
N-NO, IT'S NOTHING ...
SIGH.
SIP
PHEW... MAYBE I DRANK TOO MUCH.
OH!

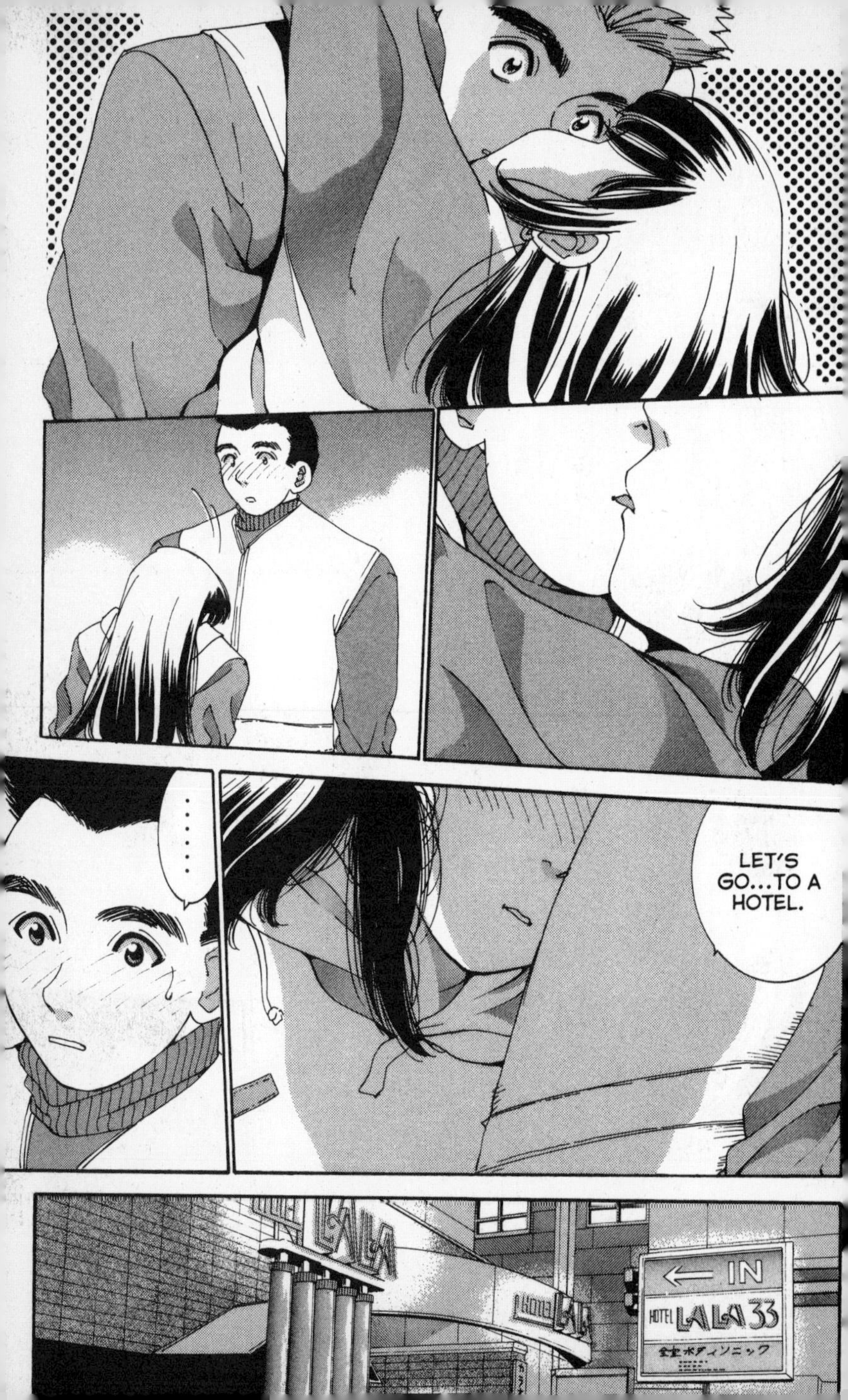
LET'S GO...TO A HOTEL.
......
LALA
← IN
HOTEL LALA 33

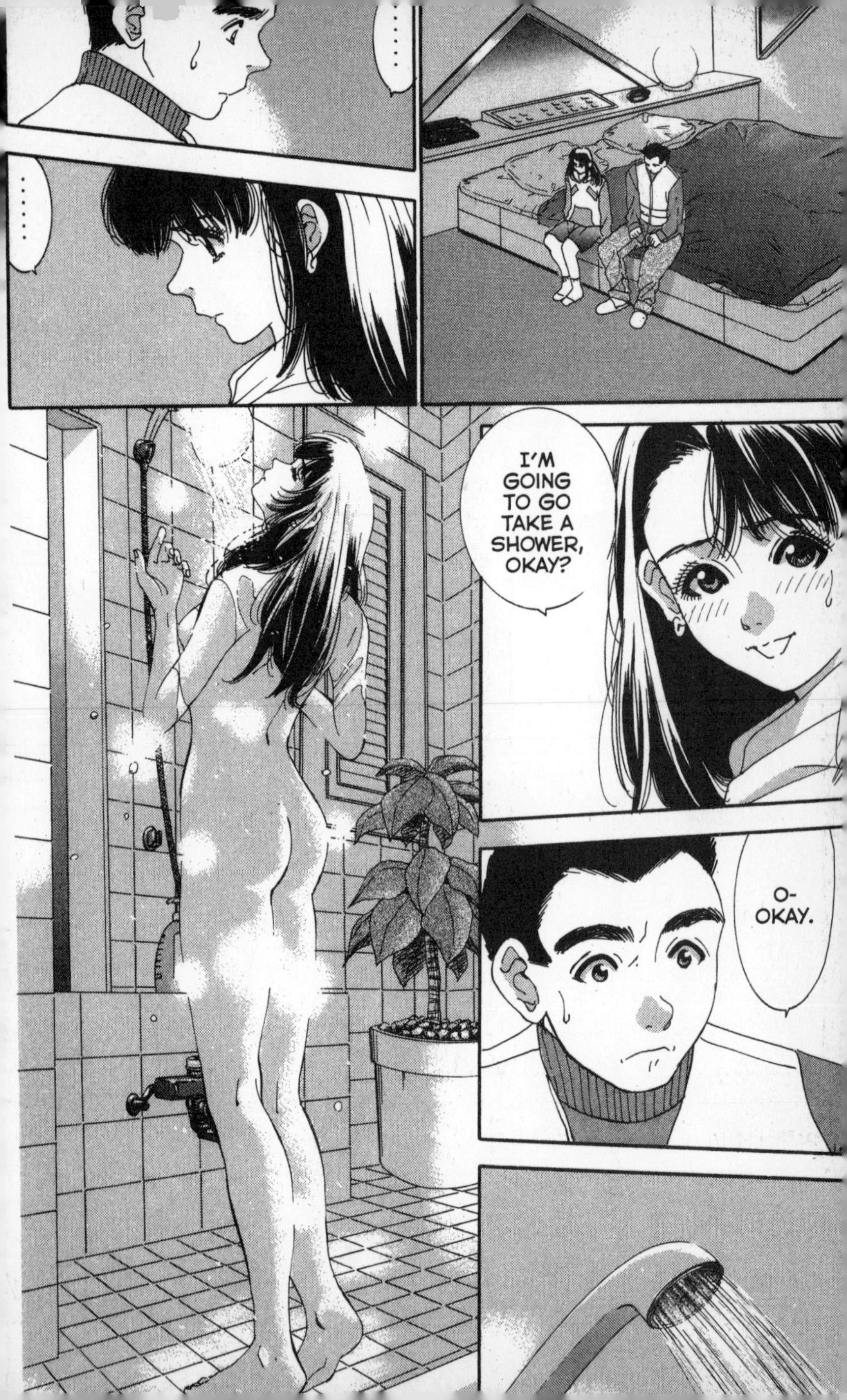
...
......
I'M GOING TO GO TAKE A SHOWER, OKAY?
O-OKAY.

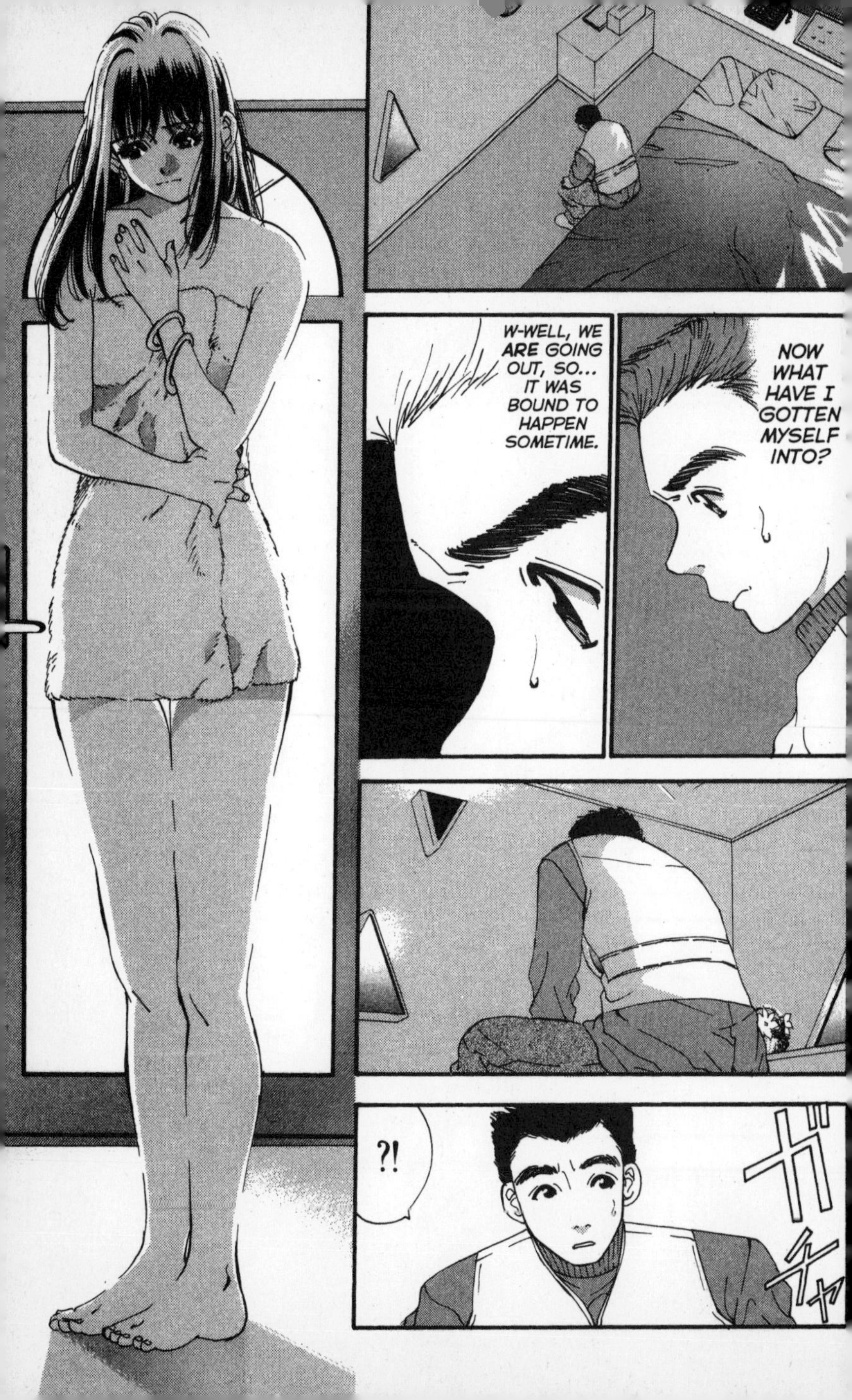
NOW WHAT HAVE I GOTTEN MYSELF INTO?
W-WELL, WE ARE GOING OUT, SO... IT WAS BOUND TO HAPPEN SOMETIME.
?!
ガチャ

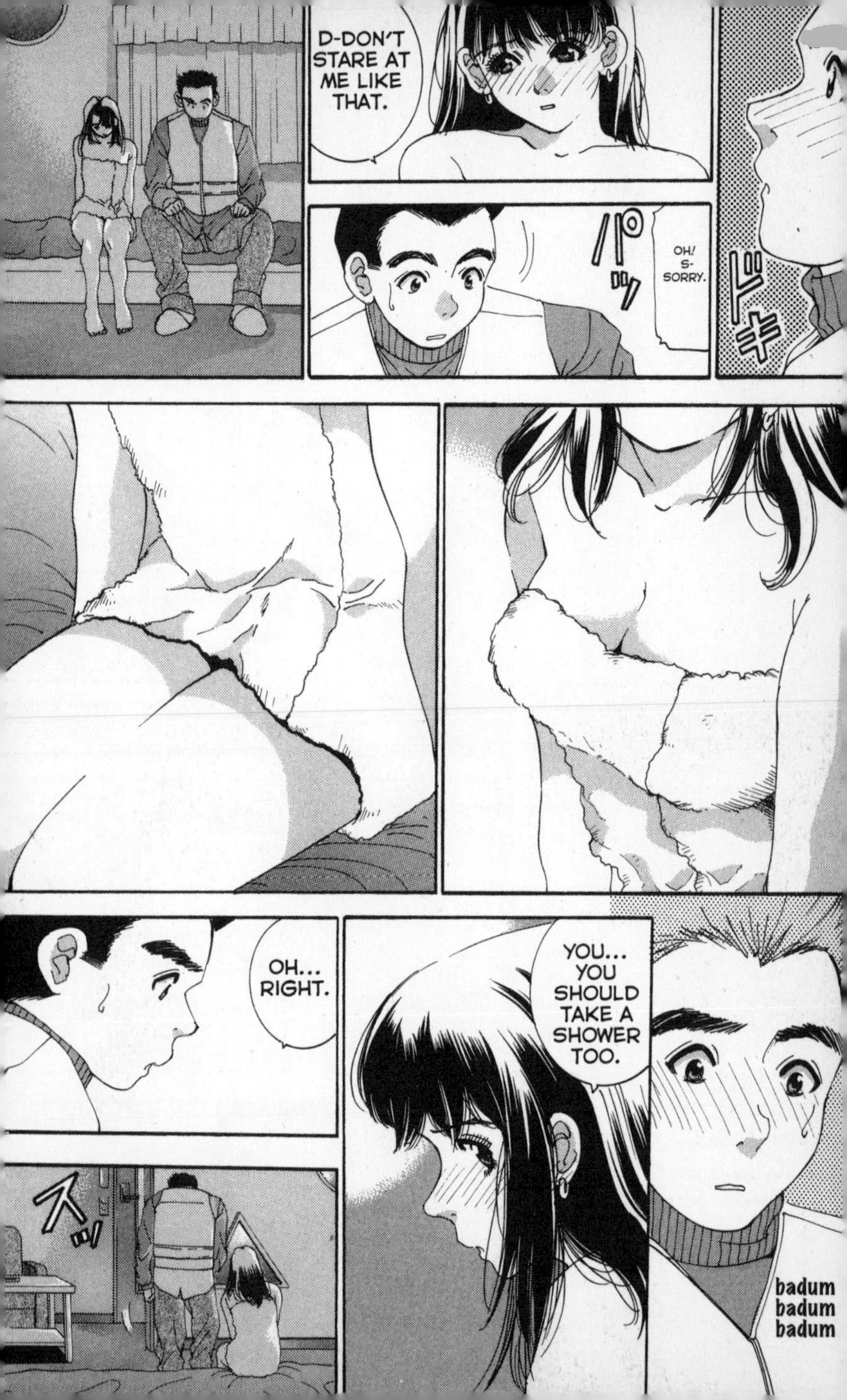

ドキ
D-DON'T STARE AT ME LIKE THAT.
OH! S-SORRY.
パッ
YOU... YOU SHOULD TAKE A SHOWER TOO.
badum badum badum
OH... RIGHT.
スッ

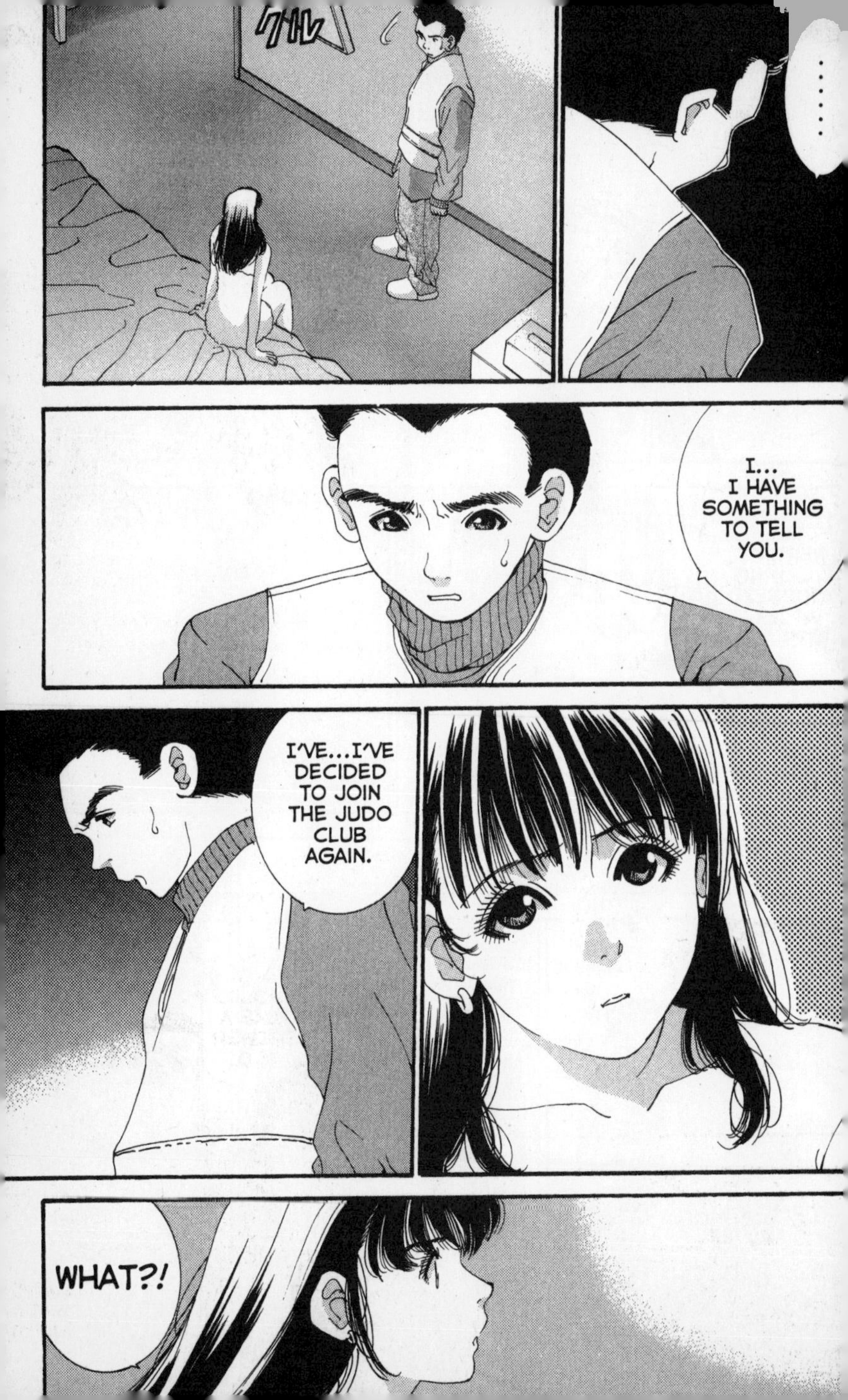
......
I... I HAVE SOMETHING TO TELL YOU.
I'VE...I'VE DECIDED TO JOIN THE JUDO CLUB AGAIN.
WHAT?!

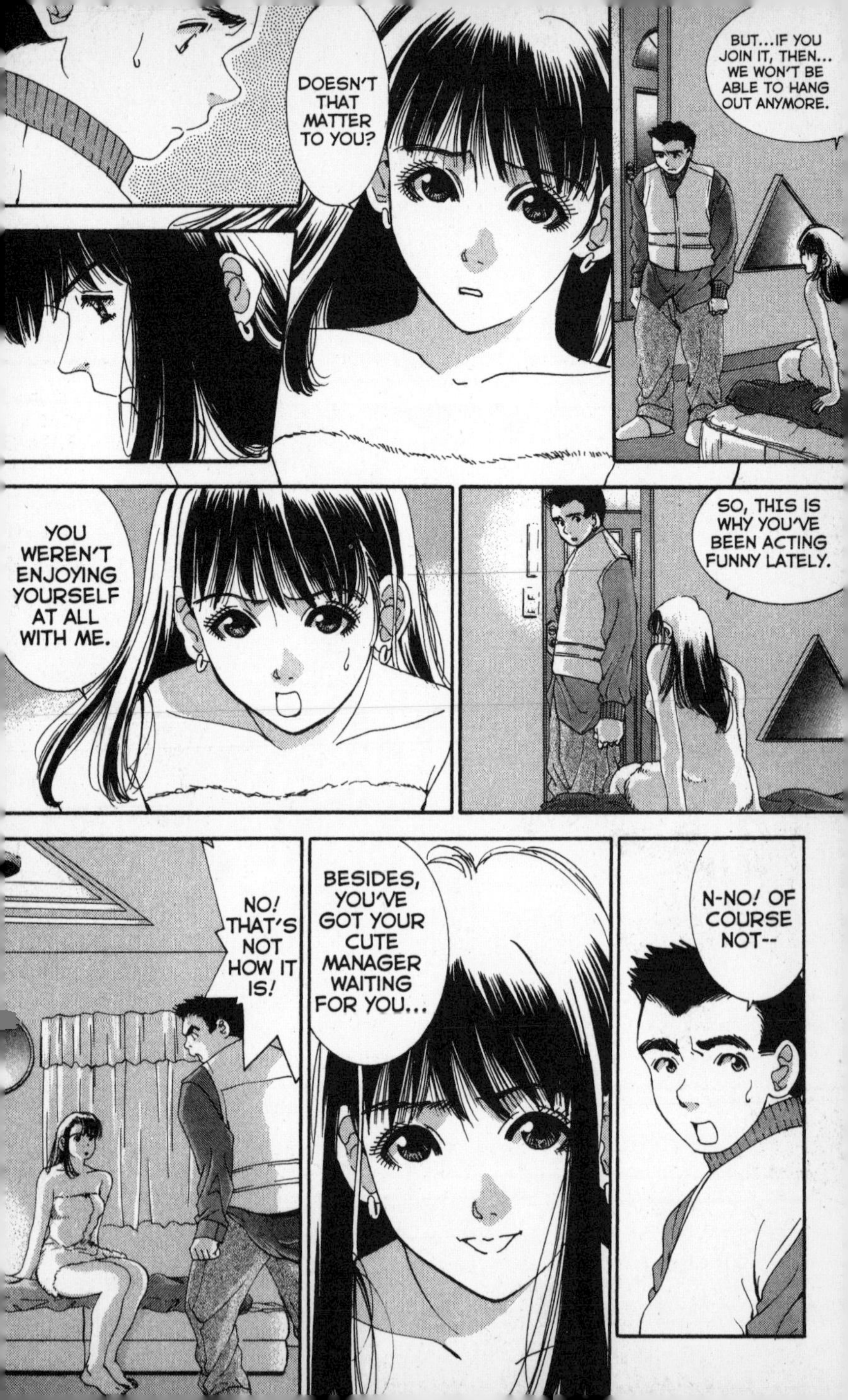
BUT...IF YOU JOIN IT, THEN... WE WON'T BE ABLE TO HANG OUT ANYMORE.
DOESN'T THAT MATTER TO YOU?
SO, THIS IS WHY YOU'VE BEEN ACTING FUNNY LATELY.
YOU WEREN'T ENJOYING YOURSELF AT ALL WITH ME.
N-NO! OF COURSE NOT--
BESIDES, YOU'VE GOT YOUR CUTE MANAGER WAITING FOR YOU...
NO! THAT'S NOT HOW IT IS!

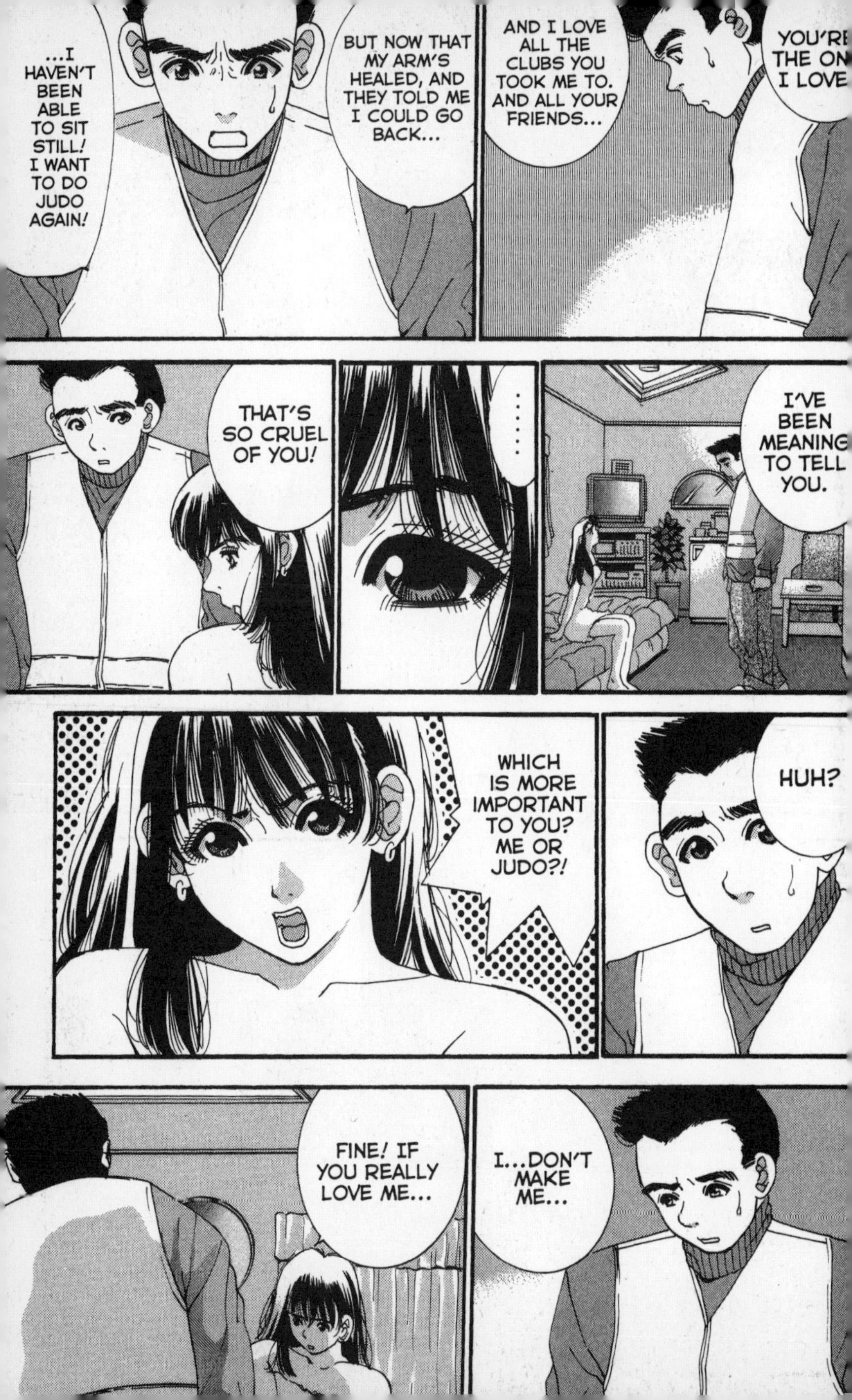
YOU'RE THE ON I LOVE
AND I LOVE ALL THE CLUBS YOU TOOK ME TO. AND ALL YOUR FRIENDS...
BUT NOW THAT MY ARM'S HEALED, AND THEY TOLD ME I COULD GO BACK...
...I HAVEN'T BEEN ABLE TO SIT STILL! I WANT TO DO JUDO AGAIN!
I'VE BEEN MEANING TO TELL YOU.
......
THAT'S SO CRUEL OF YOU!
HUH?
WHICH IS MORE IMPORTANT TO YOU? ME OR JUDO?!
I...DON'T MAKE ME...
FINE! IF YOU REALLY LOVE ME...

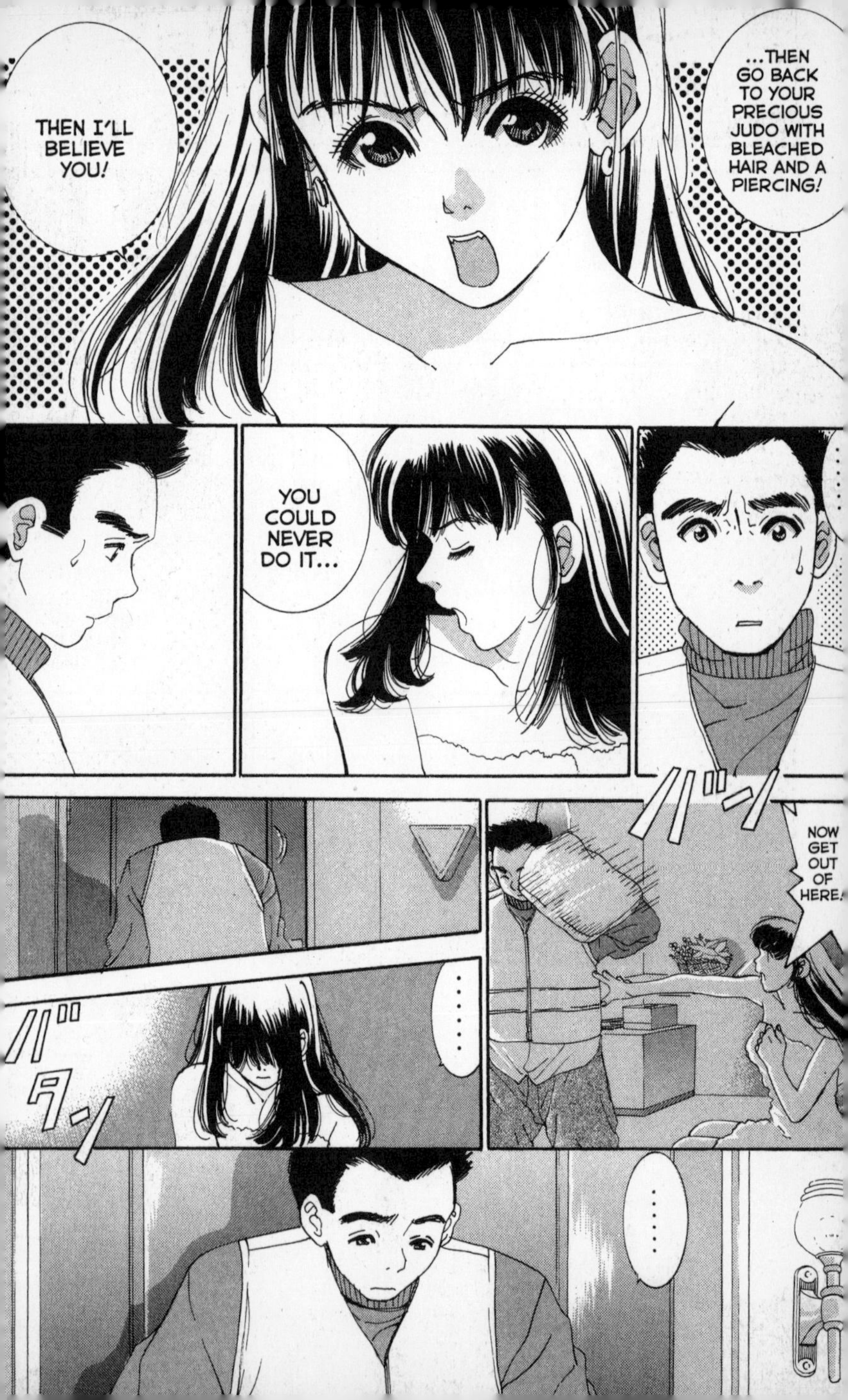
...THEN GO BACK TO YOUR PRECIOUS JUDO WITH BLEACHED HAIR AND A PIERCING!
THEN I'LL BELIEVE YOU!
...
YOU COULD NEVER DO IT...
バン
NOW GET OUT OF HERE!
......
バタン
......

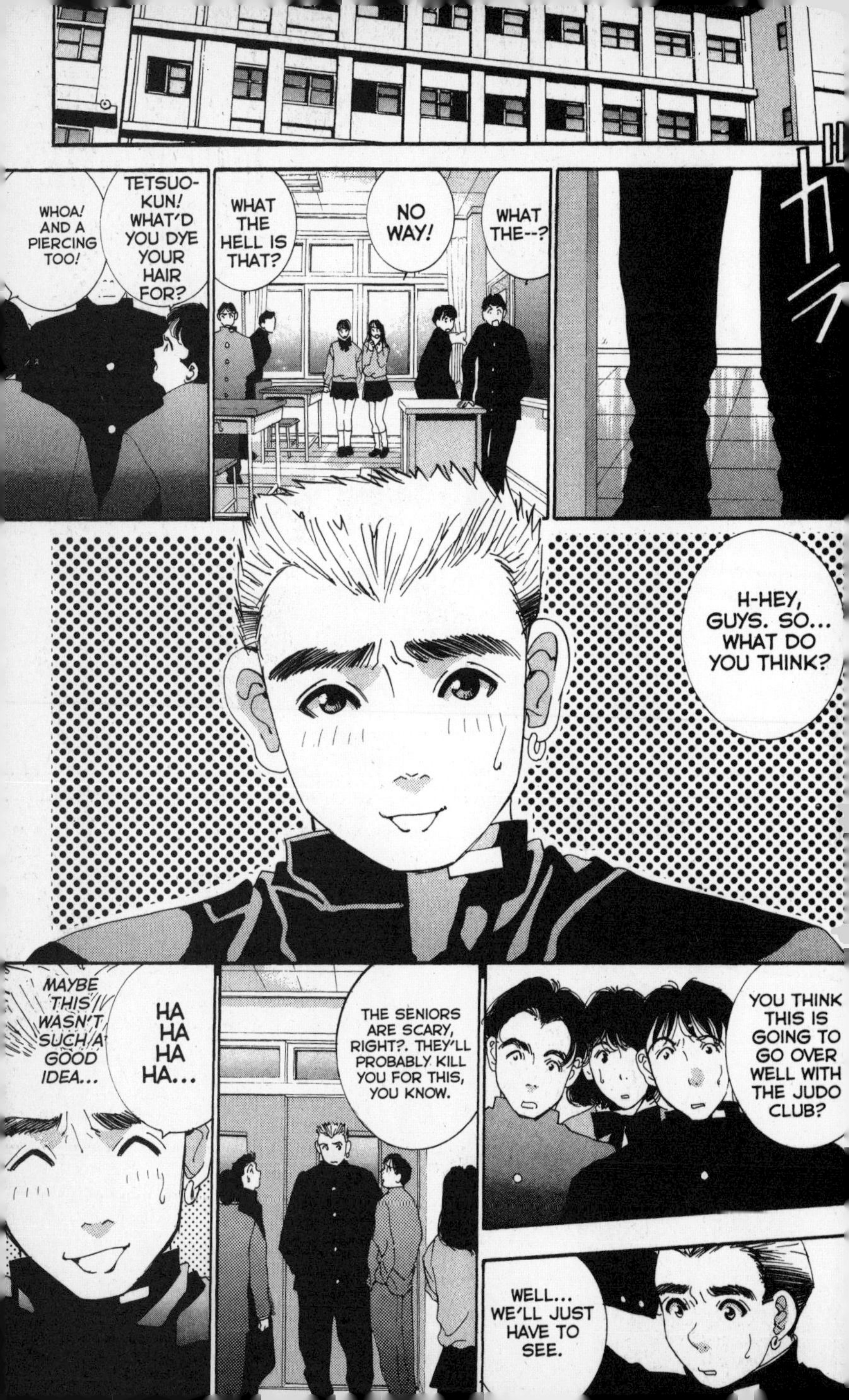
WHAT THE--?
NO WAY!
WHAT THE HELL IS THAT?
TETSUO-KUN! WHAT'D YOU DYE YOUR HAIR FOR?
WHOA! AND A PIERCING TOO!
H-HEY, GUYS. SO... WHAT DO YOU THINK?
YOU THINK THIS IS GOING TO GO OVER WELL WITH THE JUDO CLUB?
WELL... WE'LL JUST HAVE TO SEE.
THE SENIORS ARE SCARY, RIGHT?. THEY'LL PROBABLY KILL YOU FOR THIS, YOU KNOW.
HA HA HA HA...
MAYBE THIS WASN'T SUCH A GOOD IDEA...

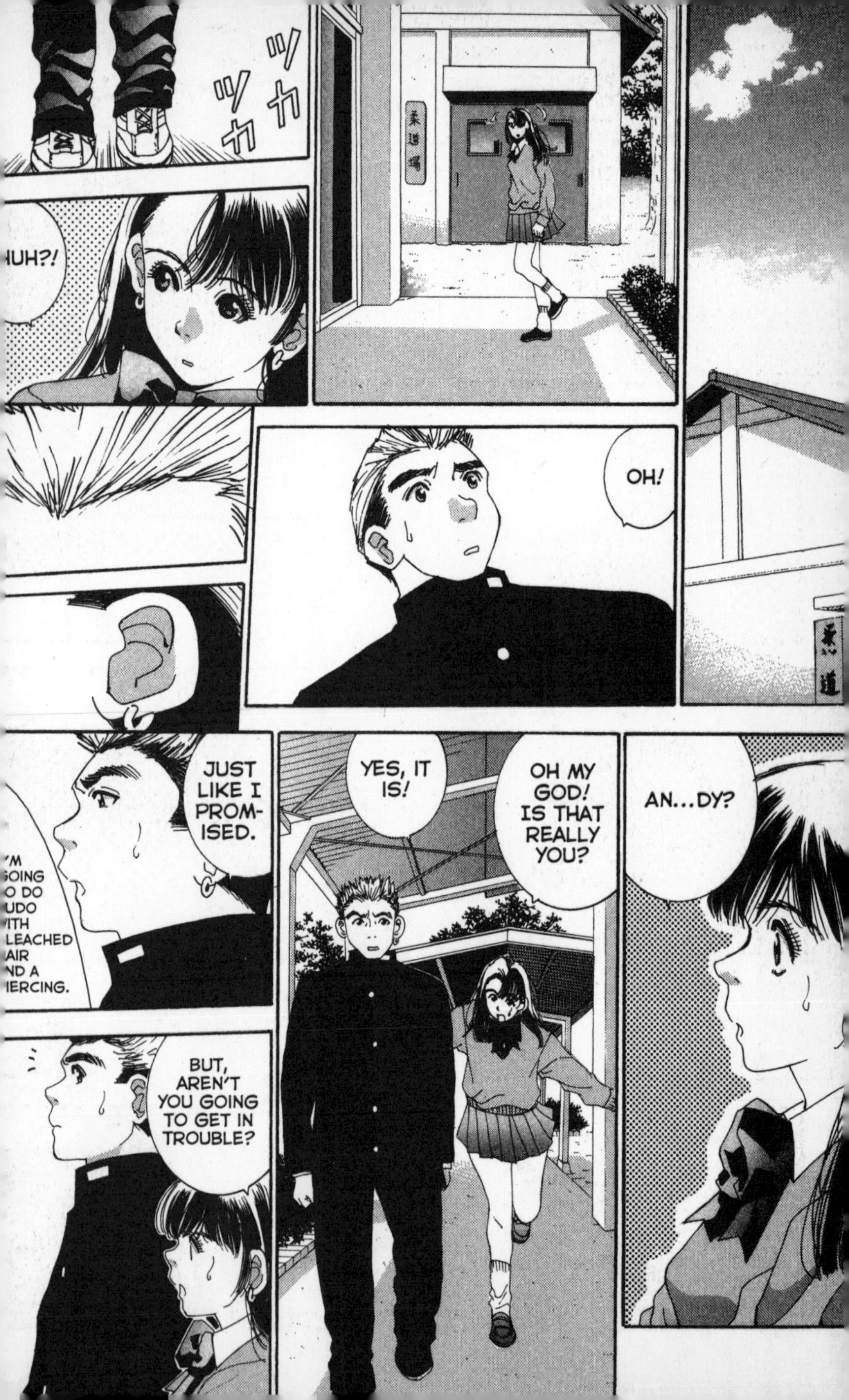
ツカツカ
HUH?!
OH!
AN...DY?
OH MY GOD! IS THAT REALLY YOU?
YES, IT IS!
JUST LIKE I PROMISED.
'M GOING O DO UDO WITH LEACHED AIR ND A IERCING.
BUT, AREN'T YOU GOING TO GET IN TROUBLE?

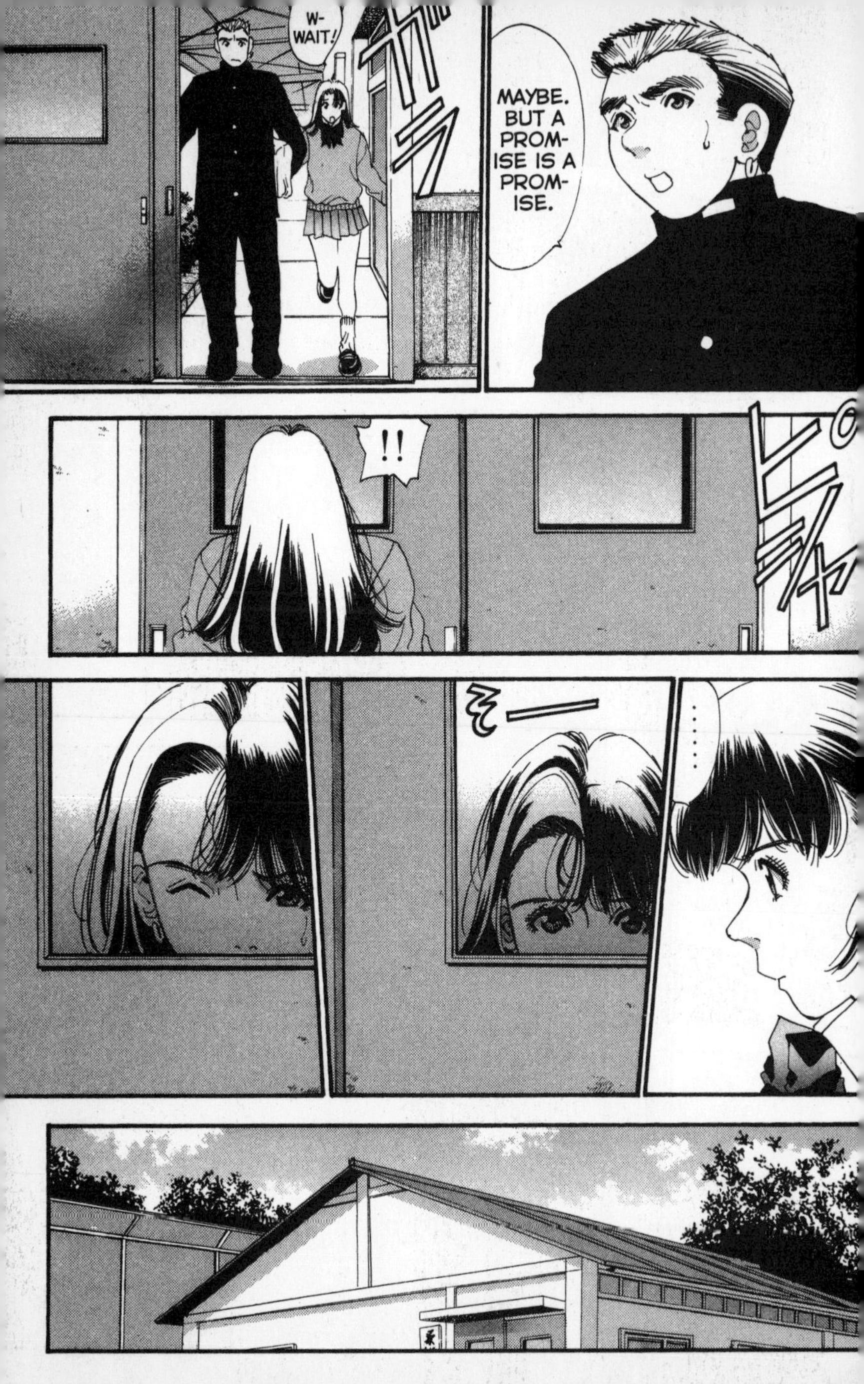
MAYBE. BUT A PROMISE IS A PROMISE.
W-WAIT!
!!
......

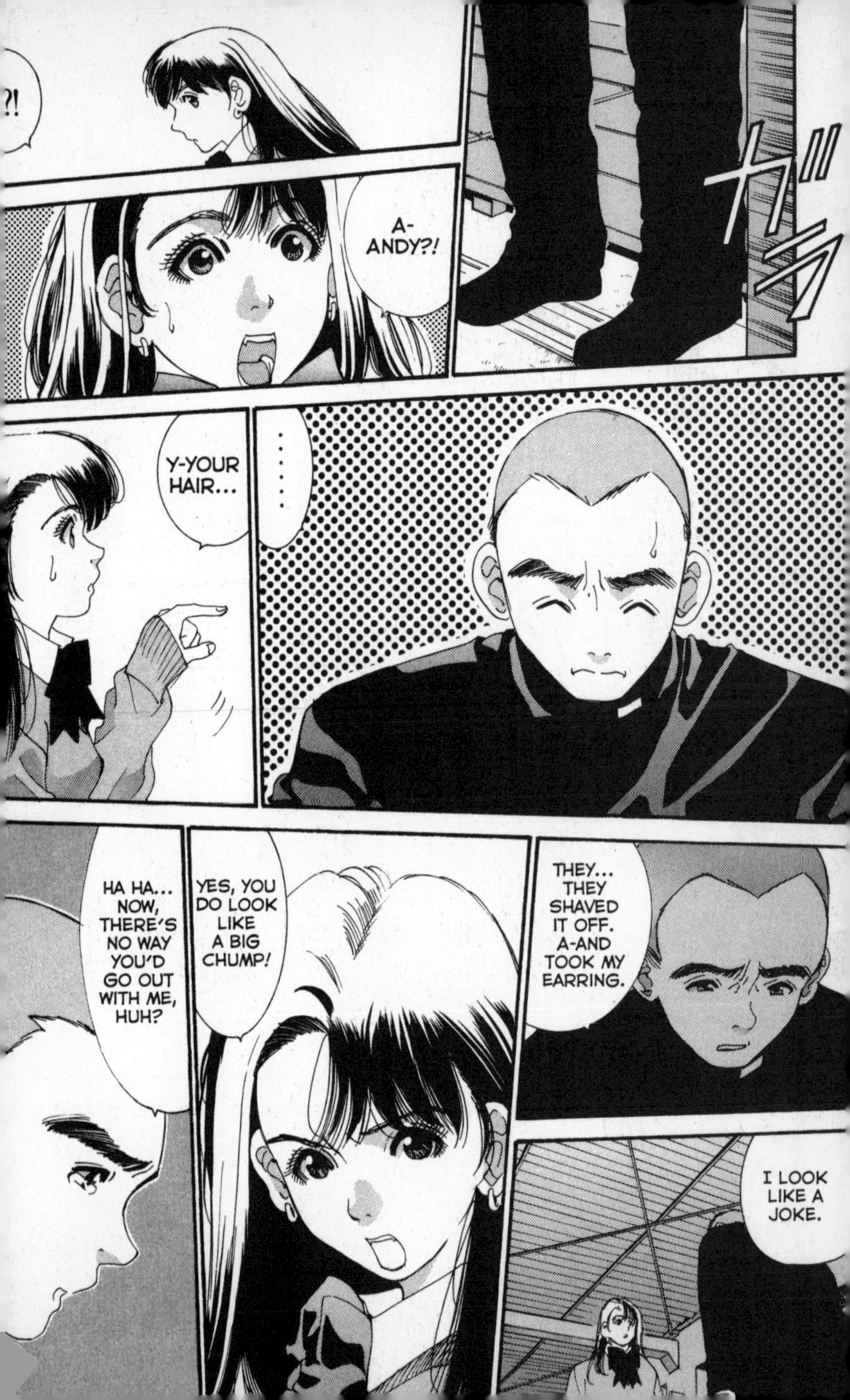
ガラ
?!
A-ANDY?!
......
Y-YOUR HAIR...
THEY... THEY SHAVED IT OFF. A-AND TOOK MY EARRING.
I LOOK LIKE A JOKE.
YES, YOU DO LOOK LIKE A BIG CHUMP!
HA HA... NOW, THERE'S NO WAY YOU'D GO OUT WITH ME, HUH?

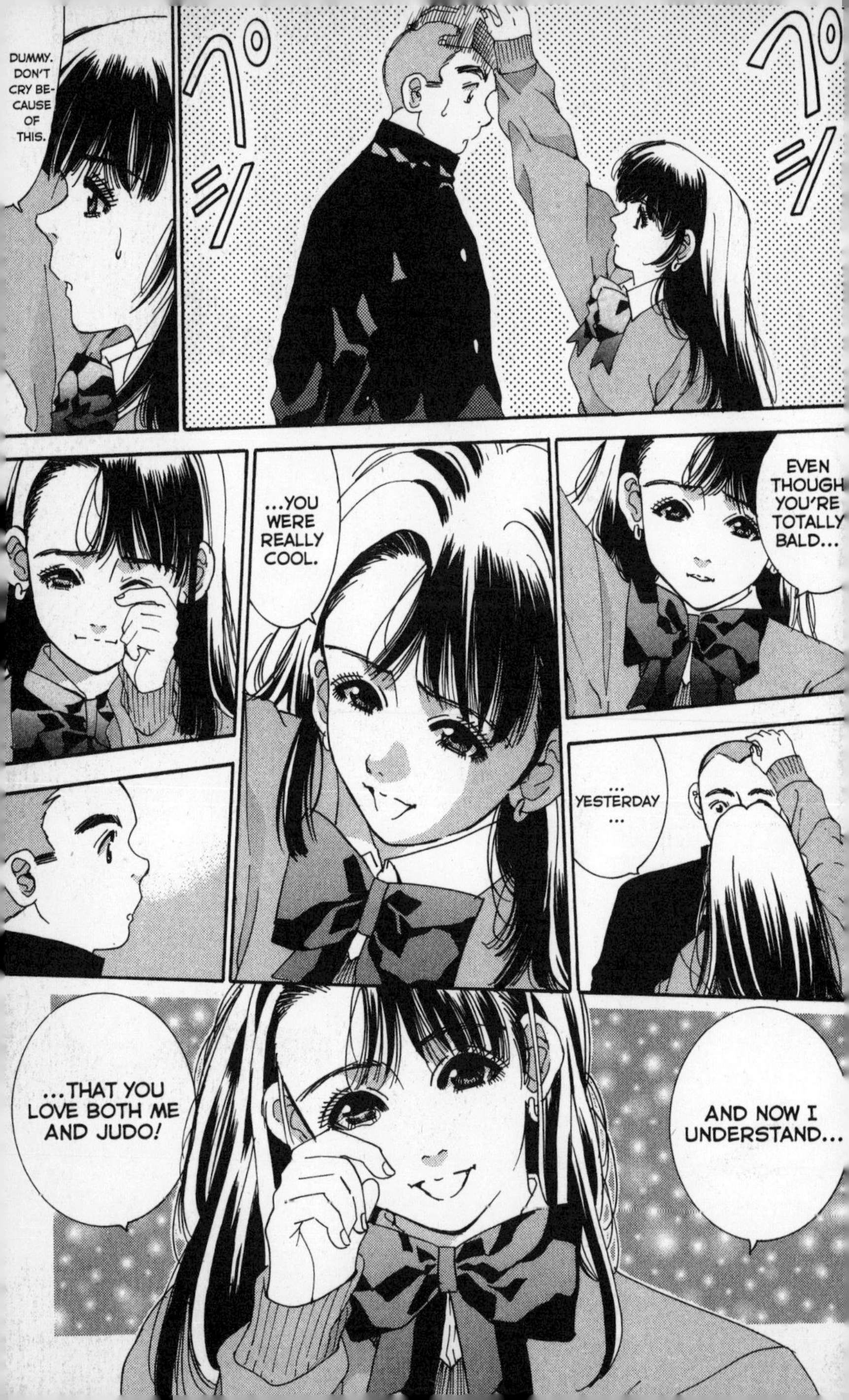
DUMMY. DON'T CRY BE-CAUSE OF THIS.
EVEN THOUGH YOU'RE TOTALLY BALD...
... YESTERDAY ...
...YOU WERE REALLY COOL.
AND NOW I UNDERSTAND...
...THAT YOU LOVE BOTH ME AND JUDO!

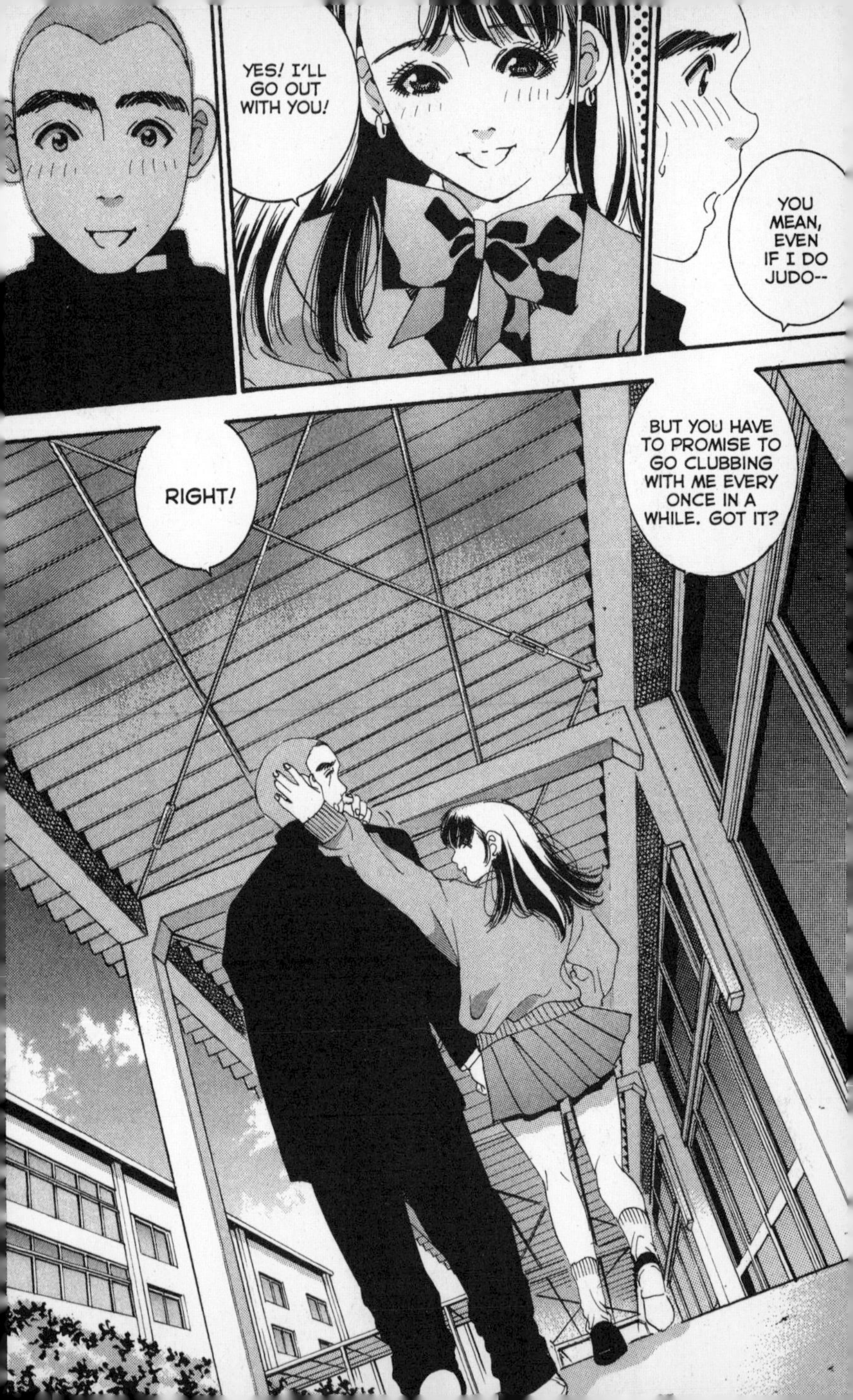
YOU MEAN, EVEN IF I DO JUDO--
YES! I'LL GO OUT WITH YOU!
BUT YOU HAVE TO PROMISE TO GO CLUBBING WITH ME EVERY ONCE IN A WHILE. GOT IT?
RIGHT!

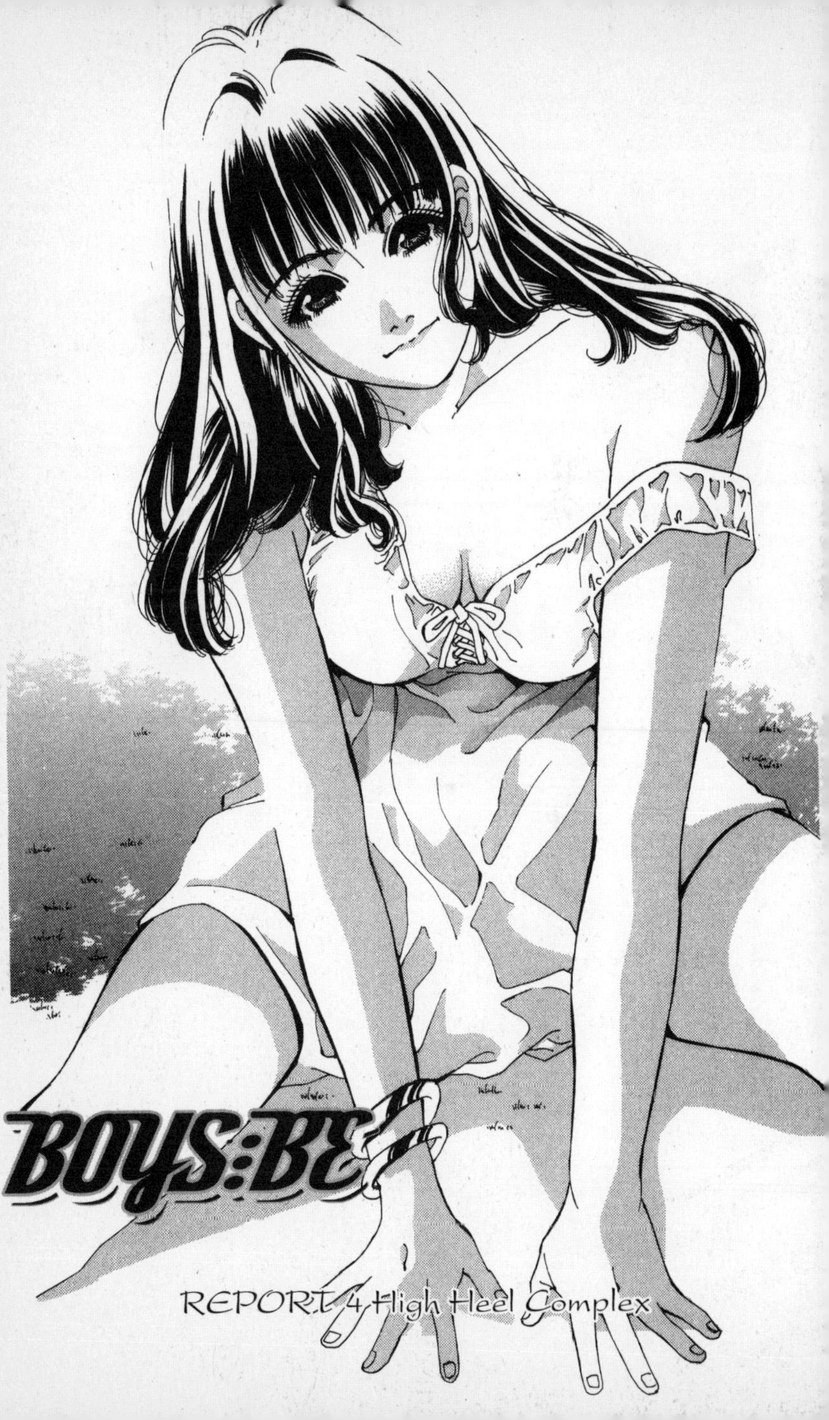
BOYS BE
REPORT 4 High Heel Complex

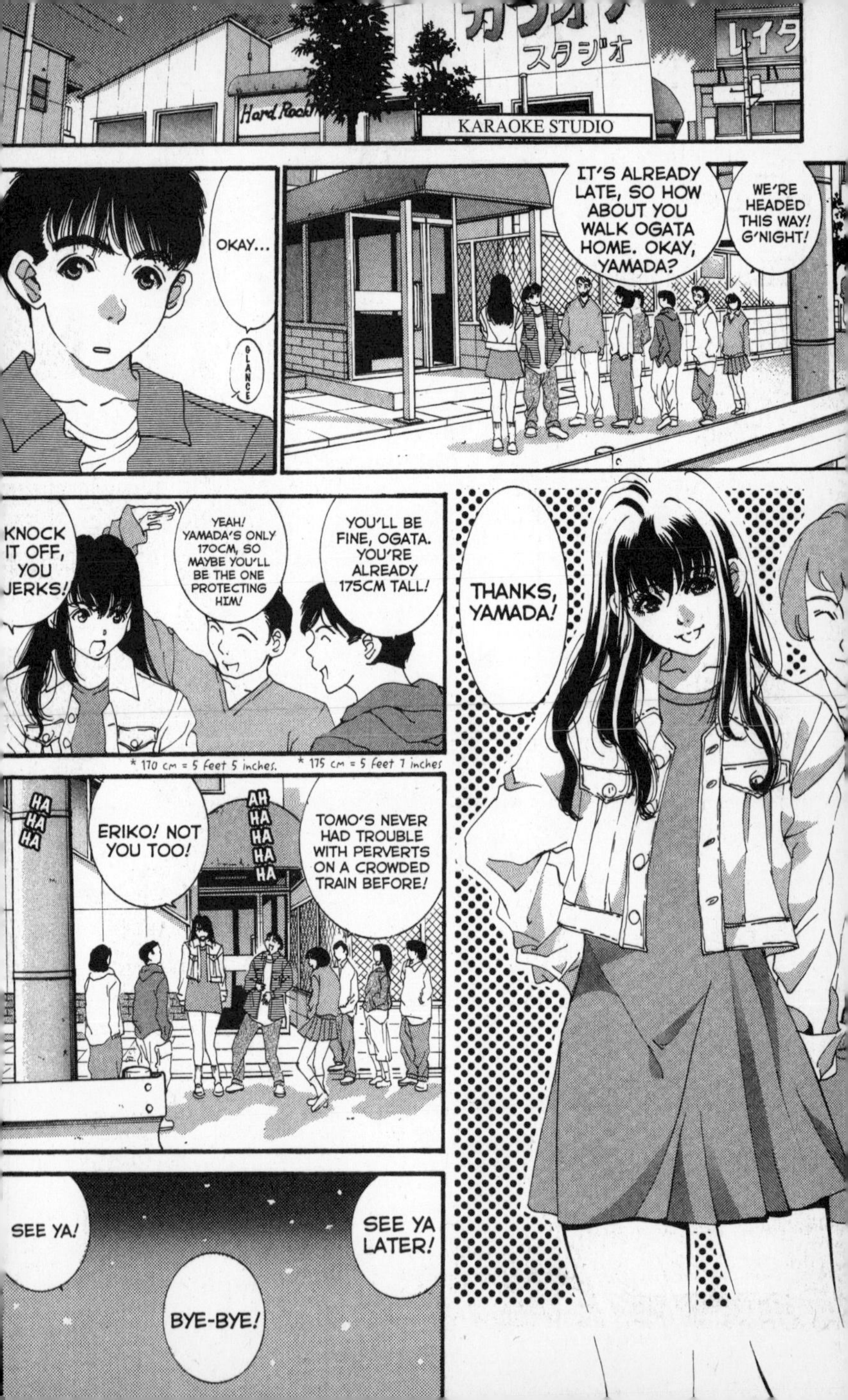
スタジオ
Hard Rock
KARAOKE STUDIO
WE'RE HEADED THIS WAY! G'NIGHT!
IT'S ALREADY LATE, SO HOW ABOUT YOU WALK OGATA HOME. OKAY, YAMADA?
OKAY...
GLANCE
THANKS, YAMADA!
YOU'LL BE FINE, OGATA. YOU'RE ALREADY 175CM TALL!
YEAH! YAMADA'S ONLY 170CM, SO MAYBE YOU'LL BE THE ONE PROTECTING HIM!
KNOCK IT OFF, YOU JERKS!
* 175 cm = 5 feet 7 inches
* 170 cm = 5 feet 5 inches.
TOMO'S NEVER HAD TROUBLE WITH PERVERTS ON A CROWDED TRAIN BEFORE!
AH HA HA HA HA HA
ERIKO! NOT YOU TOO!
HA HA HA HA
SEE YA LATER!
BYE-BYE!
SEE YA!

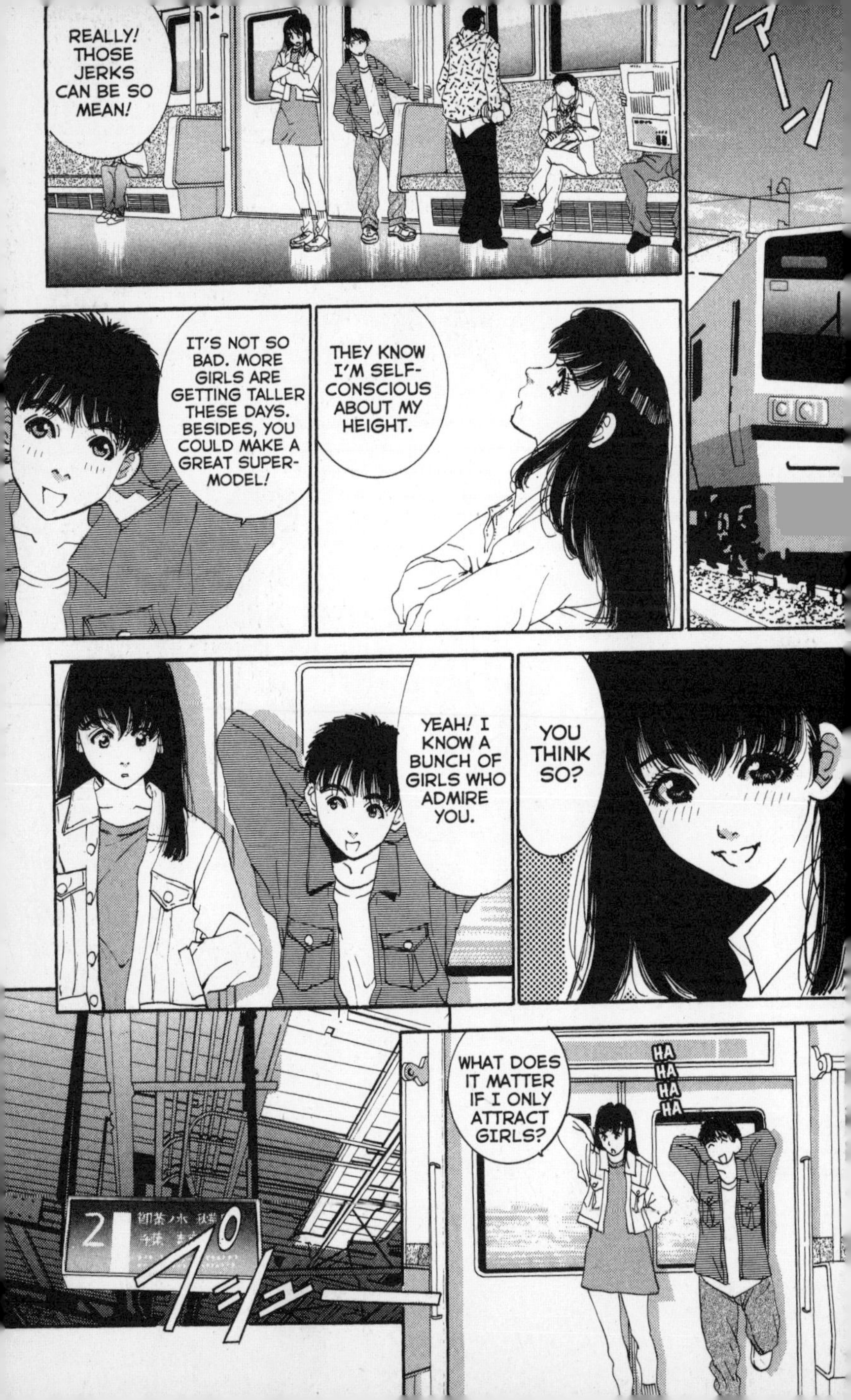
REALLY! THOSE JERKS CAN BE SO MEAN!
THEY KNOW I'M SELF-CONSCIOUS ABOUT MY HEIGHT.
IT'S NOT SO BAD. MORE GIRLS ARE GETTING TALLER THESE DAYS. BESIDES, YOU COULD MAKE A GREAT SUPER-MODEL!
YOU THINK SO?
YEAH! I KNOW A BUNCH OF GIRLS WHO ADMIRE YOU.
WHAT DOES IT MATTER IF I ONLY ATTRACT GIRLS?
HA HA HA HA
2

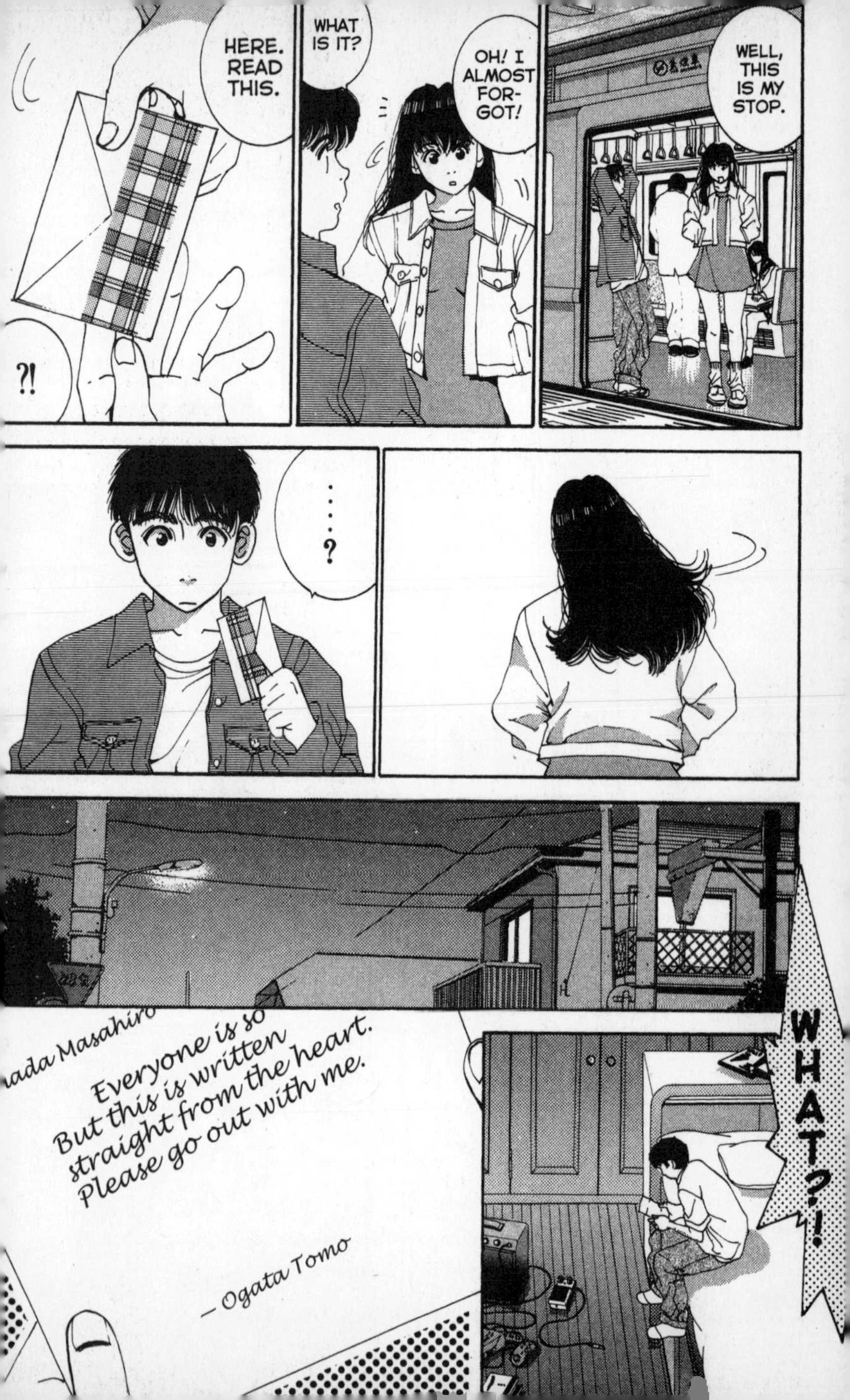
WELL, THIS IS MY STOP.
OH! I ALMOST FOR-GOT!
WHAT IS IT?
HERE. READ THIS.
?!
. . . ?
WHAT?!
ada Masahiro
Everyone is so
But this is written
straight from the heart.
Please go out with me.
—Ogata Tomo

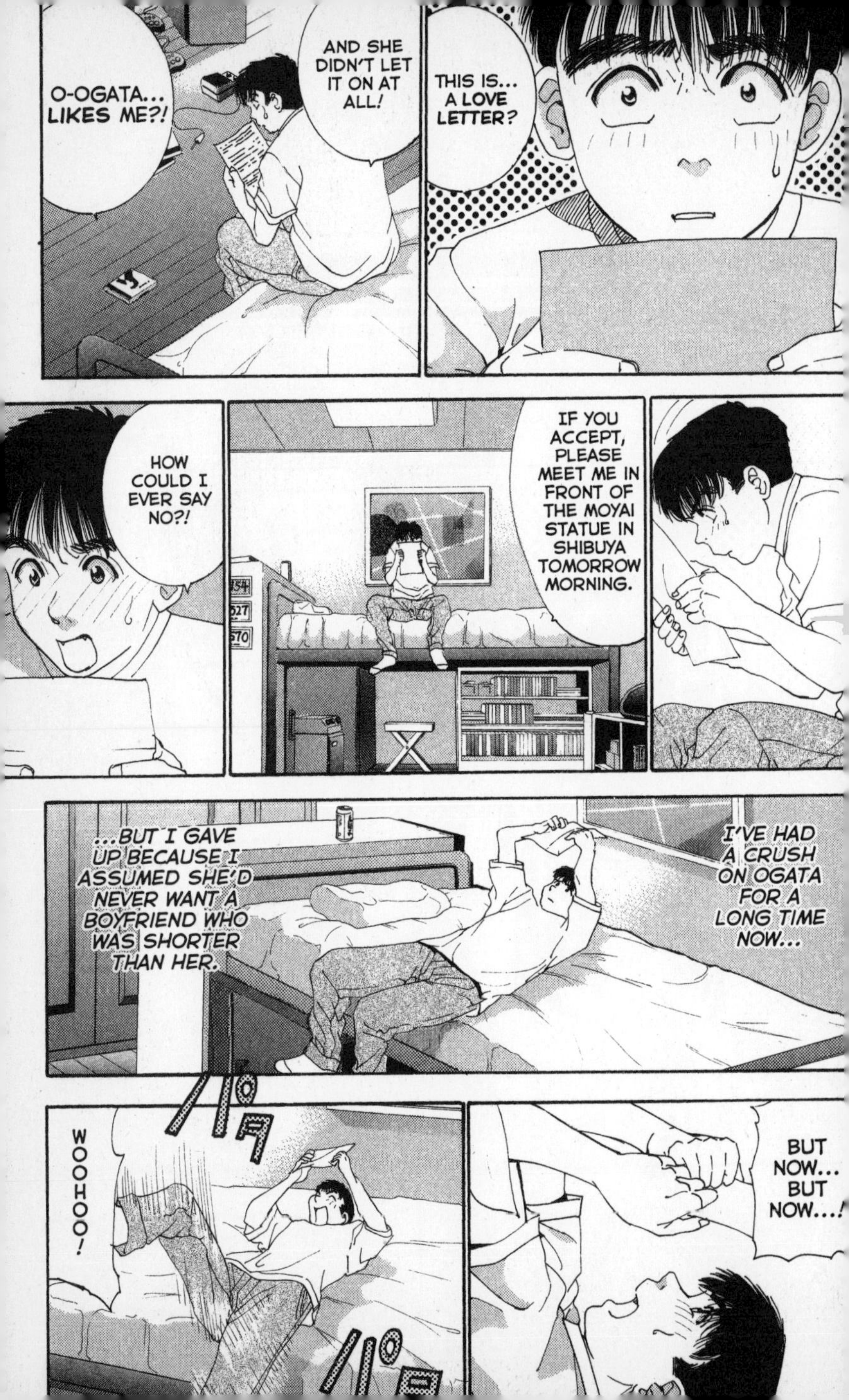
THIS IS... A LOVE LETTER?
AND SHE DIDN'T LET IT ON AT ALL!
O-OGATA... LIKES ME?!
IF YOU ACCEPT, PLEASE MEET ME IN FRONT OF THE MOYAI STATUE IN SHIBUYA TOMORROW MORNING.
HOW COULD I EVER SAY NO?!
I'VE HAD A CRUSH ON OGATA FOR A LONG TIME NOW...
...BUT I GAVE UP BECAUSE I ASSUMED SHE'D NEVER WANT A BOYFRIEND WHO WAS SHORTER THAN HER.
BUT NOW... BUT NOW...!
パタ
WOOHOO!
パタ

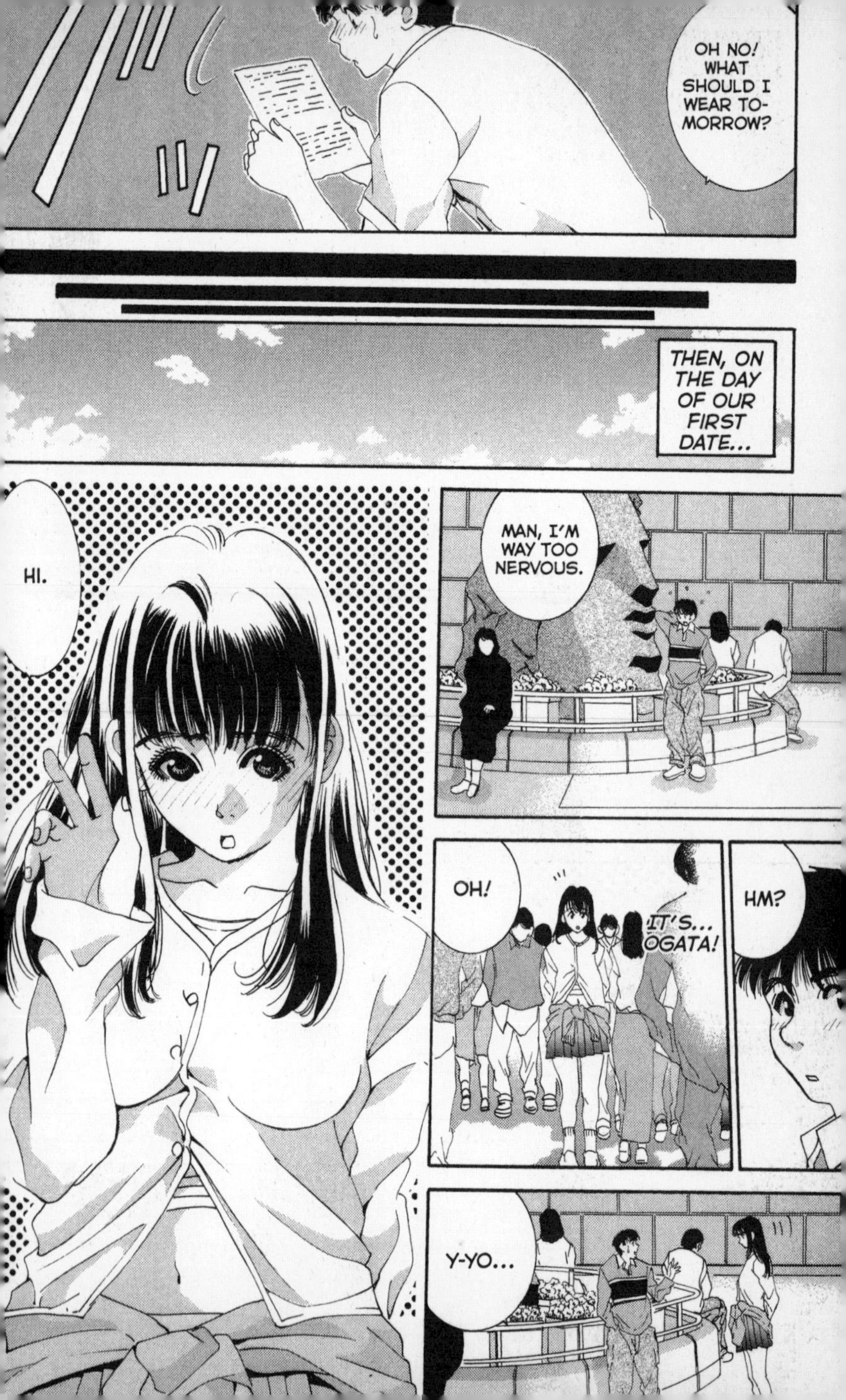
OH NO! WHAT SHOULD I WEAR TO-MORROW?
THEN, ON THE DAY OF OUR FIRST DATE...
MAN, I'M WAY TOO NERVOUS.
HM?
OH!
IT'S... OGATA!
Y-YO...
HI.

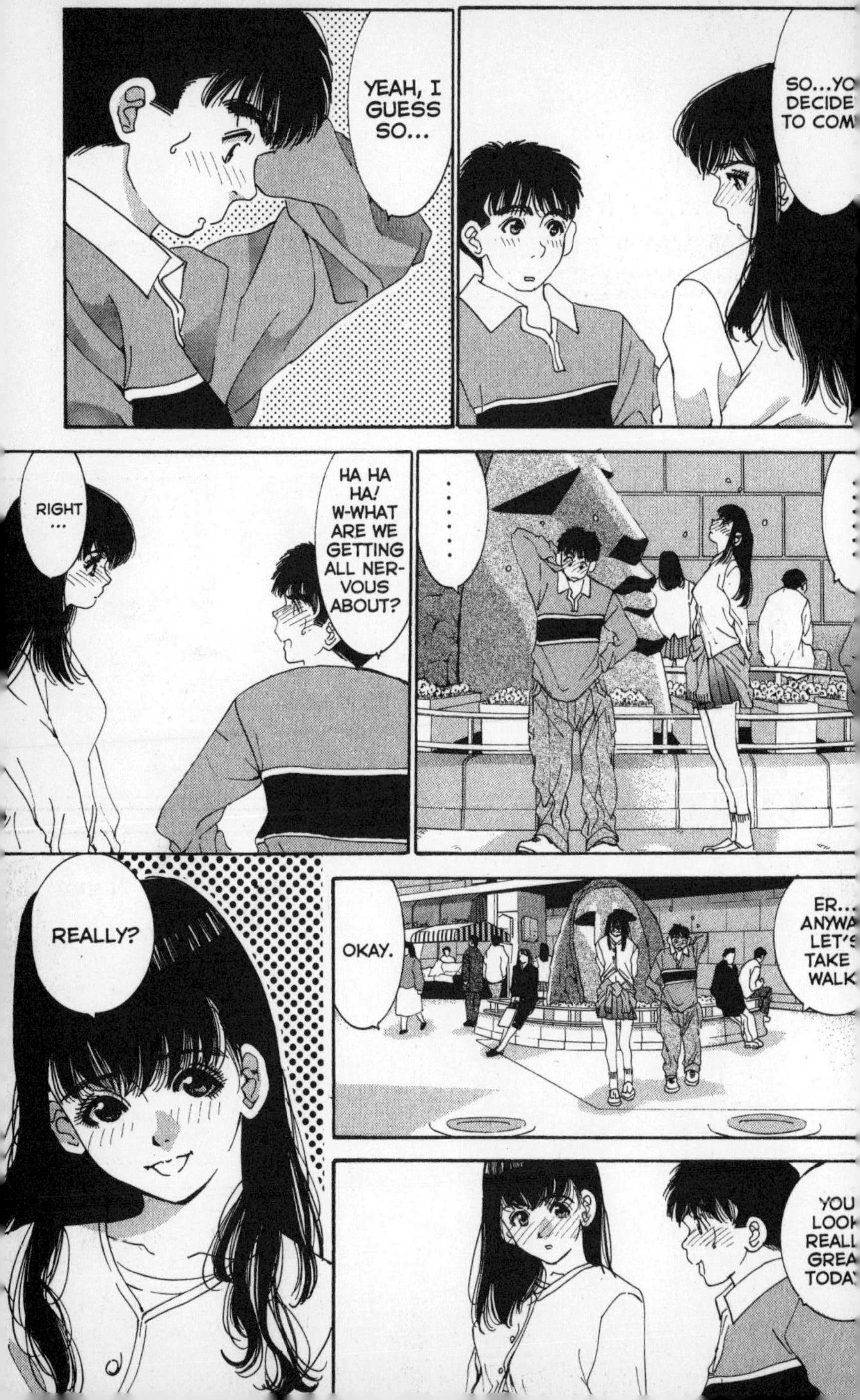
SO...YO DECIDE TO COM
YEAH, I GUESS SO...
......
HA HA HA! W-WHAT ARE WE GETTING ALL NER-VOUS ABOUT?
RIGHT ...
ER... ANYWA LET'S TAKE WALK
OKAY.
YOU LOOK REALL GREA TODAY
REALLY?

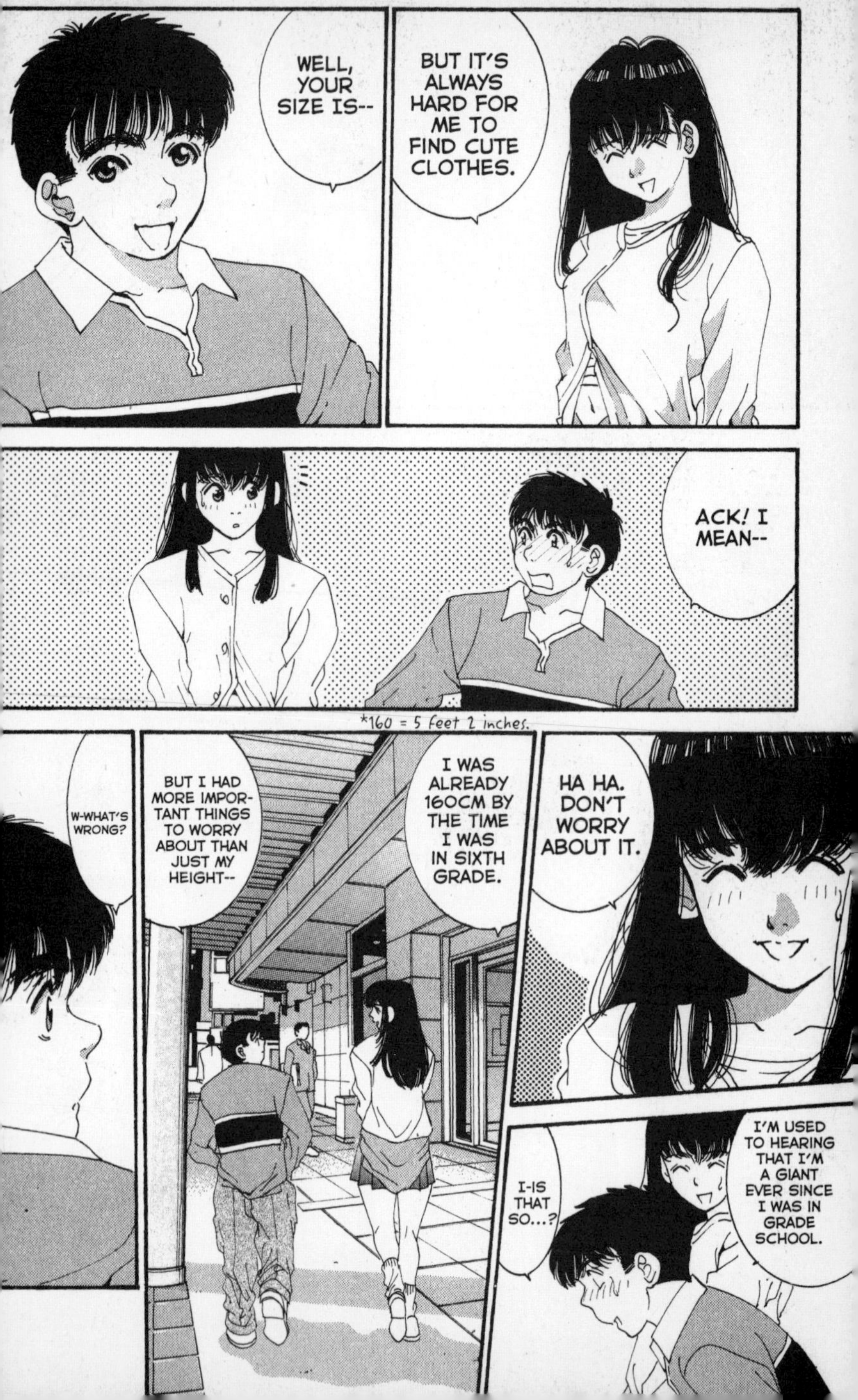
BUT IT'S ALWAYS HARD FOR ME TO FIND CUTE CLOTHES.
WELL, YOUR SIZE IS--
ACK! I MEAN--
*160 = 5 feet 2 inches.
HA HA. DON'T WORRY ABOUT IT.
I'M USED TO HEARING THAT I'M A GIANT EVER SINCE I WAS IN GRADE SCHOOL.
I-IS THAT SO...?
I WAS ALREADY 160CM BY THE TIME I WAS IN SIXTH GRADE.
BUT I HAD MORE IMPORTANT THINGS TO WORRY ABOUT THAN JUST MY HEIGHT--
W-WHAT'S WRONG?

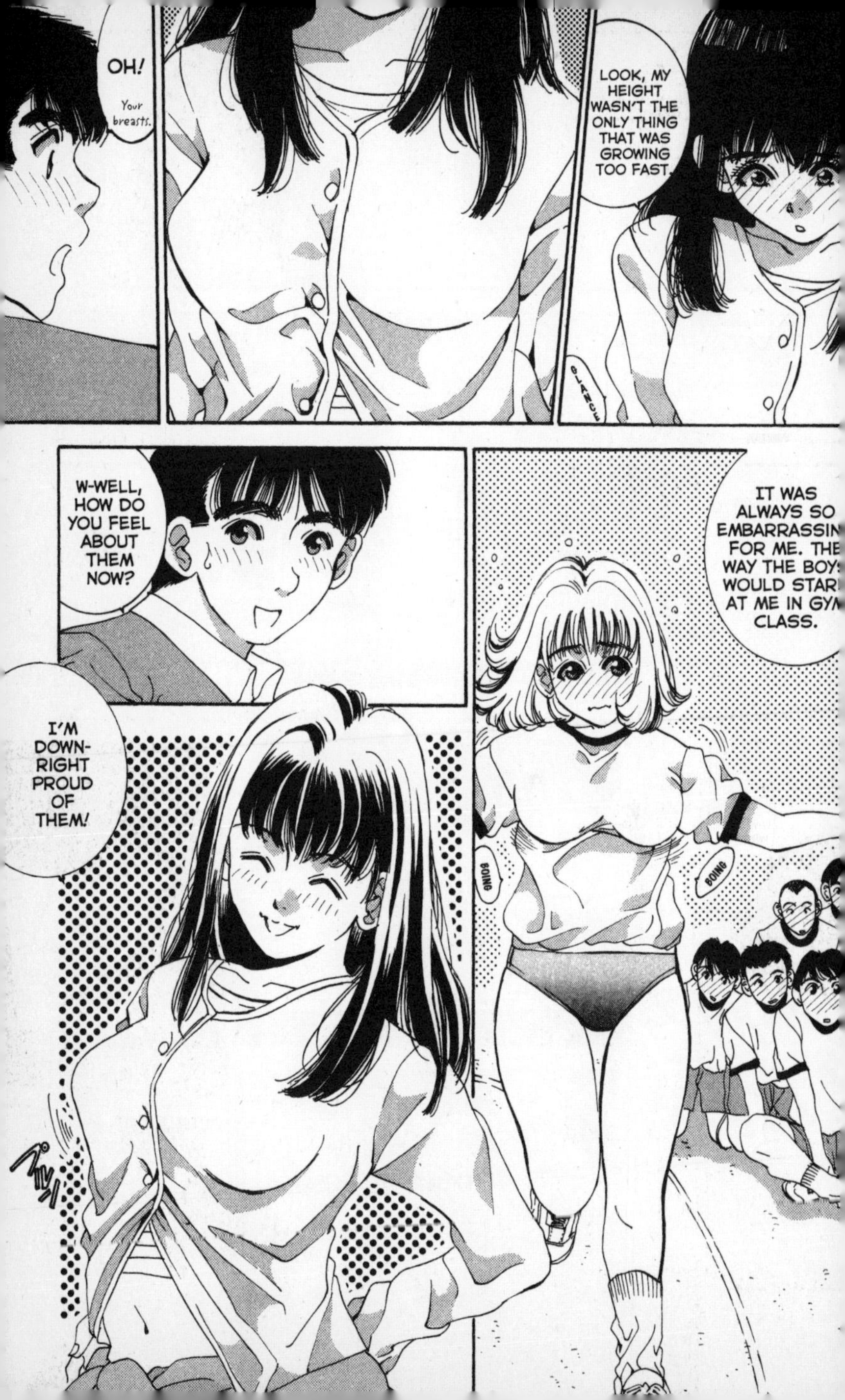
LOOK, MY HEIGHT WASN'T THE ONLY THING THAT WAS GROWING TOO FAST.
GLANCE
OH!
Your breasts.
IT WAS ALWAYS SO EMBARRASSIN FOR ME. THE WAY THE BOY WOULD STAR AT ME IN GY CLASS.
BOING
BOING
W-WELL, HOW DO YOU FEEL ABOUT THEM NOW?
I'M DOWN-RIGHT PROUD OF THEM!

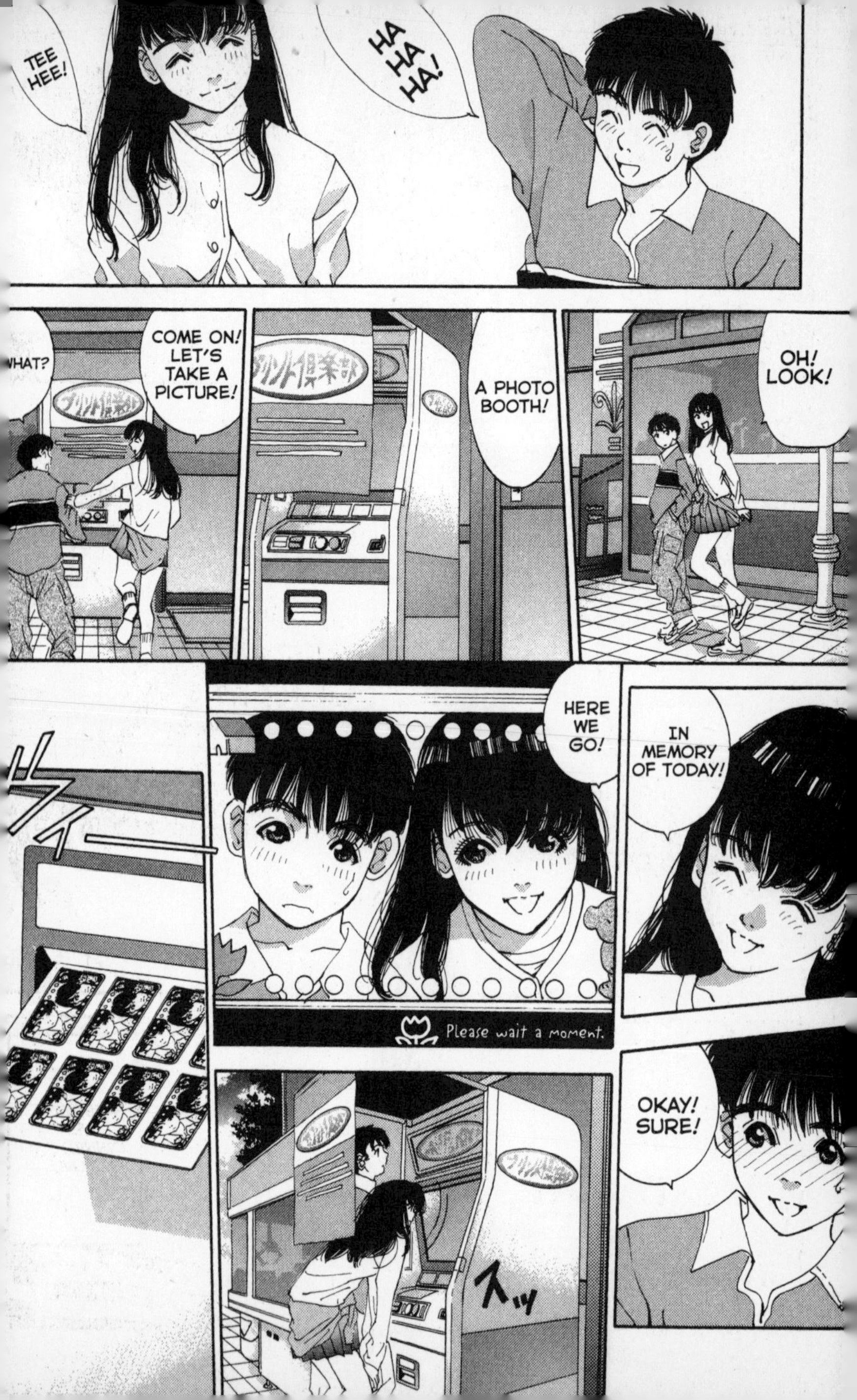
HA HA HA!
TEE HEE!
OH! LOOK!
A PHOTO BOOTH!
COME ON! LET'S TAKE A PICTURE!
HAT?
IN MEMORY OF TODAY!
OKAY! SURE!
HERE WE GO!
Please wait a moment.
スッ
ジィー

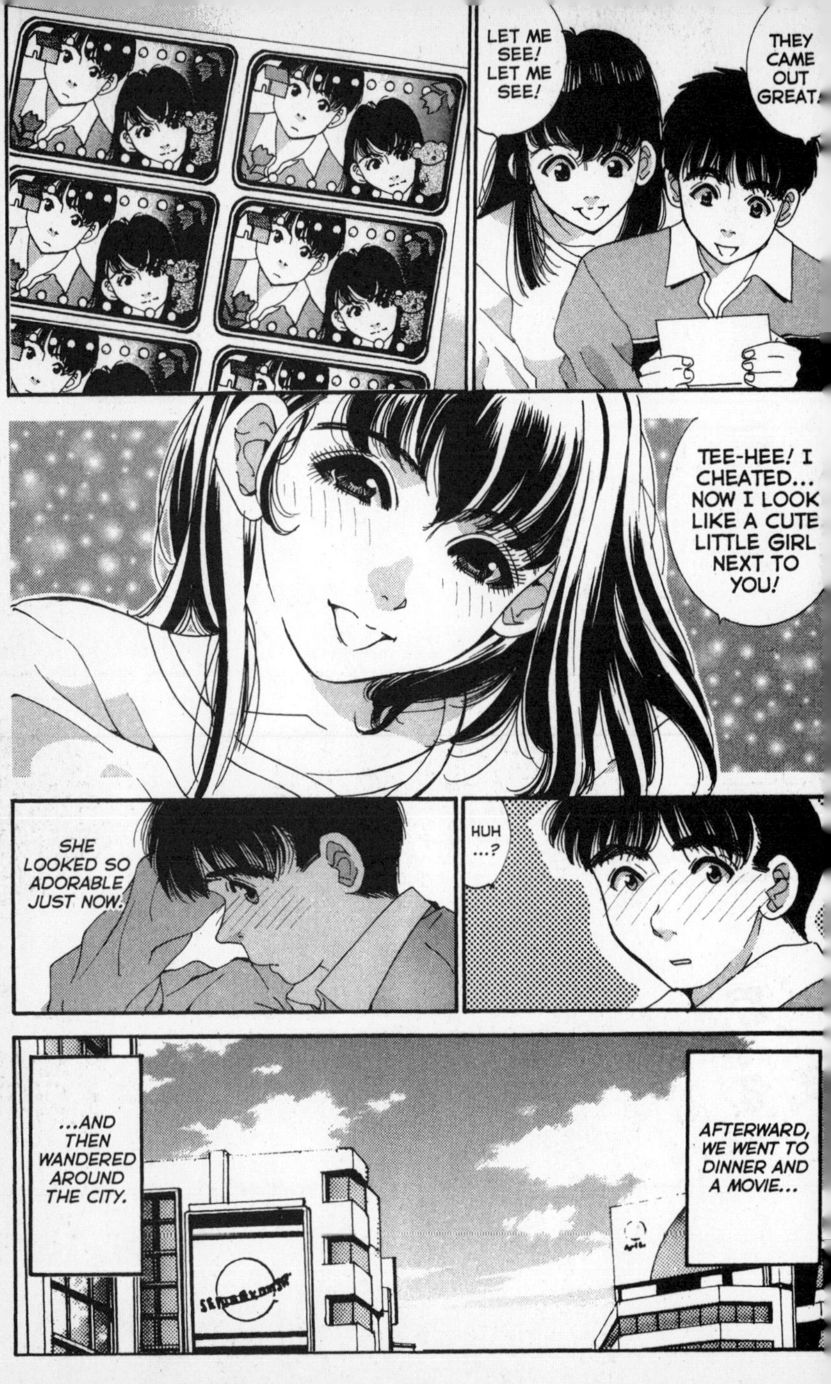
THEY CAME OUT GREAT!
LET ME SEE! LET ME SEE!
TEE-HEE! I CHEATED... NOW I LOOK LIKE A CUTE LITTLE GIRL NEXT TO YOU!
HUH ...?
SHE LOOKED SO ADORABLE JUST NOW.
AFTERWARD, WE WENT TO DINNER AND A MOVIE...
...AND THEN WANDERED AROUND THE CITY.

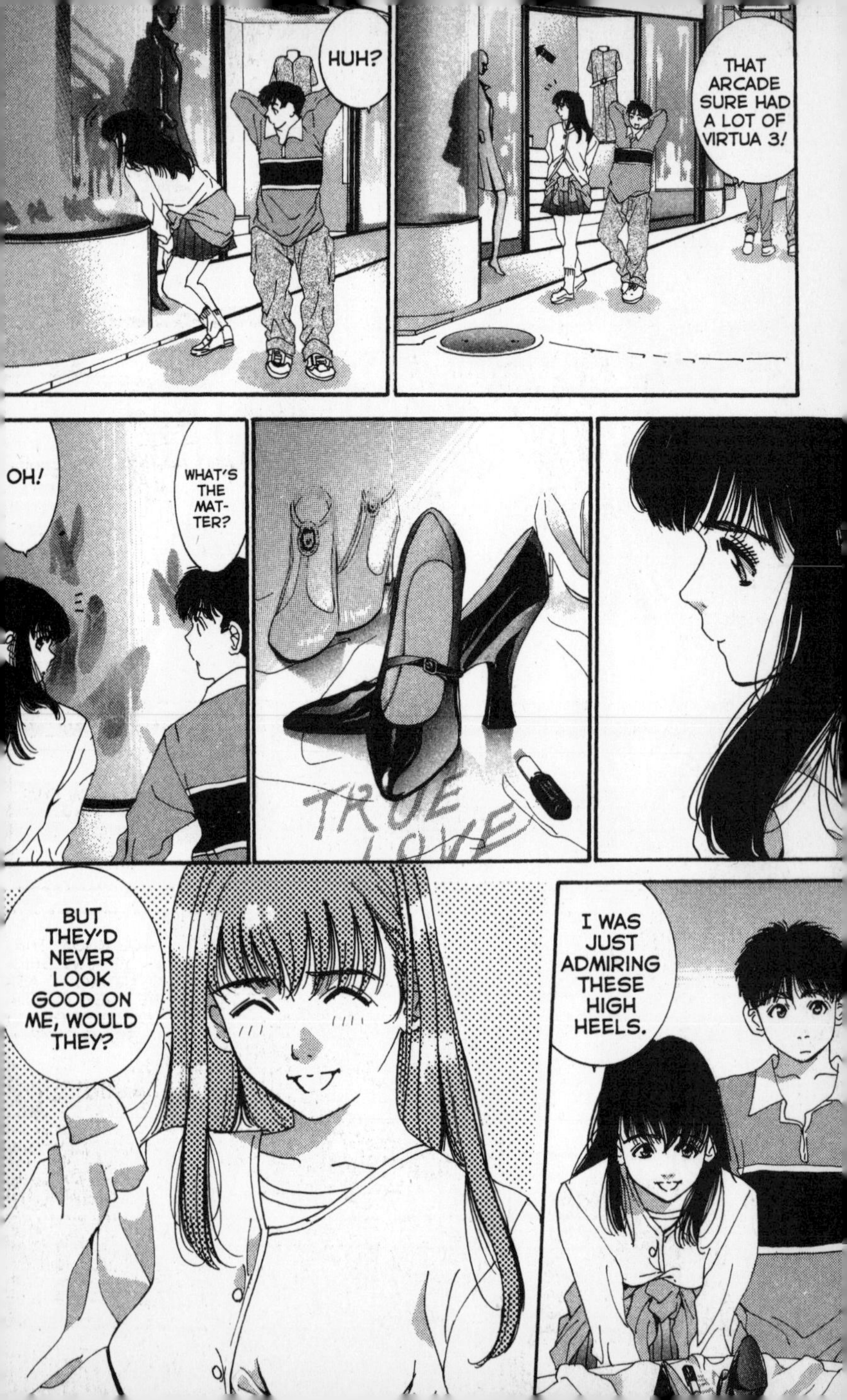
THAT ARCADE SURE HAD A LOT OF VIRTUA 3!
HUH?
TRUE
WHAT'S THE MAT-TER?
OH!
I WAS JUST ADMIRING THESE HIGH HEELS.
BUT THEY'D NEVER LOOK GOOD ON ME, WOULD THEY?

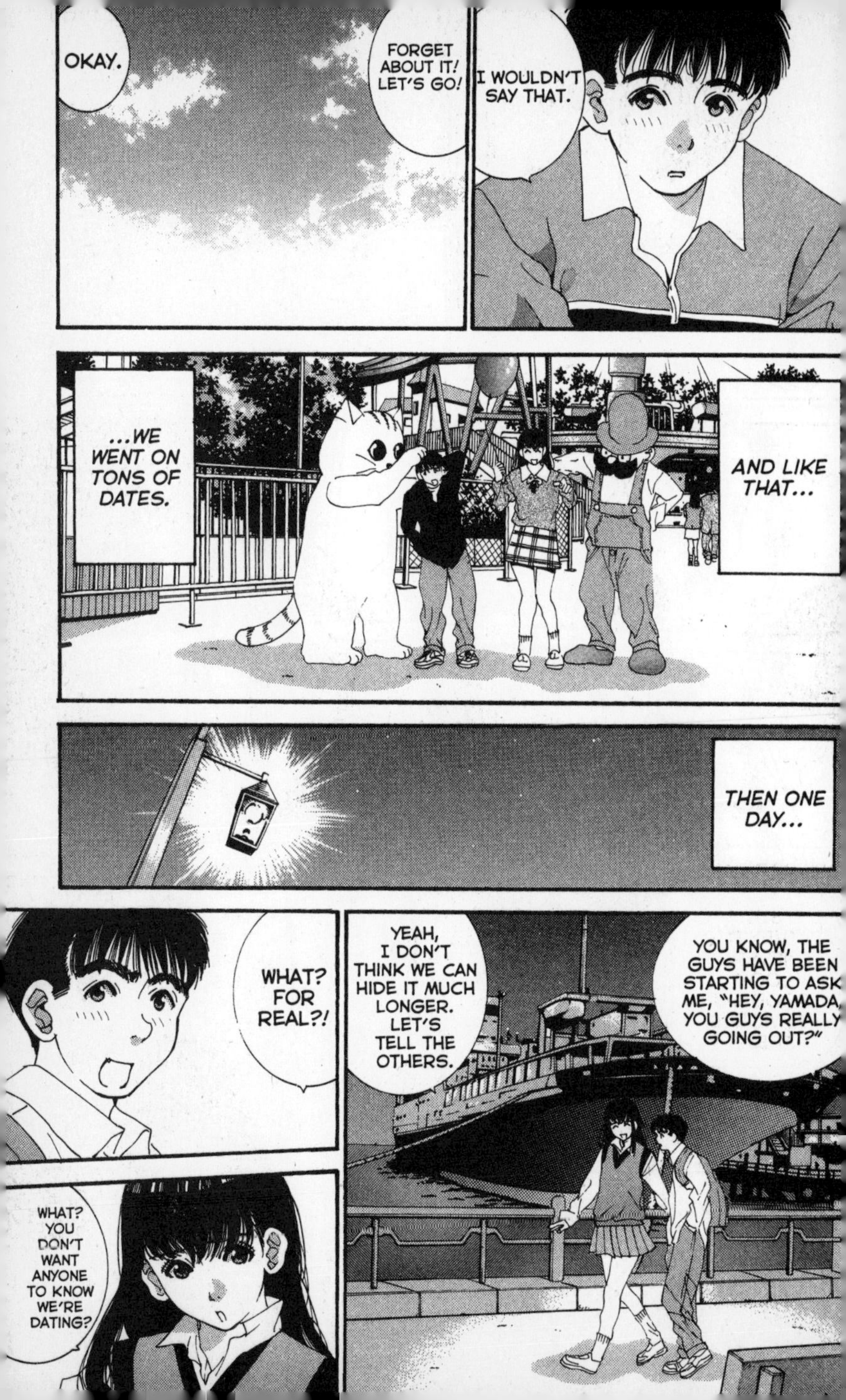
I WOULDN'T SAY THAT.
FORGET ABOUT IT! LET'S GO!
OKAY.
AND LIKE THAT...
...WE WENT ON TONS OF DATES.
THEN ONE DAY...
YOU KNOW, THE GUYS HAVE BEEN STARTING TO ASK ME, "HEY, YAMADA, YOU GUYS REALLY GOING OUT?"
YEAH, I DON'T THINK WE CAN HIDE IT MUCH LONGER. LET'S TELL THE OTHERS.
WHAT? FOR REAL?!
WHAT? YOU DON'T WANT ANYONE TO KNOW WE'RE DATING?

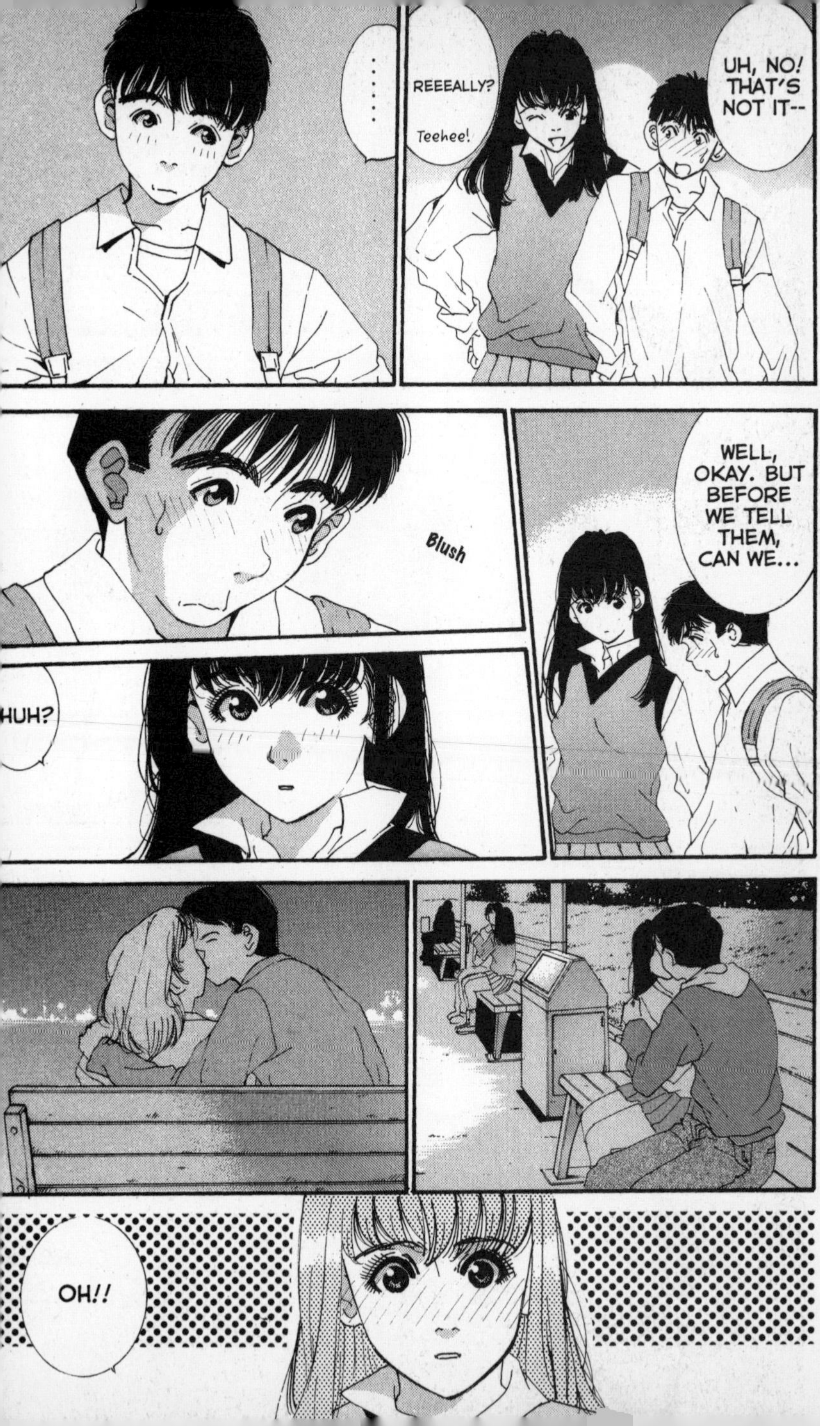
UH, NO! THAT'S NOT IT--
REEEALLY?
Teehee!
......
WELL, OKAY. BUT BEFORE WE TELL THEM, CAN WE...
Blush
HUH?
OH!!

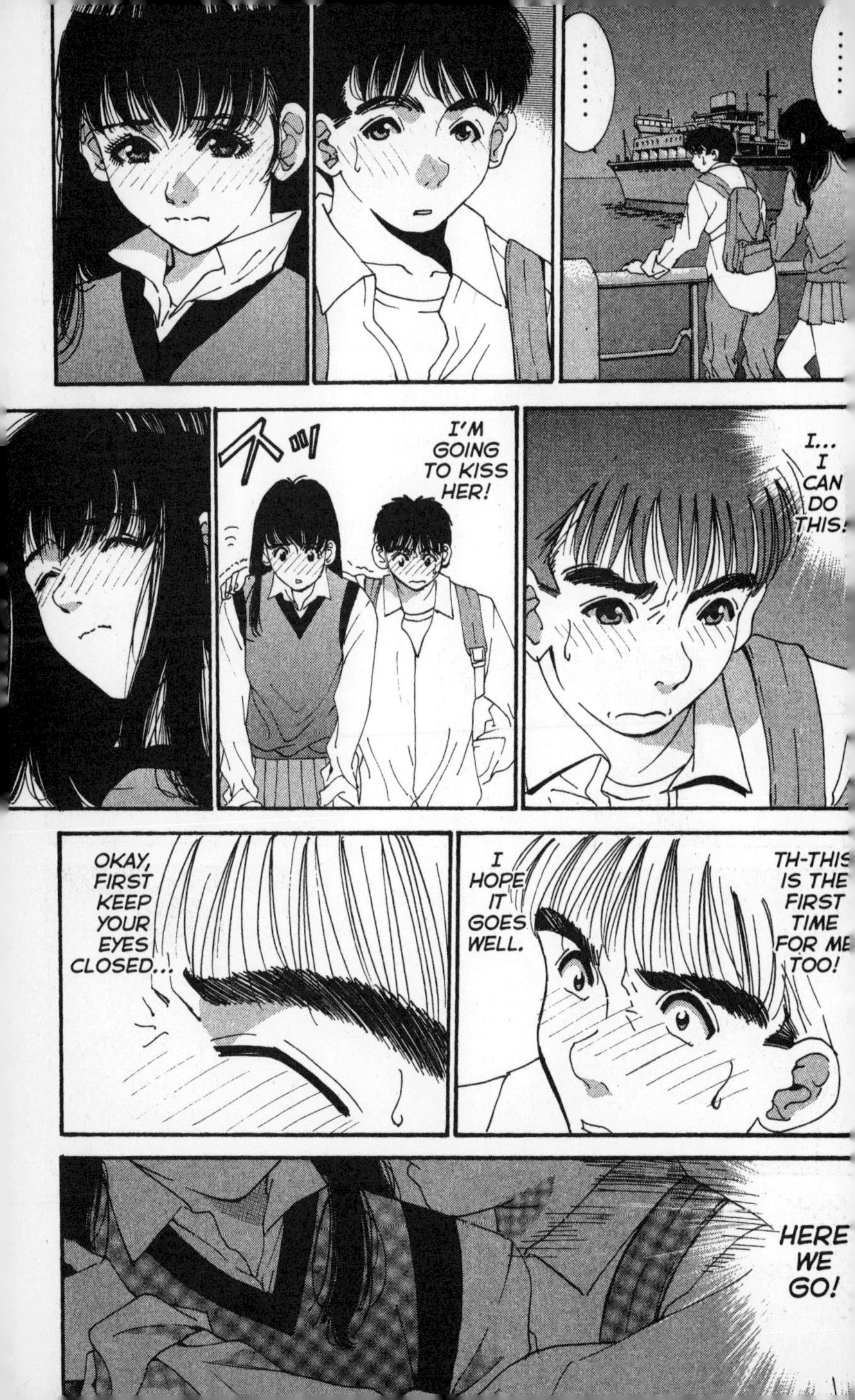
....
....
I... I CAN DO THIS!
I'M GOING TO KISS HER!
TH-THIS IS THE FIRST TIME FOR ME TOO!
I HOPE IT GOES WELL.
OKAY, FIRST KEEP YOUR EYES CLOSED...
HERE WE GO!

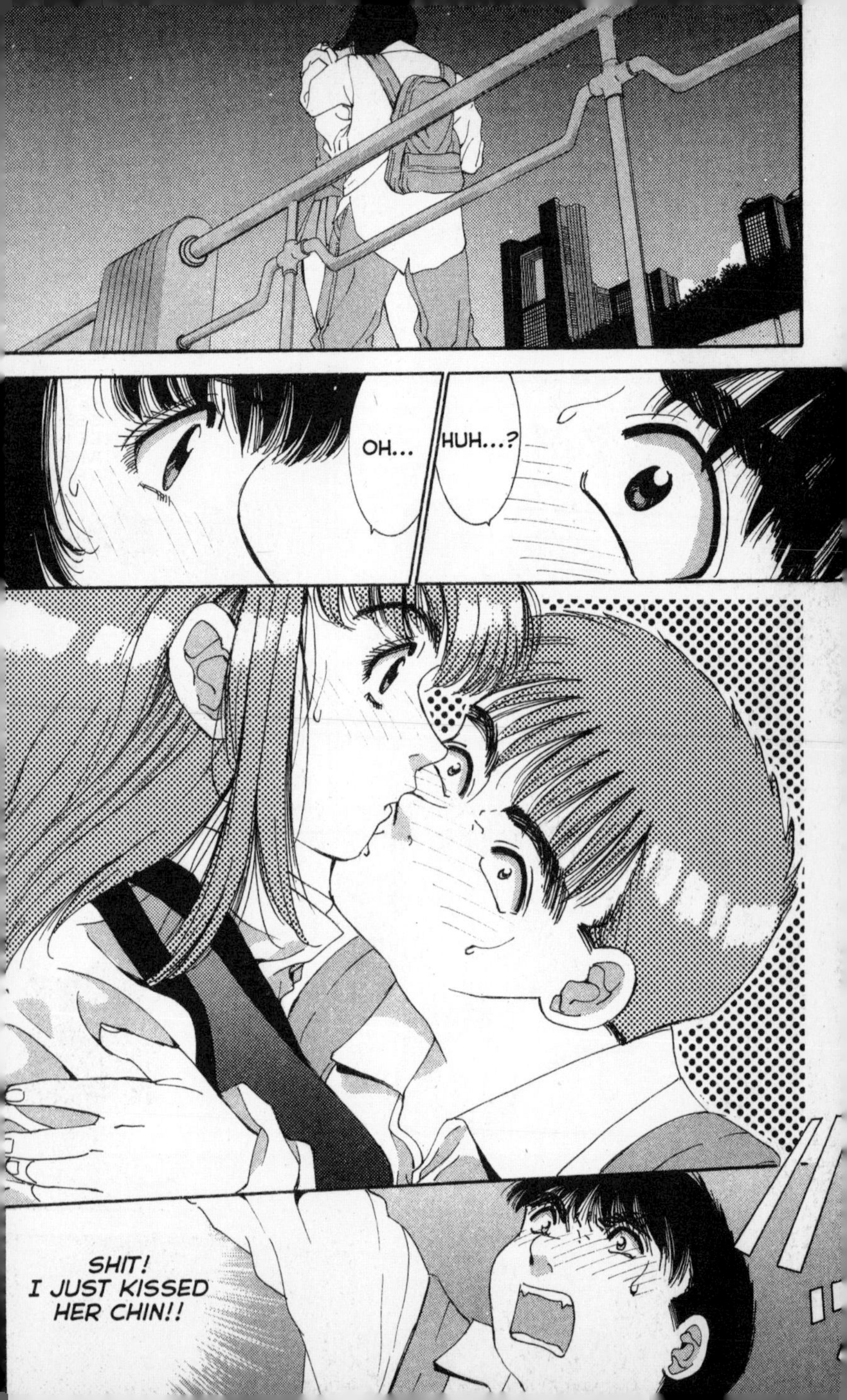
HUH...?
OH...
SHIT! I JUST KISSED HER CHIN!!

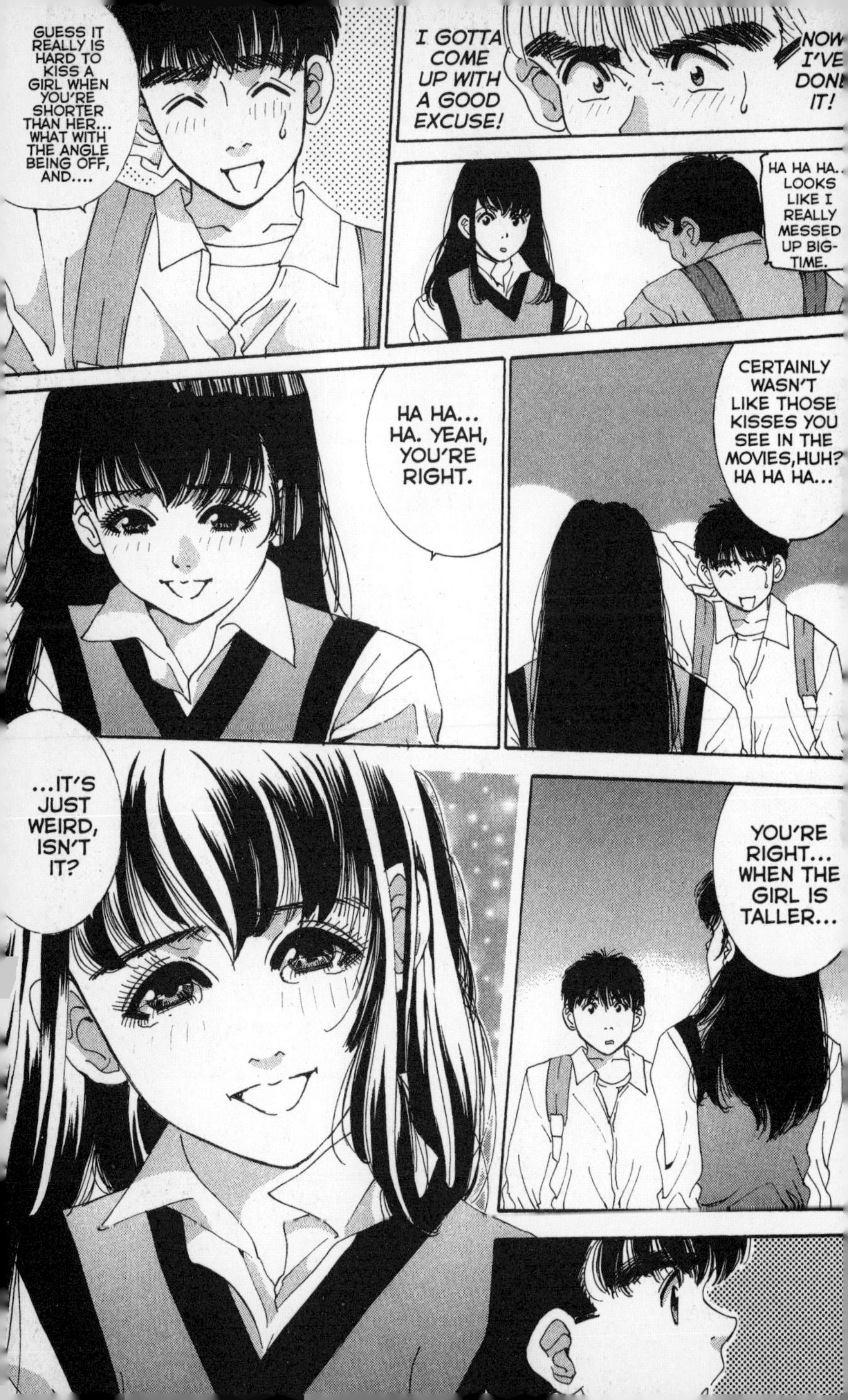
NOW I'VE DONE IT!
I GOTTA COME UP WITH A GOOD EXCUSE!
HA HA HA.. LOOKS LIKE I REALLY MESSED UP BIG-TIME.
GUESS IT REALLY IS HARD TO KISS A GIRL WHEN YOU'RE SHORTER THAN HER... WHAT WITH THE ANGLE BEING OFF, AND....
CERTAINLY WASN'T LIKE THOSE KISSES YOU SEE IN THE MOVIES,HUH? HA HA HA...
HA HA... HA. YEAH, YOU'RE RIGHT.
YOU'RE RIGHT... WHEN THE GIRL IS TALLER...
...IT'S JUST WEIRD, ISN'T IT?

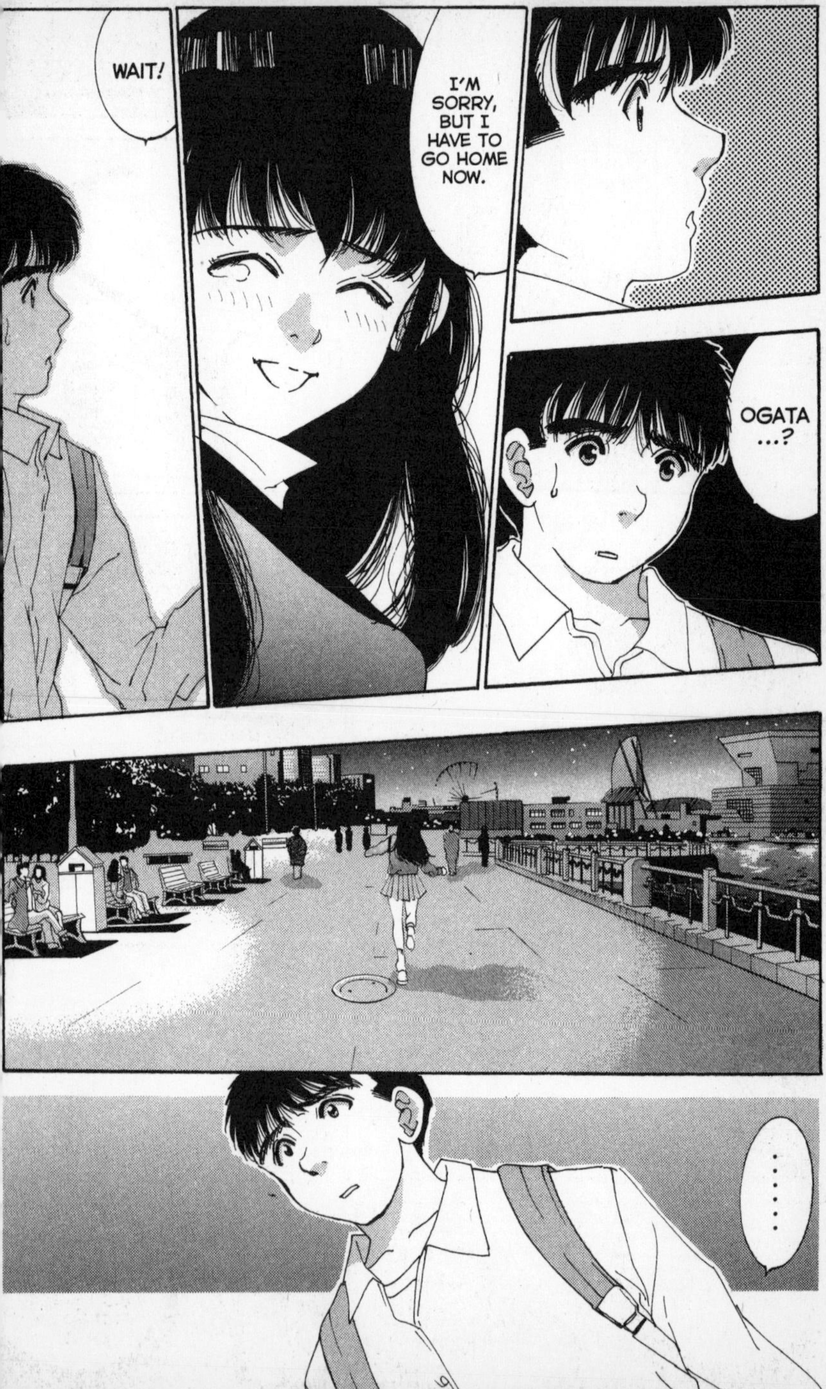
OGATA ...?
I'M SORRY, BUT I HAVE TO GO HOME NOW.
WAIT!
......

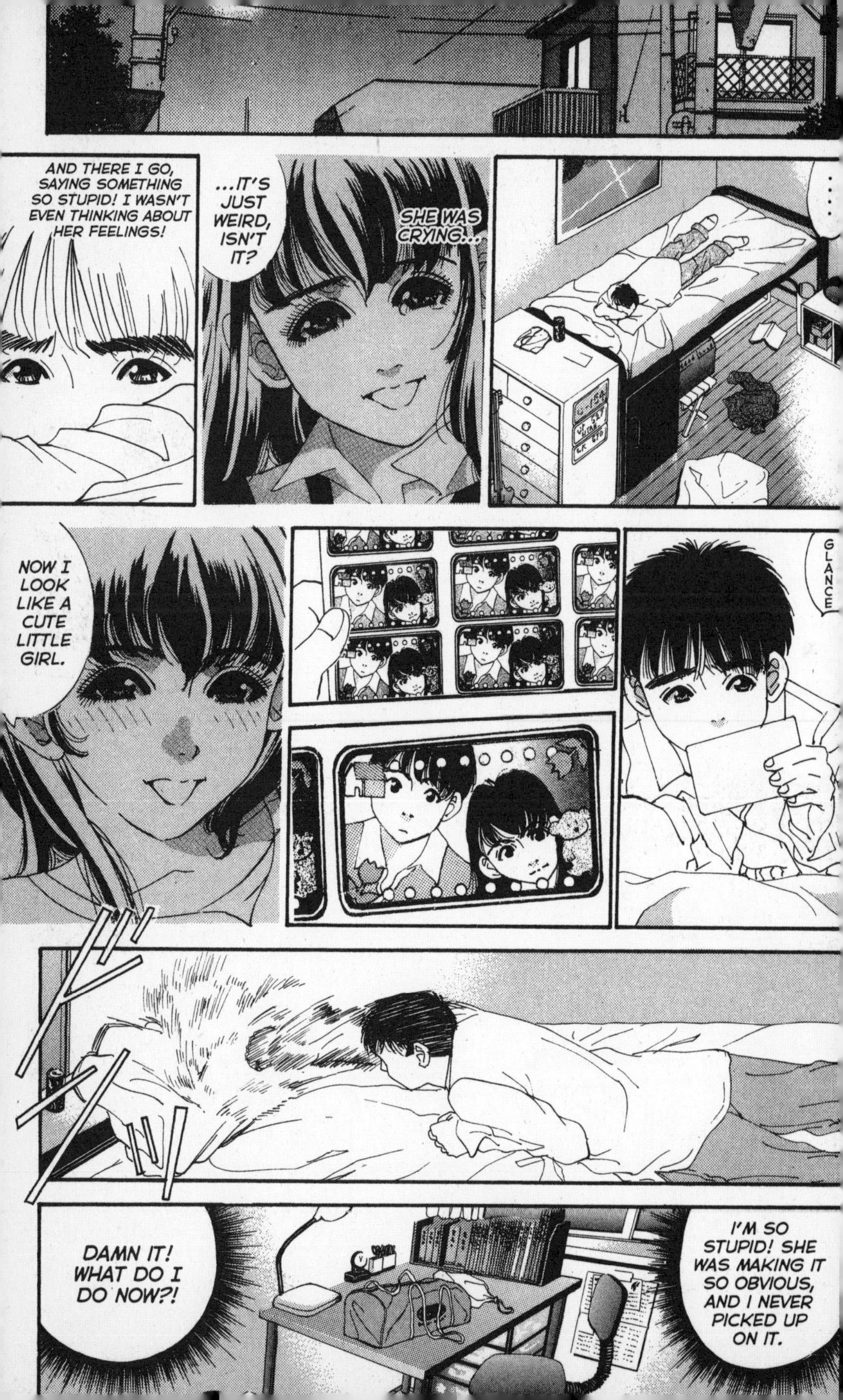
....
SHE WAS CRYING...
...IT'S JUST WEIRD, ISN'T IT?
AND THERE I GO, SAYING SOMETHING SO STUPID! I WASN'T EVEN THINKING ABOUT HER FEELINGS!
GLANCE
NOW I LOOK LIKE A CUTE LITTLE GIRL.
I'M SO STUPID! SHE WAS MAKING IT SO OBVIOUS, AND I NEVER PICKED UP ON IT.
DAMN IT! WHAT DO I DO NOW?!

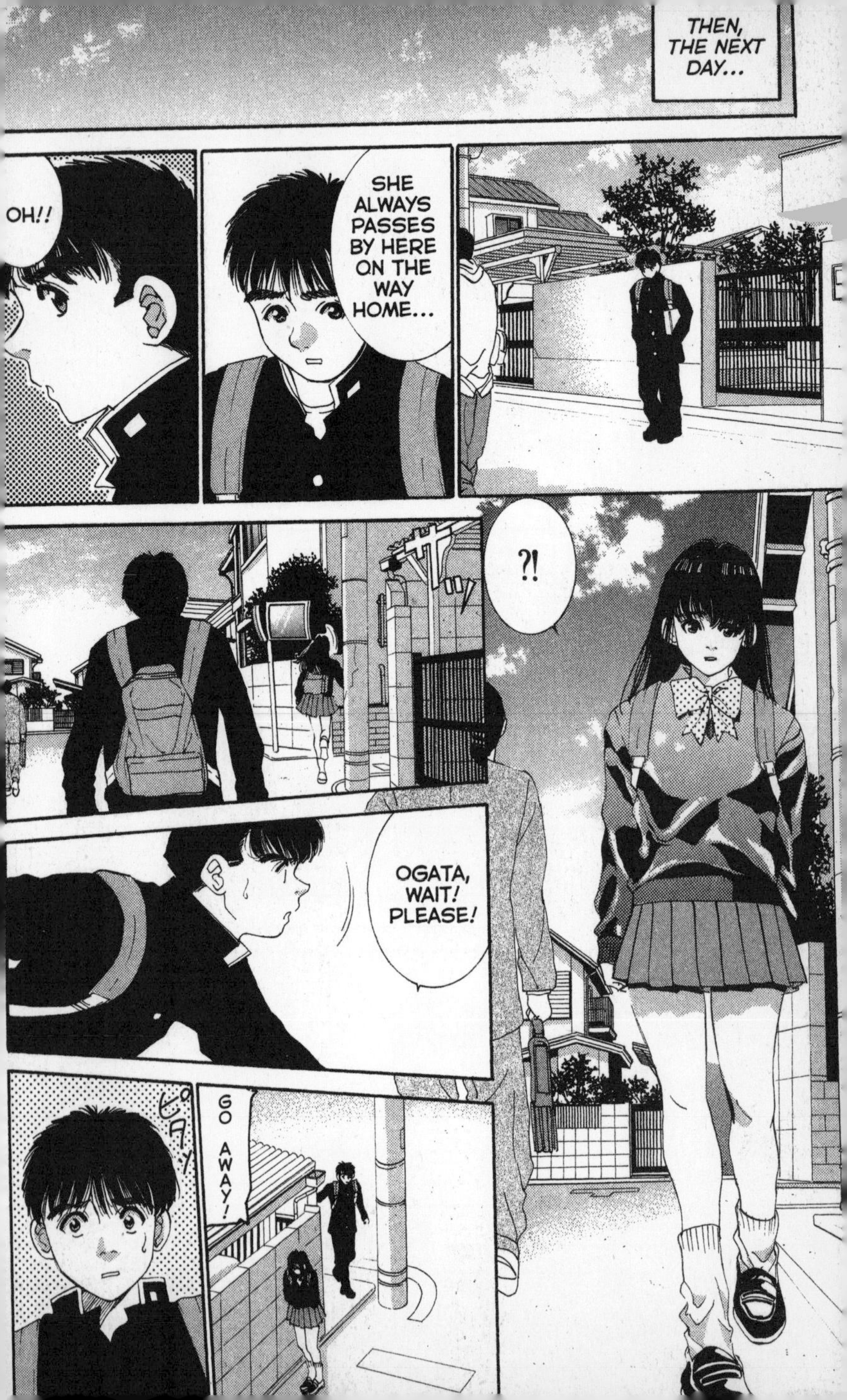
THEN, THE NEXT DAY...
SHE ALWAYS PASSES BY HERE ON THE WAY HOME...
OH!!
?!
OGATA, WAIT! PLEASE!
GO AWAY!

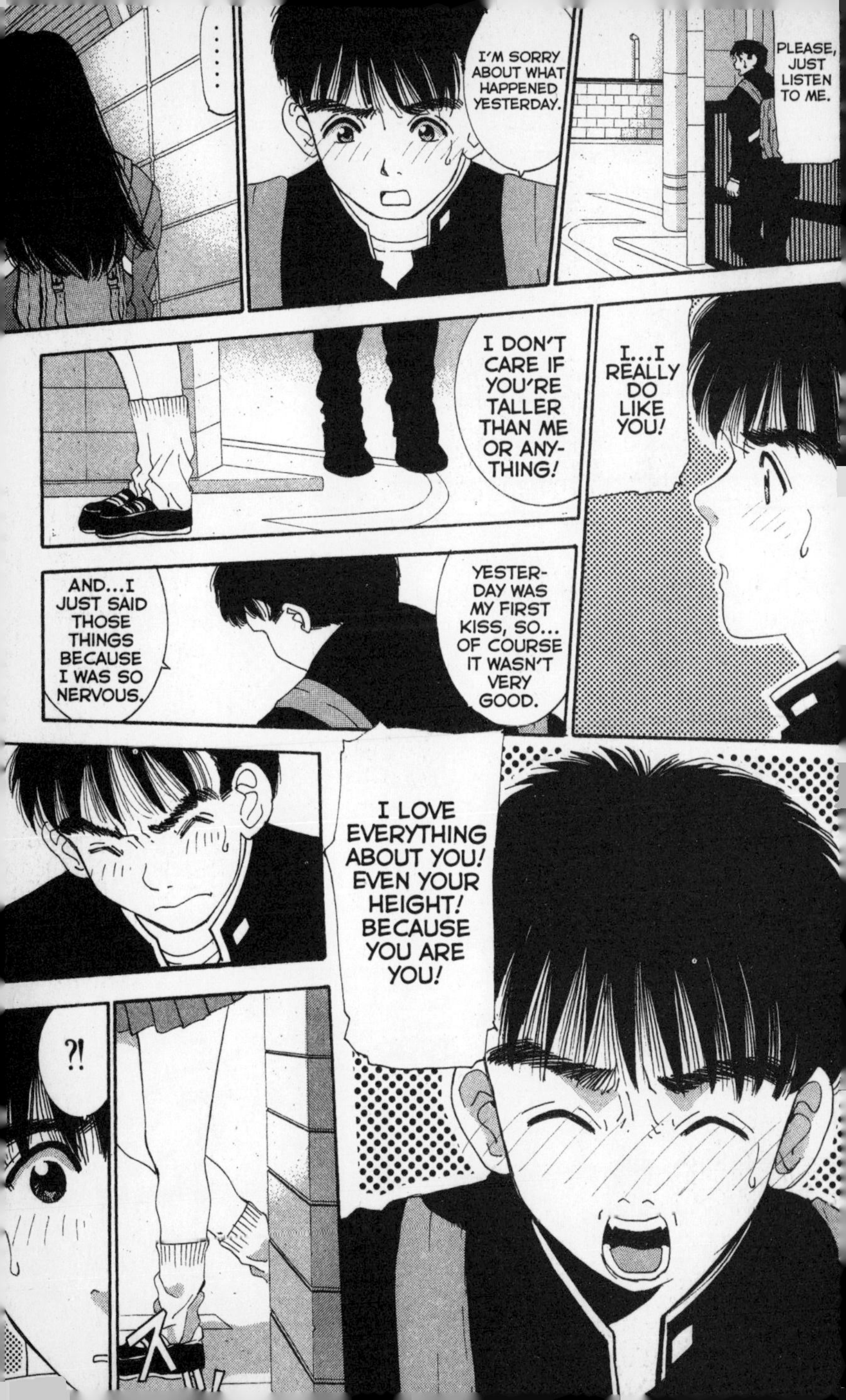
PLEASE, JUST LISTEN TO ME.
I'M SORRY ABOUT WHAT HAPPENED YESTERDAY.
......
I...I REALLY DO LIKE YOU!
I DON'T CARE IF YOU'RE TALLER THAN ME OR ANY-THING!
YESTER-DAY WAS MY FIRST KISS, SO... OF COURSE IT WASN'T VERY GOOD.
AND...I JUST SAID THOSE THINGS BECAUSE I WAS SO NERVOUS.
I LOVE EVERYTHING ABOUT YOU! EVEN YOUR HEIGHT! BECAUSE YOU ARE YOU!
?!

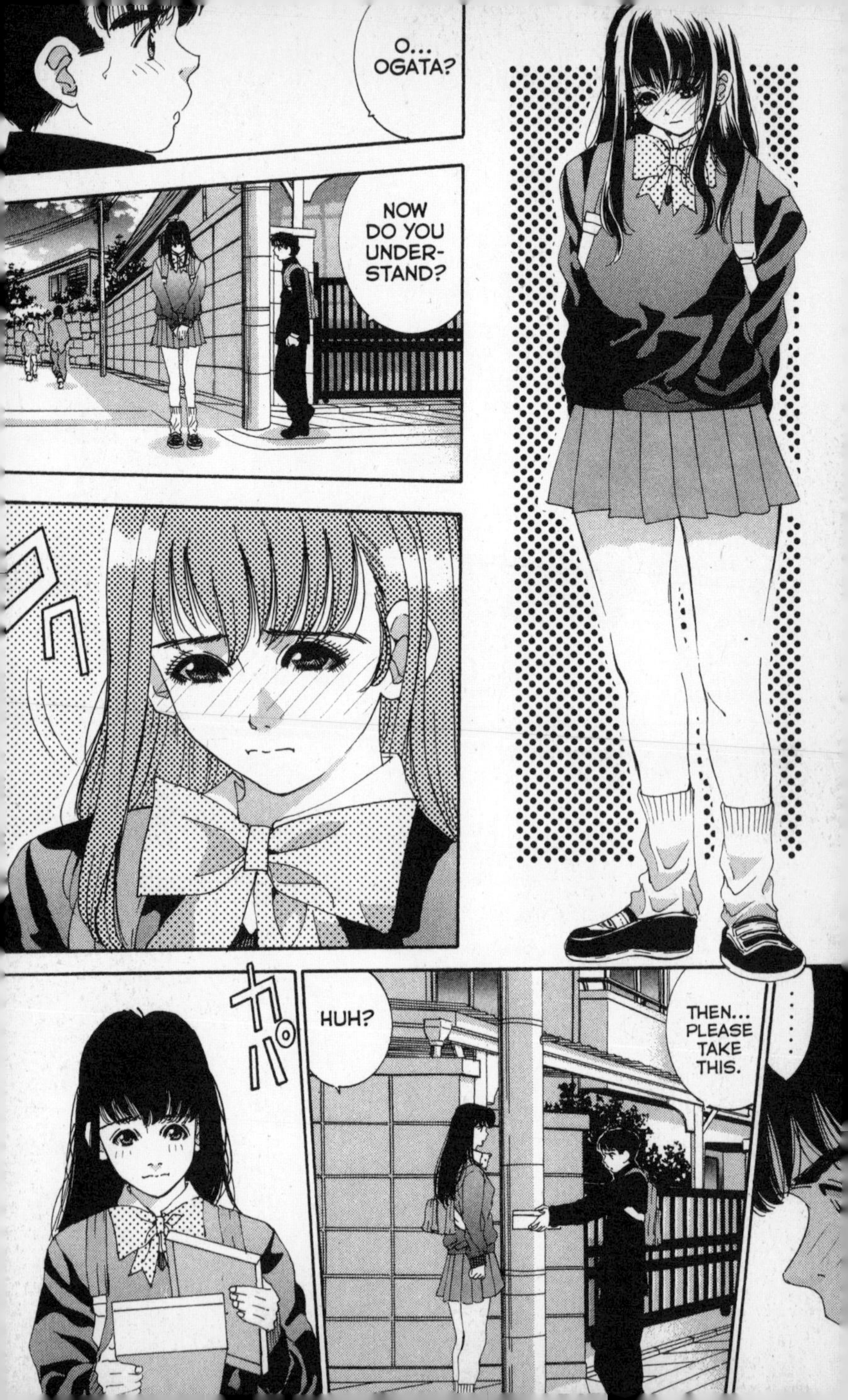
O... OGATA?
NOW DO YOU UNDER-STAND?
......
THEN... PLEASE TAKE THIS.
HUH?
カパ

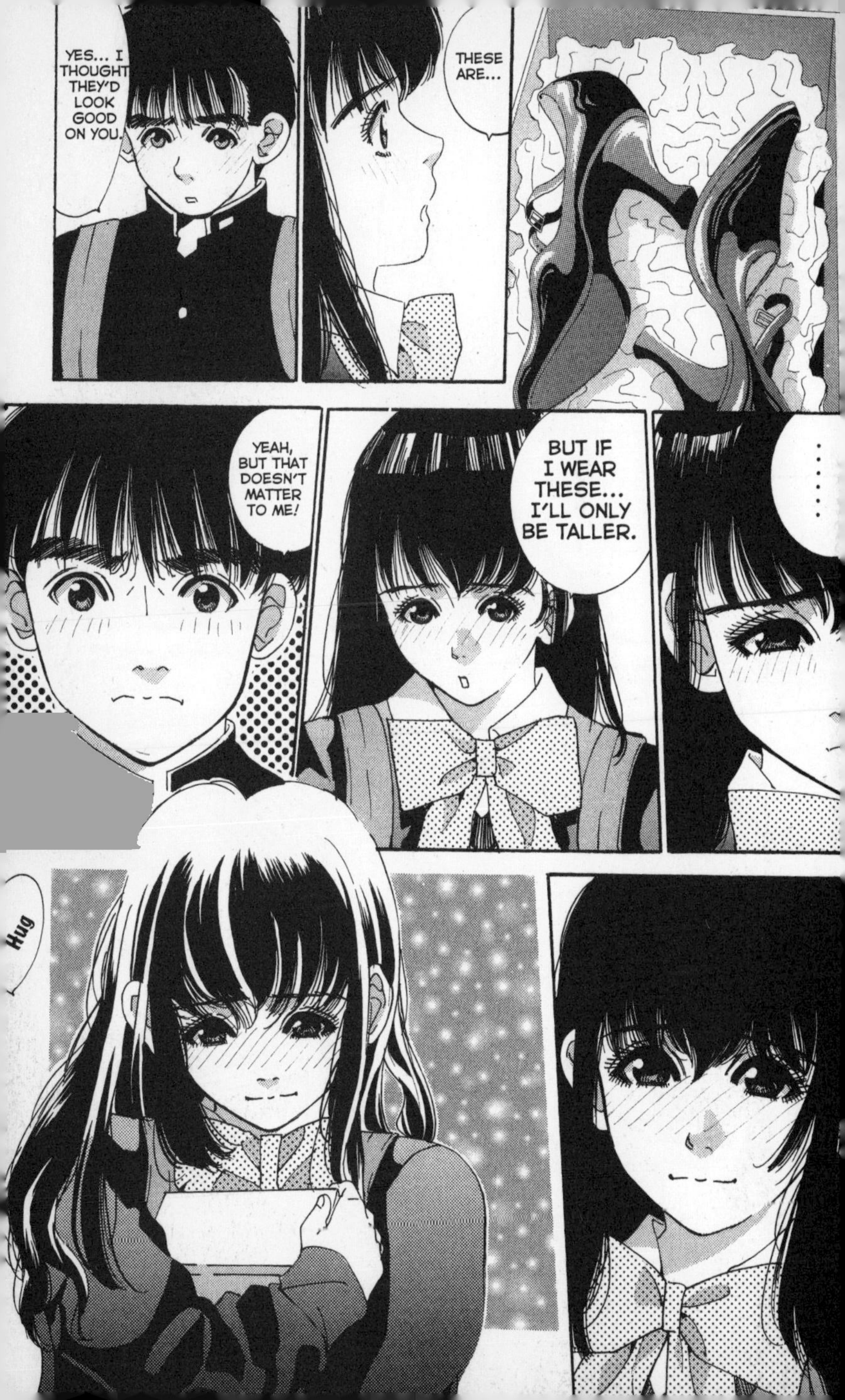
THESE ARE...
YES... I THOUGHT THEY'D LOOK GOOD ON YOU.
......
BUT IF I WEAR THESE... I'LL ONLY BE TALLER.
YEAH, BUT THAT DOESN'T MATTER TO ME!
Hug

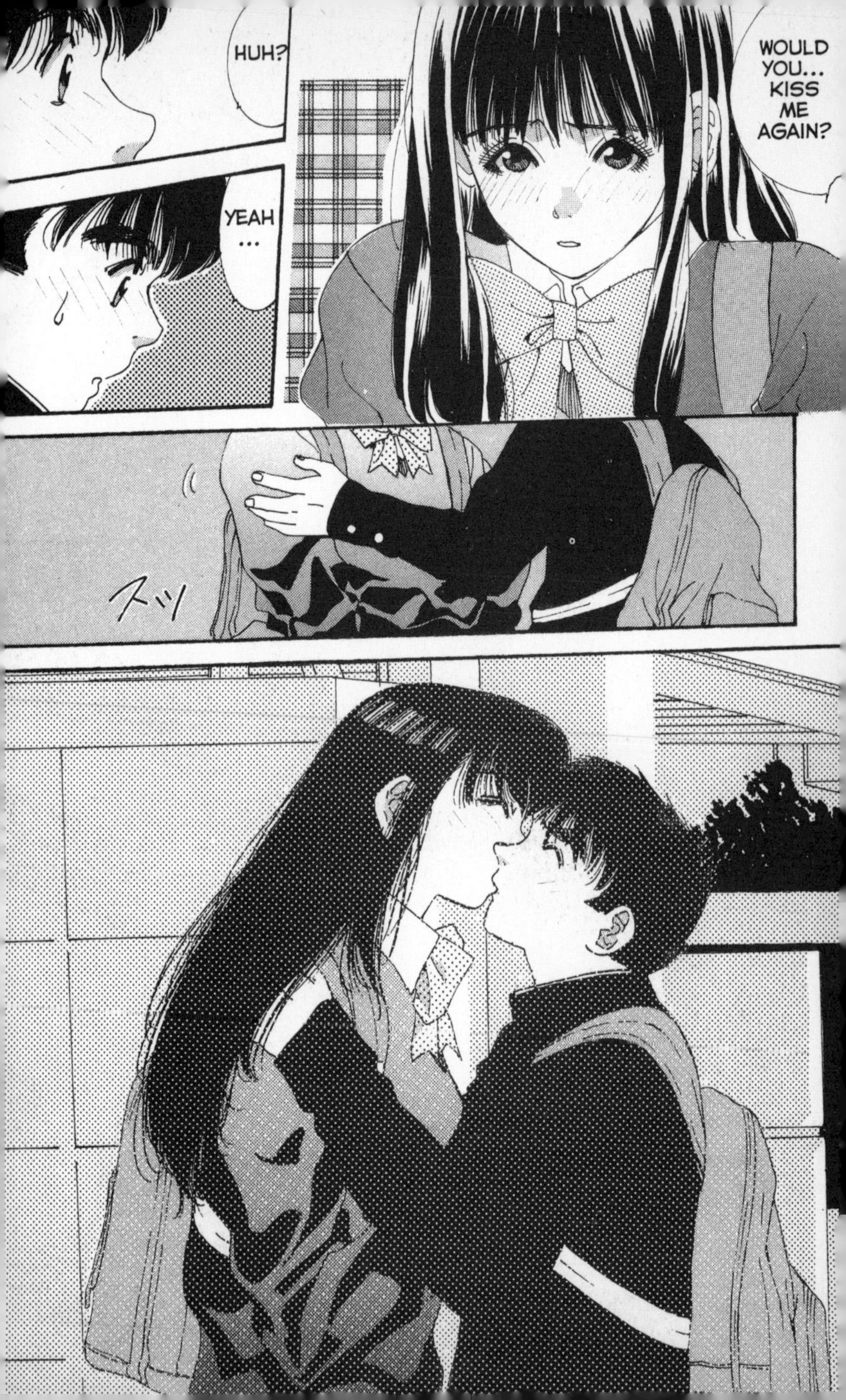
WOULD YOU... KISS ME AGAIN?
HUH?
YEAH ...
スッ

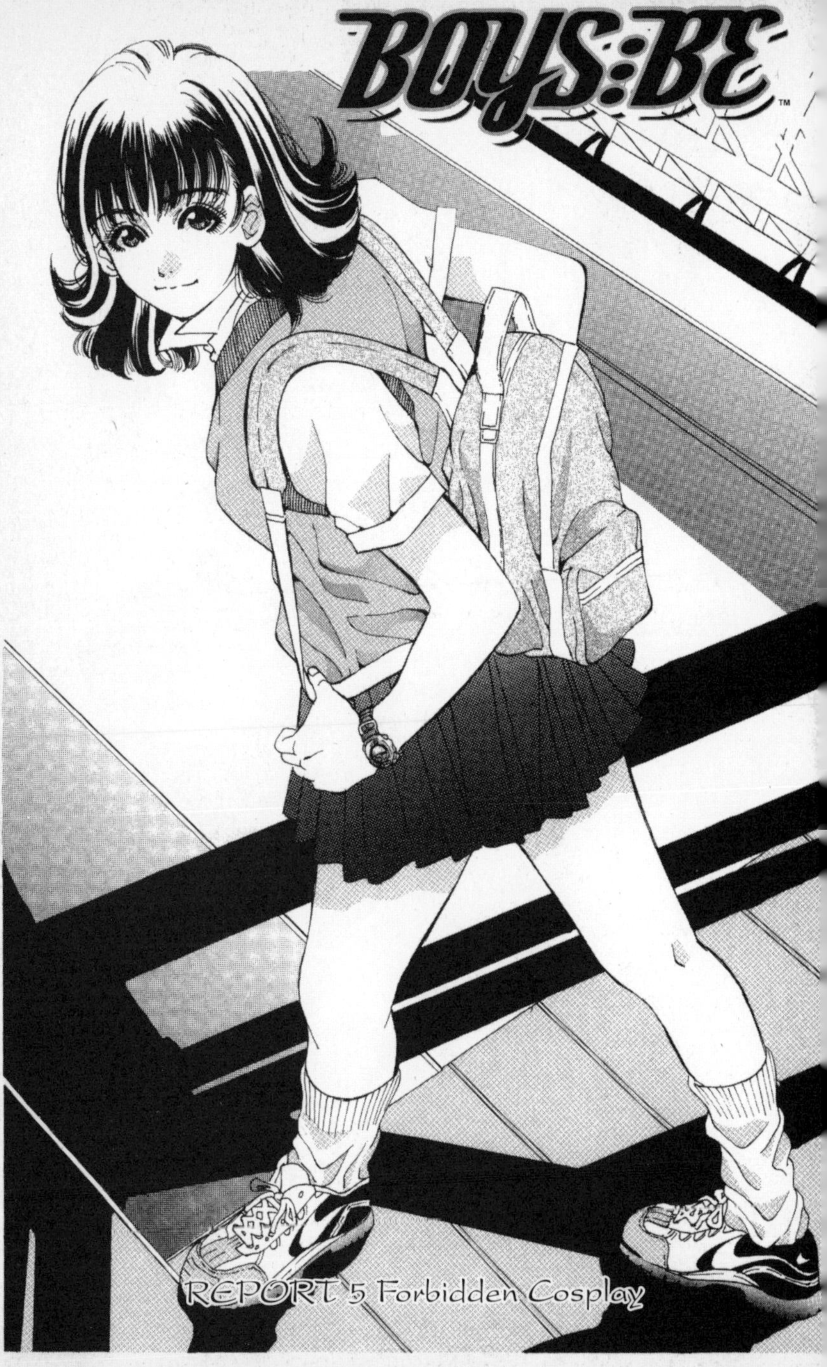
BOYS BE™
REPORT 5 Forbidden Cosplay

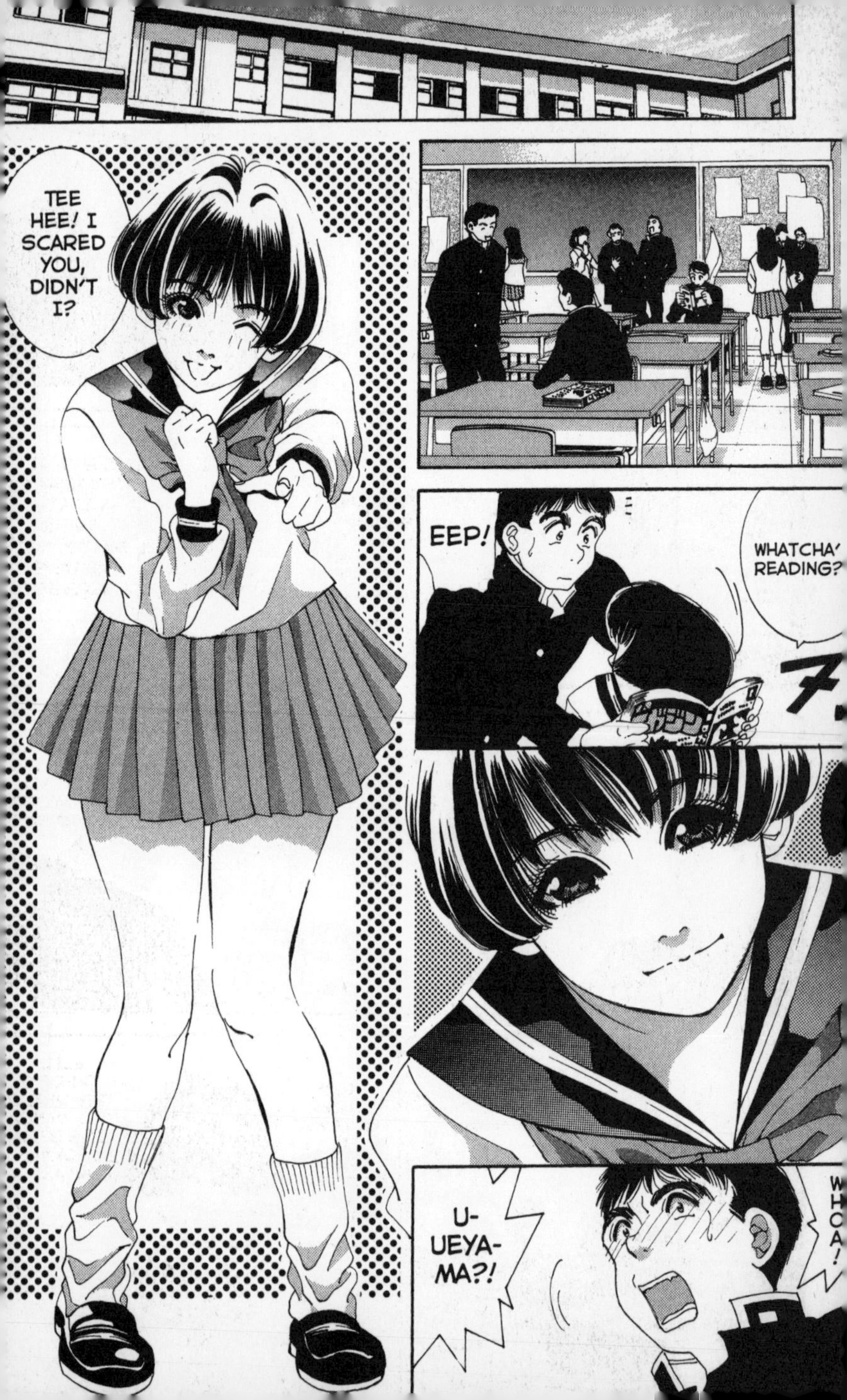
WHATCHA' READING?
EEP!
WHOA!
U-UEYAMA?!
TEE HEE! I SCARED YOU, DIDN'T I?

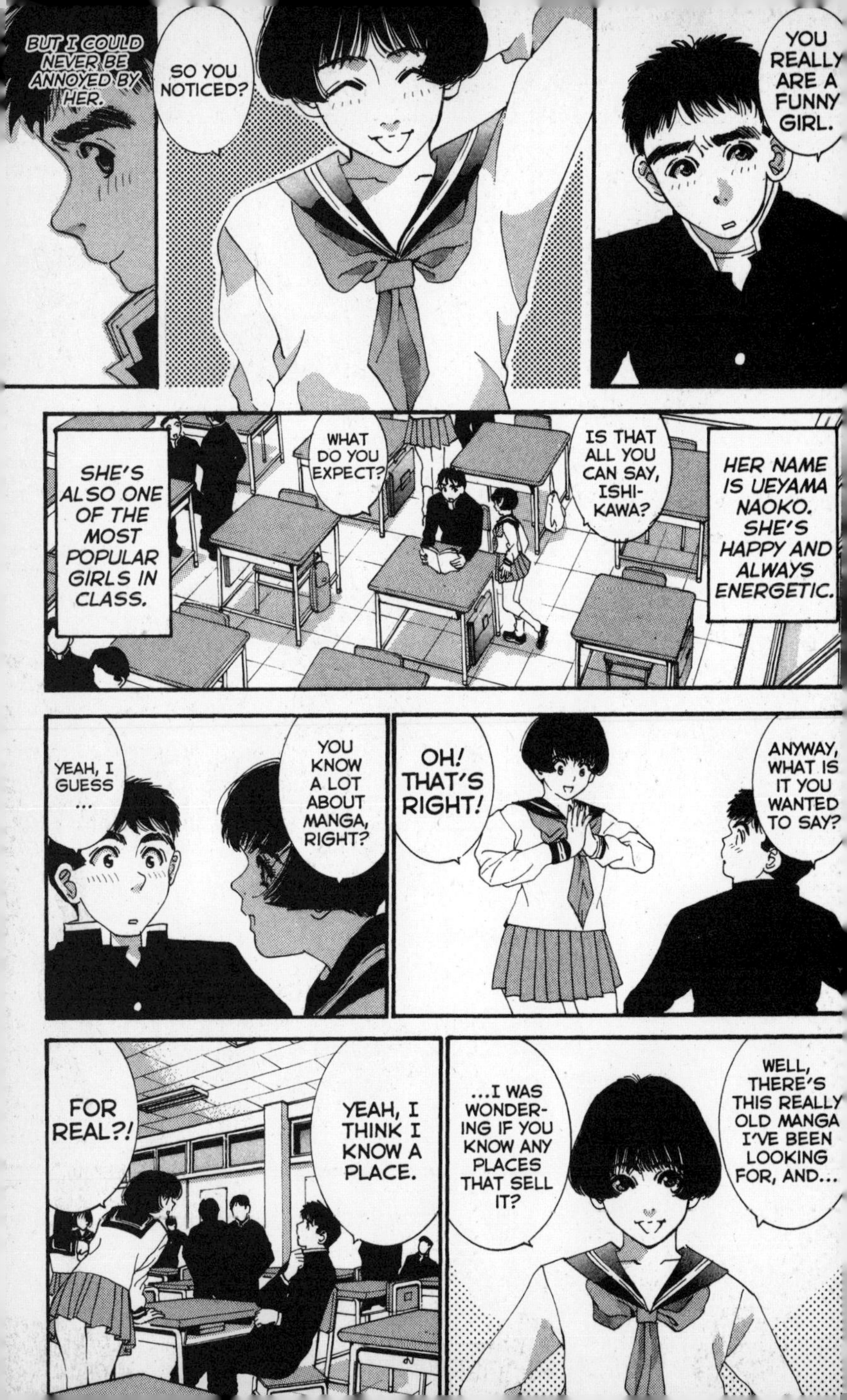
YOU REALLY ARE A FUNNY GIRL.
SO YOU NOTICED?
BUT I COULD NEVER BE ANNOYED BY HER.
HER NAME IS UEYAMA NAOKO. SHE'S HAPPY AND ALWAYS ENERGETIC.
IS THAT ALL YOU CAN SAY, ISHI-KAWA?
WHAT DO YOU EXPECT?
SHE'S ALSO ONE OF THE MOST POPULAR GIRLS IN CLASS.
ANYWAY, WHAT IS IT YOU WANTED TO SAY?
OH! THAT'S RIGHT!
YOU KNOW A LOT ABOUT MANGA, RIGHT?
YEAH, I GUESS ...
WELL, THERE'S THIS REALLY OLD MANGA I'VE BEEN LOOKING FOR, AND...
...I WAS WONDERING IF YOU KNOW ANY PLACES THAT SELL IT?
YEAH, I THINK I KNOW A PLACE.
FOR REAL?!

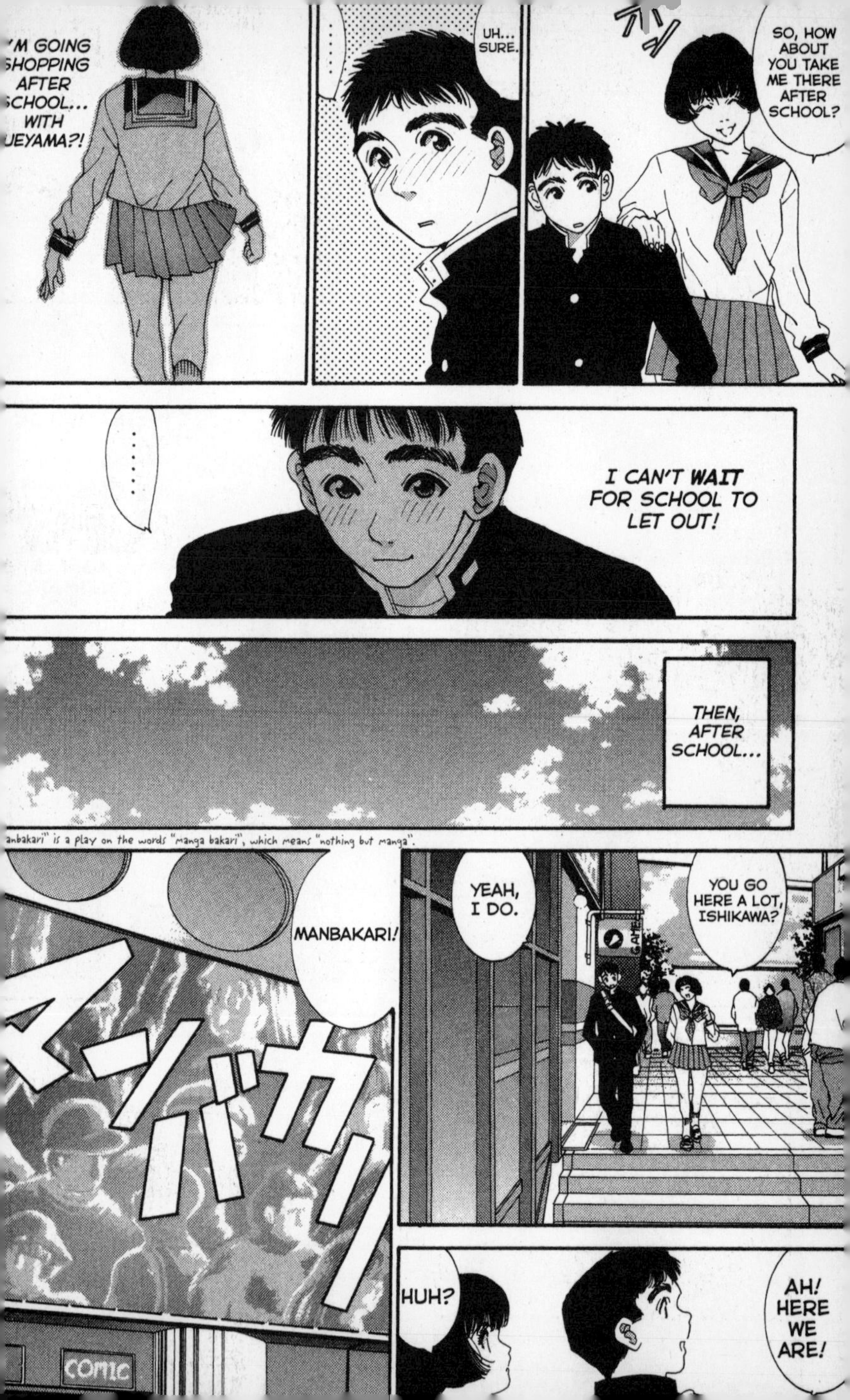
SO, HOW ABOUT YOU TAKE ME THERE AFTER SCHOOL?
UH... SURE.
......
'M GOING SHOPPING AFTER SCHOOL... WITH UEYAMA?!
I CAN'T WAIT FOR SCHOOL TO LET OUT!
......
THEN, AFTER SCHOOL...
YOU GO HERE A LOT, ISHIKAWA?
YEAH, I DO.
AH! HERE WE ARE!
HUH?
MANBAKARI!
COMIC

anbakari" is a play on the words "manga bakari", which means "nothing but manga".

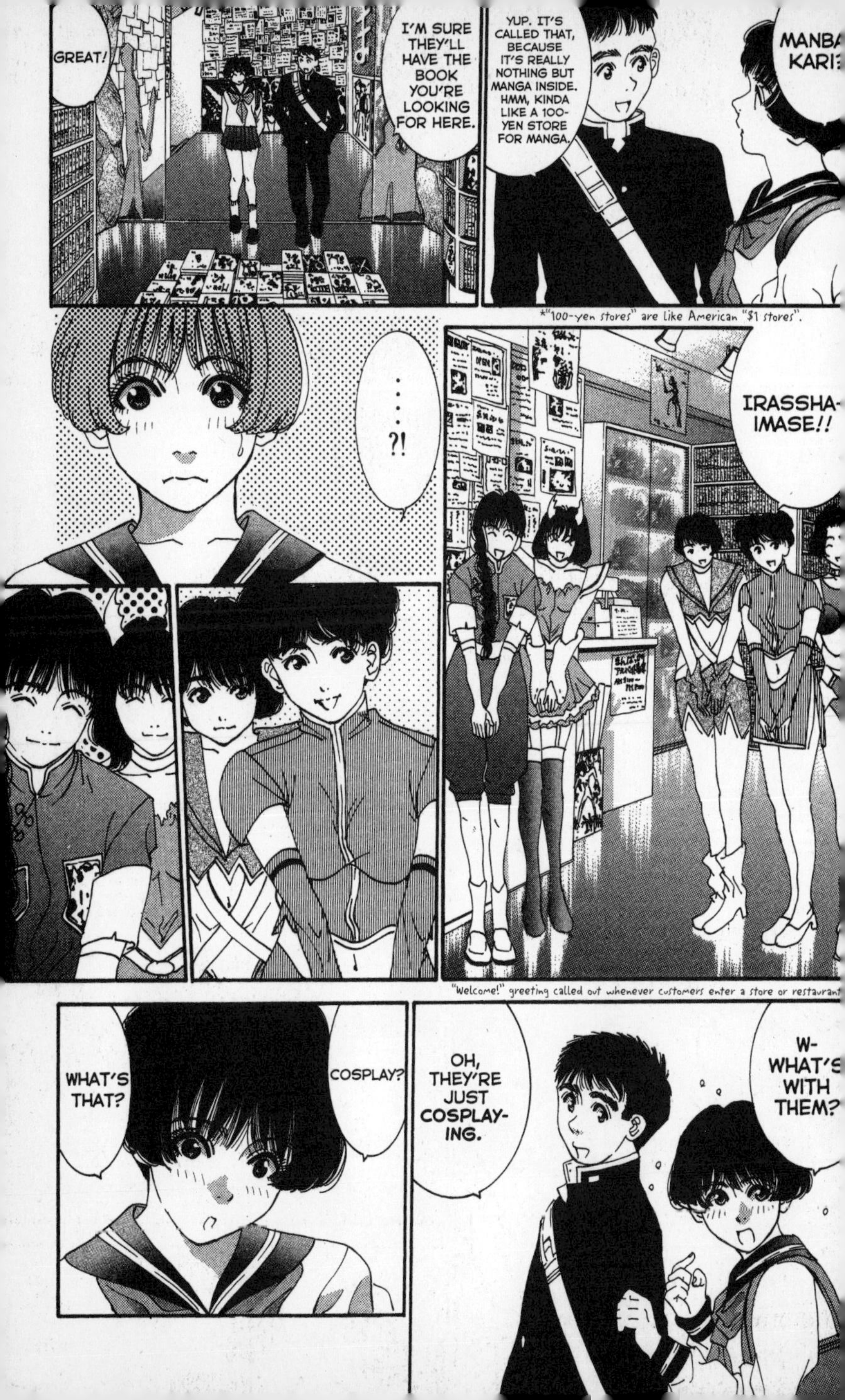
MANBA KARI?
YUP. IT'S CALLED THAT, BECAUSE IT'S REALLY NOTHING BUT MANGA INSIDE. HMM, KINDA LIKE A 100-YEN STORE FOR MANGA.
I'M SURE THEY'LL HAVE THE BOOK YOU'RE LOOKING FOR HERE.
GREAT!
*"100-yen stores" are like American "$1 stores".
IRASSHA-IMASE!!
......?!
"Welcome!" greeting called out whenever customers enter a store or restaurant
W-WHAT'S WITH THEM?
OH, THEY'RE JUST COSPLAYING.
COSPLAY?
WHAT'S THAT?

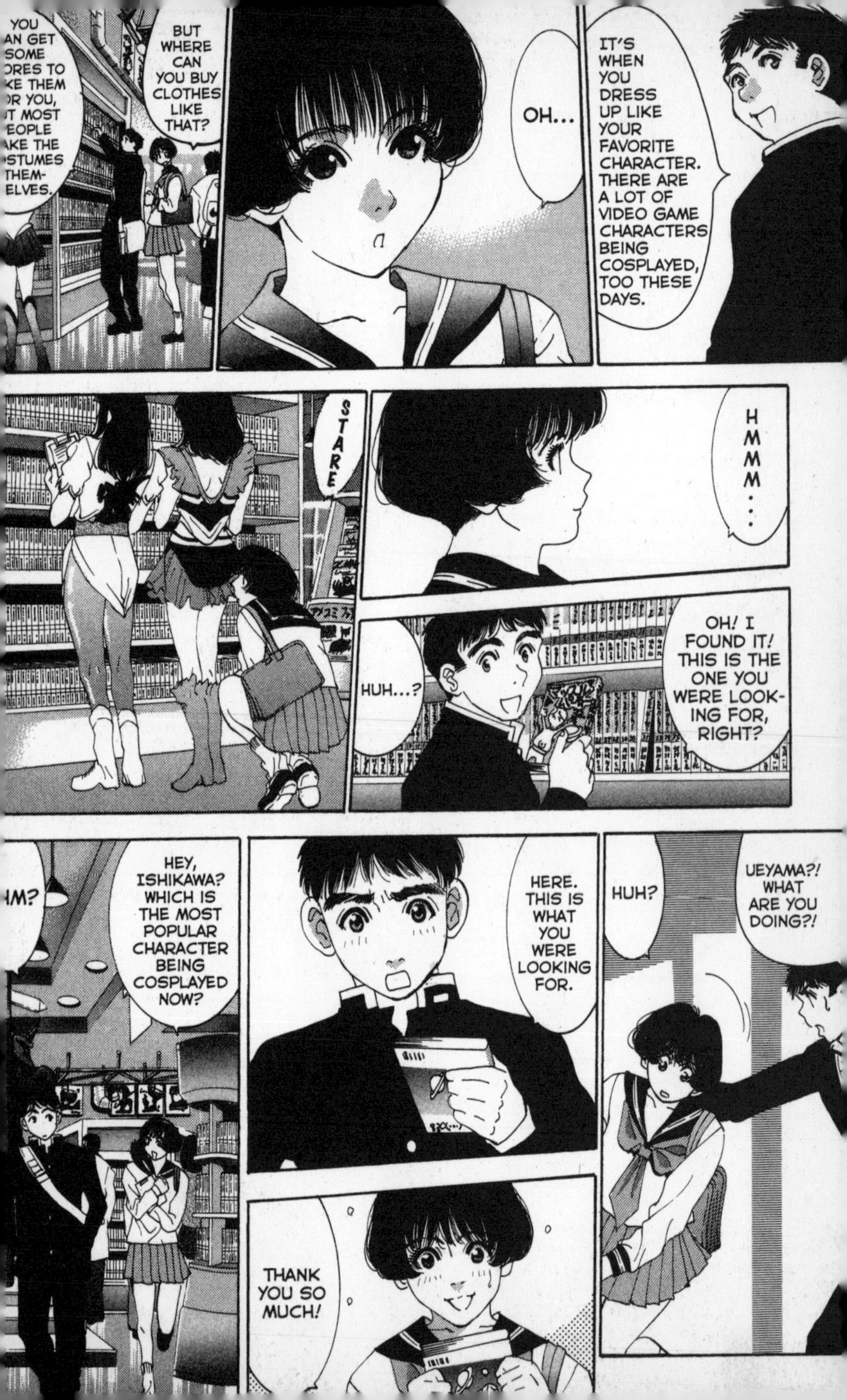
IT'S WHEN YOU DRESS UP LIKE YOUR FAVORITE CHARACTER. THERE ARE A LOT OF VIDEO GAME CHARACTERS BEING COSPLAYED, TOO THESE DAYS.
OH...
BUT WHERE CAN YOU BUY CLOTHES LIKE THAT?
YOU AN GET SOME ORES TO KE THEM OR YOU, T MOST EOPLE AKE THE STUMES THEM- ELVES.
HMMM...
OH! I FOUND IT! THIS IS THE ONE YOU WERE LOOK- ING FOR, RIGHT?
HUH...?
STARE
UEYAMA?! WHAT ARE YOU DOING?!
HUH?
HERE. THIS IS WHAT YOU WERE LOOKING FOR.
THANK YOU SO MUCH!
HEY, ISHIKAWA? WHICH IS THE MOST POPULAR CHARACTER BEING COSPLAYED NOW?
HM?

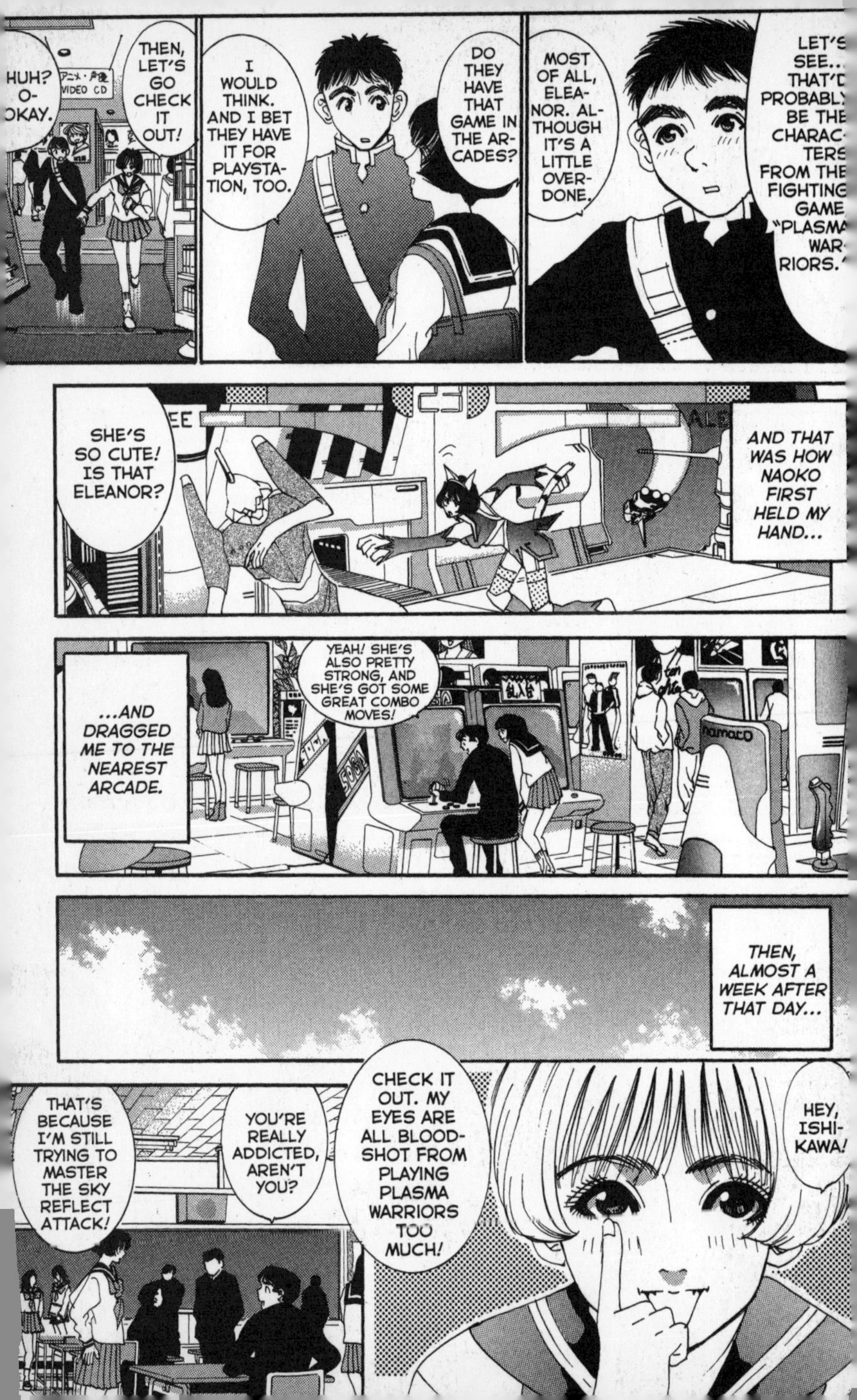
LET'S SEE... THAT'D PROBABLY BE THE CHARACTERS FROM THE FIGHTING GAME "PLASMA WARRIORS."
MOST OF ALL, ELEANOR. ALTHOUGH IT'S A LITTLE OVERDONE.
DO THEY HAVE THAT GAME IN THE ARCADES?
I WOULD THINK. AND I BET THEY HAVE IT FOR PLAYSTATION, TOO.
THEN, LET'S GO CHECK IT OUT!
HUH? O-OKAY.
AND THAT WAS HOW NAOKO FIRST HELD MY HAND...
SHE'S SO CUTE! IS THAT ELEANOR?
YEAH! SHE'S ALSO PRETTY STRONG, AND SHE'S GOT SOME GREAT COMBO MOVES!
...AND DRAGGED ME TO THE NEAREST ARCADE.
THEN, ALMOST A WEEK AFTER THAT DAY...
HEY, ISHIKAWA!
CHECK IT OUT. MY EYES ARE ALL BLOODSHOT FROM PLAYING PLASMA WARRIORS TOO MUCH!
YOU'RE REALLY ADDICTED, AREN'T YOU?
THAT'S BECAUSE I'M STILL TRYING TO MASTER THE SKY REFLECT ATTACK!

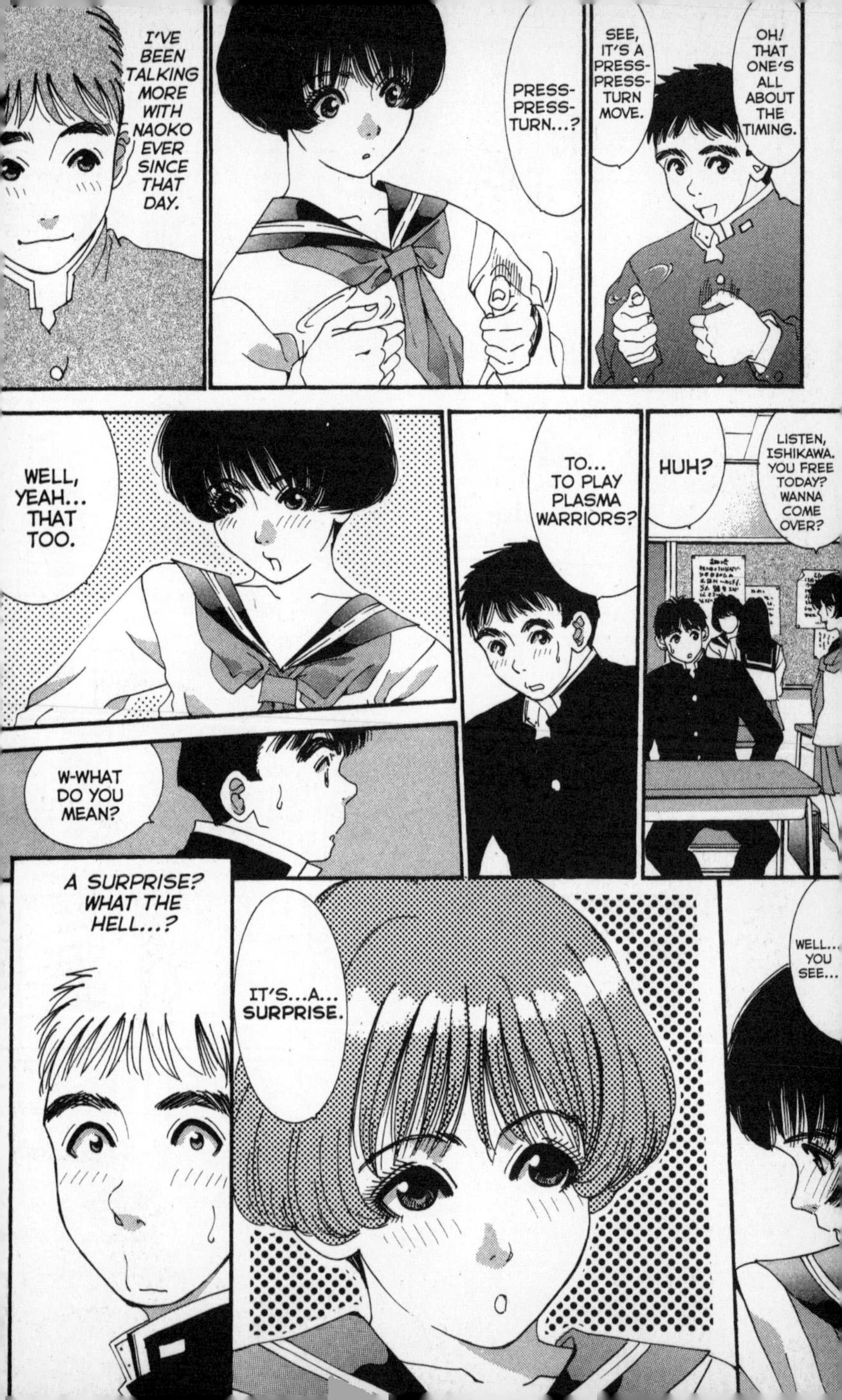
OH! THAT ONE'S ALL ABOUT THE TIMING.
SEE, IT'S A PRESS-PRESS-TURN MOVE.
PRESS-PRESS-TURN...?
I'VE BEEN TALKING MORE WITH NAOKO EVER SINCE THAT DAY.
LISTEN, ISHIKAWA. YOU FREE TODAY? WANNA COME OVER?
HUH?
TO... TO PLAY PLASMA WARRIORS?
WELL, YEAH... THAT TOO.
W-WHAT DO YOU MEAN?
WELL... YOU SEE...
IT'S...A... SURPRISE.
A SURPRISE? WHAT THE HELL...?

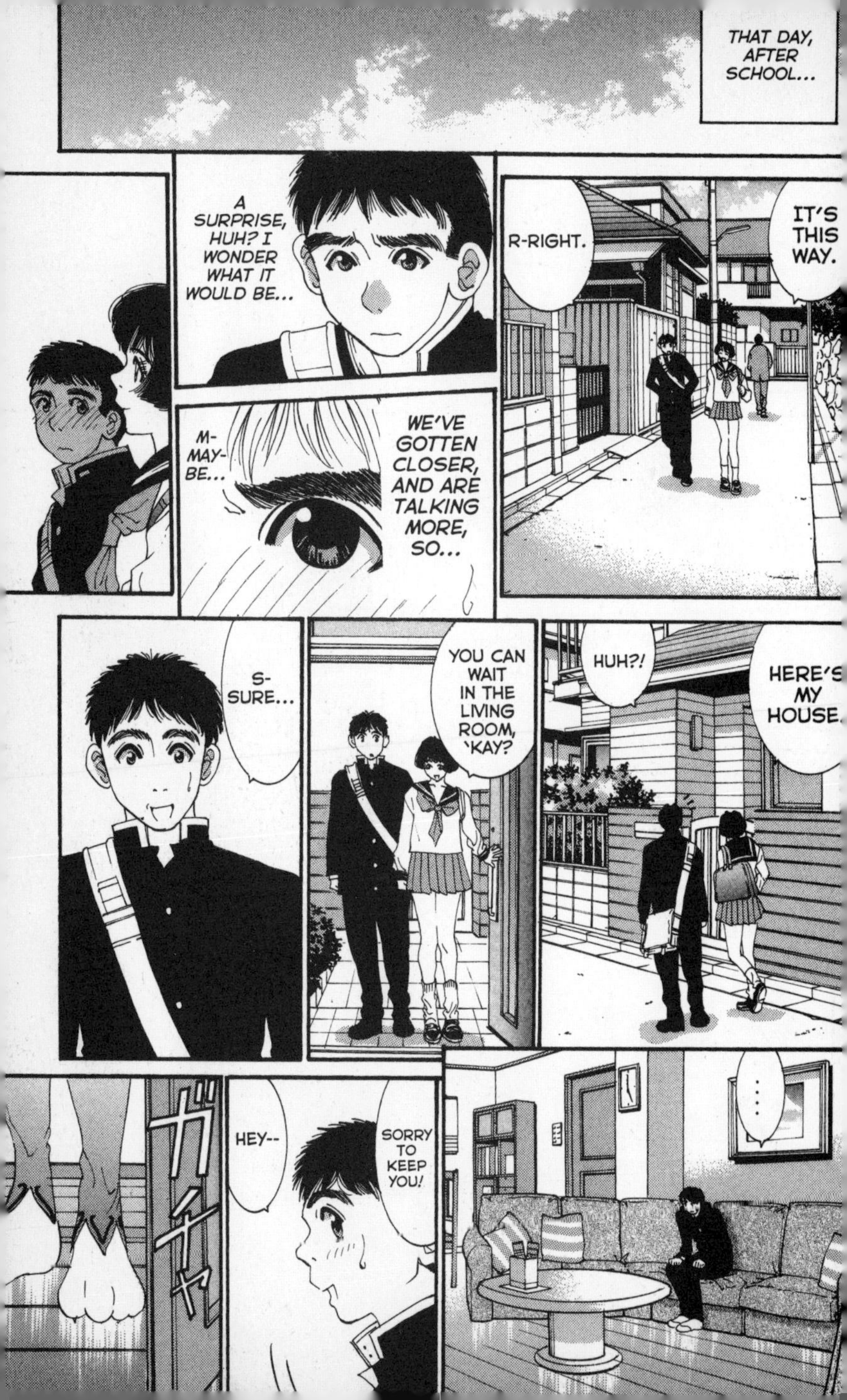
THAT DAY, AFTER SCHOOL...
IT'S THIS WAY.
R-RIGHT.
A SURPRISE, HUH? I WONDER WHAT IT WOULD BE...
WE'VE GOTTEN CLOSER, AND ARE TALKING MORE, SO...
M-MAY-BE...
HERE'S MY HOUSE.
HUH?!
YOU CAN WAIT IN THE LIVING ROOM, 'KAY?
S-SURE...
....
SORRY TO KEEP YOU!
HEY--
ガチャ

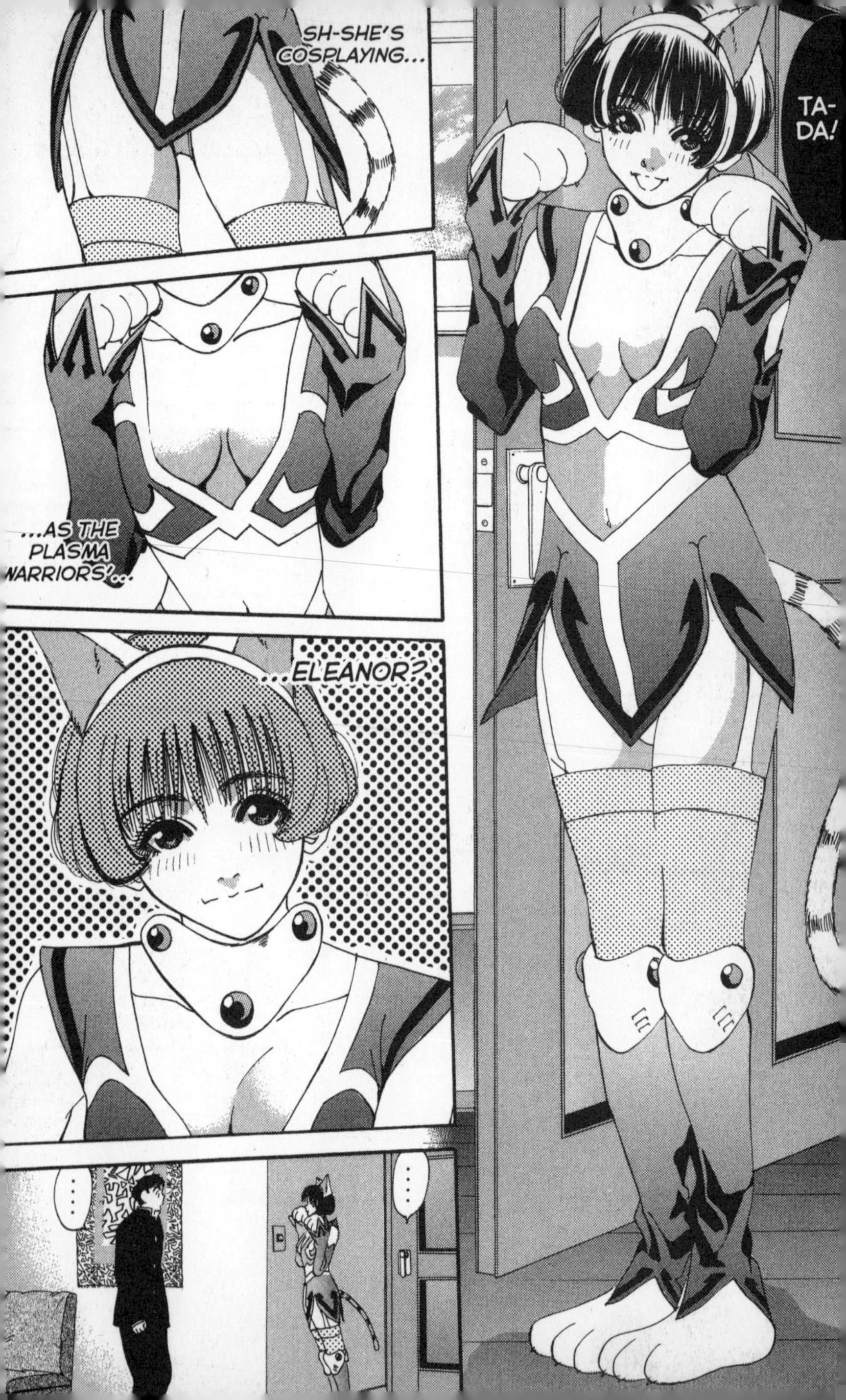
TA-DA!
SH-SHE'S COSPLAYING...
...AS THE PLASMA WARRIORS!...
...ELEANOR?
....
....

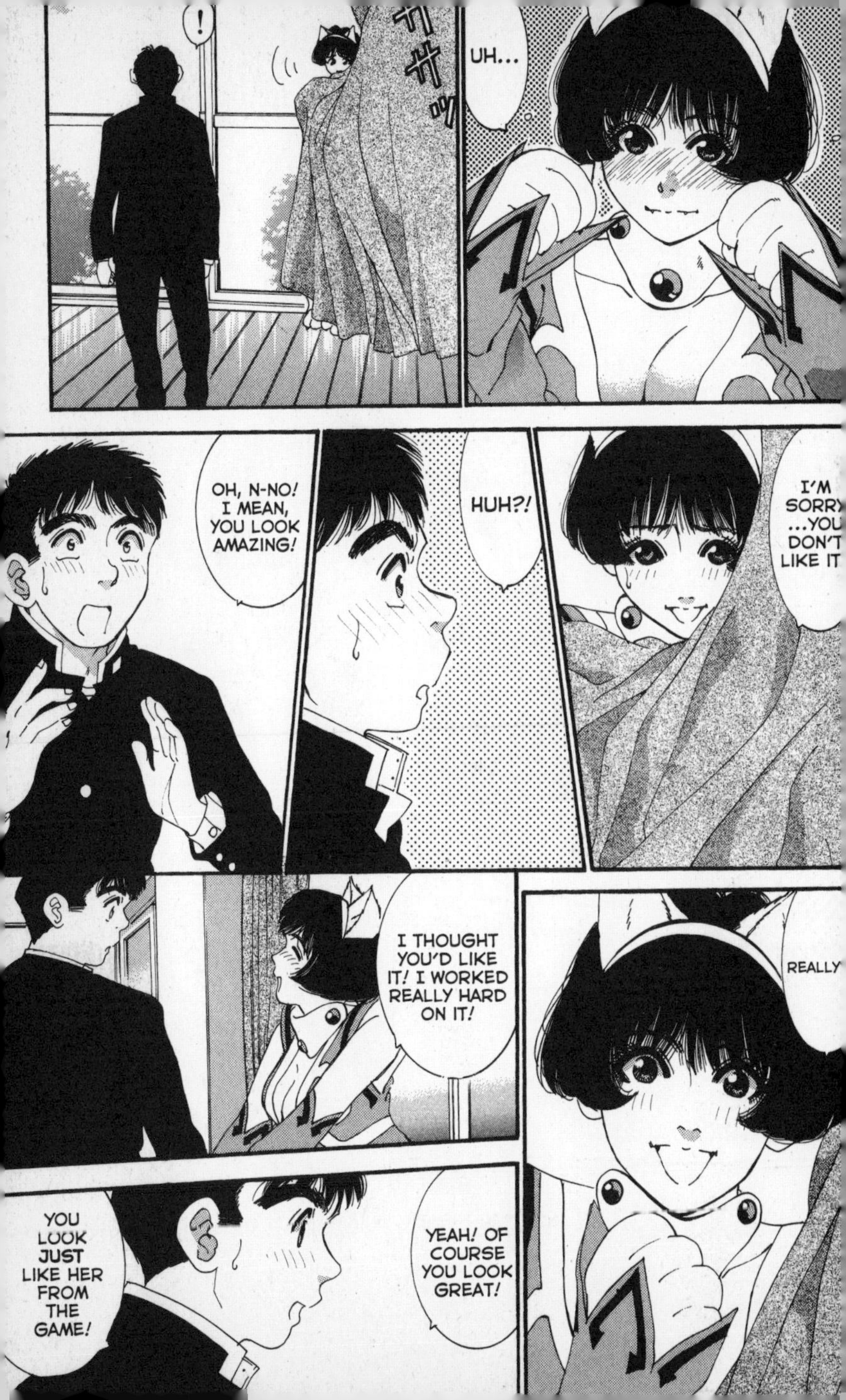
UH...
!
I'M SORRY ...YOU DON'T LIKE IT
HUH?!
OH, N-NO! I MEAN, YOU LOOK AMAZING!
REALLY
I THOUGHT YOU'D LIKE IT! I WORKED REALLY HARD ON IT!
YEAH! OF COURSE YOU LOOK GREAT!
YOU LOOK JUST LIKE HER FROM THE GAME!

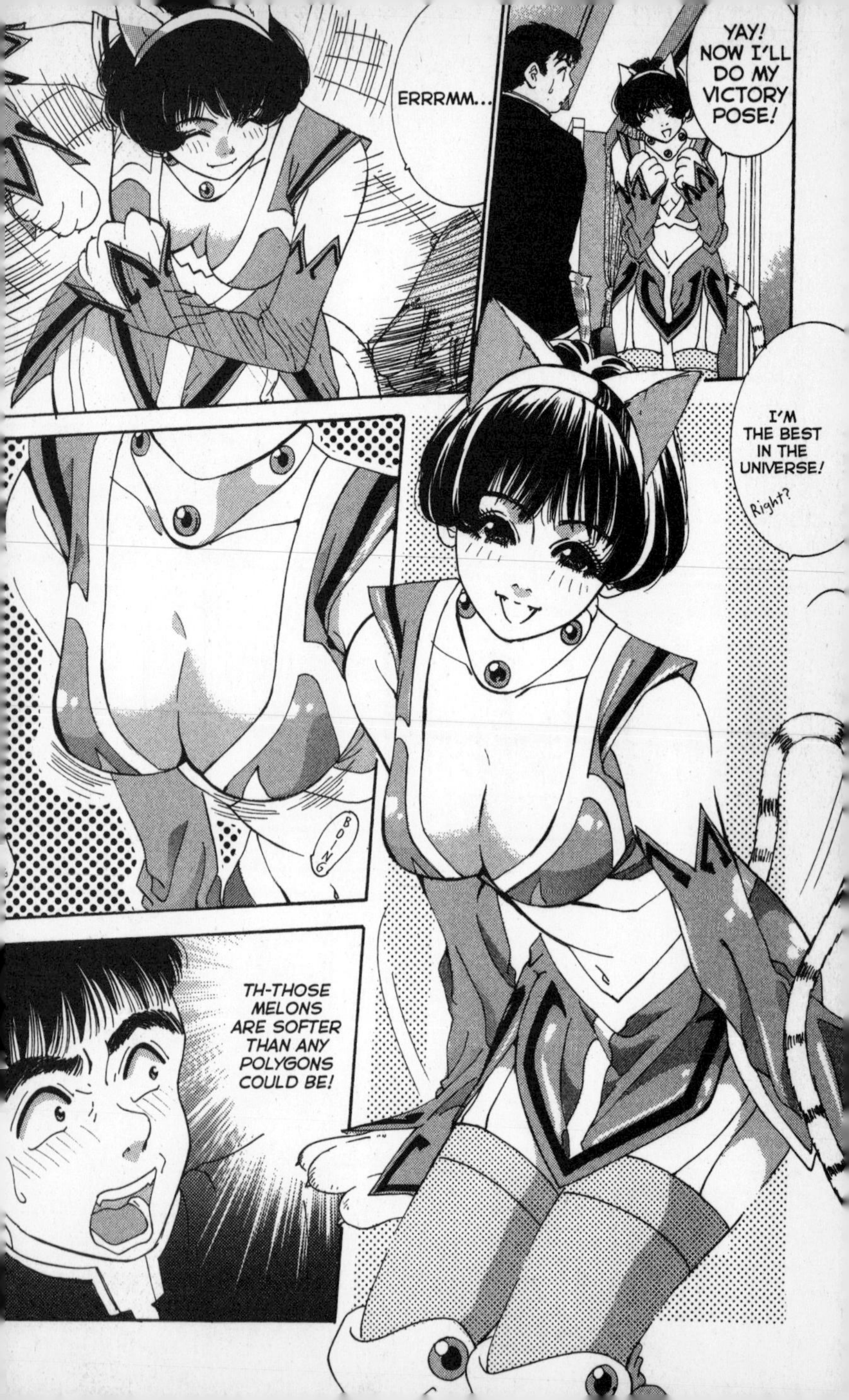
YAY! NOW I'LL DO MY VICTORY POSE!
ERRRMM...
I'M THE BEST IN THE UNIVERSE!
Right?
BOING
TH-THOSE MELONS ARE SOFTER THAN ANY POLYGONS COULD BE!

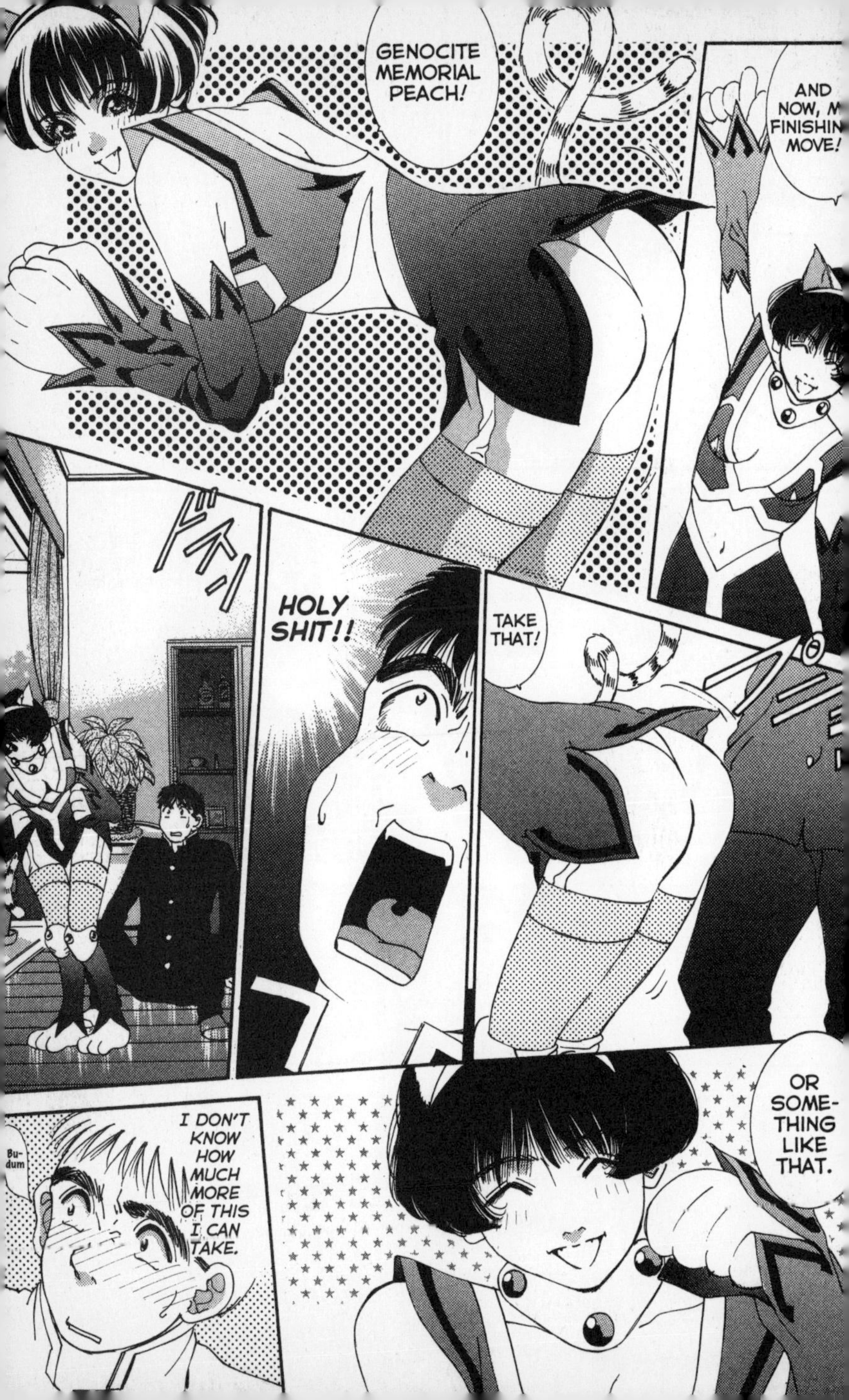
AND NOW, M FINISHIN MOVE!
GENOCITE MEMORIAL PEACH!
TAKE THAT!
HOLY SHIT!!
OR SOME-THING LIKE THAT.
I DON'T KNOW HOW MUCH MORE OF THIS I CAN TAKE.
Bu-dum

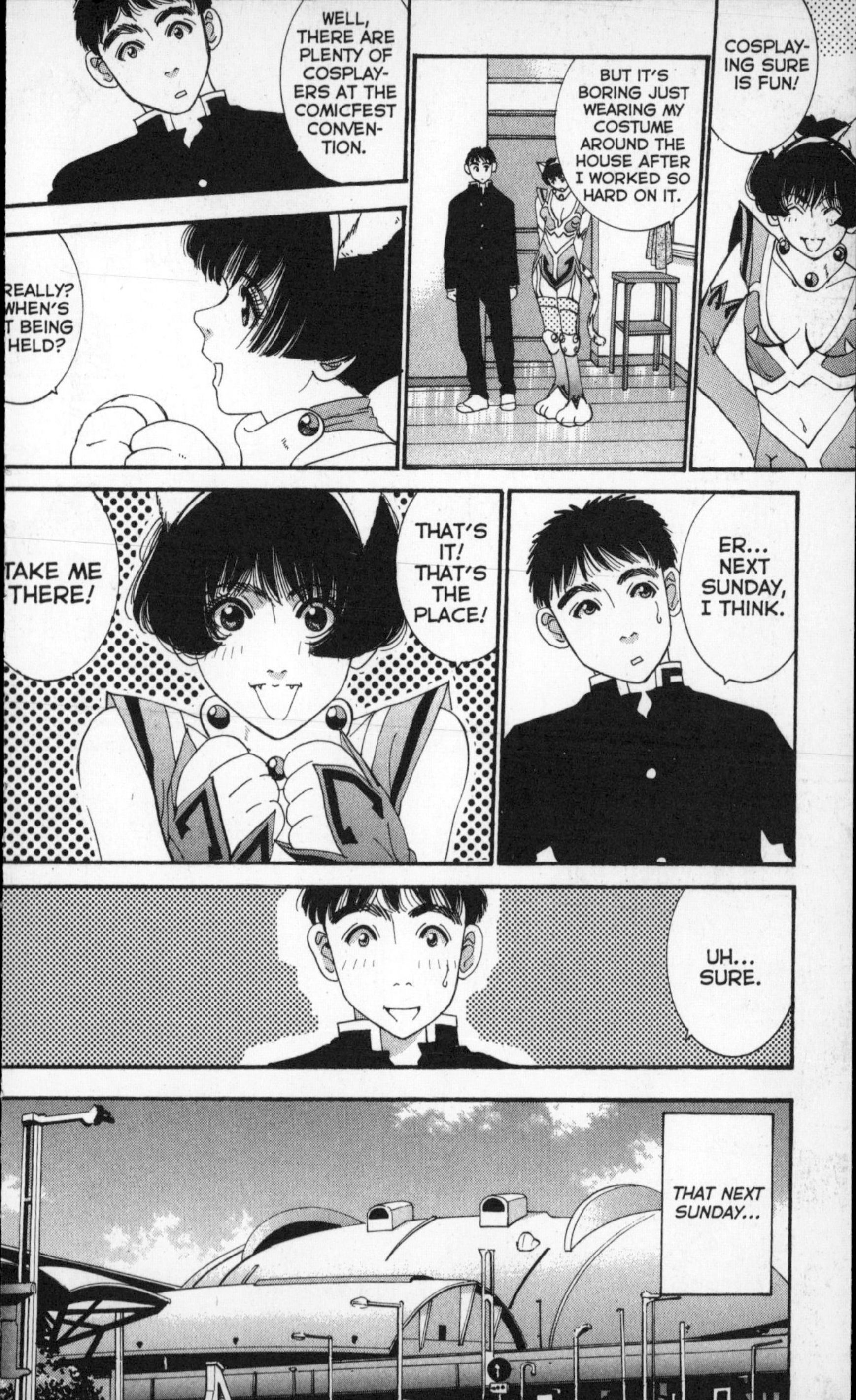
COSPLAYING SURE IS FUN!
BUT IT'S BORING JUST WEARING MY COSTUME AROUND THE HOUSE AFTER I WORKED SO HARD ON IT.
WELL, THERE ARE PLENTY OF COSPLAYERS AT THE COMICFEST CONVENTION.
REALLY? WHEN'S T BEING HELD?
ER... NEXT SUNDAY, I THINK.
THAT'S IT! THAT'S THE PLACE!
TAKE ME THERE!
UH... SURE.
THAT NEXT SUNDAY...

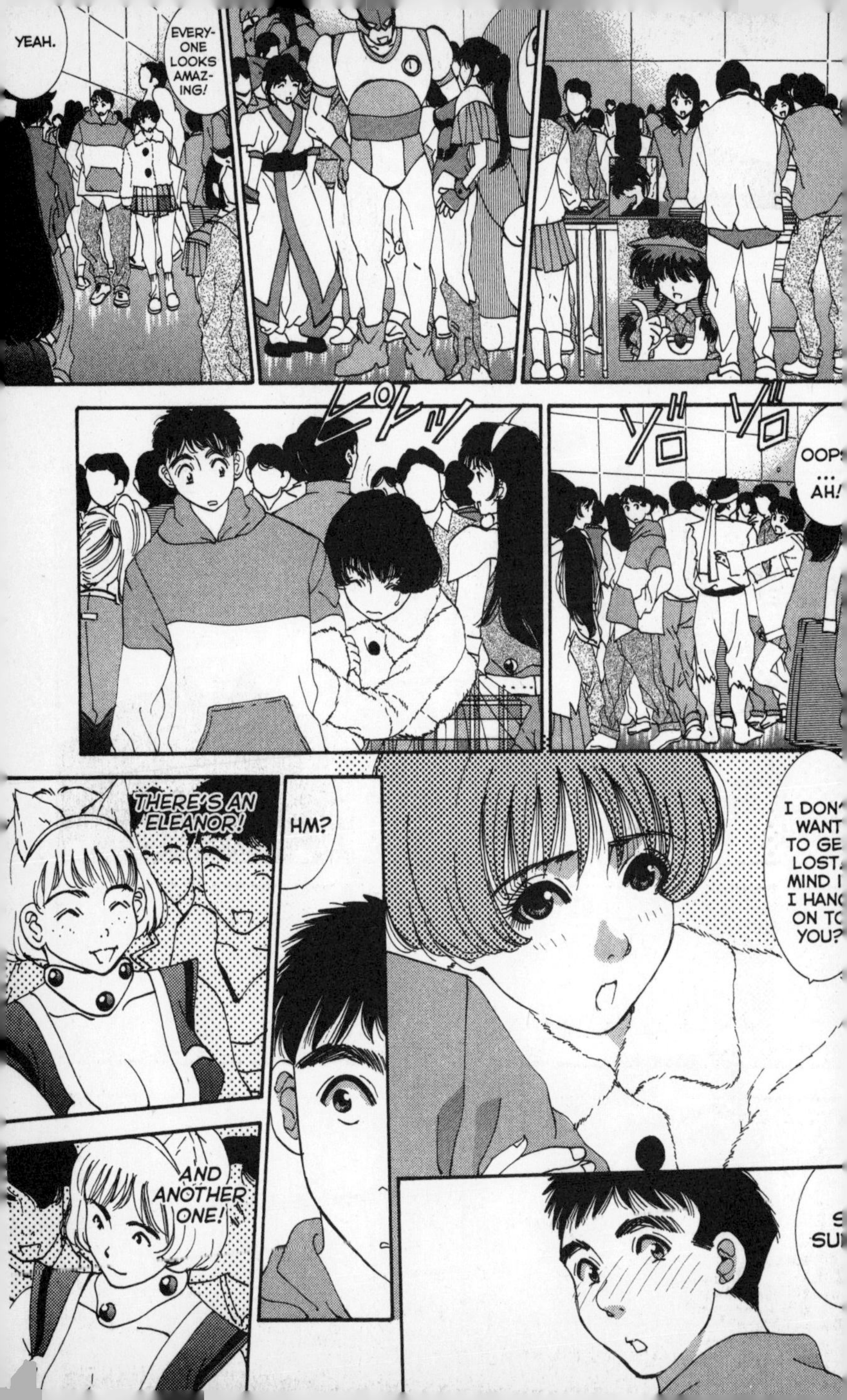
EVERY-ONE LOOKS AMAZ-ING!
YEAH.
ゾロ ゾロ
OOP ... AH!
ピクッ
I DON' WANT TO GE LOST. MIND I I HANG ON TO YOU?
S SU
HM?
THERE'S AN ELEANOR!
AND ANOTHER ONE!

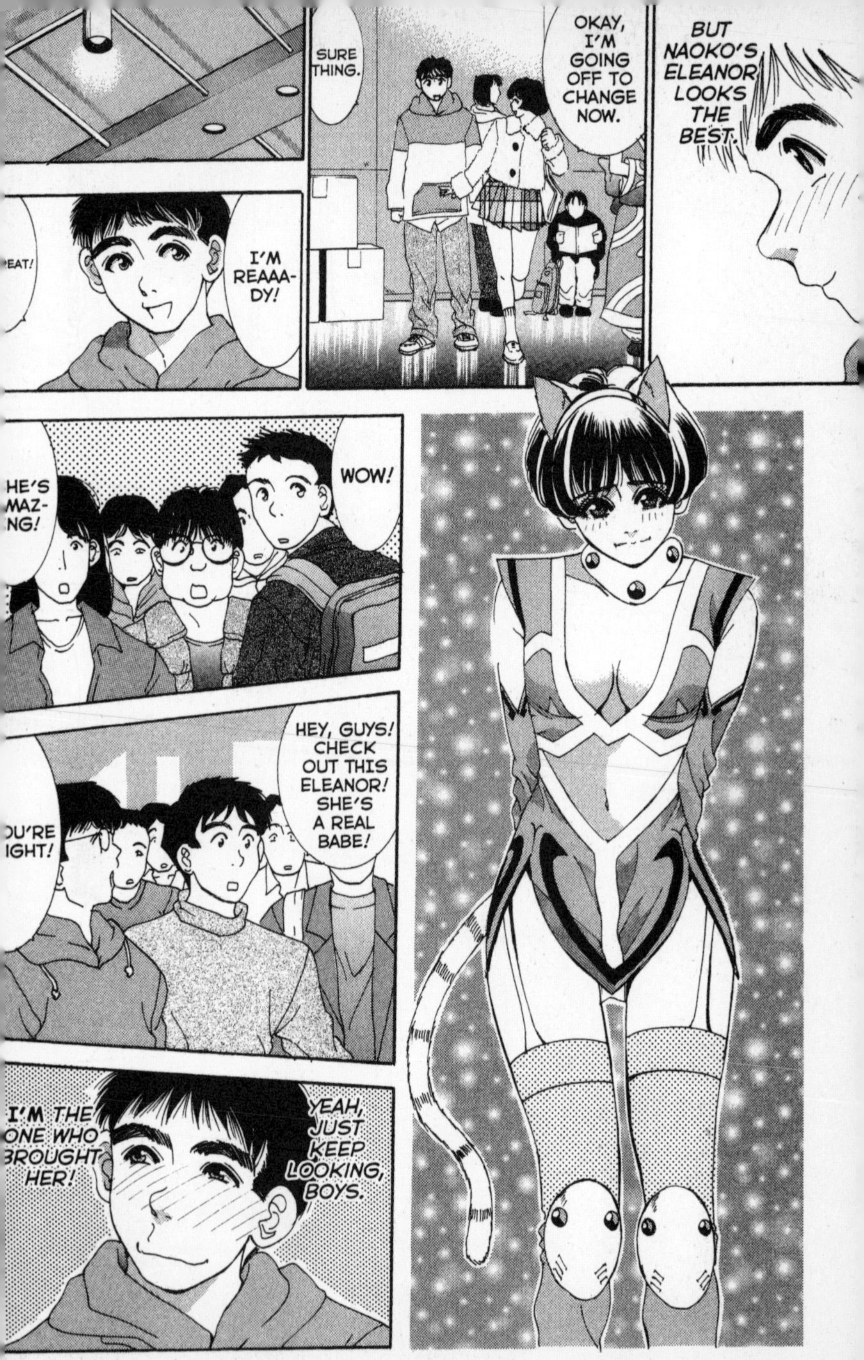
BUT NAOKO'S ELEANOR LOOKS THE BEST.
OKAY, I'M GOING OFF TO CHANGE NOW.
SURE THING.
I'M REAAAA-DY!
EAT!
WOW!
HE'S MAZ-NG!
HEY, GUYS! CHECK OUT THIS ELEANOR! SHE'S A REAL BABE!
OU'RE IGHT!
YEAH, JUST KEEP LOOKING, BOYS.
I'M THE ONE WHO BROUGHT HER!

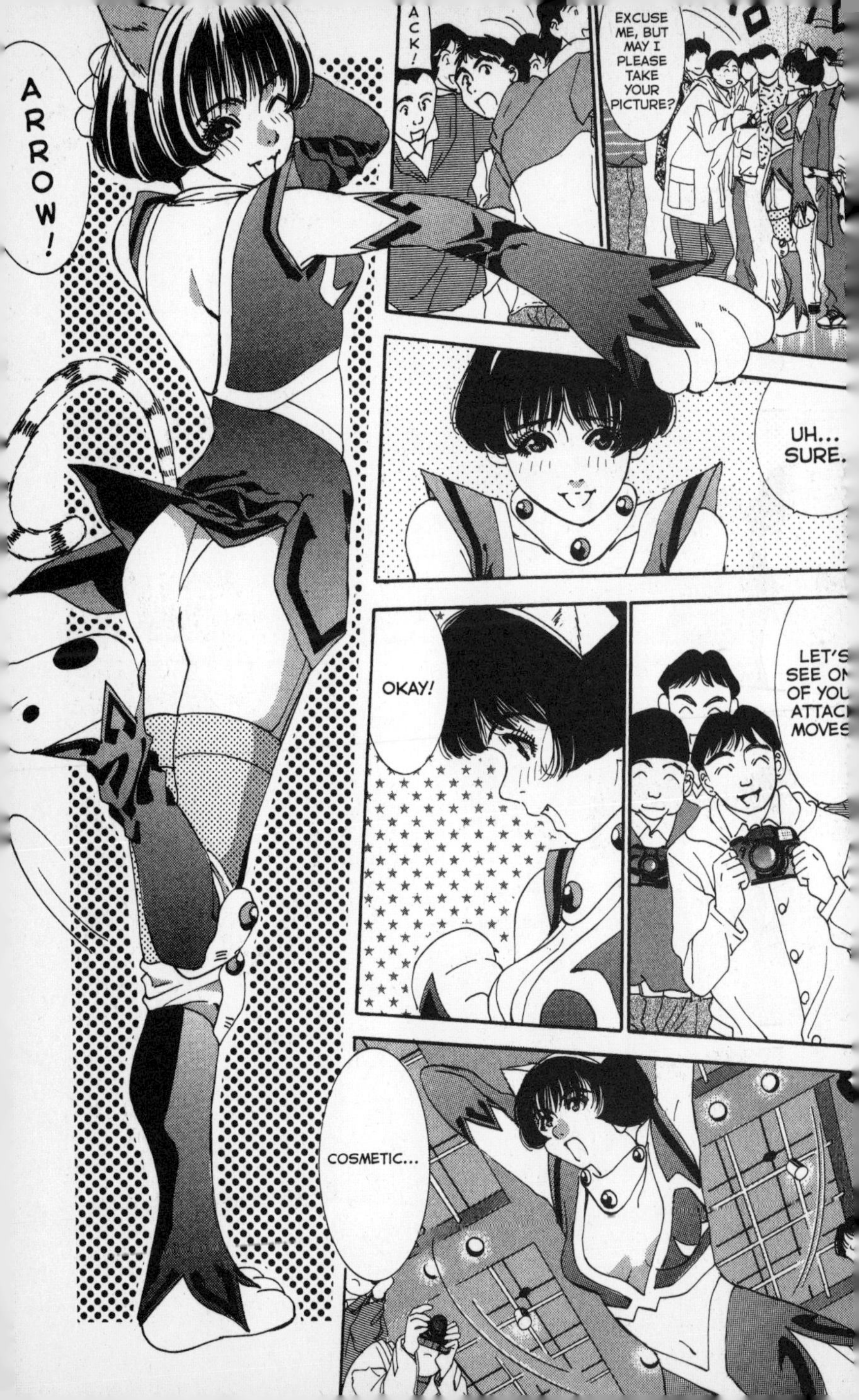
EXCUSE ME, BUT MAY I PLEASE TAKE YOUR PICTURE?
ACK!
UH... SURE.
LET'S SEE ON OF YOU ATTACK MOVES
OKAY!
COSMETIC...
ARROW!

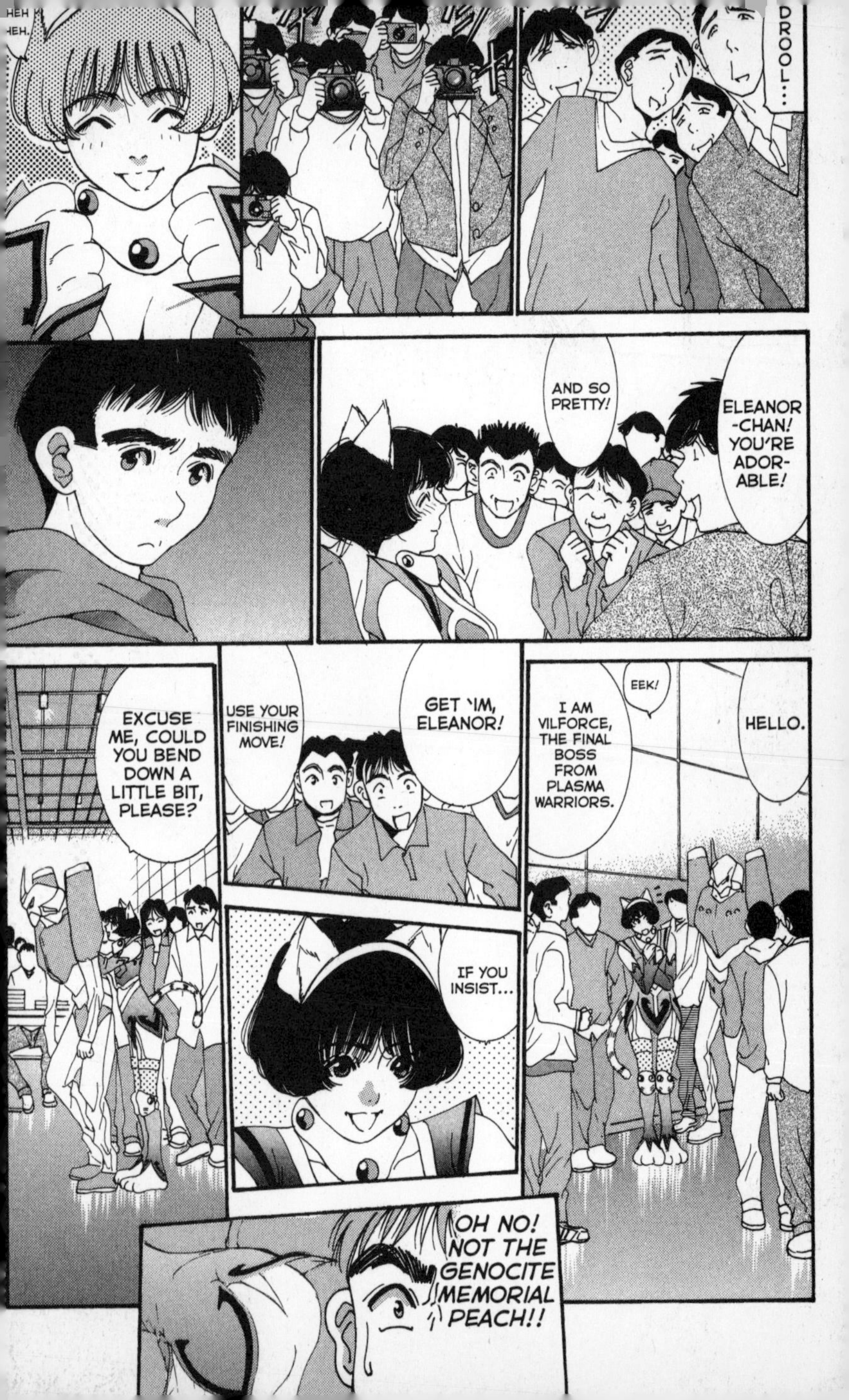
DROOL...
HEH
HEH.
ELEANOR-CHAN! YOU'RE ADORABLE!
AND SO PRETTY!
HELLO.
EEK!
I AM VILFORCE, THE FINAL BOSS FROM PLASMA WARRIORS.
GET 'IM, ELEANOR!
USE YOUR FINISHING MOVE!
IF YOU INSIST...
EXCUSE ME, COULD YOU BEND DOWN A LITTLE BIT, PLEASE?
OH NO! NOT THE GENOCITE MEMORIAL PEACH!!

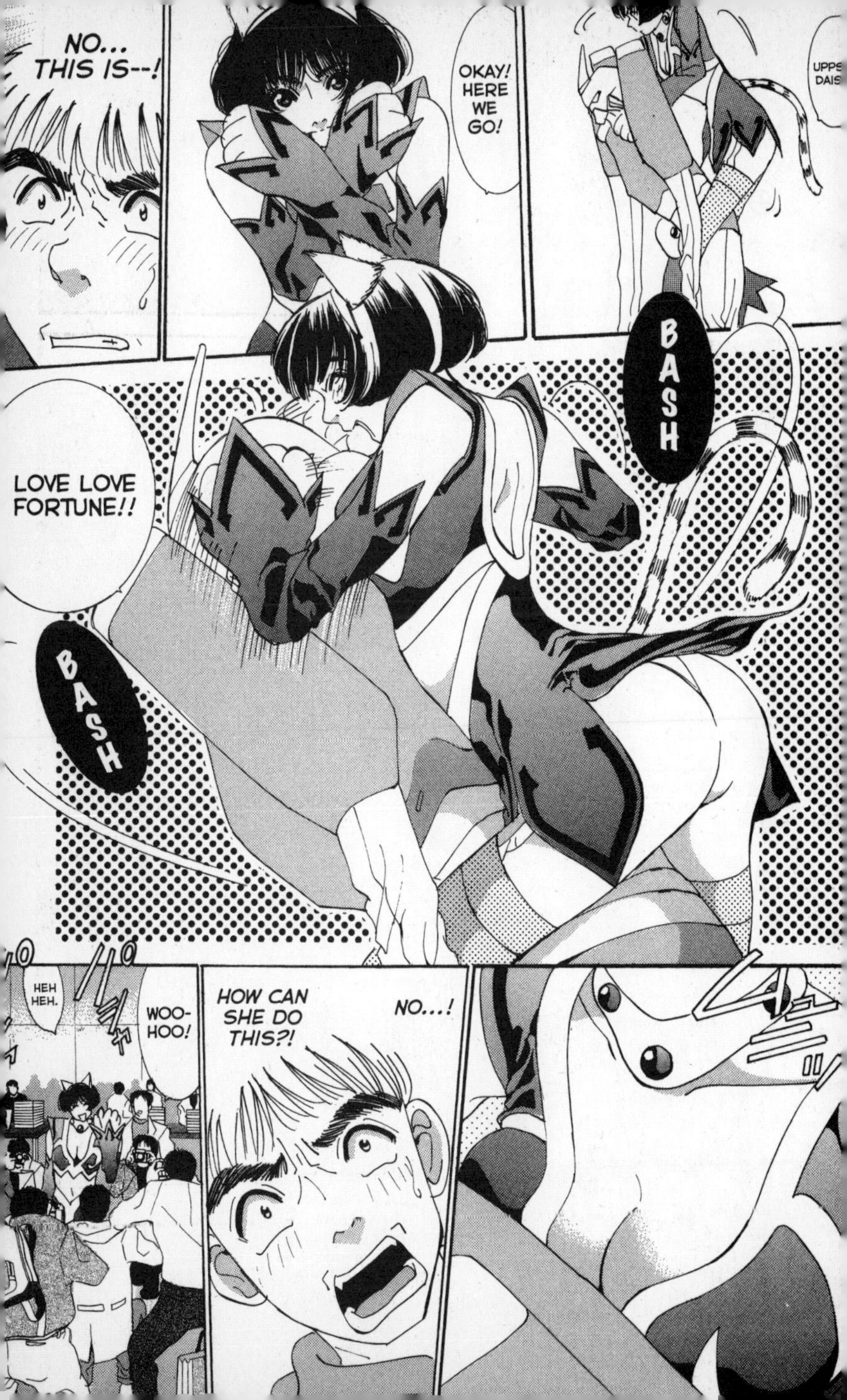
UPPS DAIS
OKAY! HERE WE GO!
NO... THIS IS--!
BASH
LOVE LOVE FORTUNE!!
BASH
NO...!
HOW CAN SHE DO THIS?!
WOO-HOO!
HEH HEH.

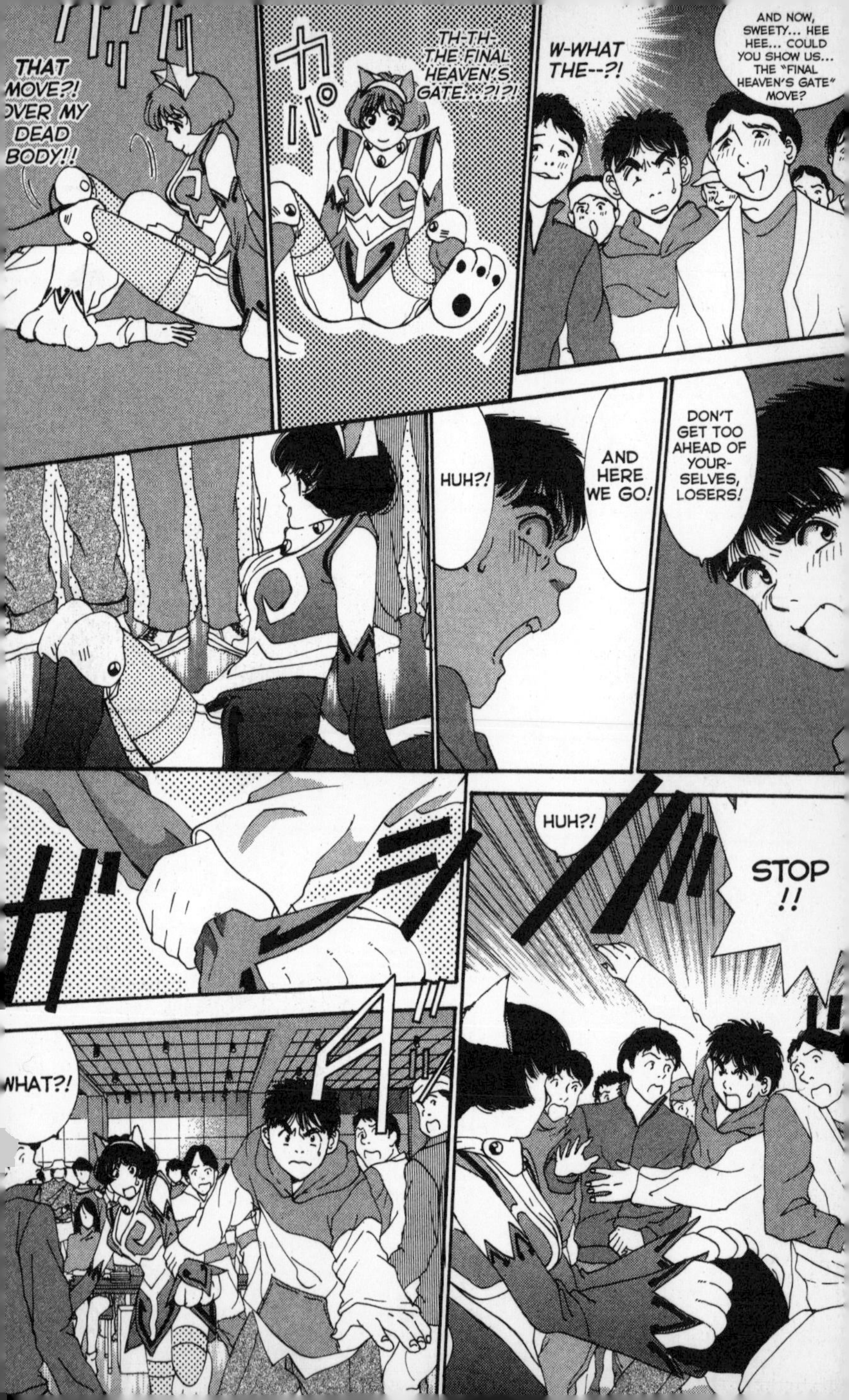
AND NOW, SWEETY... HEE HEE... COULD YOU SHOW US... THE "FINAL HEAVEN'S GATE" MOVE?
W-WHAT THE--?!
TH-TH-THE FINAL HEAVEN'S GATE...?!?!
THAT MOVE?! OVER MY DEAD BODY!!
DON'T GET TOO AHEAD OF YOURSELVES, LOSERS!
AND HERE WE GO!
HUH?!
HUH?!
STOP !!
WHAT?!

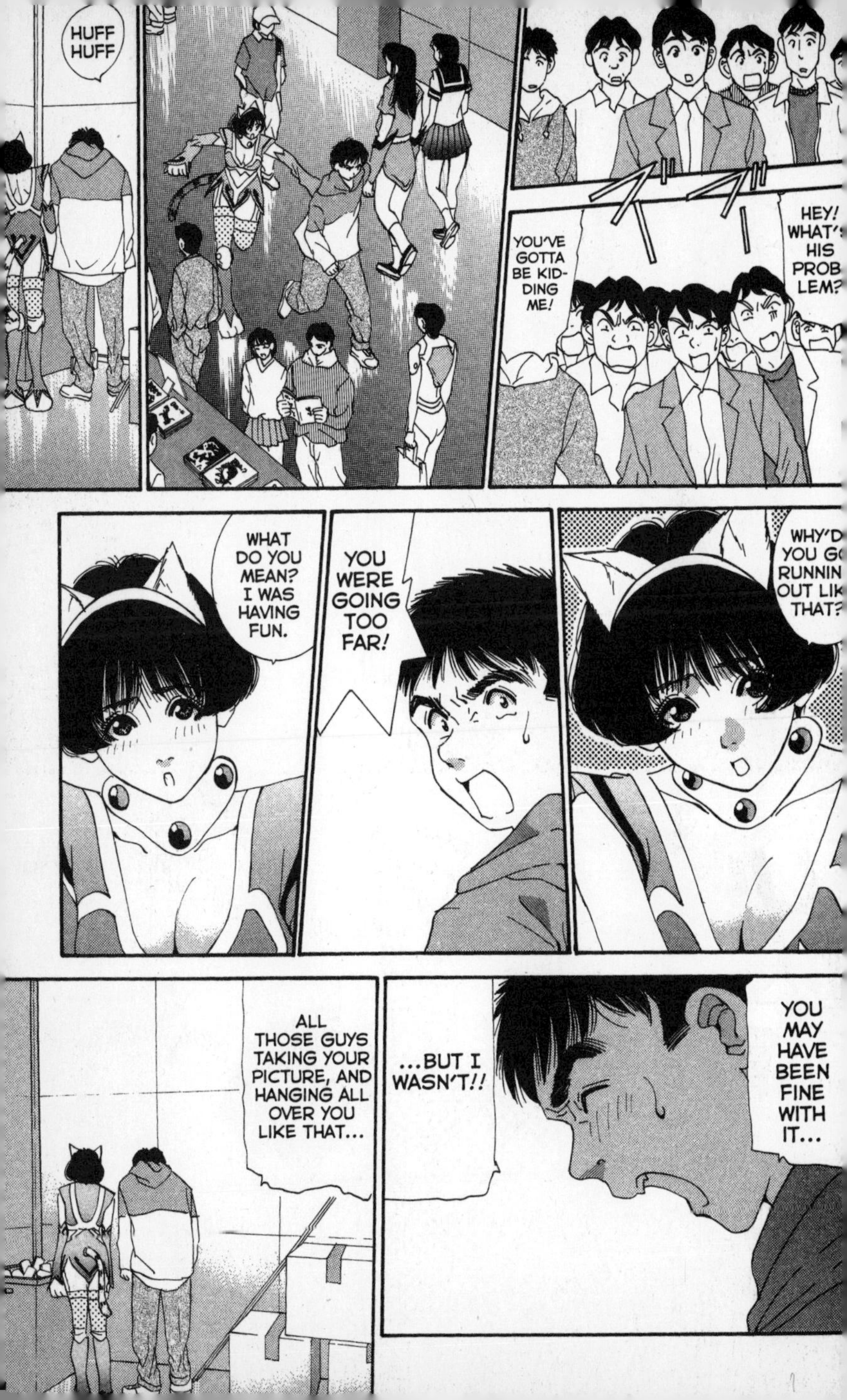
HEY! WHAT'S HIS PROB-LEM?
YOU'VE GOTTA BE KID-DING ME!
HUFF HUFF
WHY'D YOU GO RUNNIN OUT LIK THAT?
YOU WERE GOING TOO FAR!
WHAT DO YOU MEAN? I WAS HAVING FUN.
YOU MAY HAVE BEEN FINE WITH IT...
...BUT I WASN'T!!
ALL THOSE GUYS TAKING YOUR PICTURE, AND HANGING ALL OVER YOU LIKE THAT...

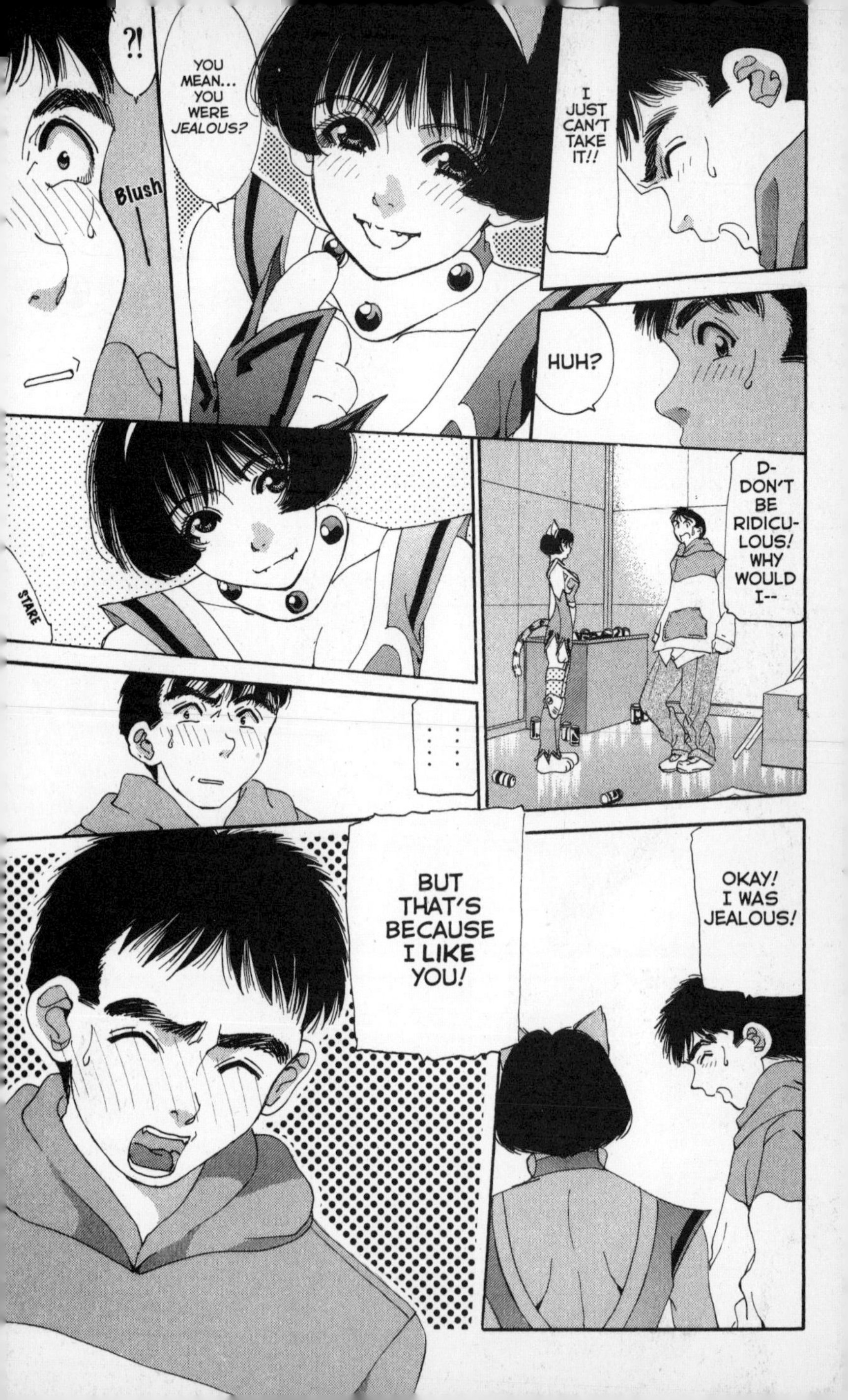
I JUST CAN'T TAKE IT!!
HUH?
YOU MEAN... YOU WERE JEALOUS?
?!
Blush
D-DON'T BE RIDICULOUS! WHY WOULD I--
STARE
OKAY! I WAS JEALOUS!
BUT THAT'S BECAUSE I LIKE YOU!

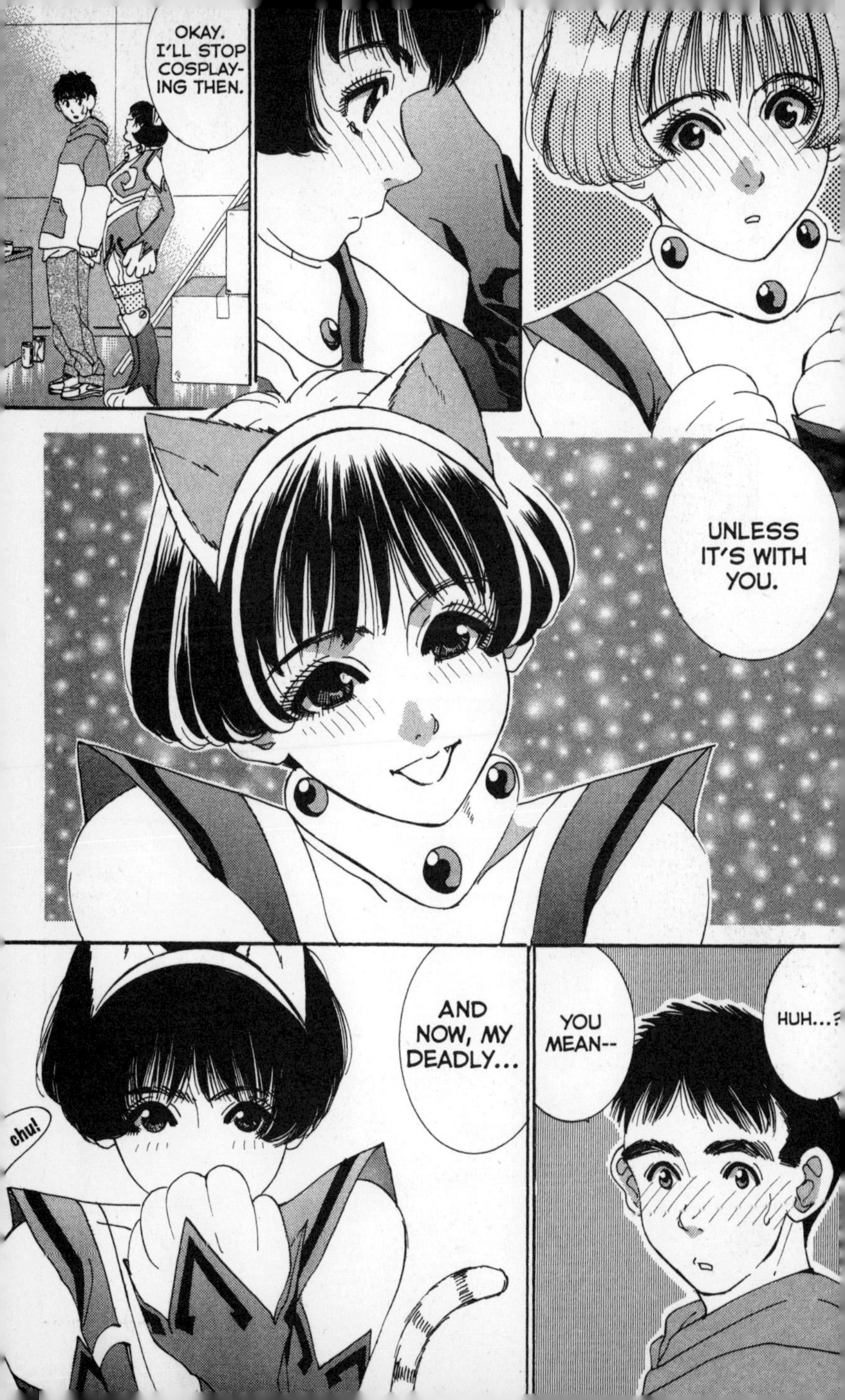
OKAY. I'LL STOP COSPLAYING THEN.
UNLESS IT'S WITH YOU.
HUH...?
YOU MEAN--
AND NOW, MY DEADLY...
chu!

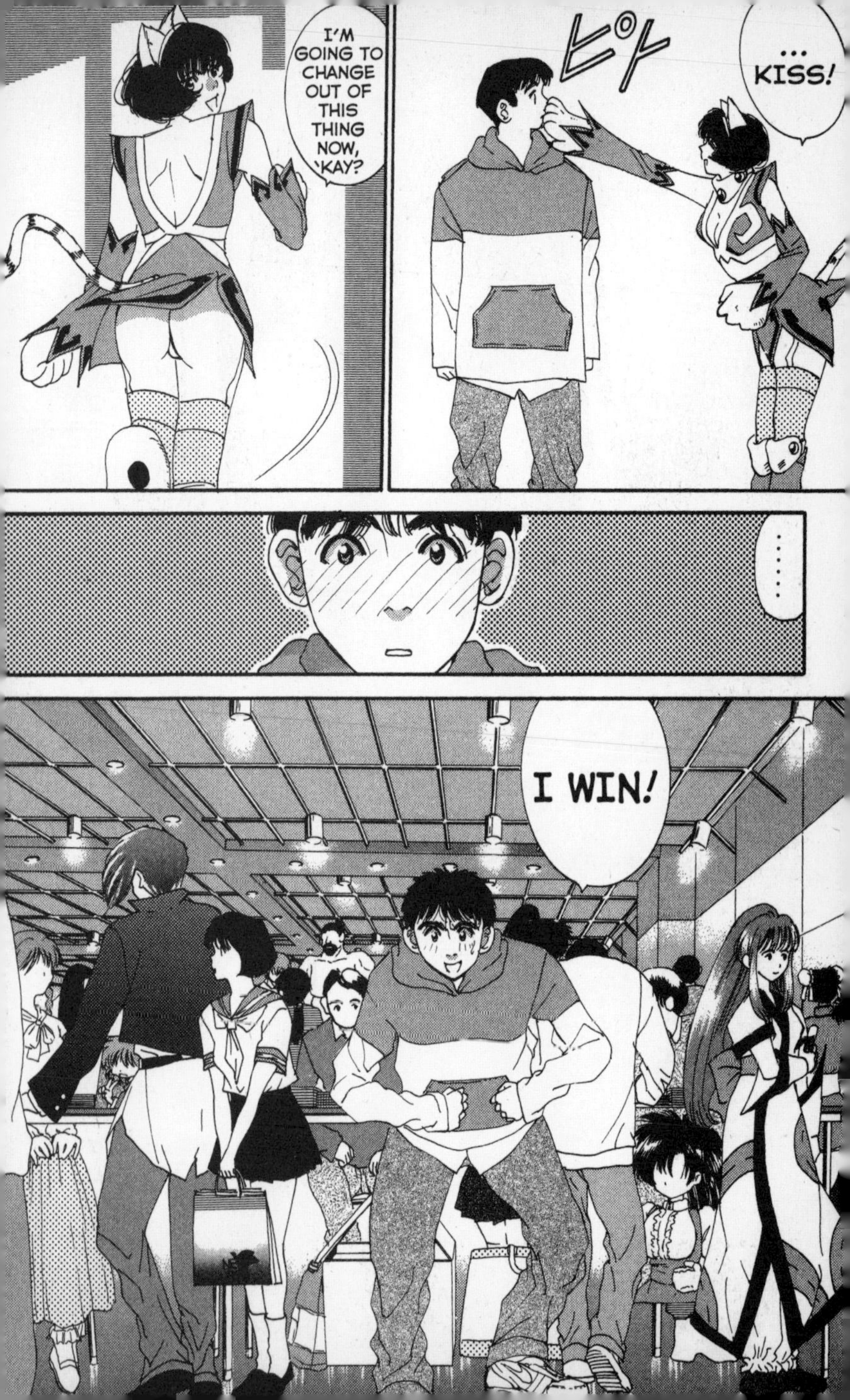
...KISS!
ピッ
I'M GOING TO CHANGE OUT OF THIS THING NOW, 'KAY?
......
I WIN!

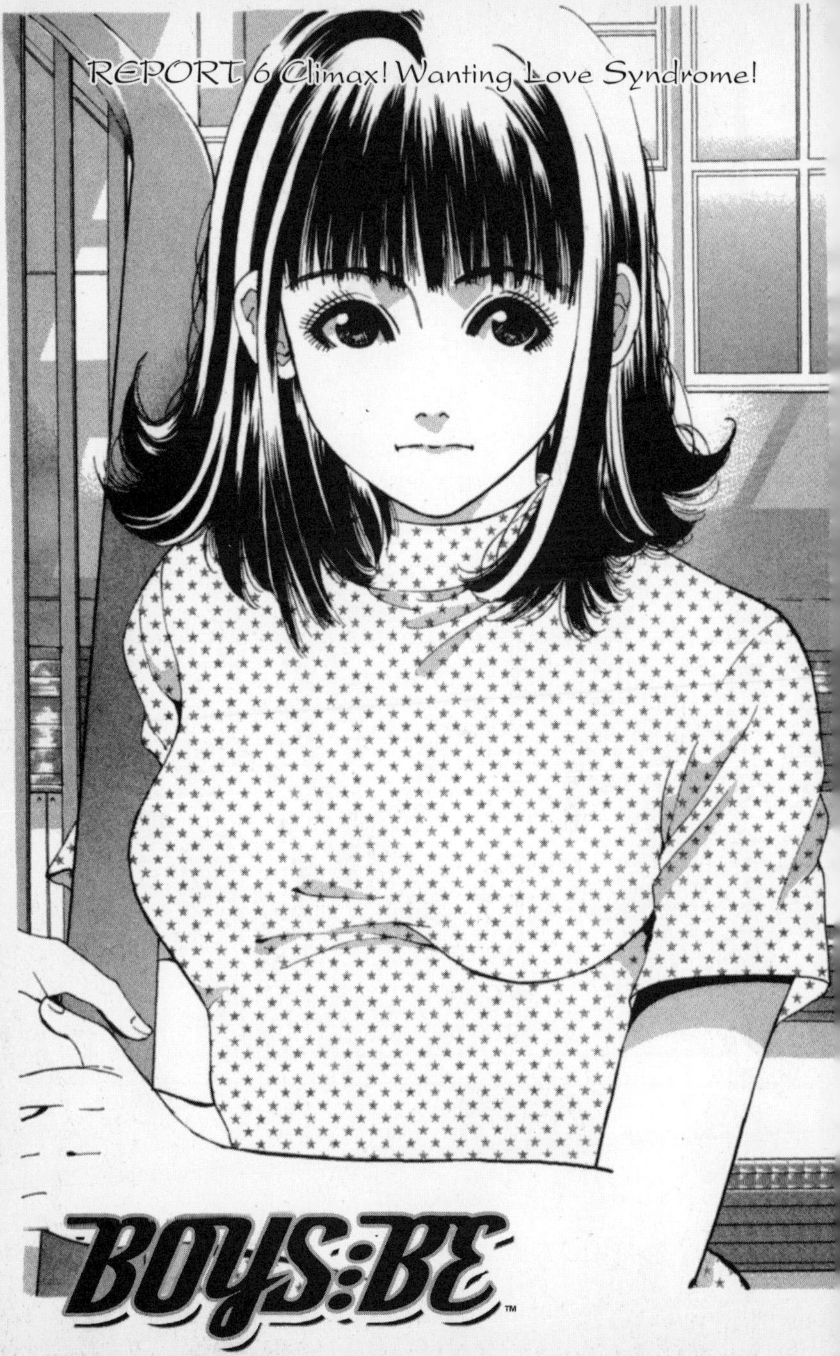
REPORT 6 Climax! Wanting Love Syndrome!
BOYS BE™

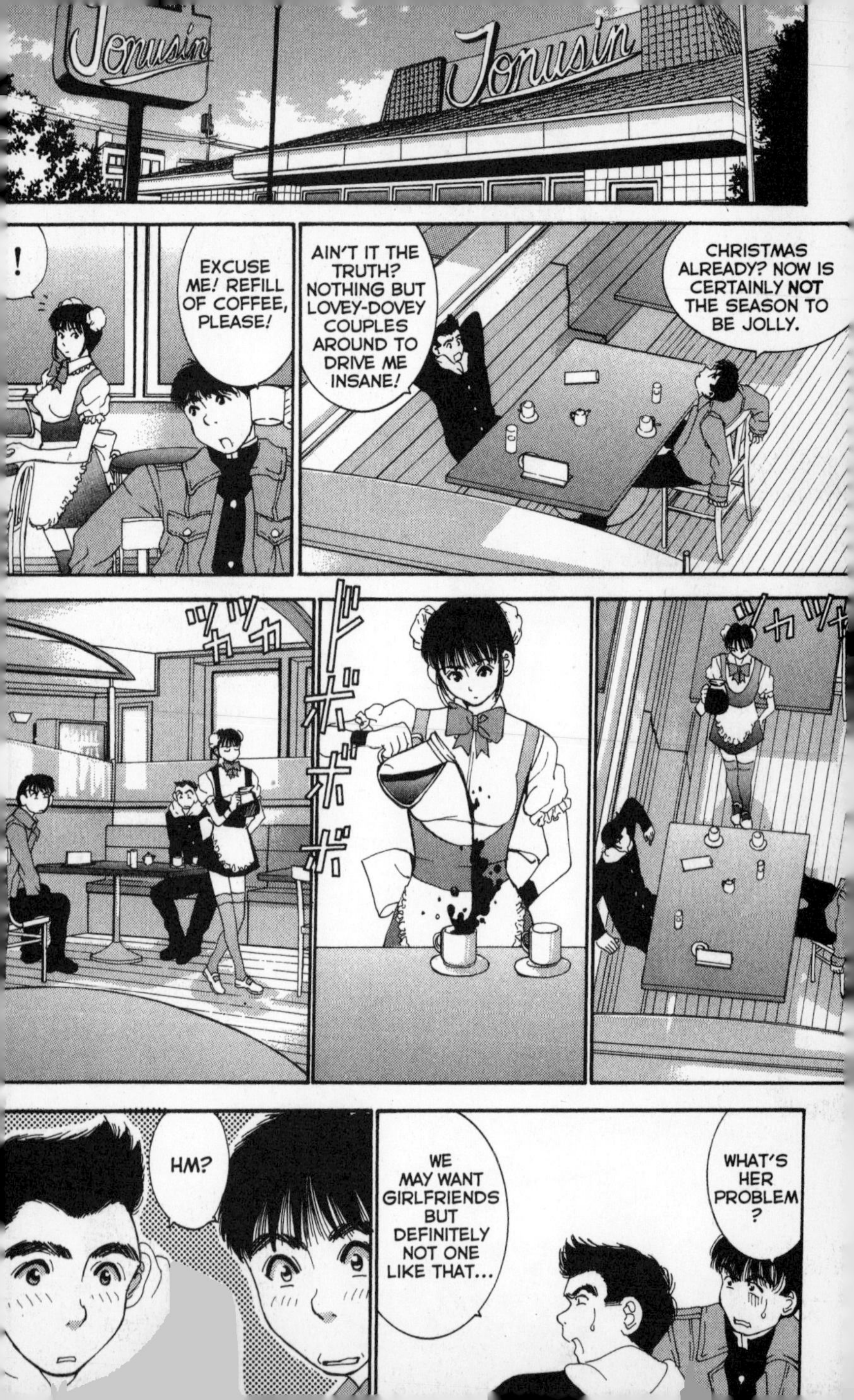
Jonusin
Jonusin
CHRISTMAS ALREADY? NOW IS CERTAINLY **NOT** THE SEASON TO BE JOLLY.
AIN'T IT THE TRUTH? NOTHING BUT LOVEY-DOVEY COUPLES AROUND TO DRIVE ME INSANE!
EXCUSE ME! REFILL OF COFFEE, PLEASE!
!
WHAT'S HER PROBLEM ?
WE MAY WANT GIRLFRIENDS BUT DEFINITELY NOT ONE LIKE THAT...
HM?

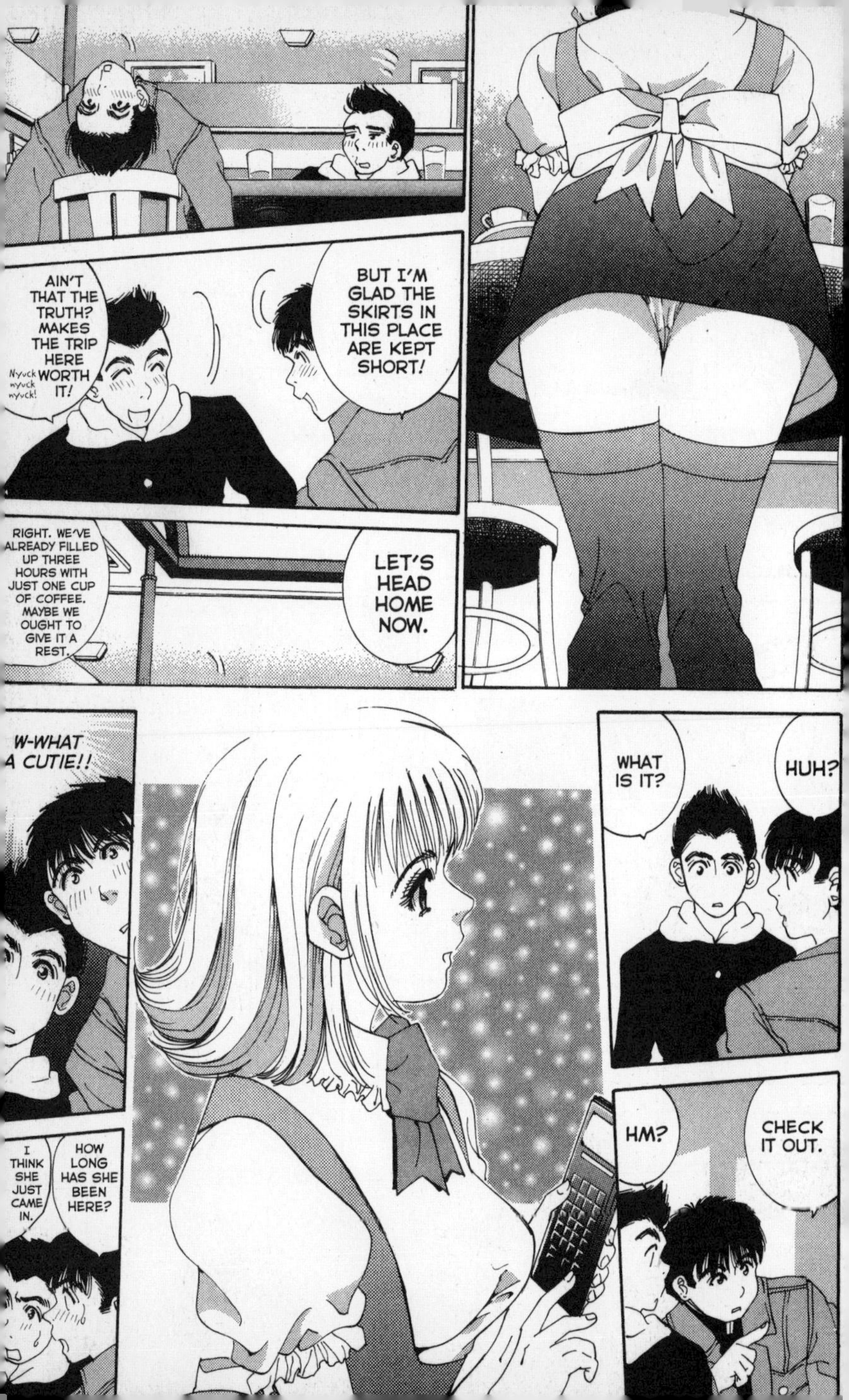
BUT I'M GLAD THE SKIRTS IN THIS PLACE ARE KEPT SHORT!
AIN'T THAT THE TRUTH? MAKES THE TRIP HERE WORTH IT!
Nyuck nyuck nyuck!
LET'S HEAD HOME NOW.
RIGHT. WE'VE ALREADY FILLED UP THREE HOURS WITH JUST ONE CUP OF COFFEE. MAYBE WE OUGHT TO GIVE IT A REST.
HUH?
WHAT IS IT?
CHECK IT OUT.
HM?
W-WHAT A CUTIE!!
HOW LONG HAS SHE BEEN HERE?
I THINK SHE JUST CAME IN.

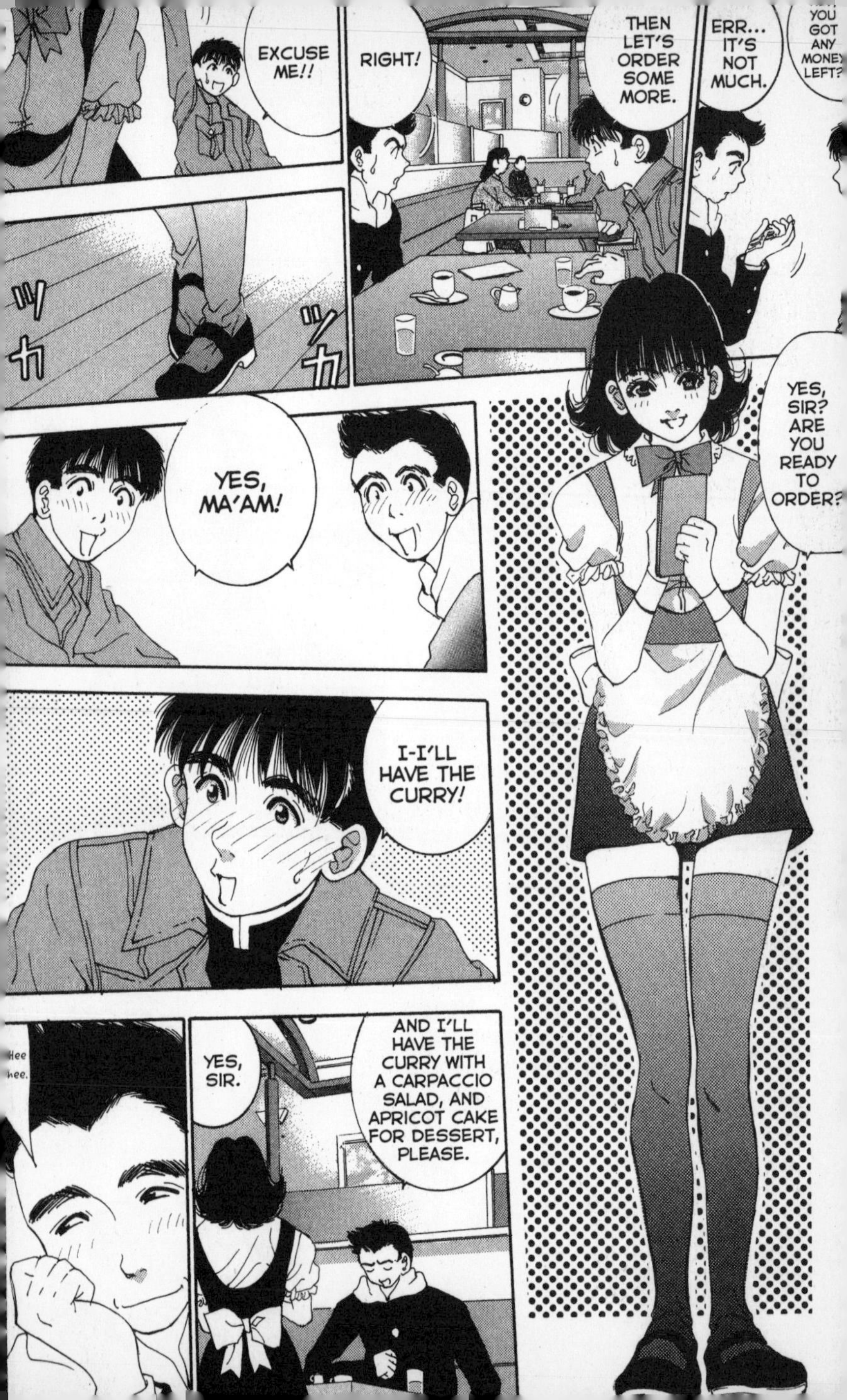

YOU GOT ANY MONEY LEFT?
ERR... IT'S NOT MUCH.
THEN LET'S ORDER SOME MORE.
RIGHT!
EXCUSE ME!!
ツカ
ツカ
YES, SIR? ARE YOU READY TO ORDER?
YES, MA'AM!
I-I'LL HAVE THE CURRY!
AND I'LL HAVE THE CURRY WITH A CARPACCIO SALAD, AND APRICOT CAKE FOR DESSERT, PLEASE.
YES, SIR.
Hee hee.

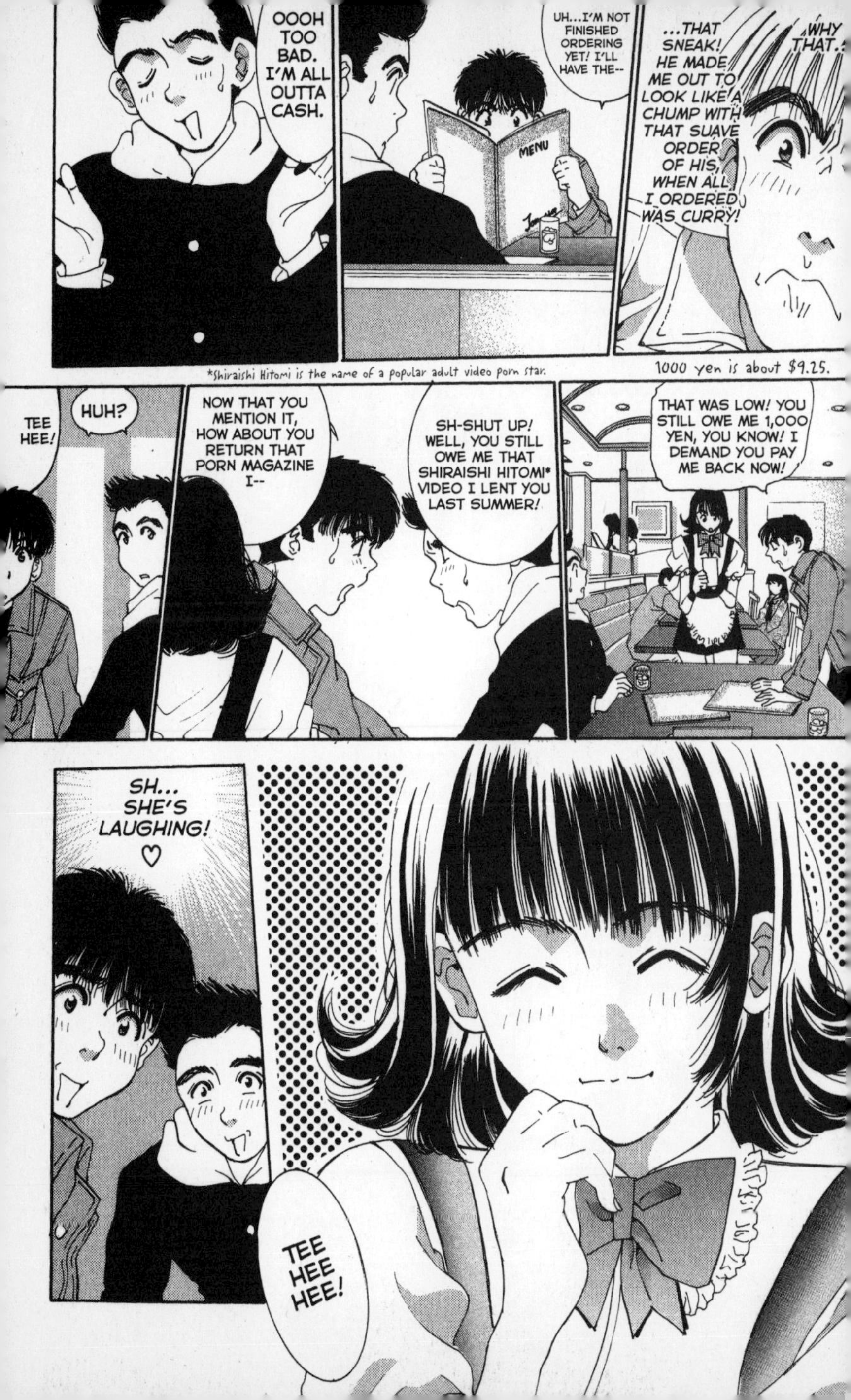
WHY THAT...
...THAT SNEAK! HE MADE ME OUT TO LOOK LIKE A CHUMP WITH THAT SUAVE ORDER OF HIS, WHEN ALL I ORDERED WAS CURRY!
UH...I'M NOT FINISHED ORDERING YET! I'LL HAVE THE--
MENU
OOOH TOO BAD. I'M ALL OUTTA CASH.
1000 yen is about $9.25.
*Shiraishi Hitomi is the name of a popular adult video porn star.
THAT WAS LOW! YOU STILL OWE ME 1,000 YEN, YOU KNOW! I DEMAND YOU PAY ME BACK NOW!
SH-SHUT UP! WELL, YOU STILL OWE ME THAT SHIRAISHI HITOMI* VIDEO I LENT YOU LAST SUMMER!
NOW THAT YOU MENTION IT, HOW ABOUT YOU RETURN THAT PORN MAGAZINE I--
HUH?
TEE HEE!
TEE HEE HEE!
SH... SHE'S LAUGHING! ♡

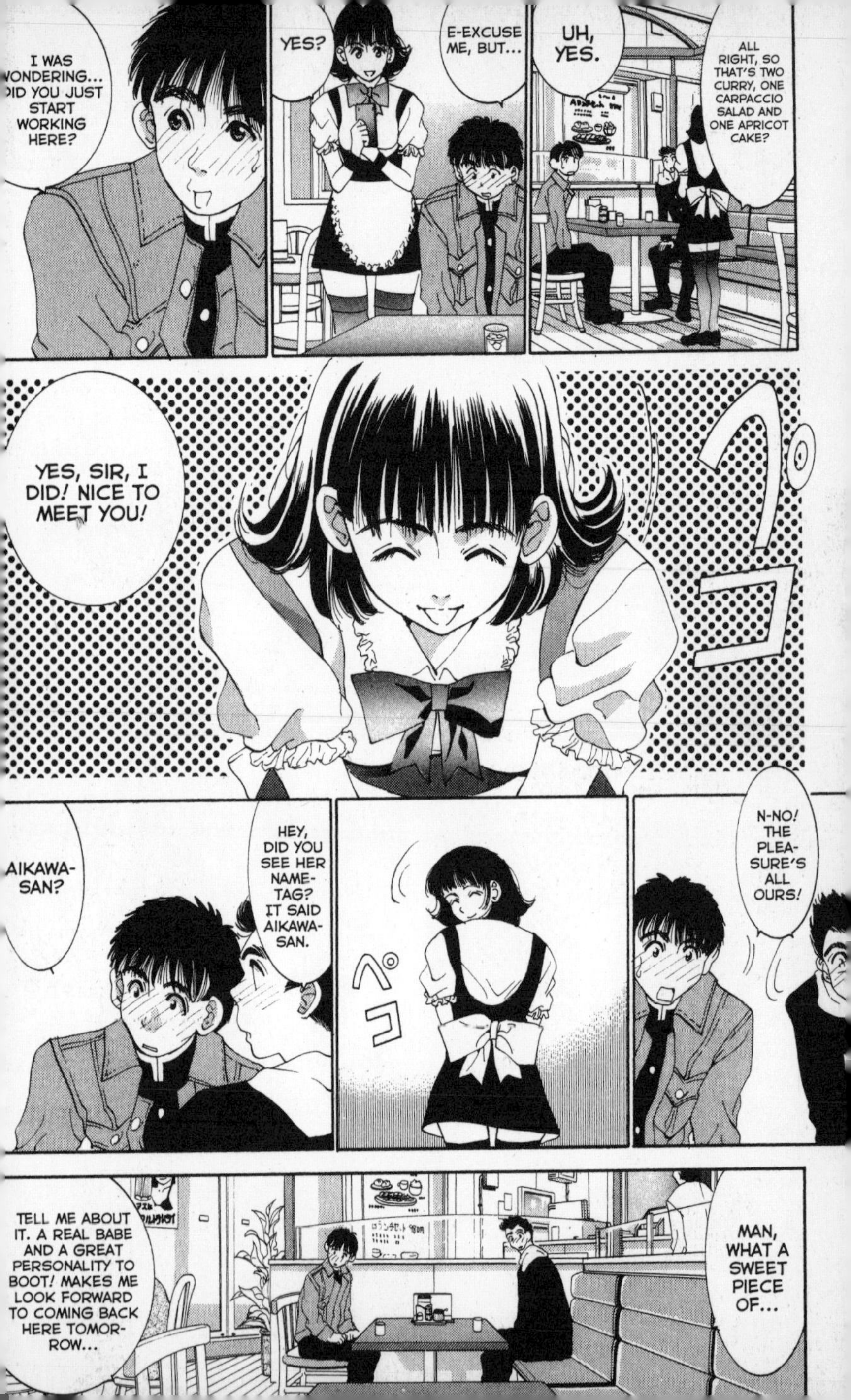
ALL RIGHT, SO THAT'S TWO CURRY, ONE CARPACCIO SALAD AND ONE APRICOT CAKE?
UH, YES.
E-EXCUSE ME, BUT...
YES?
I WAS WONDERING... DID YOU JUST START WORKING HERE?
YES, SIR, I DID! NICE TO MEET YOU!
ペコ
N-NO! THE PLEASURE'S ALL OURS!
ペコ
HEY, DID YOU SEE HER NAME-TAG? IT SAID AIKAWA-SAN.
AIKAWA-SAN?
MAN, WHAT A SWEET PIECE OF...
TELL ME ABOUT IT. A REAL BABE AND A GREAT PERSONALITY TO BOOT! MAKES ME LOOK FORWARD TO COMING BACK HERE TOMORROW...

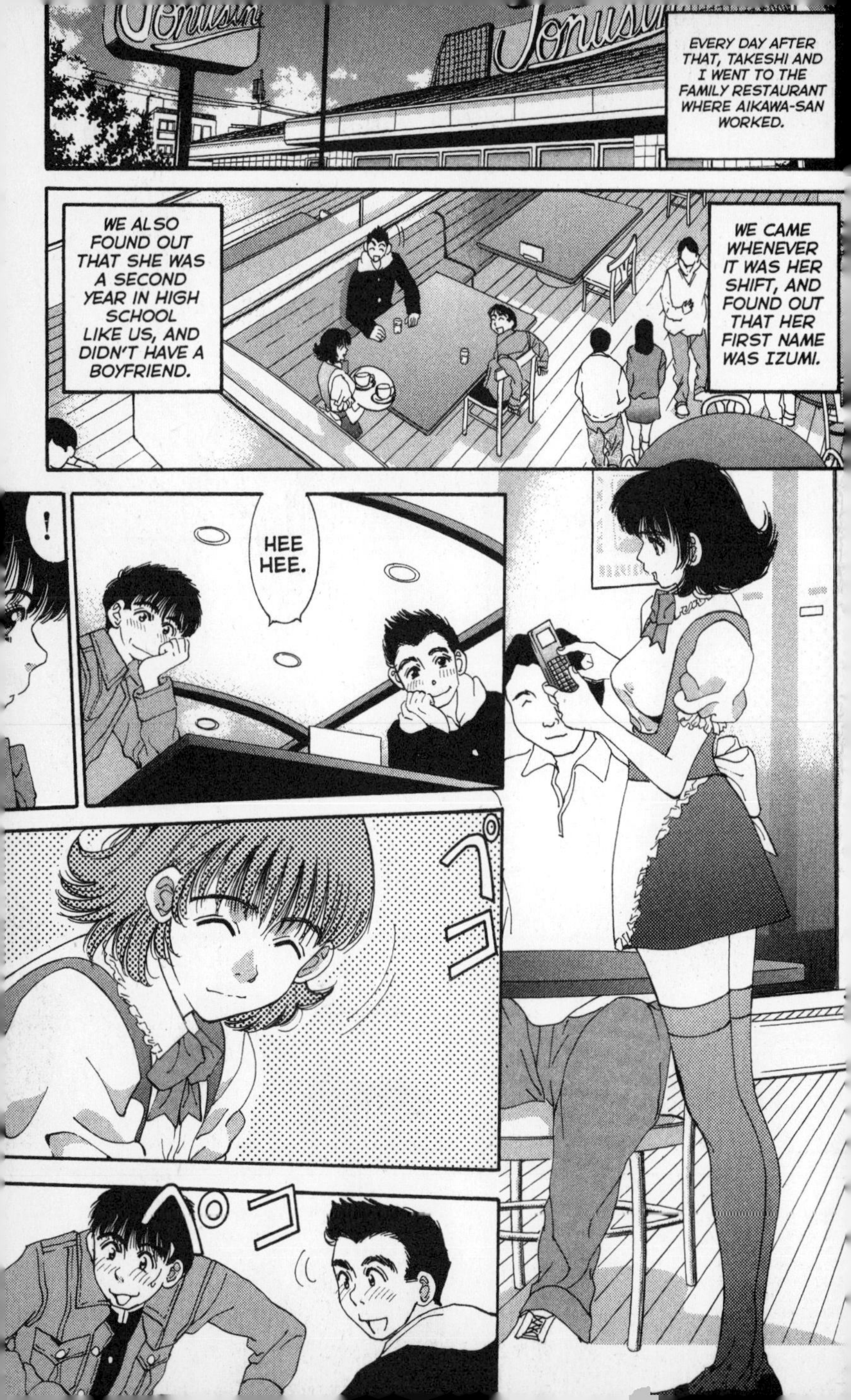
EVERY DAY AFTER THAT, TAKESHI AND I WENT TO THE FAMILY RESTAURANT WHERE AIKAWA-SAN WORKED.
WE CAME WHENEVER IT WAS HER SHIFT, AND FOUND OUT THAT HER FIRST NAME WAS IZUMI.
WE ALSO FOUND OUT THAT SHE WAS A SECOND YEAR IN HIGH SCHOOL LIKE US, AND DIDN'T HAVE A BOYFRIEND.
HEE HEE.
!
ペコ
ペコ

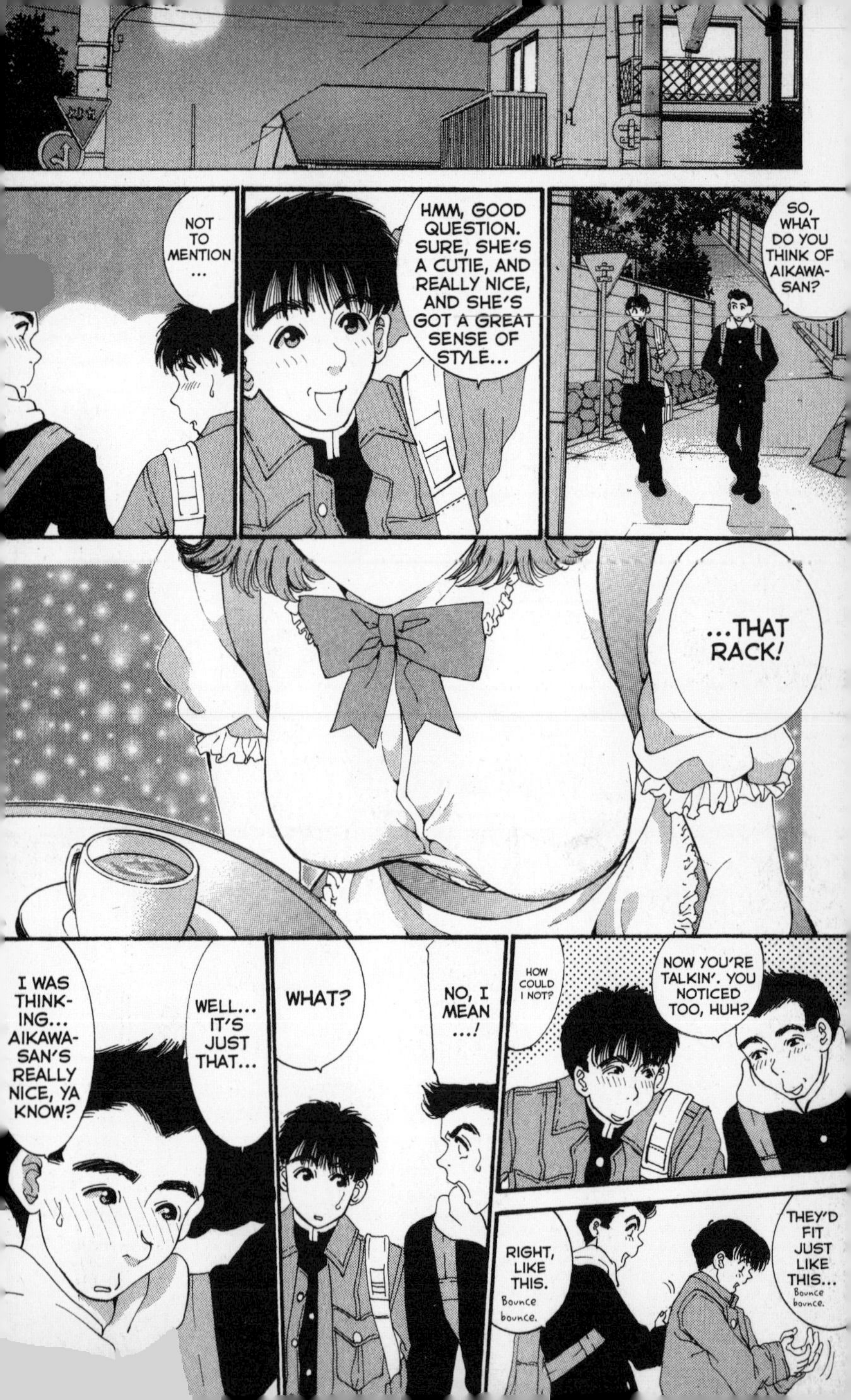
SO, WHAT DO YOU THINK OF AIKAWA-SAN?
HMM, GOOD QUESTION. SURE, SHE'S A CUTIE, AND REALLY NICE, AND SHE'S GOT A GREAT SENSE OF STYLE...
NOT TO MENTION ...
...THAT RACK!
NOW YOU'RE TALKIN'. YOU NOTICED TOO, HUH?
HOW COULD I NOT?
THEY'D FIT JUST LIKE THIS...
Bounce bounce.
RIGHT, LIKE THIS.
Bounce bounce.
NO, I MEAN ...!
WHAT?
WELL... IT'S JUST THAT...
I WAS THINKING... AIKAWA-SAN'S REALLY NICE, YA KNOW?

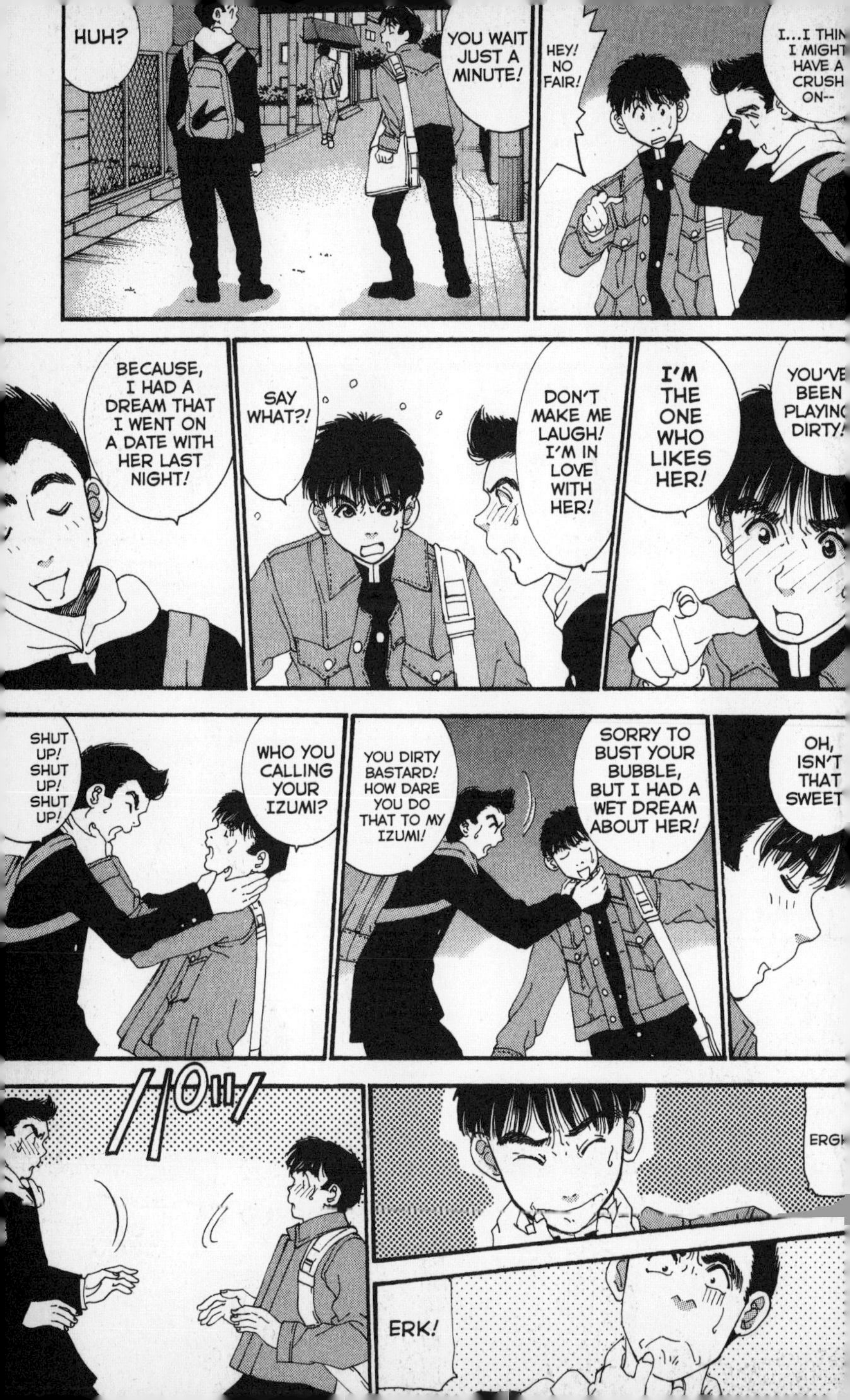

I...I THIN I MIGHT HAVE A CRUSH ON--
HEY! NO FAIR!
YOU WAIT JUST A MINUTE!
HUH?
YOU'VE BEEN PLAYIN DIRTY!
I'M THE ONE WHO LIKES HER!
DON'T MAKE ME LAUGH! I'M IN LOVE WITH HER!
SAY WHAT?!
BECAUSE, I HAD A DREAM THAT I WENT ON A DATE WITH HER LAST NIGHT!
OH, ISN'T THAT SWEET
SORRY TO BUST YOUR BUBBLE, BUT I HAD A WET DREAM ABOUT HER!
YOU DIRTY BASTARD! HOW DARE YOU DO THAT TO MY IZUMI!
WHO YOU CALLING YOUR IZUMI?
SHUT UP! SHUT UP! SHUT UP!
ERG
ERK!

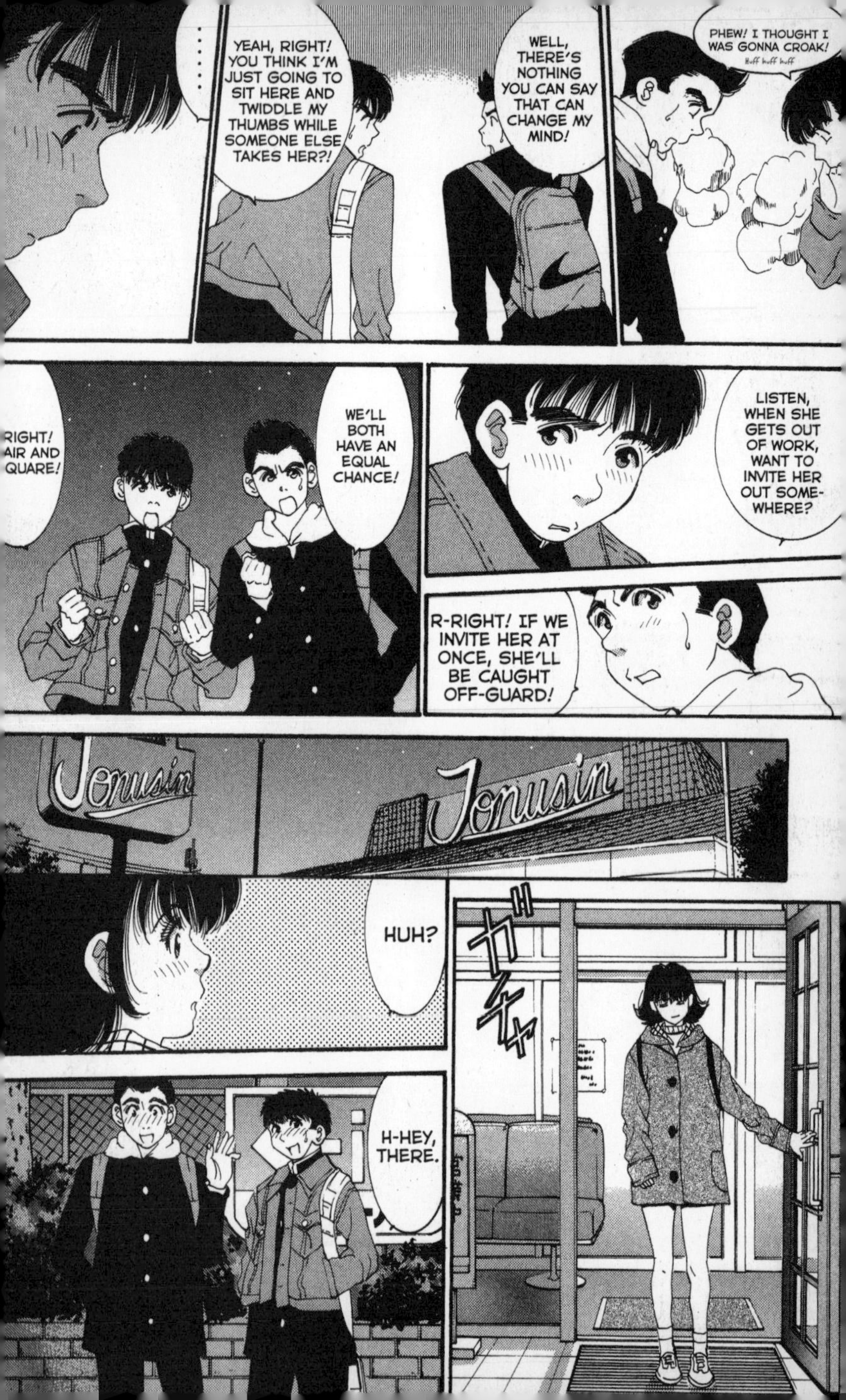
PHEW! I THOUGHT I WAS GONNA CROAK!
huff huff huff
WELL, THERE'S NOTHING YOU CAN SAY THAT CAN CHANGE MY MIND!
YEAH, RIGHT! YOU THINK I'M JUST GOING TO SIT HERE AND TWIDDLE MY THUMBS WHILE SOMEONE ELSE TAKES HER?!
.....
LISTEN, WHEN SHE GETS OUT OF WORK, WANT TO INVITE HER OUT SOME-WHERE?
R-RIGHT! IF WE INVITE HER AT ONCE, SHE'LL BE CAUGHT OFF-GUARD!
WE'LL BOTH HAVE AN EQUAL CHANCE!
RIGHT! AIR AND QUARE!
Jonusin
Jonusin
ガチャ
HUH?
H-HEY, THERE.

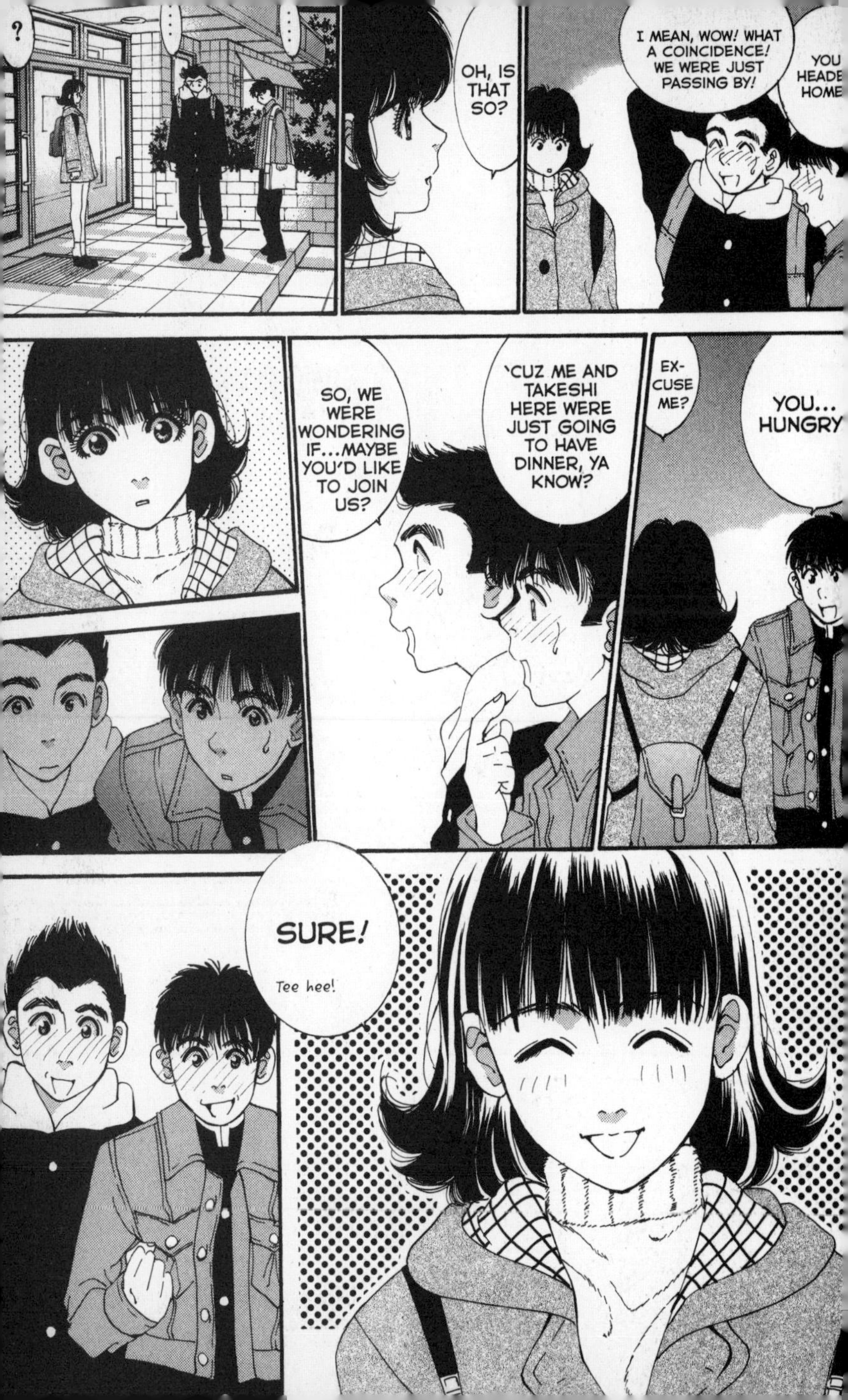
I MEAN, WOW! WHAT A COINCIDENCE! WE WERE JUST PASSING BY!
YOU HEADE HOME
OH, IS THAT SO?
?
...
...
YOU... HUNGRY
EX-CUSE ME?
'CUZ ME AND TAKESHI HERE WERE JUST GOING TO HAVE DINNER, YA KNOW?
SO, WE WERE WONDERING IF...MAYBE YOU'D LIKE TO JOIN US?
SURE!
Tee hee!

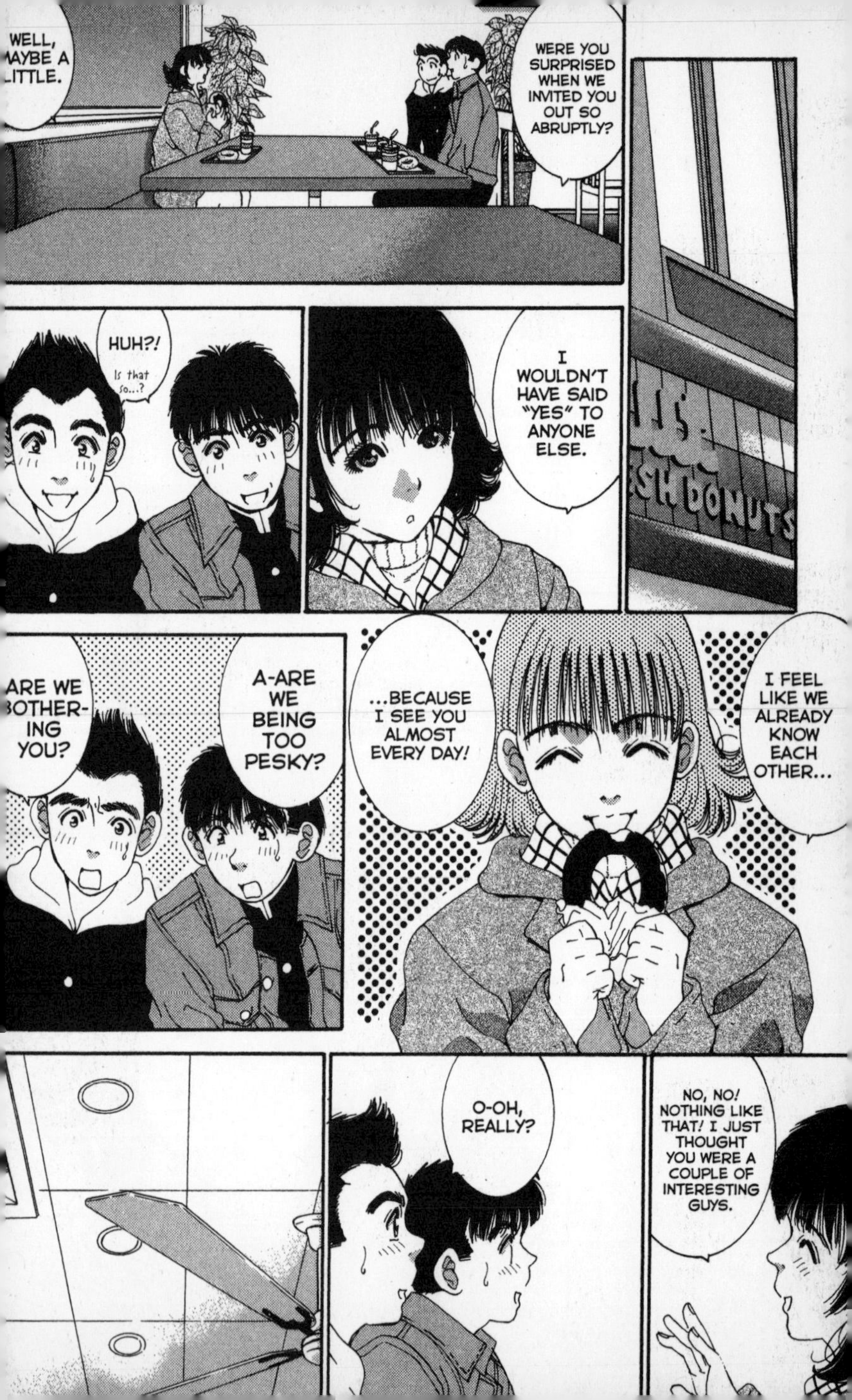
SH DONUTS
WERE YOU SURPRISED WHEN WE INVITED YOU OUT SO ABRUPTLY?
WELL, MAYBE A LITTLE.
I WOULDN'T HAVE SAID "YES" TO ANYONE ELSE.
HUH?!
Is that so...?
I FEEL LIKE WE ALREADY KNOW EACH OTHER...
...BECAUSE I SEE YOU ALMOST EVERY DAY!
A-ARE WE BEING TOO PESKY?
ARE WE BOTHERING YOU?
NO, NO! NOTHING LIKE THAT! I JUST THOUGHT YOU WERE A COUPLE OF INTERESTING GUYS.
O-OH, REALLY?

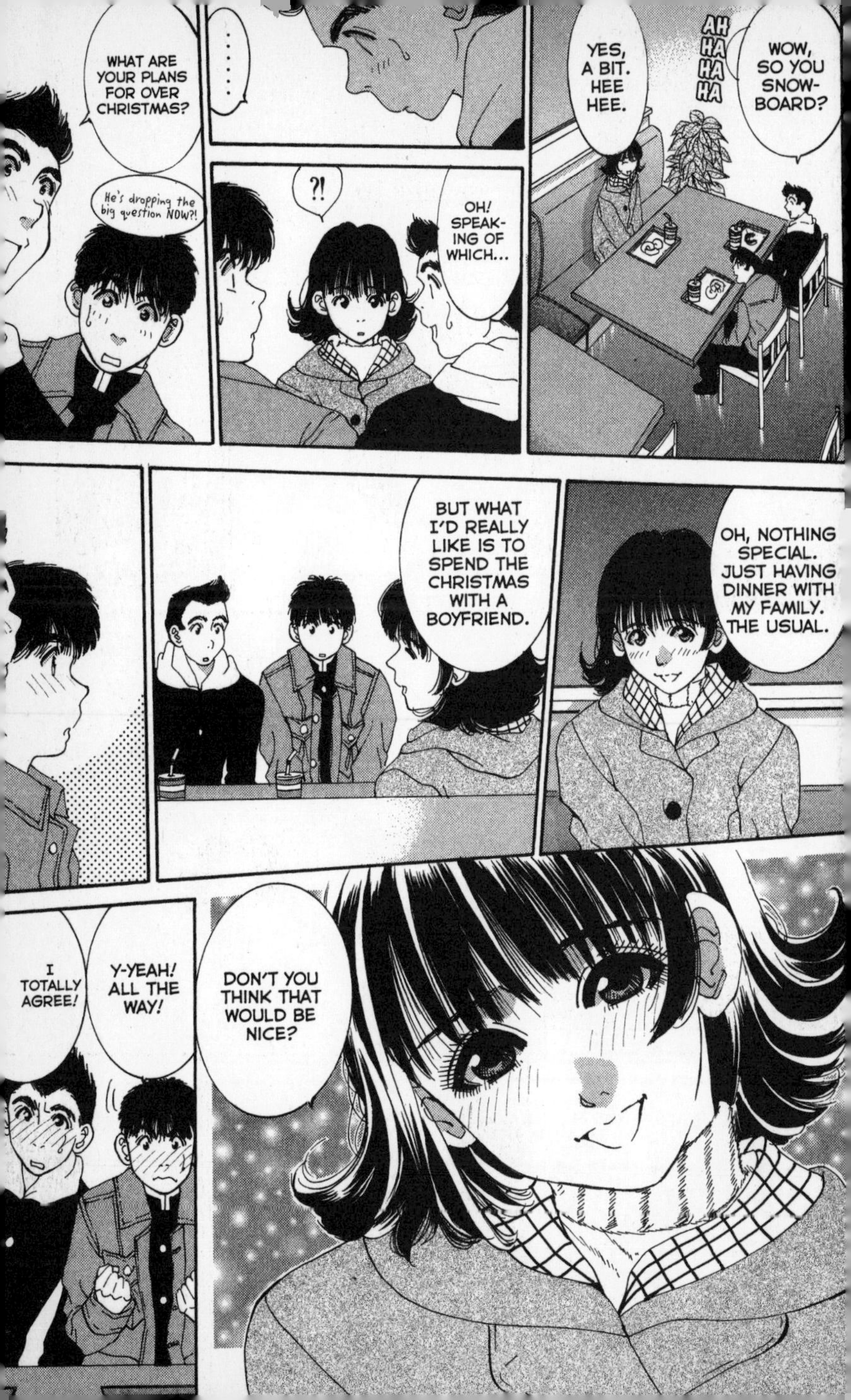
WOW, SO YOU SNOW-BOARD?
AH HA HA HA
YES, A BIT. HEE HEE.
......
OH! SPEAKING OF WHICH...
?!
WHAT ARE YOUR PLANS FOR OVER CHRISTMAS?
He's dropping the big question NOW?!
OH, NOTHING SPECIAL. JUST HAVING DINNER WITH MY FAMILY. THE USUAL.
BUT WHAT I'D REALLY LIKE IS TO SPEND THE CHRISTMAS WITH A BOYFRIEND.
DON'T YOU THINK THAT WOULD BE NICE?
Y-YEAH! ALL THE WAY!
I TOTALLY AGREE!

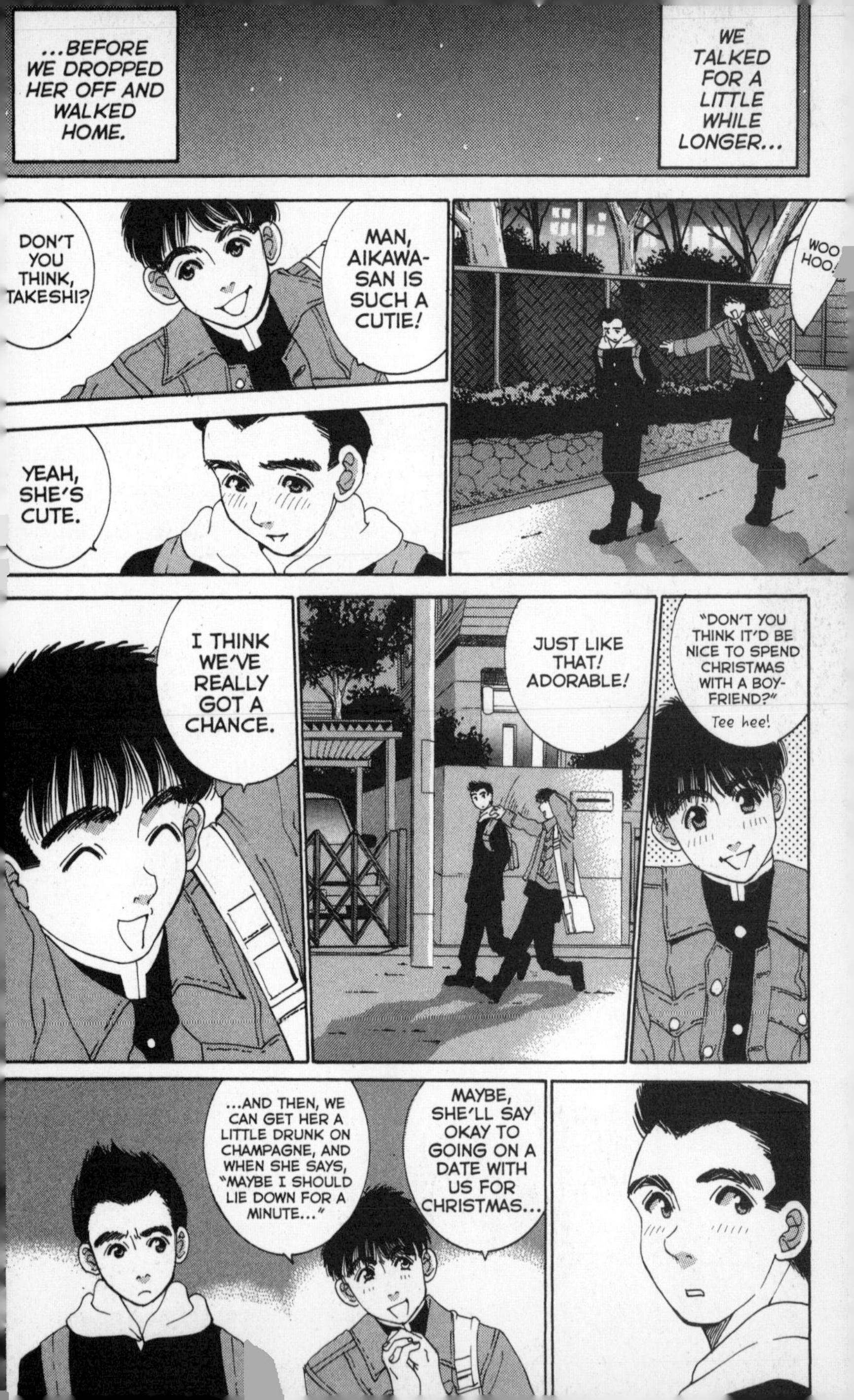
WE TALKED FOR A LITTLE WHILE LONGER...
...BEFORE WE DROPPED HER OFF AND WALKED HOME.
WOO HOO!
MAN, AIKAWA-SAN IS SUCH A CUTIE!
DON'T YOU THINK, TAKESHI?
YEAH, SHE'S CUTE.
"DON'T YOU THINK IT'D BE NICE TO SPEND CHRISTMAS WITH A BOY-FRIEND?" Tee hee!
JUST LIKE THAT! ADORABLE!
I THINK WE'VE REALLY GOT A CHANCE.
MAYBE, SHE'LL SAY OKAY TO GOING ON A DATE WITH US FOR CHRISTMAS...
...AND THEN, WE CAN GET HER A LITTLE DRUNK ON CHAMPAGNE, AND WHEN SHE SAYS, "MAYBE I SHOULD LIE DOWN FOR A MINUTE..."

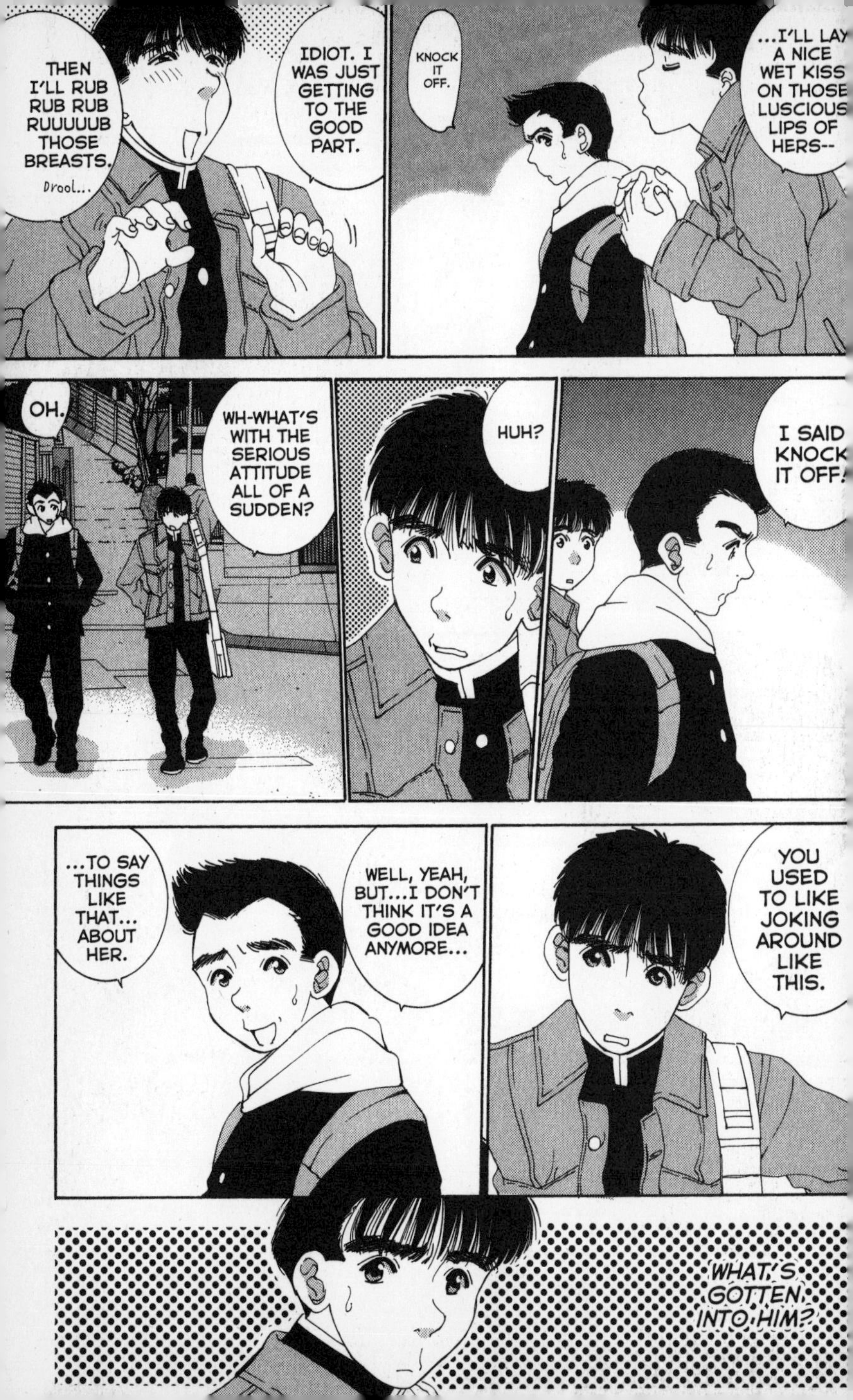
...I'LL LAY A NICE WET KISS ON THOSE LUSCIOUS LIPS OF HERS--
KNOCK IT OFF.
IDIOT. I WAS JUST GETTING TO THE GOOD PART.
THEN I'LL RUB RUB RUB RUUUUUB THOSE BREASTS.
Drool...
I SAID KNOCK IT OFF!
HUH?
WH-WHAT'S WITH THE SERIOUS ATTITUDE ALL OF A SUDDEN?
OH.
YOU USED TO LIKE JOKING AROUND LIKE THIS.
WELL, YEAH, BUT...I DON'T THINK IT'S A GOOD IDEA ANYMORE...
...TO SAY THINGS LIKE THAT... ABOUT HER.
WHAT'S GOTTEN INTO HIM?

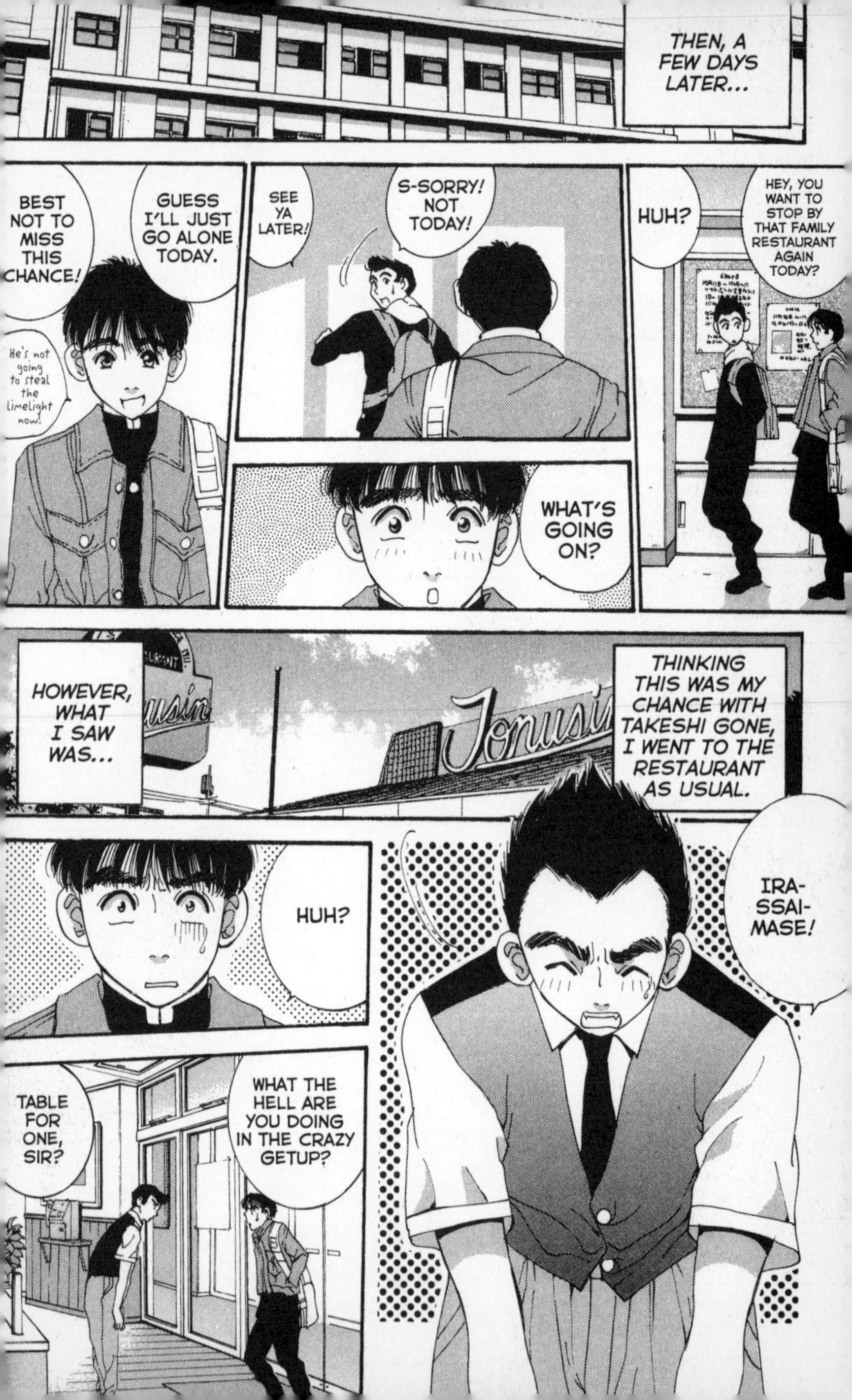
THEN, A FEW DAYS LATER...
HEY, YOU WANT TO STOP BY THAT FAMILY RESTAURANT AGAIN TODAY?
HUH?
S-SORRY! NOT TODAY!
SEE YA LATER!
WHAT'S GOING ON?
GUESS I'LL JUST GO ALONE TODAY.
BEST NOT TO MISS THIS CHANCE!
He's not going to steal the limelight now!
THINKING THIS WAS MY CHANCE WITH TAKESHI GONE, I WENT TO THE RESTAURANT AS USUAL.
HOWEVER, WHAT I SAW WAS...
IRA-SSAI-MASE!
HUH?
WHAT THE HELL ARE YOU DOING IN THE CRAZY GETUP?
TABLE FOR ONE, SIR?

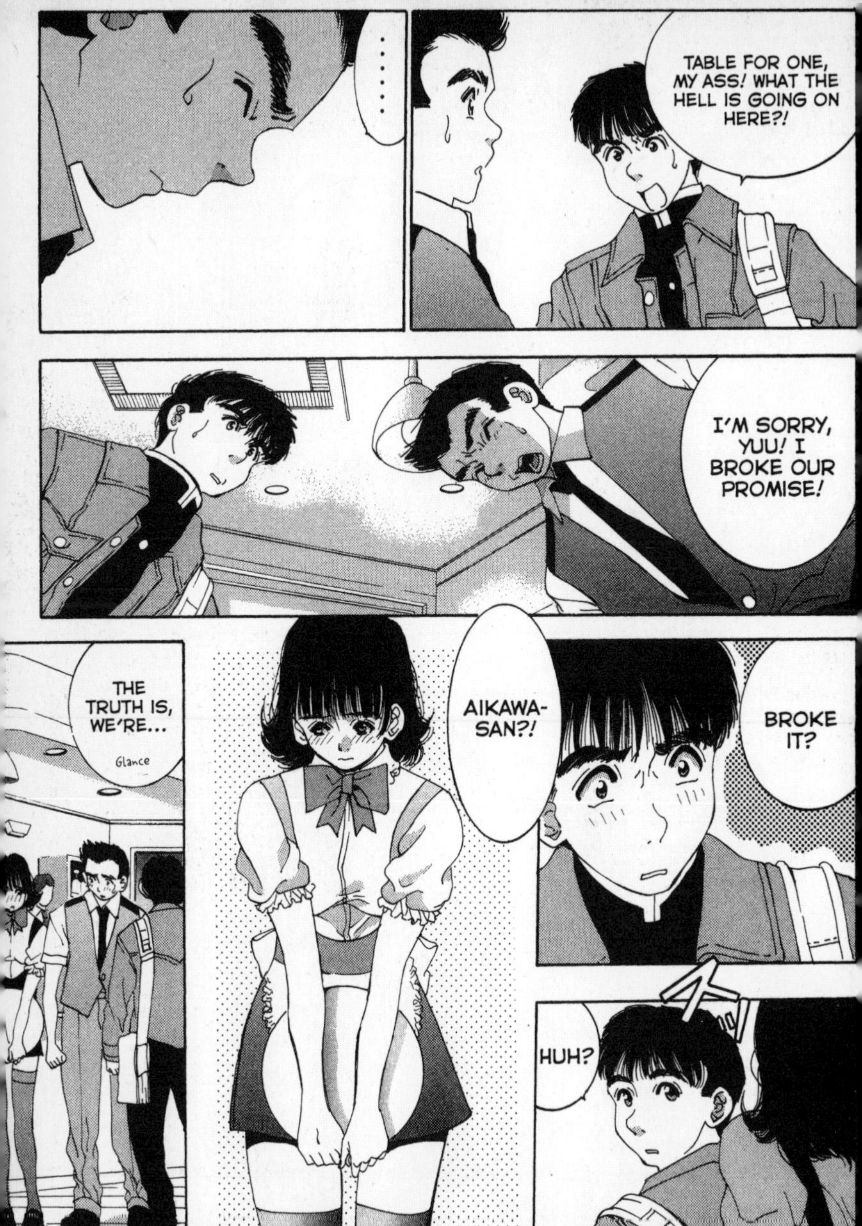
TABLE FOR ONE, MY ASS! WHAT THE HELL IS GOING ON HERE?!
......
I'M SORRY, YUU! I BROKE OUR PROMISE!
BROKE IT?
HUH?
AIKAWA-SAN?!
THE TRUTH IS, WE'RE...
Glance

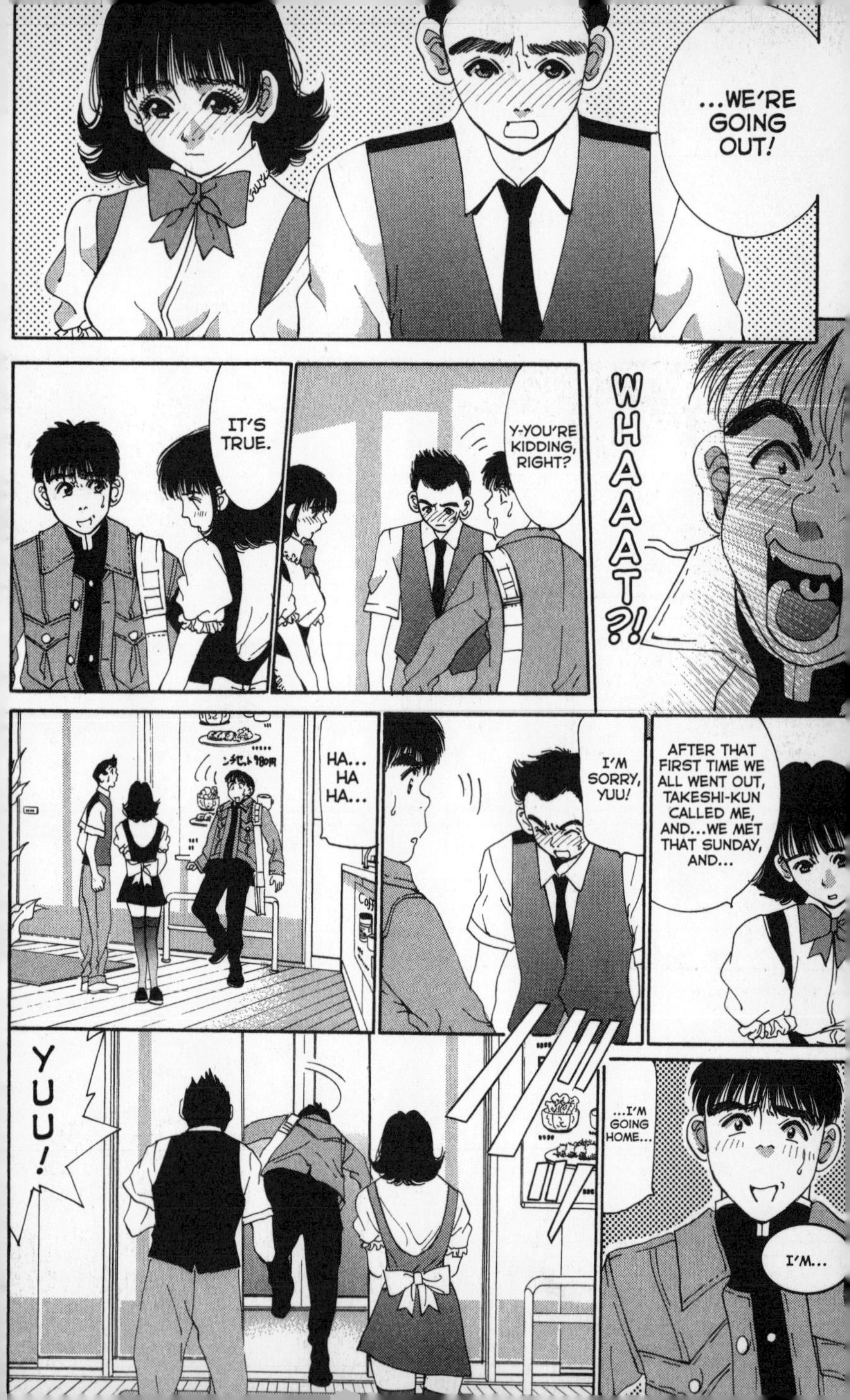

...WE'RE GOING OUT!
WHAAAAT?!
Y-YOU'RE KIDDING, RIGHT?
IT'S TRUE.
AFTER THAT FIRST TIME WE ALL WENT OUT, TAKESHI-KUN CALLED ME, AND...WE MET THAT SUNDAY, AND...
I'M SORRY, YUU!
HA... HA HA...
...I'M GOING HOME...
I'M...
YUU!

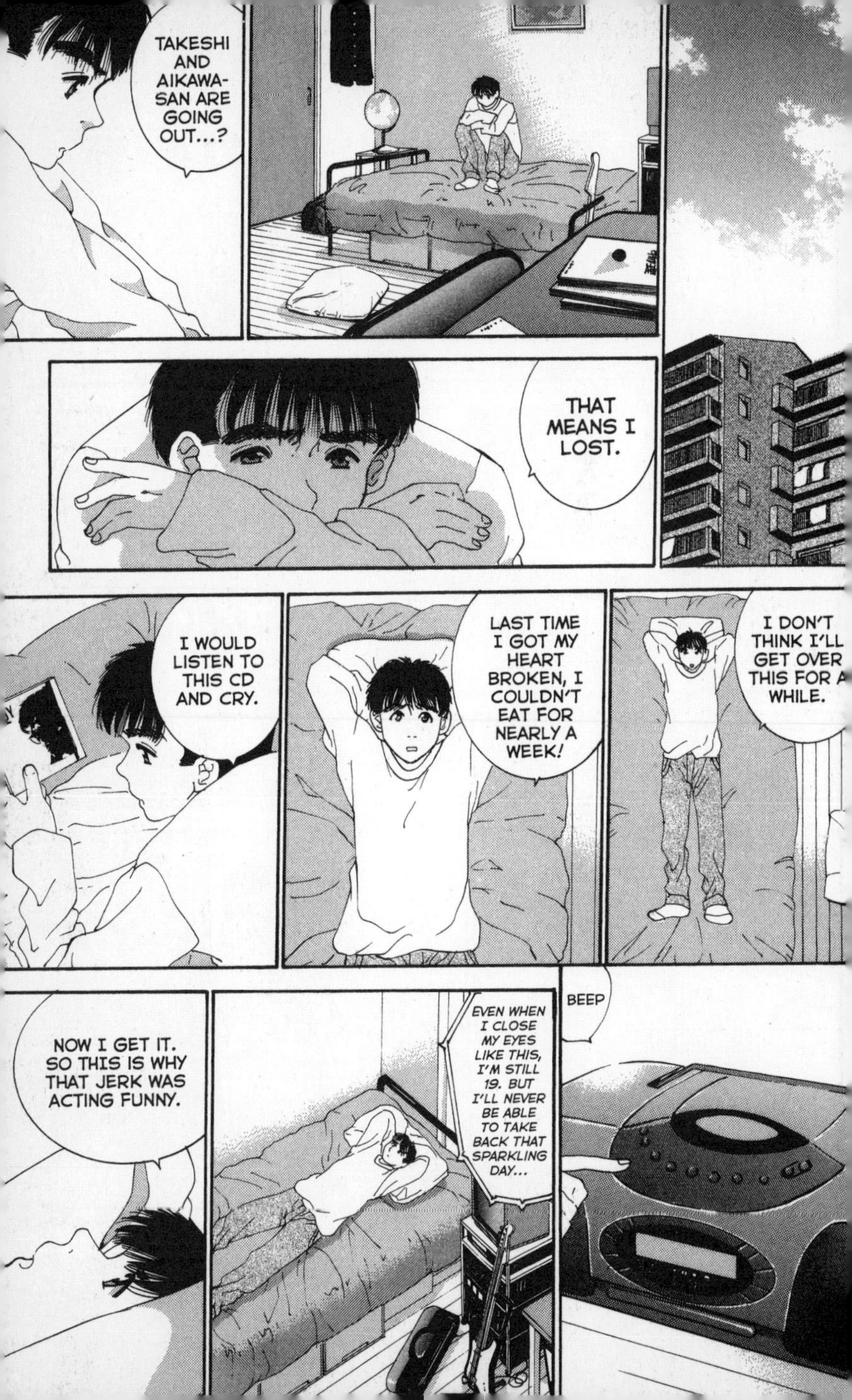
TAKESHI AND AIKAWA-SAN ARE GOING OUT...?
THAT MEANS I LOST.
I DON'T THINK I'LL GET OVER THIS FOR A WHILE.
LAST TIME I GOT MY HEART BROKEN, I COULDN'T EAT FOR NEARLY A WEEK!
I WOULD LISTEN TO THIS CD AND CRY.
BEEP
EVEN WHEN I CLOSE MY EYES LIKE THIS, I'M STILL 19. BUT I'LL NEVER BE ABLE TO TAKE BACK THAT SPARKLING DAY...
NOW I GET IT. SO THIS IS WHY THAT JERK WAS ACTING FUNNY.

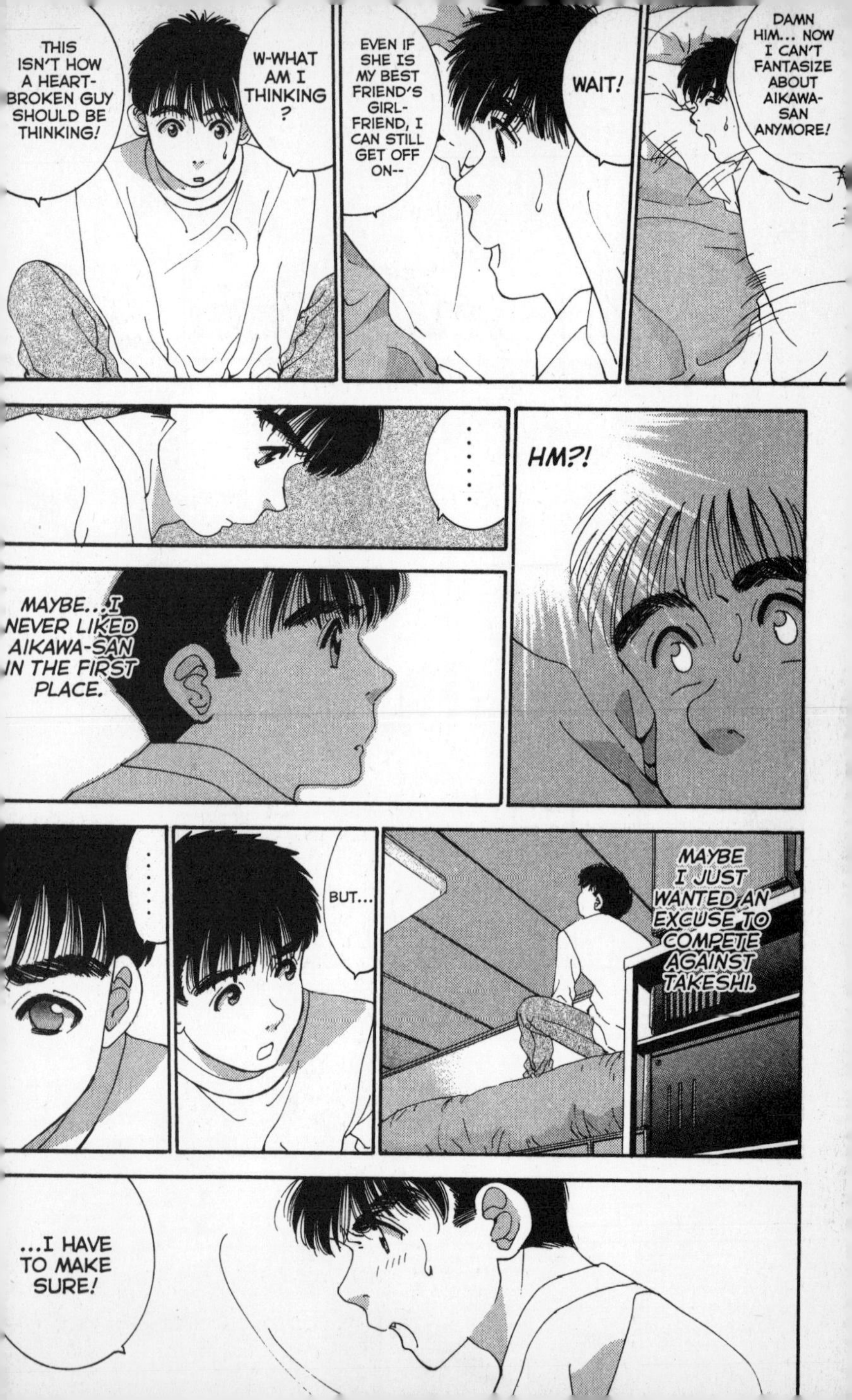
DAMN HIM... NOW I CAN'T FANTASIZE ABOUT AIKAWA-SAN ANYMORE!
WAIT!
EVEN IF SHE IS MY BEST FRIEND'S GIRL-FRIEND, I CAN STILL GET OFF ON--
W-WHAT AM I THINKING?
THIS ISN'T HOW A HEART-BROKEN GUY SHOULD BE THINKING!
HM?!
......
MAYBE... I NEVER LIKED AIKAWA-SAN IN THE FIRST PLACE.
MAYBE I JUST WANTED AN EXCUSE TO COMPETE AGAINST TAKESHI.
BUT...
......
...I HAVE TO MAKE SURE!

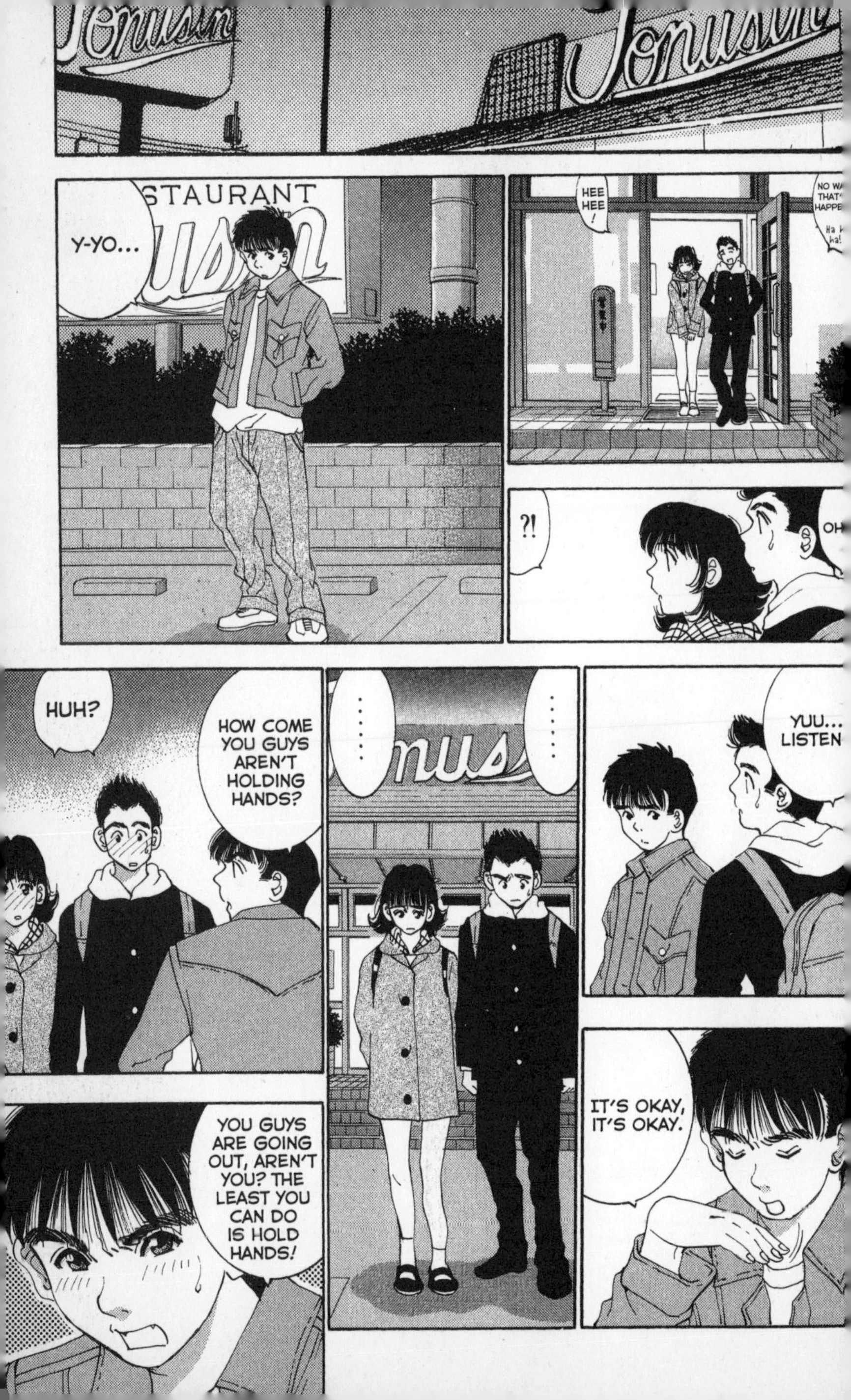
HEE HEE!
?!
STAURANT
Y-YO...
YUU... LISTEN
IT'S OKAY, IT'S OKAY.
......
......
HOW COME YOU GUYS AREN'T HOLDING HANDS?
HUH?
YOU GUYS ARE GOING OUT, AREN'T YOU? THE LEAST YOU CAN DO IS HOLD HANDS!

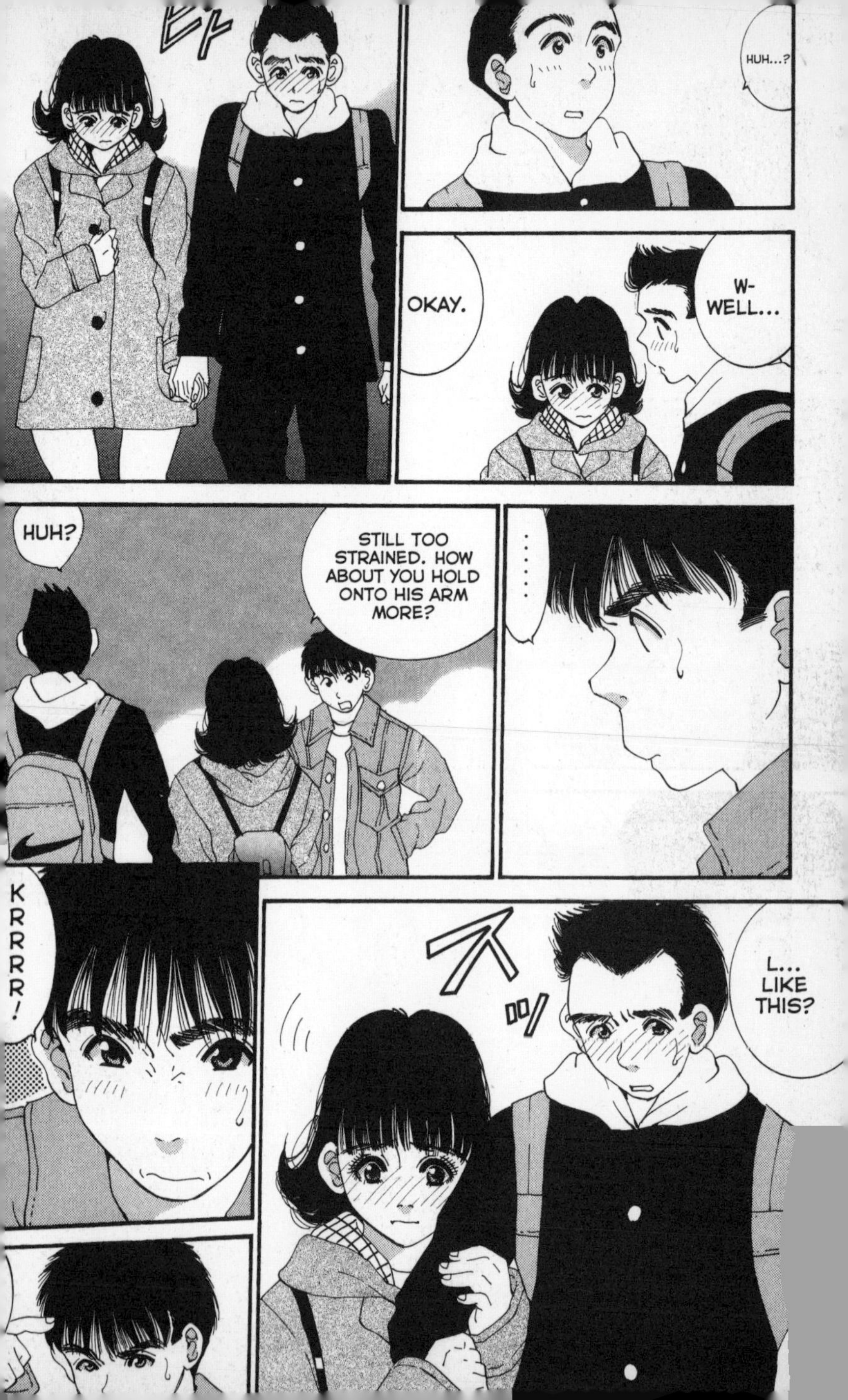
HUH...?
W- WELL...
OKAY.
......
STILL TOO STRAINED. HOW ABOUT YOU HOLD ONTO HIS ARM MORE?
HUH?
L... LIKE THIS?
KRRRRR!

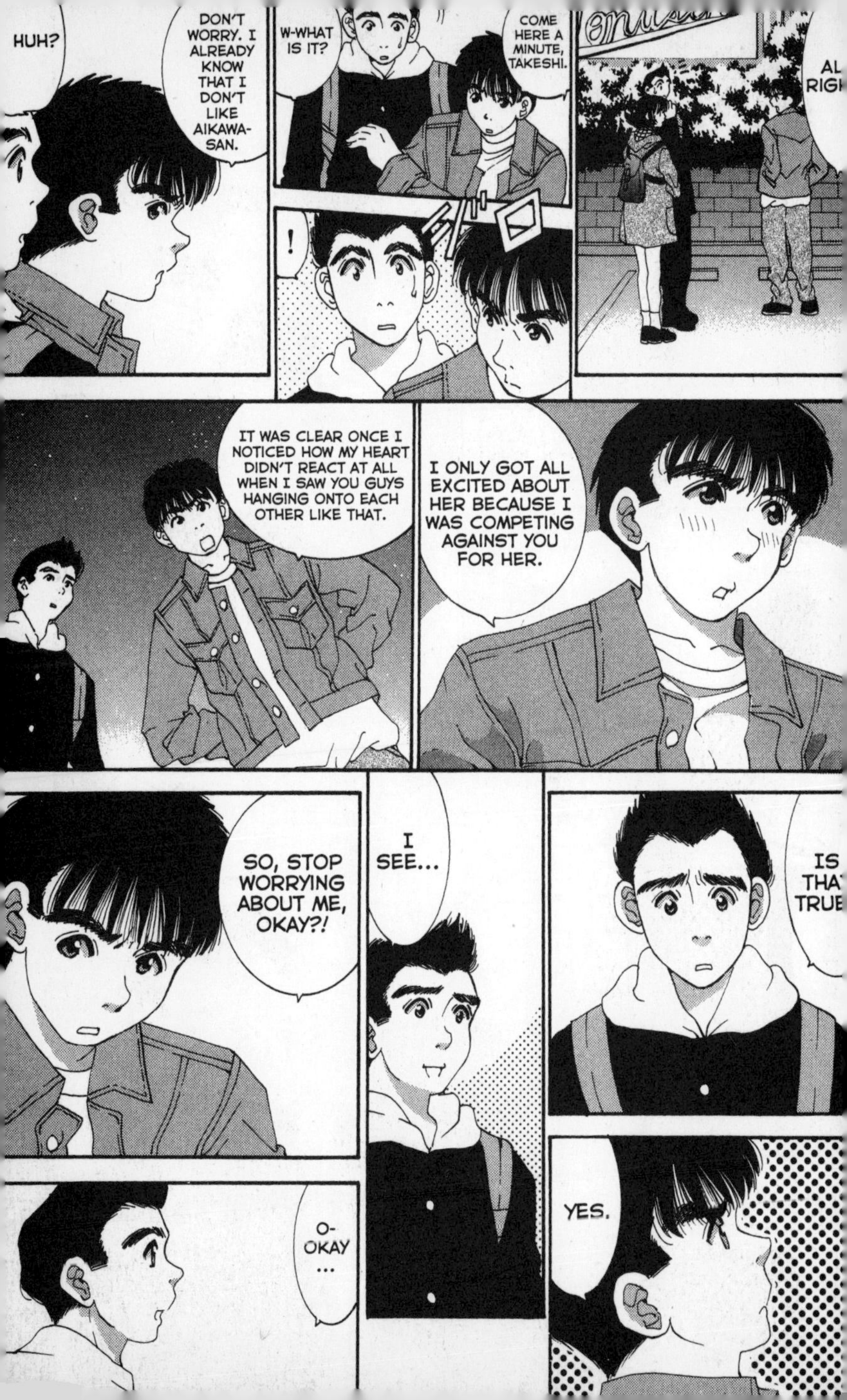
AL RIGH
COME HERE A MINUTE, TAKESHI.
W-WHAT IS IT?
!
DON'T WORRY. I ALREADY KNOW THAT I DON'T LIKE AIKAWA-SAN.
HUH?
I ONLY GOT ALL EXCITED ABOUT HER BECAUSE I WAS COMPETING AGAINST YOU FOR HER.
IT WAS CLEAR ONCE I NOTICED HOW MY HEART DIDN'T REACT AT ALL WHEN I SAW YOU GUYS HANGING ONTO EACH OTHER LIKE THAT.
IS THAT TRUE
YES.
I SEE...
SO, STOP WORRYING ABOUT ME, OKAY?!
O-OKAY ...

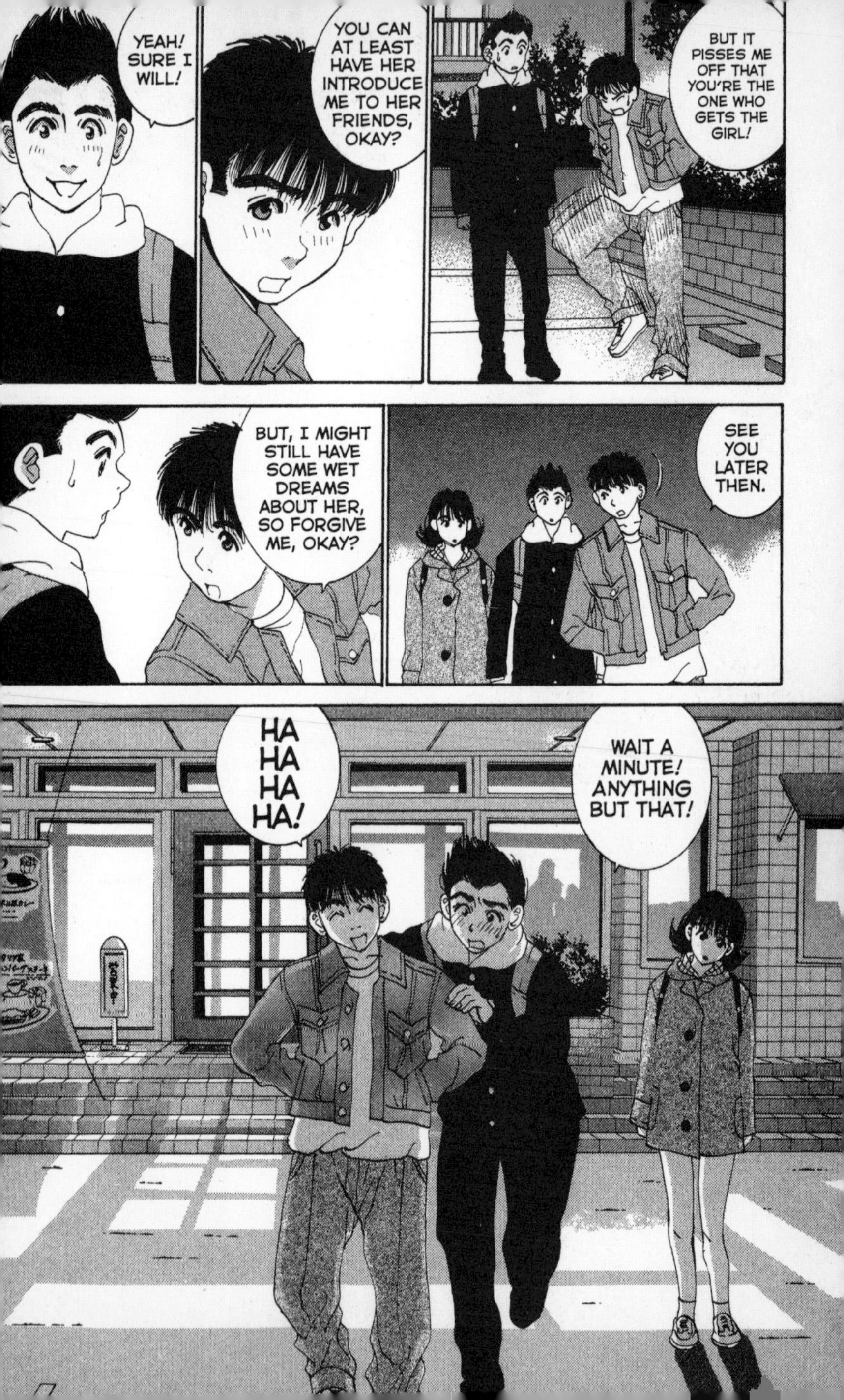
BUT IT PISSES ME OFF THAT YOU'RE THE ONE WHO GETS THE GIRL!
YOU CAN AT LEAST HAVE HER INTRODUCE ME TO HER FRIENDS, OKAY?
YEAH! SURE I WILL!
SEE YOU LATER THEN.
BUT, I MIGHT STILL HAVE SOME WET DREAMS ABOUT HER, SO FORGIVE ME, OKAY?
WAIT A MINUTE! ANYTHING BUT THAT!
HA HA HA HA!

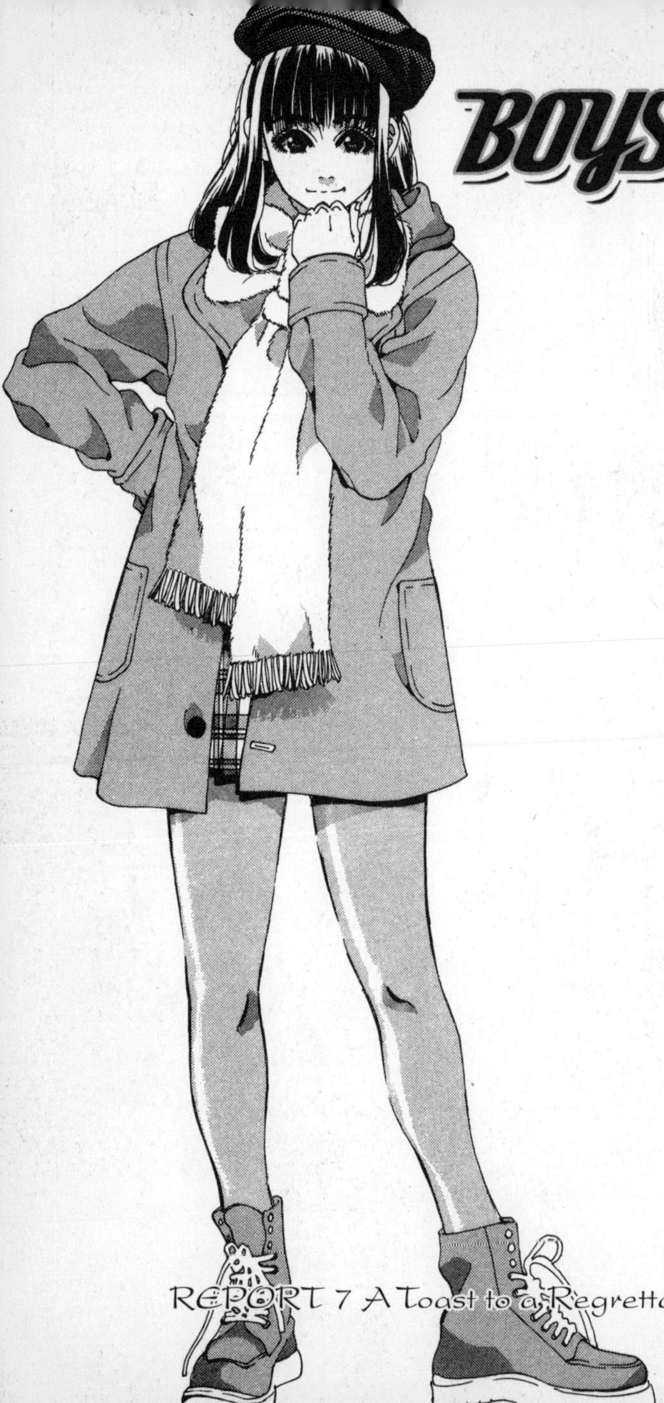

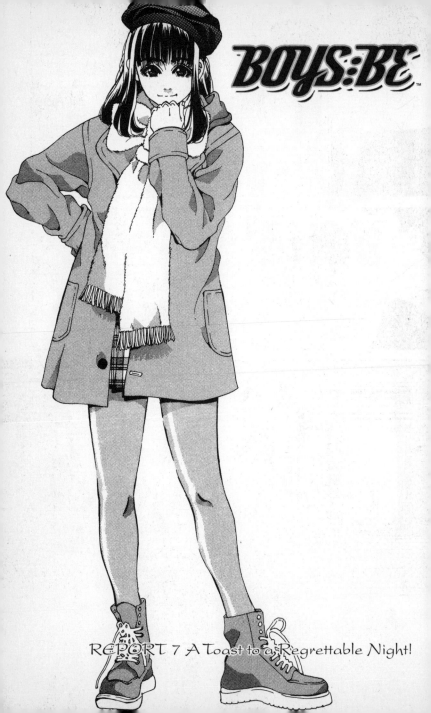

BOYS BE

REPORT 7 A Toast to a Regrettable Night!

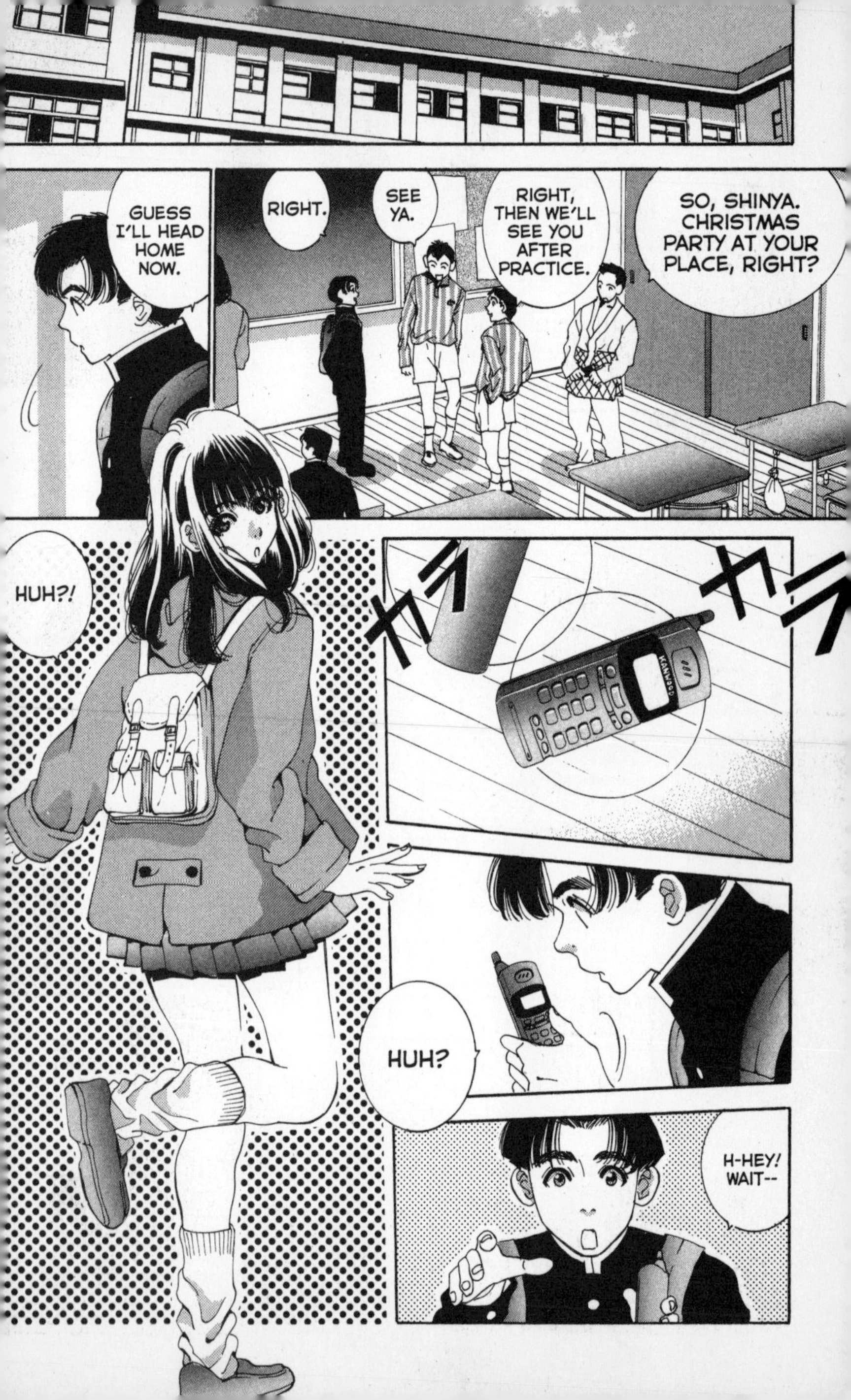
SO, SHINYA. CHRISTMAS PARTY AT YOUR PLACE, RIGHT?
RIGHT, THEN WE'LL SEE YOU AFTER PRACTICE.
SEE YA.
RIGHT.
GUESS I'LL HEAD HOME NOW.
カラ
カラ
HUH?
H-HEY! WAIT--
HUH?!

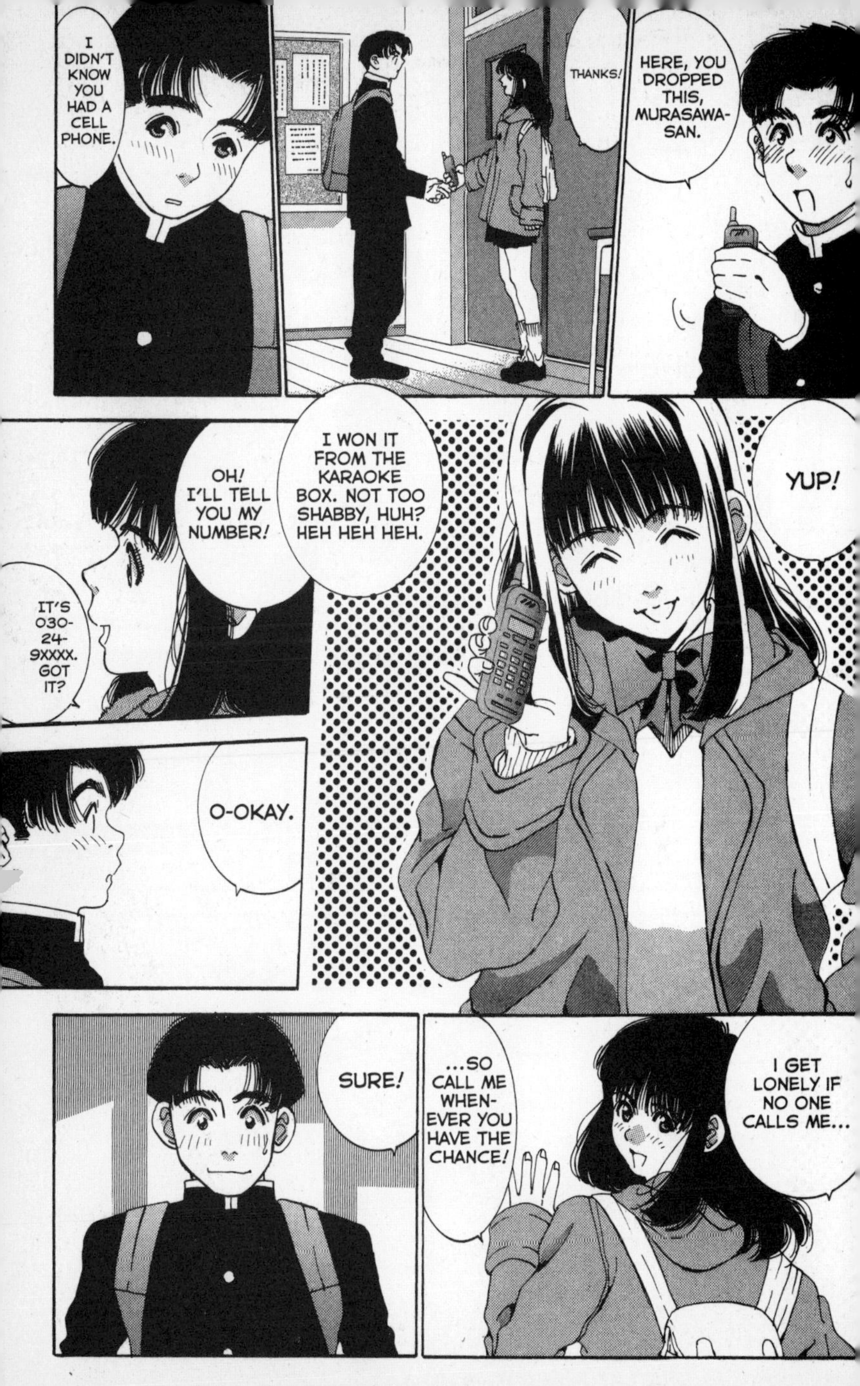
HERE, YOU DROPPED THIS, MURASAWA-SAN.
THANKS!
I DIDN'T KNOW YOU HAD A CELL PHONE.
YUP!
I WON IT FROM THE KARAOKE BOX. NOT TOO SHABBY, HUH? HEH HEH HEH.
OH! I'LL TELL YOU MY NUMBER!
IT'S 030-24-9XXXX. GOT IT?
O-OKAY.
I GET LONELY IF NO ONE CALLS ME...
...SO CALL ME WHENEVER YOU HAVE THE CHANCE!
SURE!

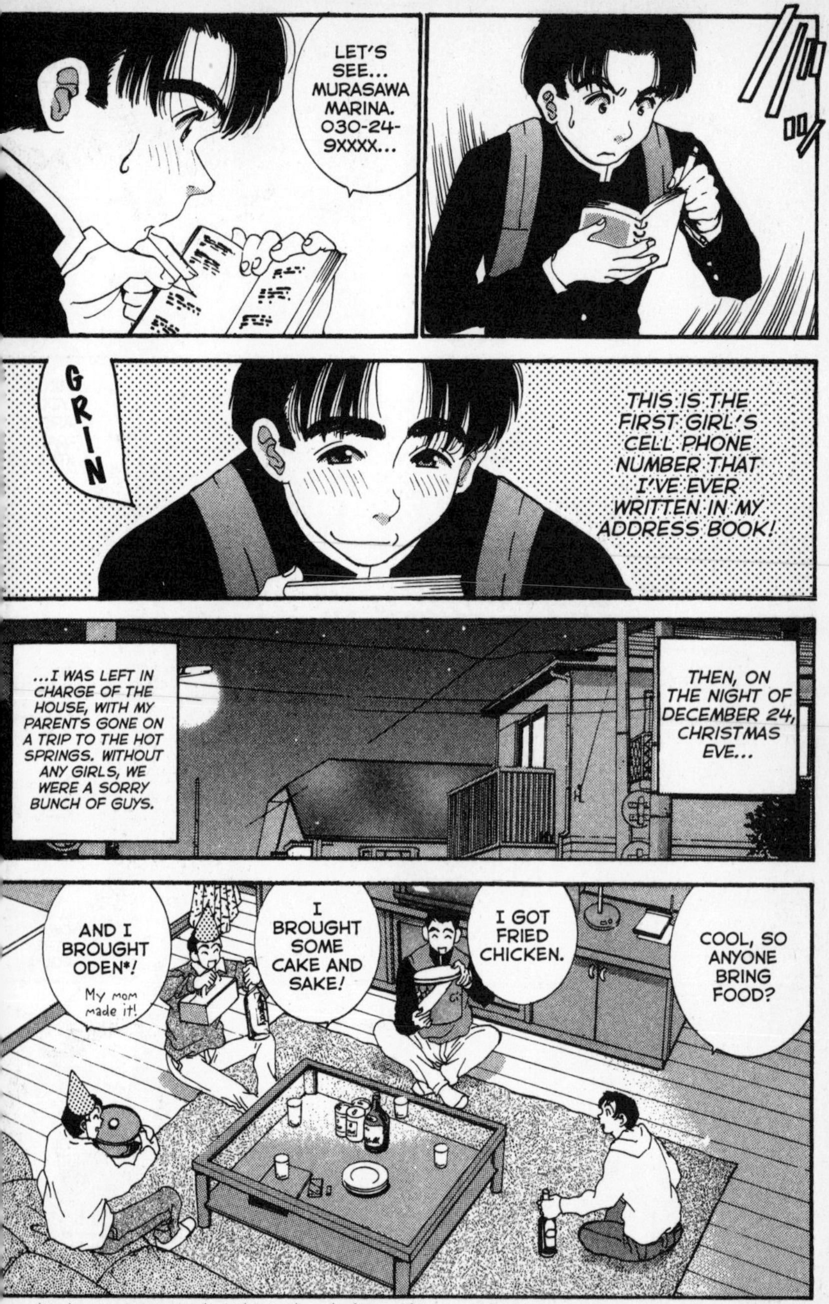
LET'S SEE... MURASAWA MARINA. 030-24-9XXXX...
THIS IS THE FIRST GIRL'S CELL PHONE NUMBER THAT I'VE EVER WRITTEN IN MY ADDRESS BOOK!
GRIN
THEN, ON THE NIGHT OF DECEMBER 24, CHRISTMAS EVE...
...I WAS LEFT IN CHARGE OF THE HOUSE, WITH MY PARENTS GONE ON A TRIP TO THE HOT SPRINGS. WITHOUT ANY GIRLS, WE WERE A SORRY BUNCH OF GUYS.
COOL, SO ANYONE BRING FOOD?
I GOT FRIED CHICKEN.
I BROUGHT SOME CAKE AND SAKE!
AND I BROUGHT ODEN*!
My mom made it!

*Oden is a popular Japanese hotpot dish that includes daikon radish, fish cakes, boiled eggs, konnyaku and more. It's often eaten in winter, but is hardly appropriate for celebrating the holidays.

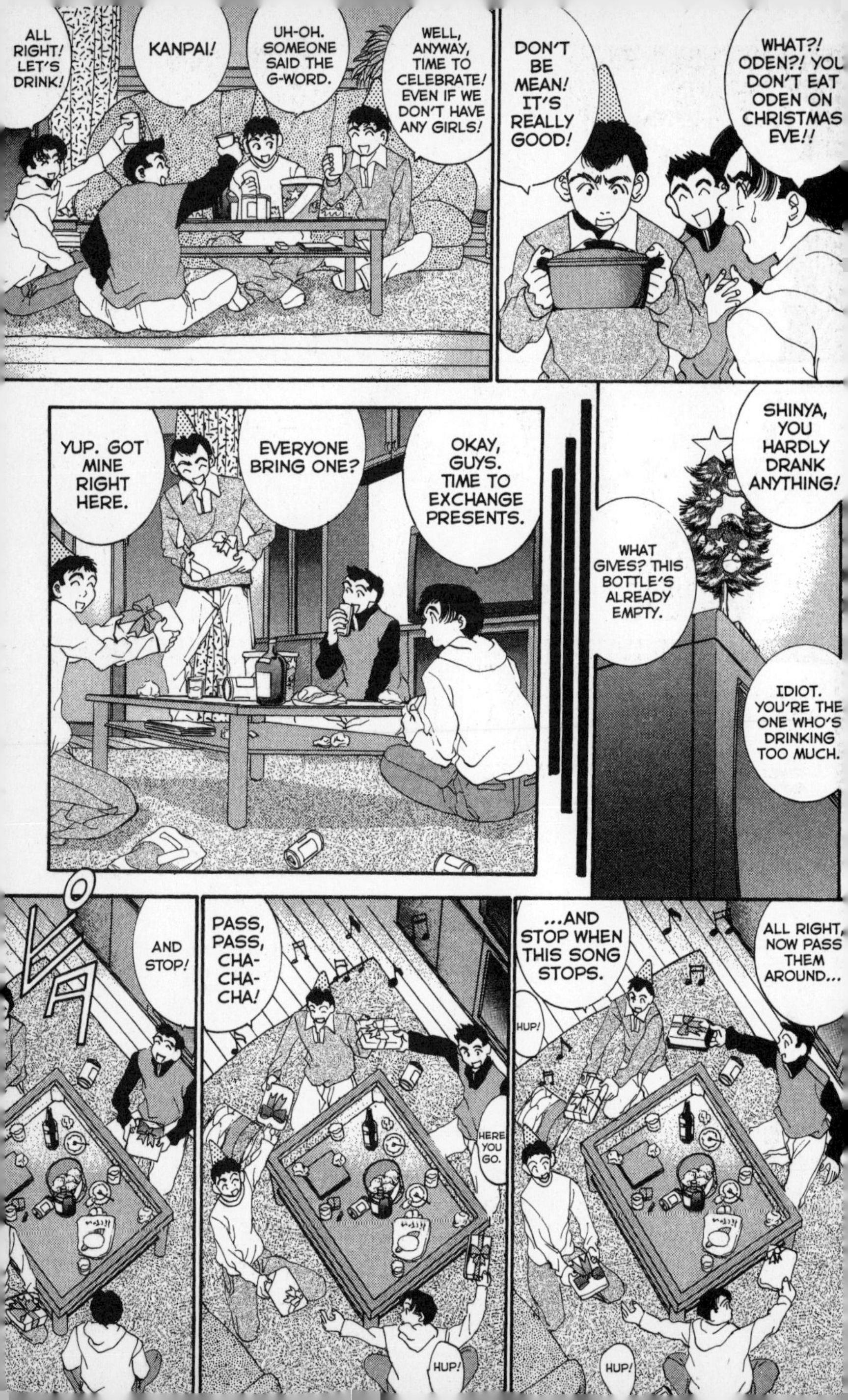
WHAT?! ODEN?! YOU DON'T EAT ODEN ON CHRISTMAS EVE!!
DON'T BE MEAN! IT'S REALLY GOOD!
WELL, ANYWAY, TIME TO CELEBRATE! EVEN IF WE DON'T HAVE ANY GIRLS!
UH-OH. SOMEONE SAID THE G-WORD.
KANPAI!
ALL RIGHT! LET'S DRINK!
SHINYA, YOU HARDLY DRANK ANYTHING!
WHAT GIVES? THIS BOTTLE'S ALREADY EMPTY.
IDIOT. YOU'RE THE ONE WHO'S DRINKING TOO MUCH.
OKAY, GUYS. TIME TO EXCHANGE PRESENTS.
EVERYONE BRING ONE?
YUP. GOT MINE RIGHT HERE.
ALL RIGHT, NOW PASS THEM AROUND...
...AND STOP WHEN THIS SONG STOPS.
HUP!
HUP!
PASS, PASS, CHA-CHA-CHA!
HERE YOU GO.
HUP!
AND STOP!

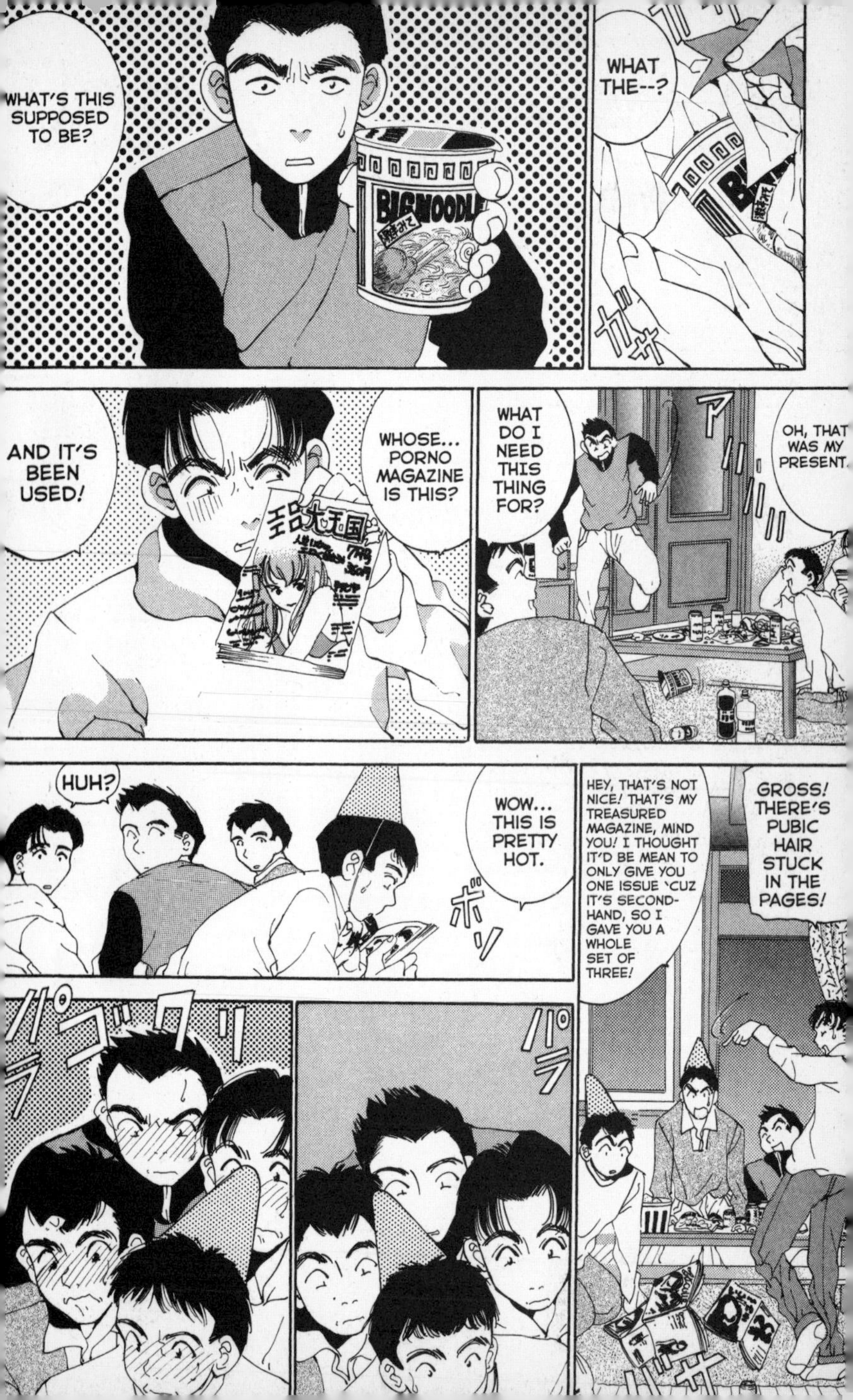
WHAT THE--?
WHAT'S THIS SUPPOSED TO BE?
OH, THAT WAS MY PRESENT.
WHAT DO I NEED THIS THING FOR?
WHOSE... PORNO MAGAZINE IS THIS?
AND IT'S BEEN USED!
GROSS! THERE'S PUBIC HAIR STUCK IN THE PAGES!
HEY, THAT'S NOT NICE! THAT'S MY TREASURED MAGAZINE, MIND YOU! I THOUGHT IT'D BE MEAN TO ONLY GIVE YOU ONE ISSUE 'CUZ IT'S SECOND-HAND, SO I GAVE YOU A WHOLE SET OF THREE!
WOW... THIS IS PRETTY HOT.
HUH?

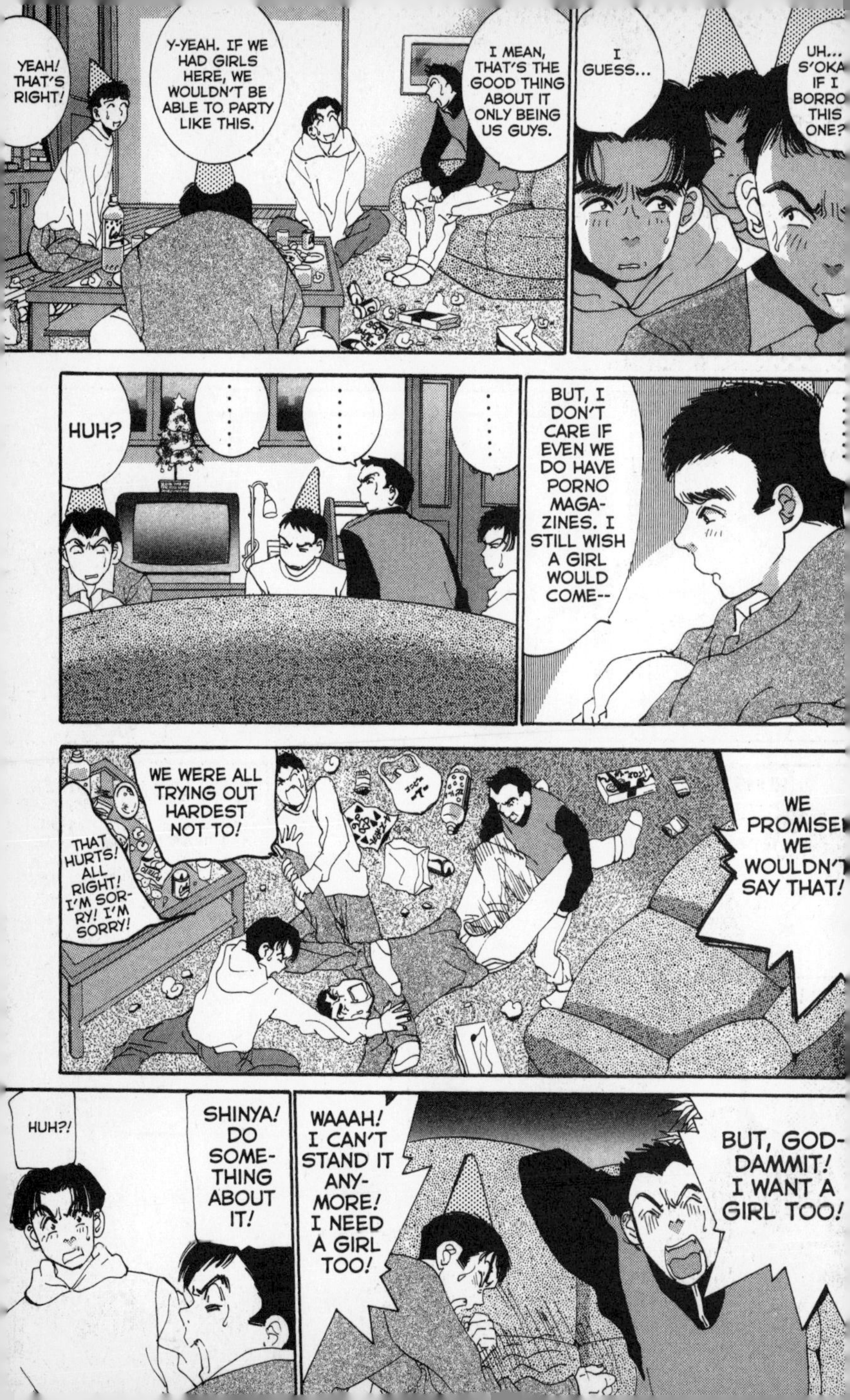
UH... S'OKA IF I BORRO THIS ONE?
I GUESS...
I MEAN, THAT'S THE GOOD THING ABOUT IT ONLY BEING US GUYS.
Y-YEAH. IF WE HAD GIRLS HERE, WE WOULDN'T BE ABLE TO PARTY LIKE THIS.
YEAH! THAT'S RIGHT!
BUT, I DON'T CARE IF EVEN WE DO HAVE PORNO MAGA-ZINES. I STILL WISH A GIRL WOULD COME--
......
......
......
HUH?
WE PROMISE WE WOULDN' SAY THAT!
WE WERE ALL TRYING OUT HARDEST NOT TO!
THAT HURTS! ALL RIGHT! I'M SOR-RY! I'M SORRY!
BUT, GOD-DAMMIT! I WANT A GIRL TOO!
WAAAH! I CAN'T STAND IT ANY-MORE! I NEED A GIRL TOO!
SHINYA! DO SOME-THING ABOUT IT!
HUH?!

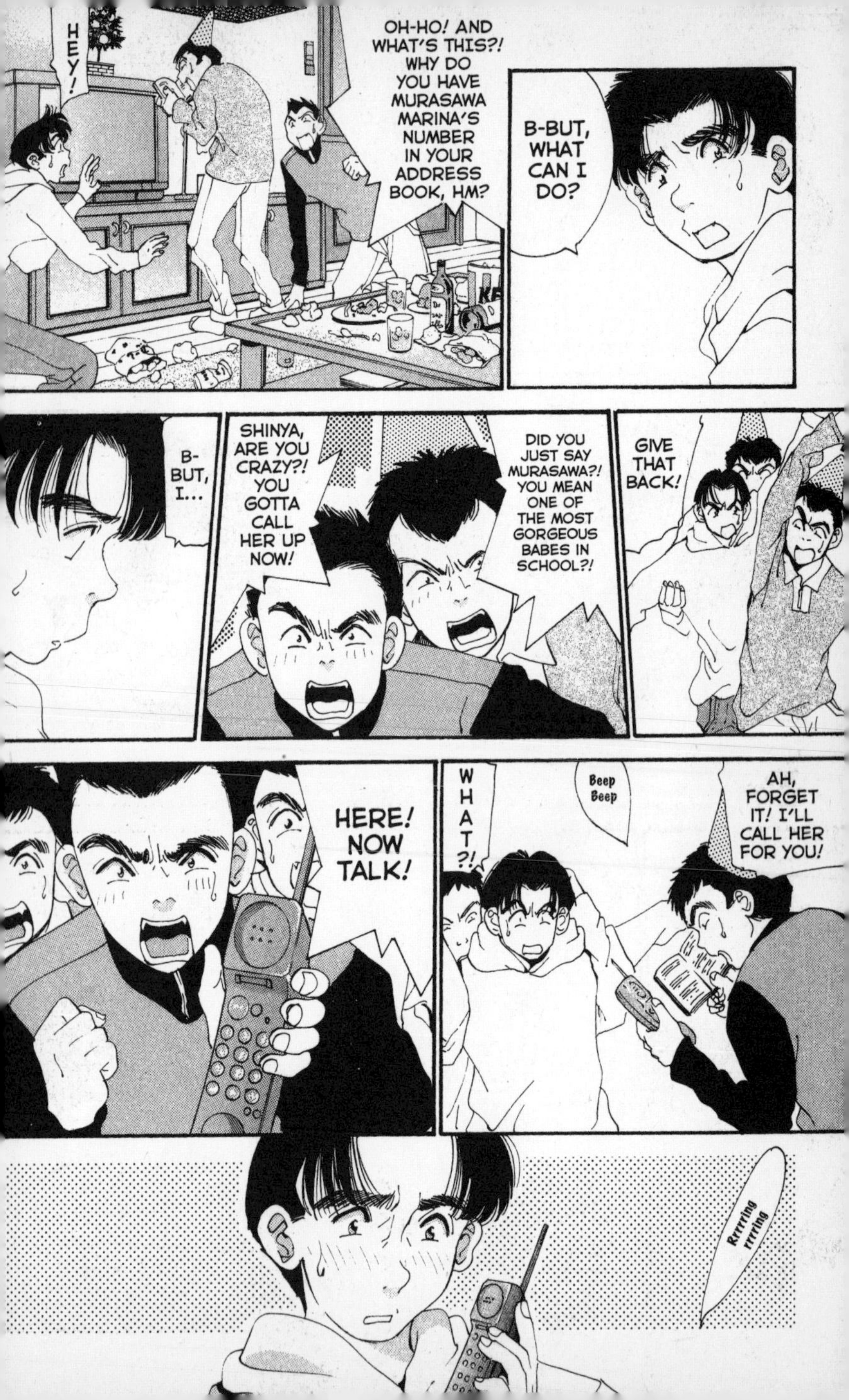
B-BUT, WHAT CAN I DO?
OH-HO! AND WHAT'S THIS?! WHY DO YOU HAVE MURASAWA MARINA'S NUMBER IN YOUR ADDRESS BOOK, HM?
HEY!
GIVE THAT BACK!
DID YOU JUST SAY MURASAWA?! YOU MEAN ONE OF THE MOST GORGEOUS BABES IN SCHOOL?!
SHINYA, ARE YOU CRAZY?! YOU GOTTA CALL HER UP NOW!
B-BUT, I...
AH, FORGET IT! I'LL CALL HER FOR YOU!
Beep Beep
WHAT?!
HERE! NOW TALK!
Rrrring rrring

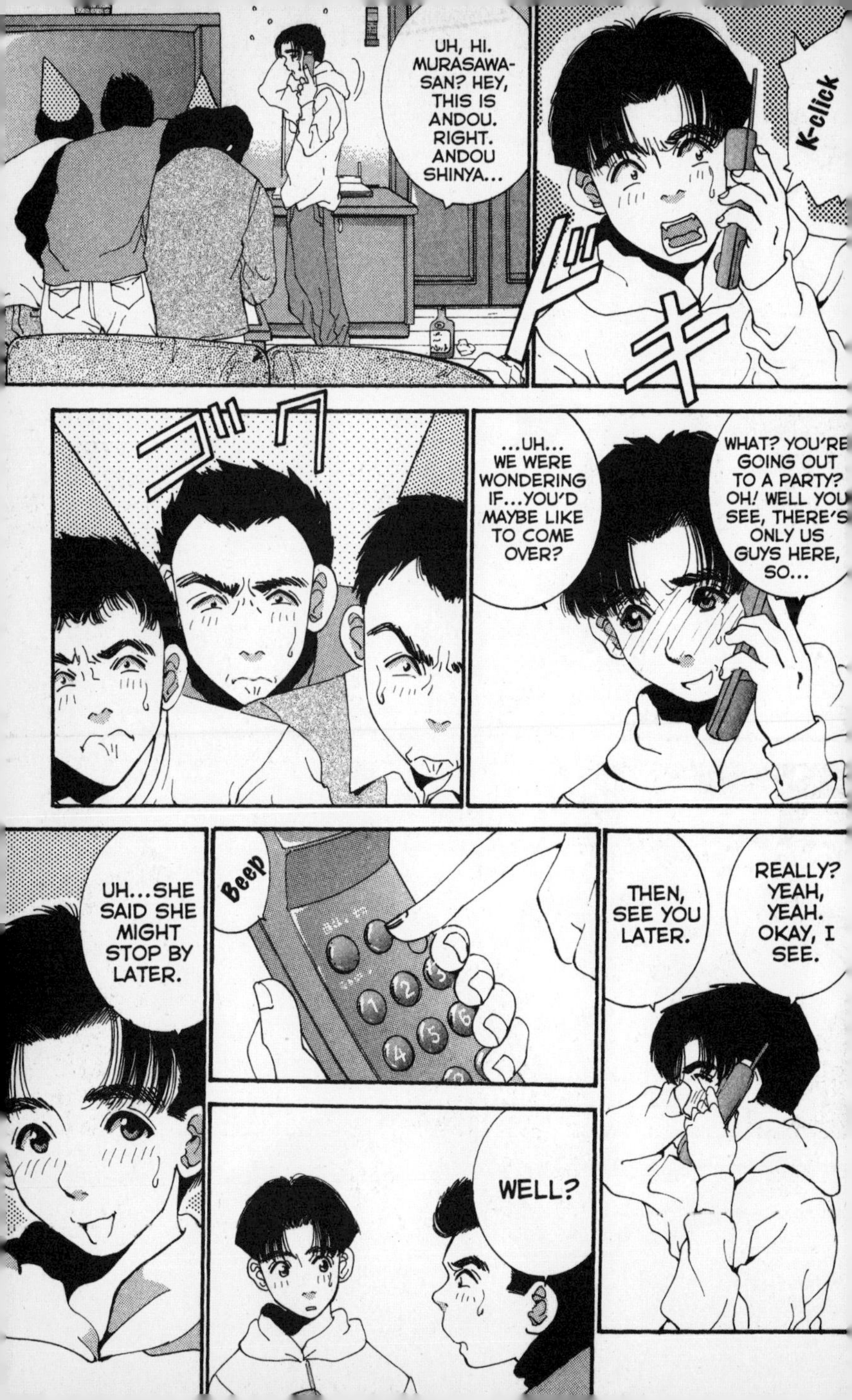
K-click
UH, HI. MURASAWA-SAN? HEY, THIS IS ANDOU. RIGHT. ANDOU SHINYA...
WHAT? YOU'RE GOING OUT TO A PARTY? OH! WELL YOU SEE, THERE'S ONLY US GUYS HERE, SO...
...UH... WE WERE WONDERING IF...YOU'D MAYBE LIKE TO COME OVER?
REALLY? YEAH, YEAH. OKAY, I SEE.
THEN, SEE YOU LATER.
Beep
WELL?
UH...SHE SAID SHE MIGHT STOP BY LATER.

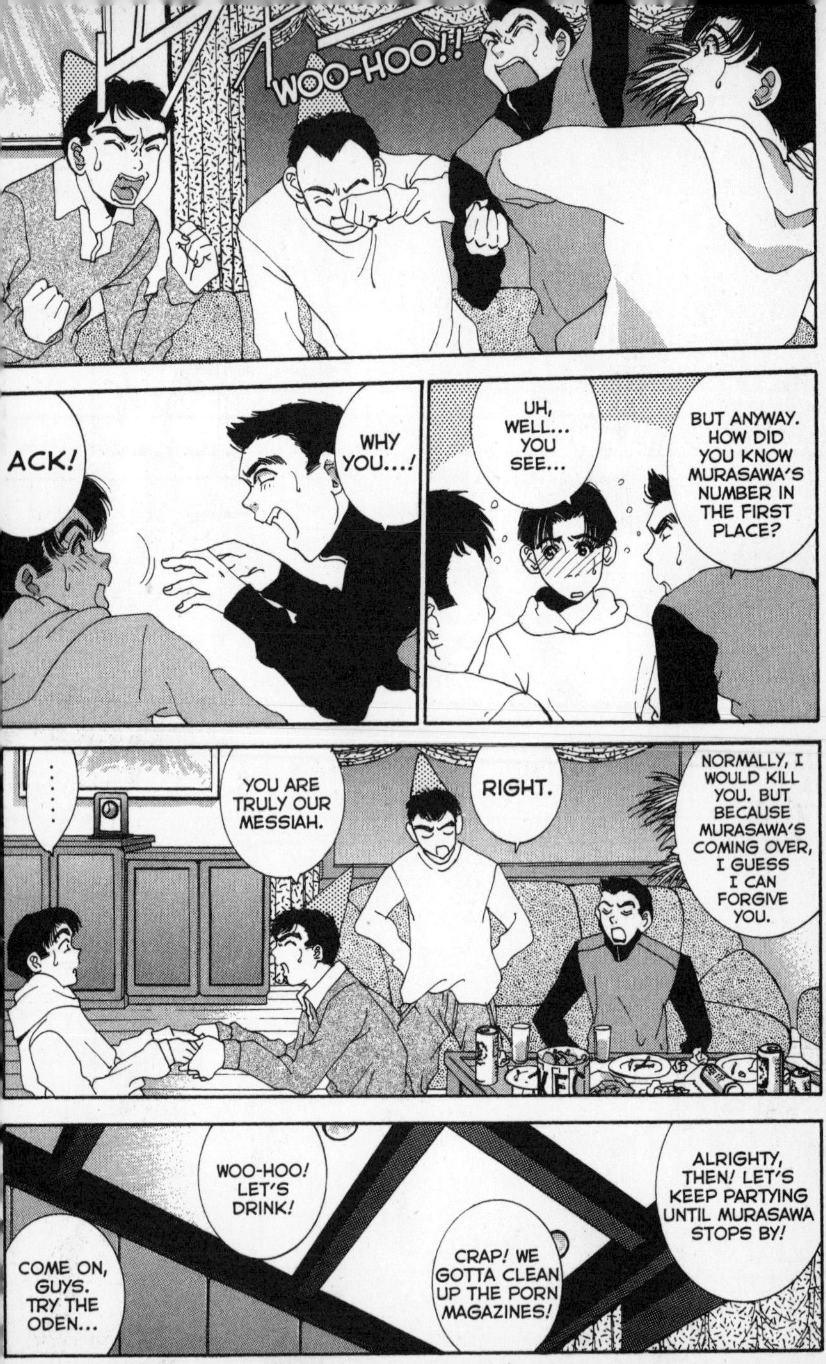
WOO-HOO!!
BUT ANYWAY. HOW DID YOU KNOW MURASAWA'S NUMBER IN THE FIRST PLACE?
UH, WELL... YOU SEE...
WHY YOU...!
ACK!
NORMALLY, I WOULD KILL YOU. BUT BECAUSE MURASAWA'S COMING OVER, I GUESS I CAN FORGIVE YOU.
RIGHT.
YOU ARE TRULY OUR MESSIAH.
......
ALRIGHTY, THEN! LET'S KEEP PARTYING UNTIL MURASAWA STOPS BY!
WOO-HOO! LET'S DRINK!
CRAP! WE GOTTA CLEAN UP THE PORN MAGAZINES!
COME ON, GUYS. TRY THE ODEN...

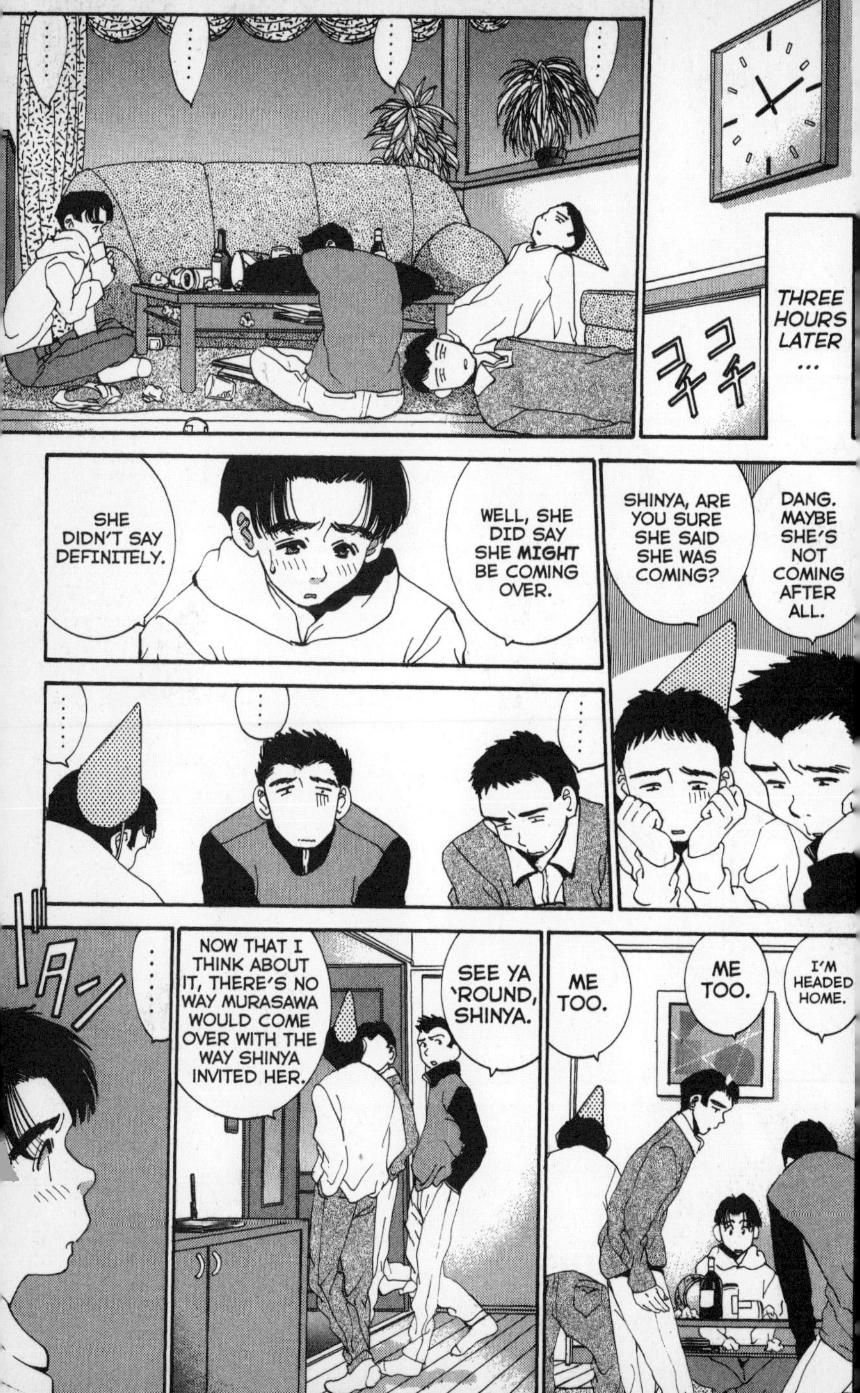
THREE HOURS LATER ...
コチコチ
......
......
......
DANG. MAYBE SHE'S NOT COMING AFTER ALL.
SHINYA, ARE YOU SURE SHE SAID SHE WAS COMING?
WELL, SHE DID SAY SHE **MIGHT** BE COMING OVER.
SHE DIDN'T SAY DEFINITELY.
......
......
......
I'M HEADED HOME.
ME TOO.
ME TOO.
SEE YA 'ROUND, SHINYA.
NOW THAT I THINK ABOUT IT, THERE'S NO WAY MURASAWA WOULD COME OVER WITH THE WAY SHINYA INVITED HER.
......
バタン

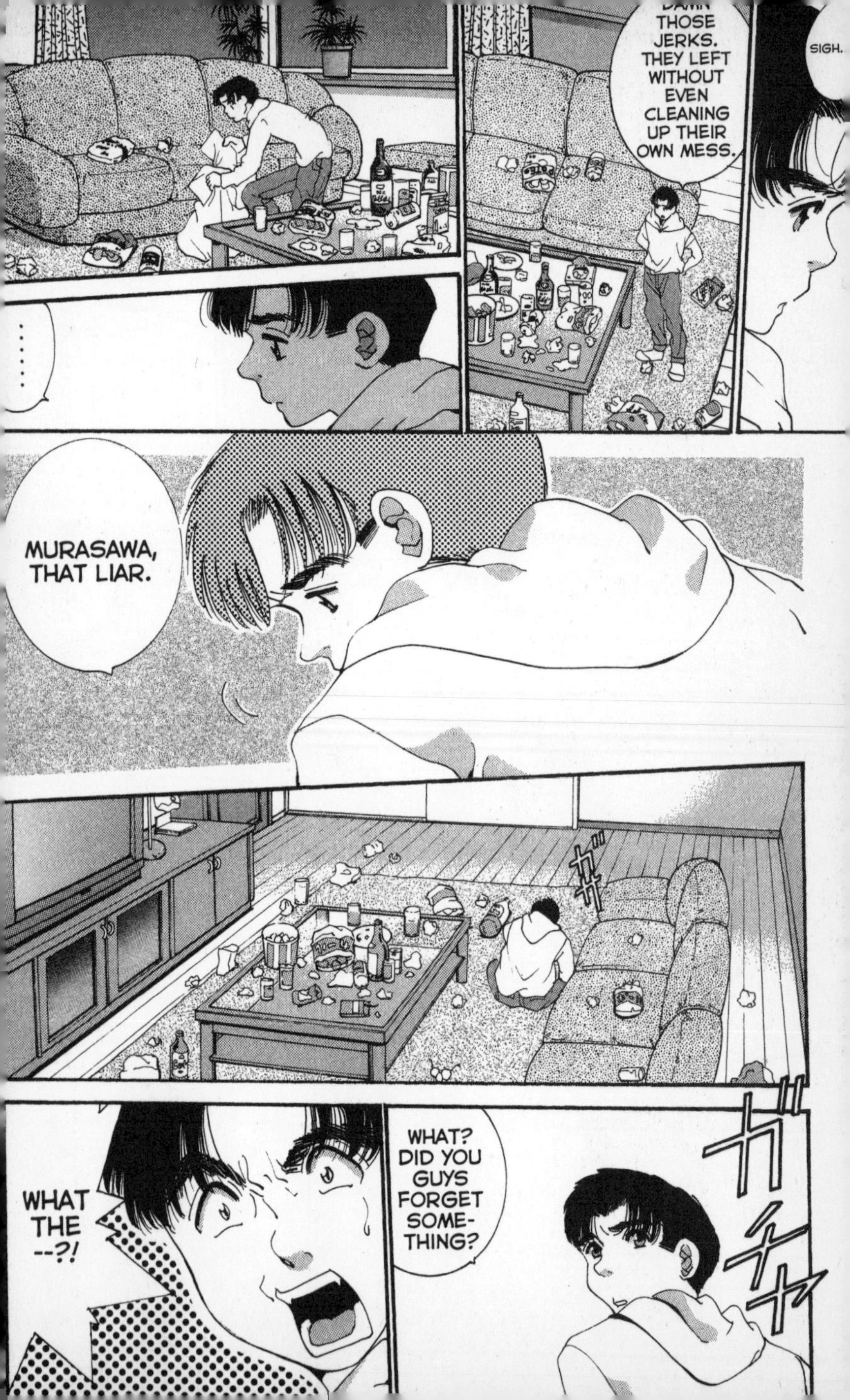
SIGH.
DAMN THOSE JERKS. THEY LEFT WITHOUT EVEN CLEANING UP THEIR OWN MESS.
......
MURASAWA, THAT LIAR.
ガチャ
WHAT? DID YOU GUYS FORGET SOME-THING?
WHAT THE --?!

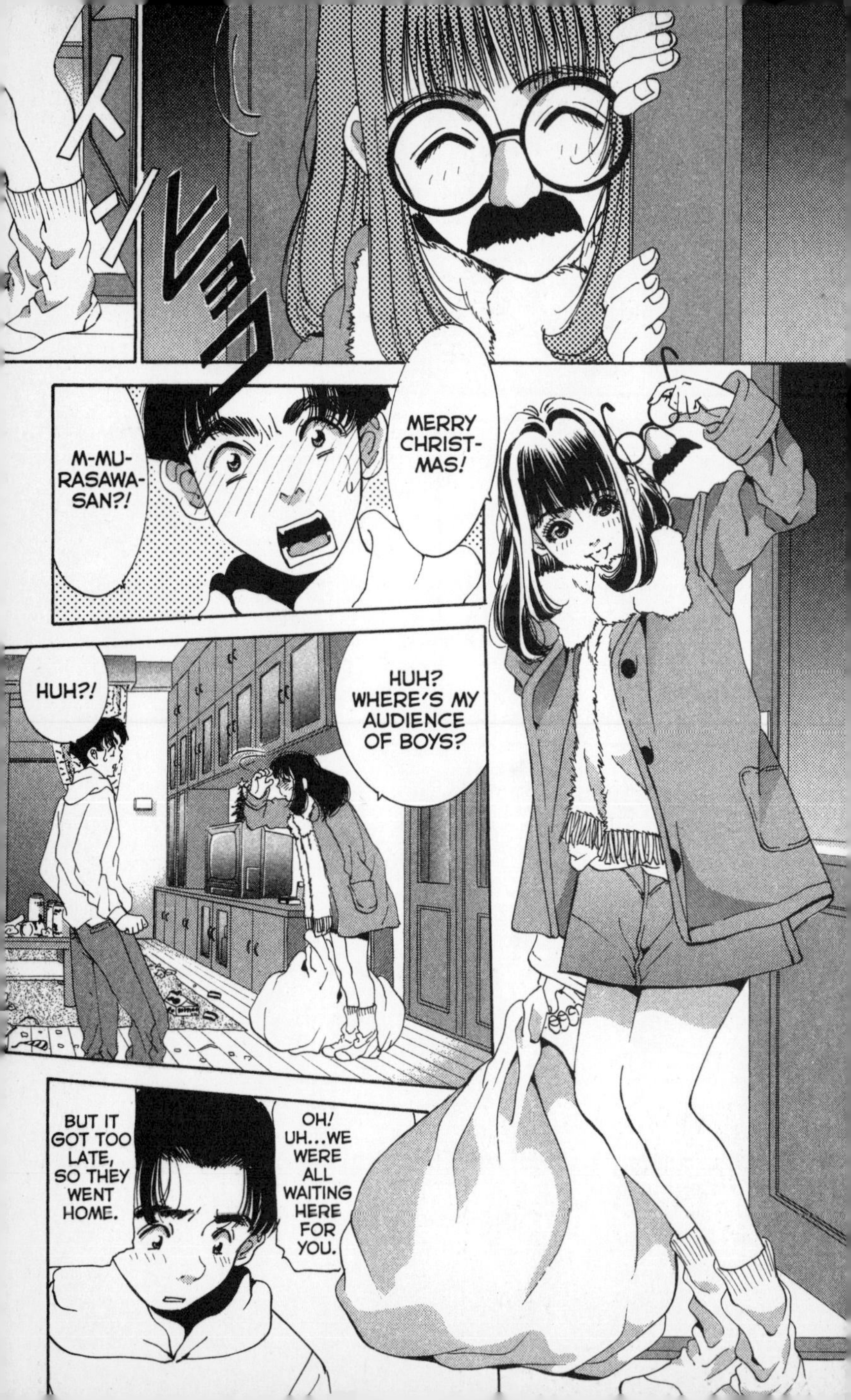
MERRY CHRIST-MAS!
M-MU-RASAWA-SAN?!
HUH? WHERE'S MY AUDIENCE OF BOYS?
HUH?!
OH! UH...WE WERE ALL WAITING HERE FOR YOU.
BUT IT GOT TOO LATE, SO THEY WENT HOME.

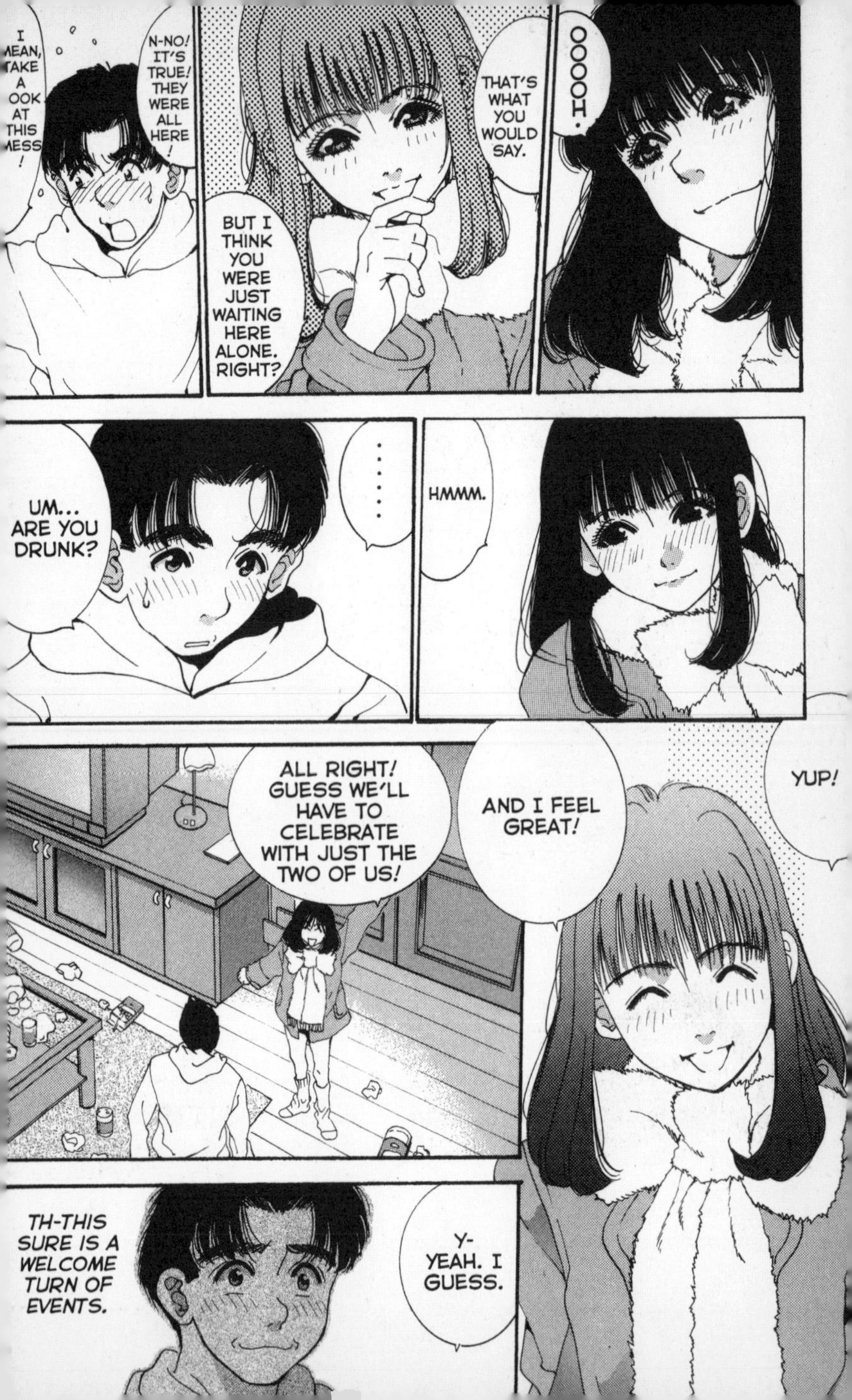
OOOOH.
THAT'S WHAT YOU WOULD SAY.
BUT I THINK YOU WERE JUST WAITING HERE ALONE. RIGHT?
N-NO! IT'S TRUE! THEY WERE ALL HERE!
I MEAN, TAKE A LOOK AT THIS MESS!
HMMM.
......
UM... ARE YOU DRUNK?
YUP!
AND I FEEL GREAT!
ALL RIGHT! GUESS WE'LL HAVE TO CELEBRATE WITH JUST THE TWO OF US!
Y-YEAH. I GUESS.
TH-THIS SURE IS A WELCOME TURN OF EVENTS.

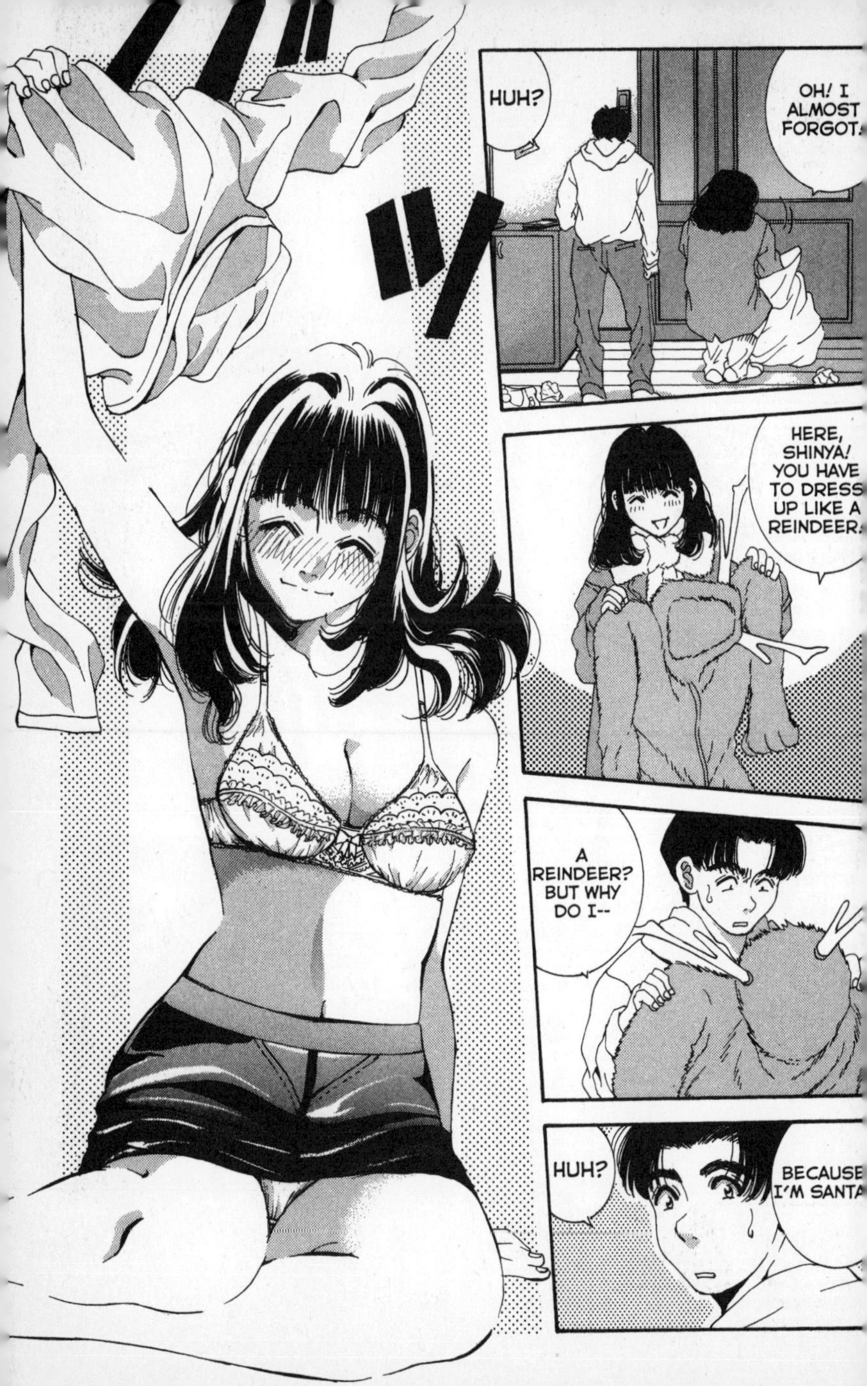
OH! I ALMOST FORGOT!
HUH?
HERE, SHINYA! YOU HAVE TO DRESS UP LIKE A REINDEER!
A REINDEER? BUT WHY DO I--
BECAUSE I'M SANTA
HUH?

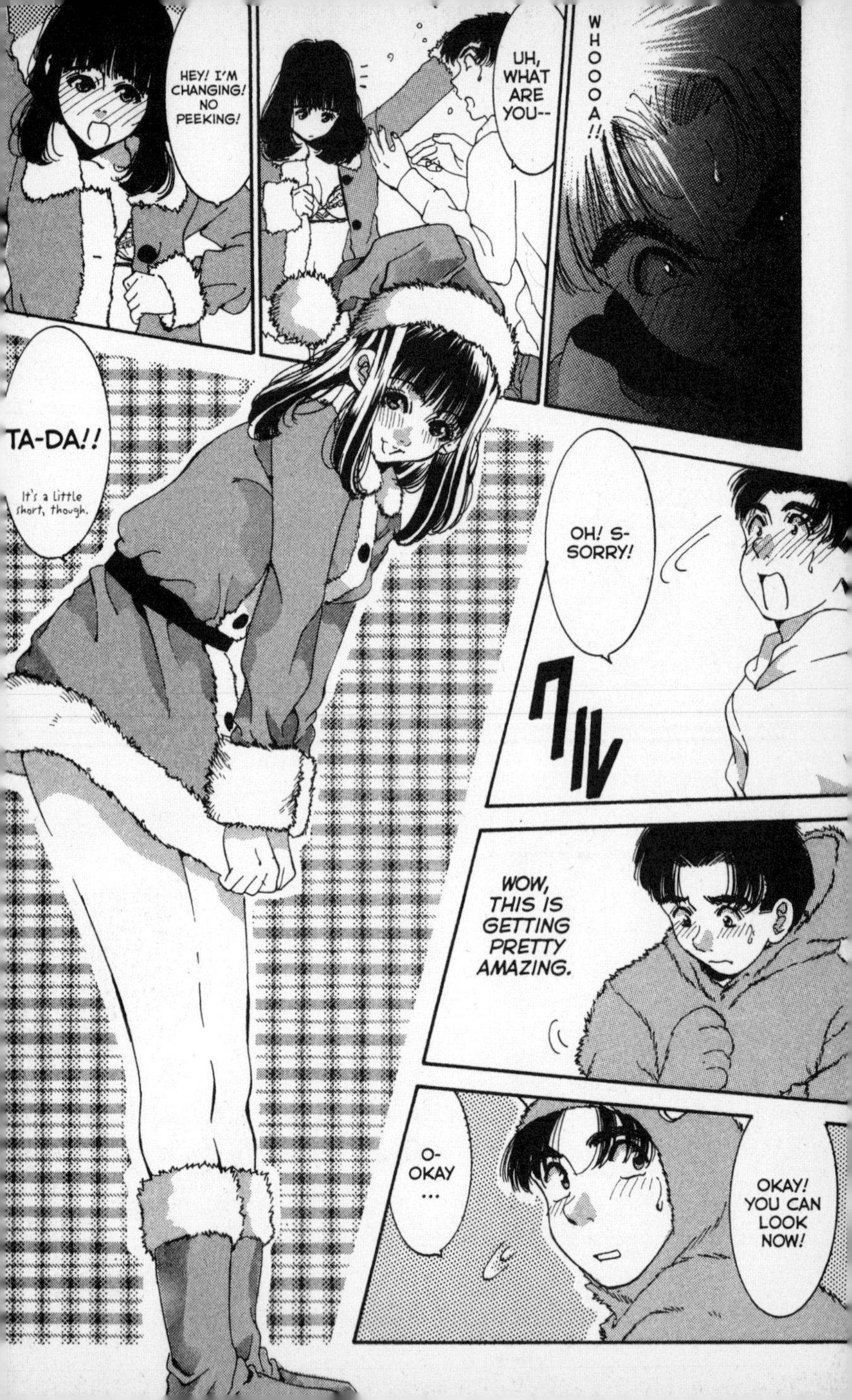
WHOOOOA!!
UH, WHAT ARE YOU--
HEY! I'M CHANGING! NO PEEKING!
OH! S-SORRY!
クル
WOW, THIS IS GETTING PRETTY AMAZING.
OKAY! YOU CAN LOOK NOW!
O-OKAY ...
TA-DA!!
It's a little short, though.

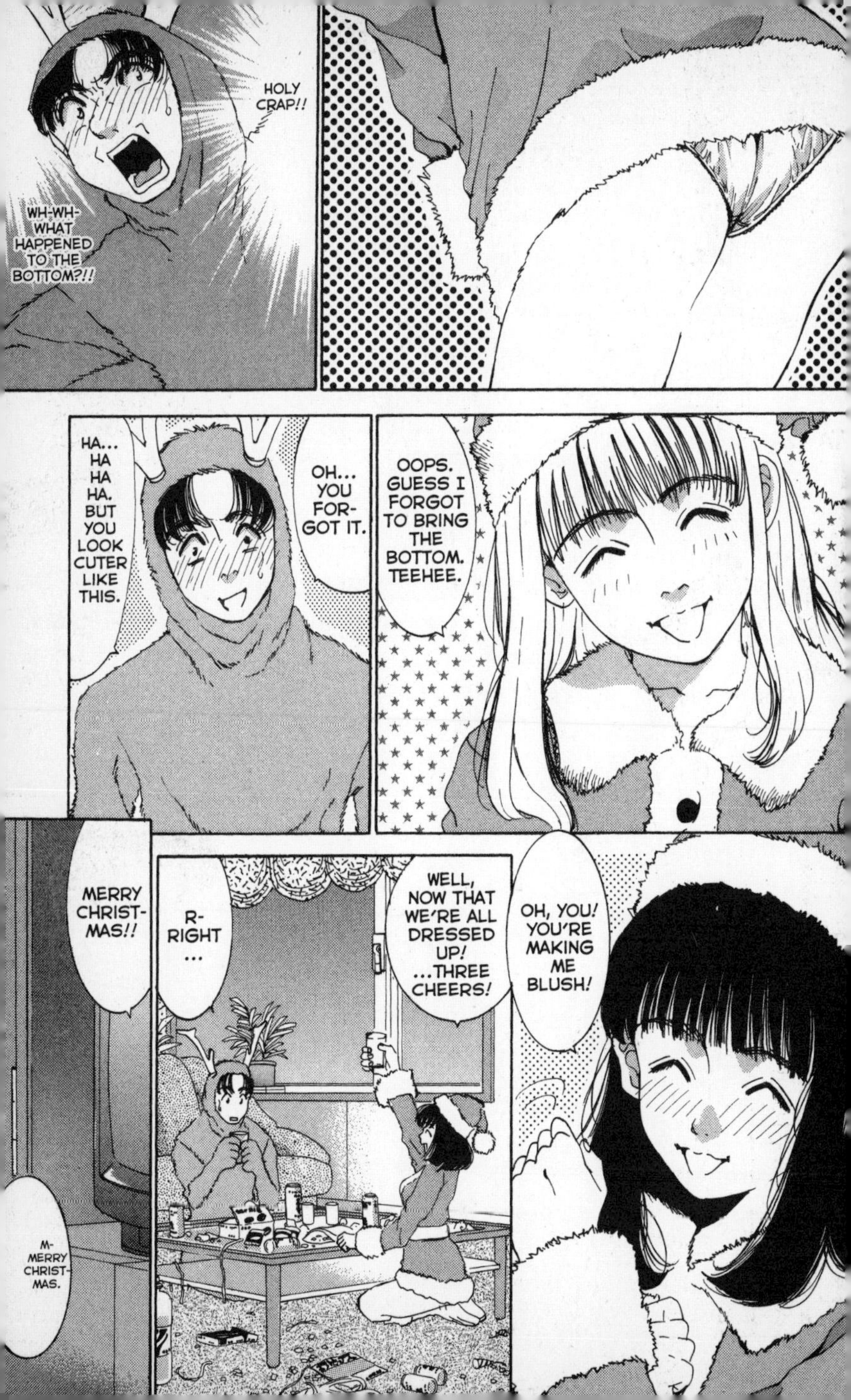
HOLY CRAP!!
WH-WH-WHAT HAPPENED TO THE BOTTOM?!!
OOPS. GUESS I FORGOT TO BRING THE BOTTOM. TEEHEE.
OH... YOU FOR-GOT IT.
HA... HA HA HA. BUT YOU LOOK CUTER LIKE THIS.
OH, YOU! YOU'RE MAKING ME BLUSH!
WELL, NOW THAT WE'RE ALL DRESSED UP! ...THREE CHEERS!
R-RIGHT ...
MERRY CHRIST-MAS!!
M-MERRY CHRIST-MAS.

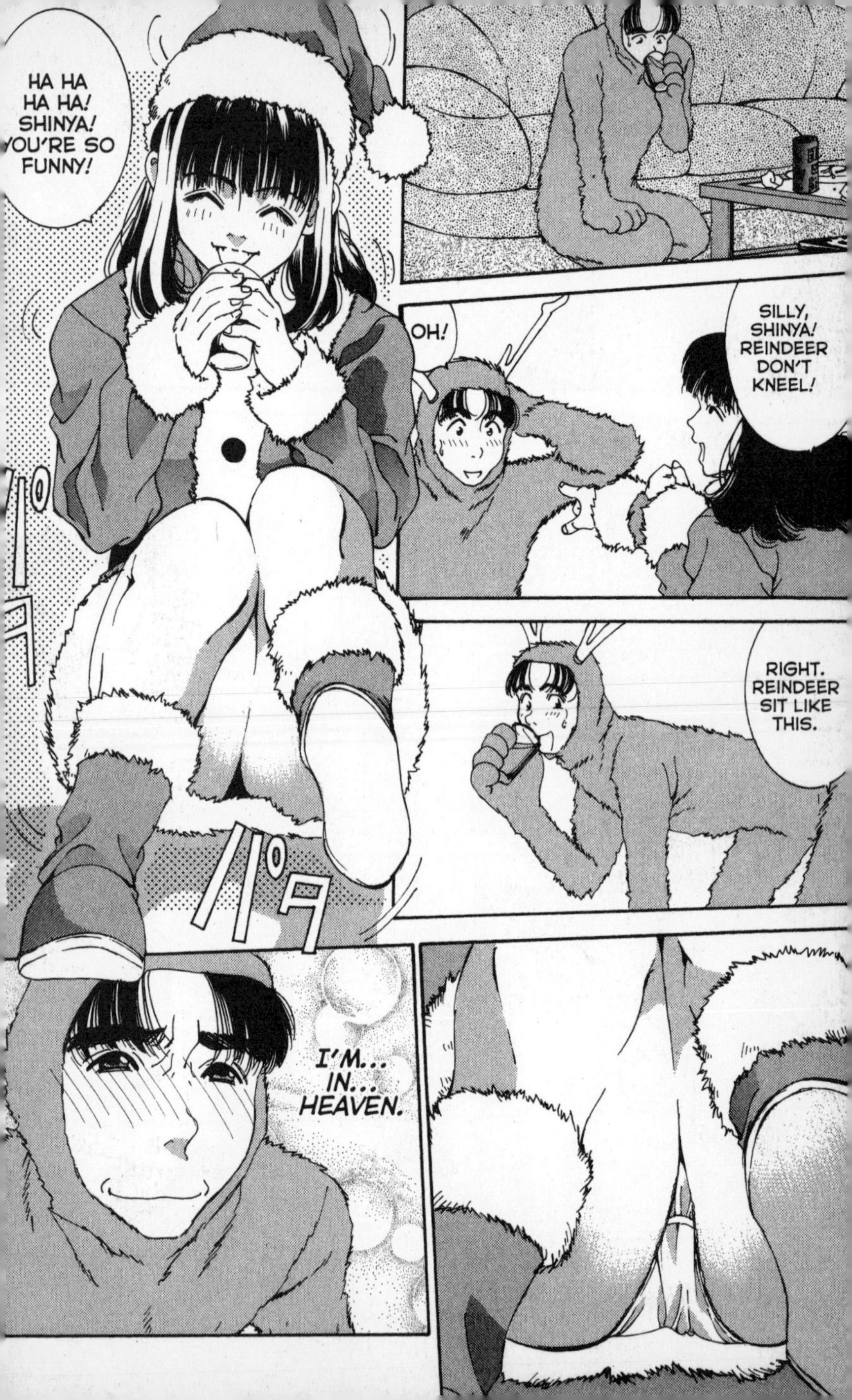
SILLY, SHINYA! REINDEER DON'T KNEEL!
OH!
RIGHT. REINDEER SIT LIKE THIS.
HA HA HA HA! SHINYA! YOU'RE SO FUNNY!
パタ
I'M... IN... HEAVEN.

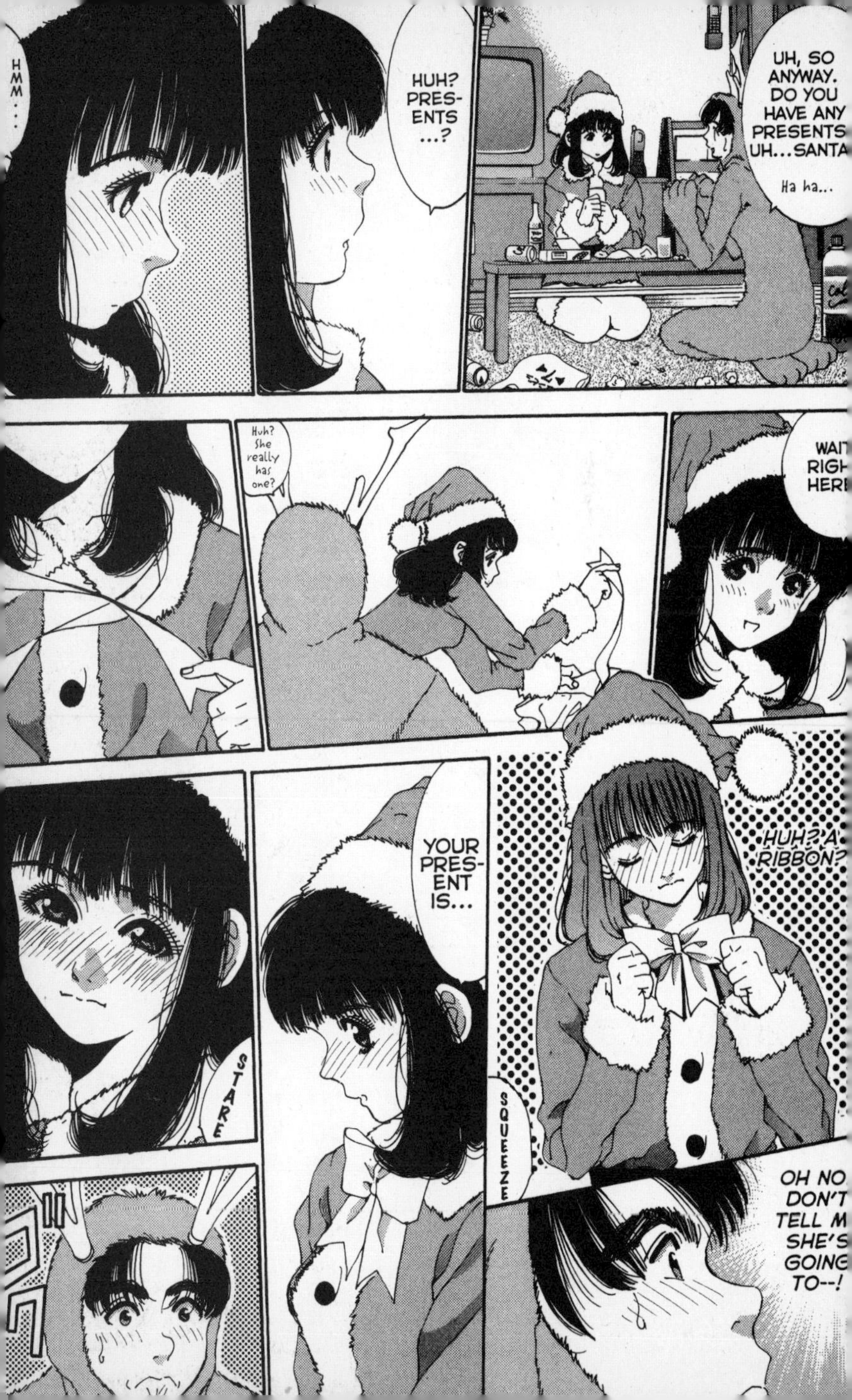
UH, SO ANYWAY. DO YOU HAVE ANY PRESENTS UH...SANTA
Ha ha...
HUH? PRES-ENTS ...?
HMM...
WAIT RIGH HERE
Huh? She really has one?
HUH? A RIBBON?
SQUEEZE
YOUR PRES-ENT IS...
STARE
OH NO DON'T TELL M SHE'S GOING TO--!

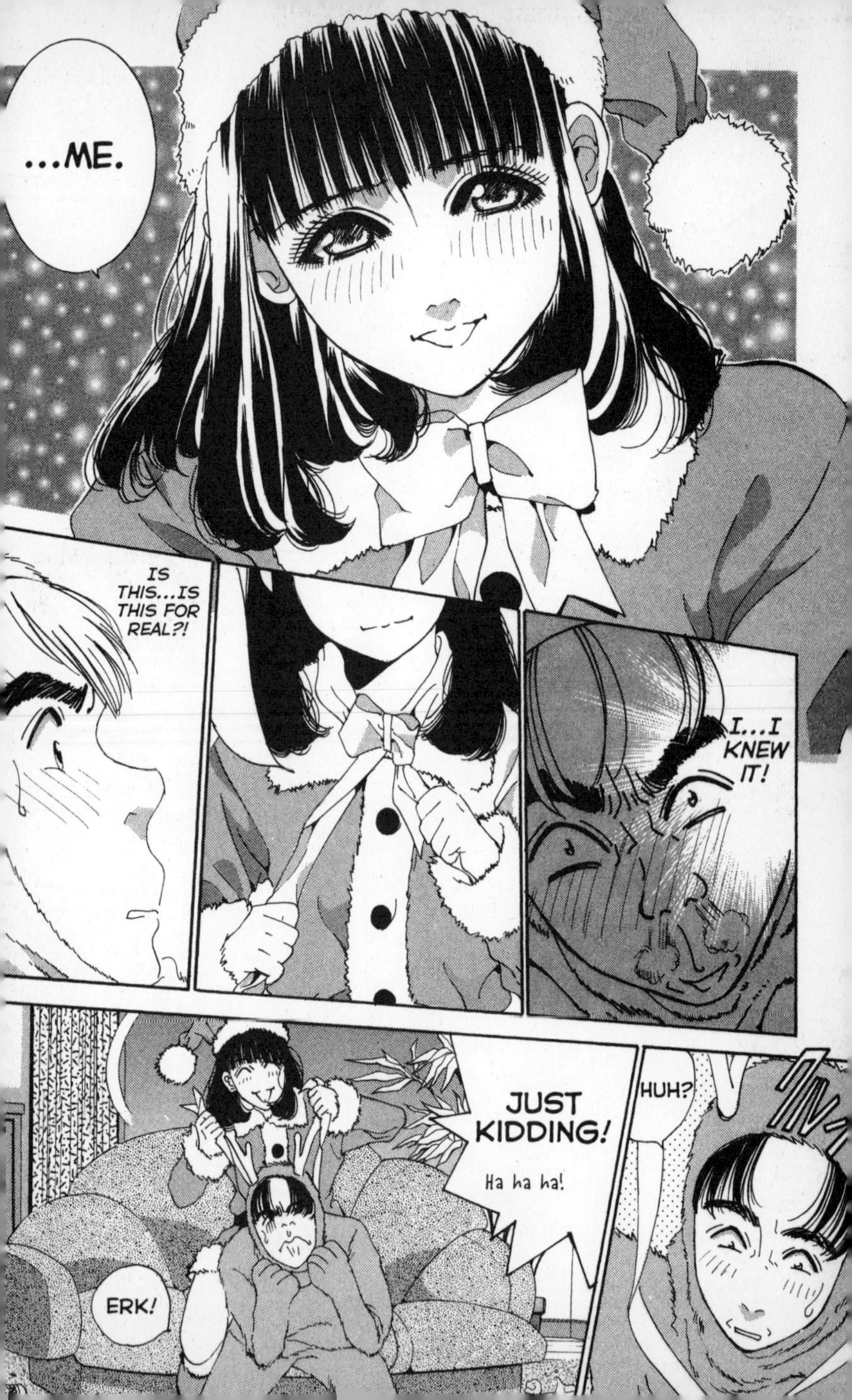
...ME.
I...I KNEW IT!
IS THIS...IS THIS FOR REAL?!
HUH?
JUST KIDDING!
Ha ha ha!
ERK!

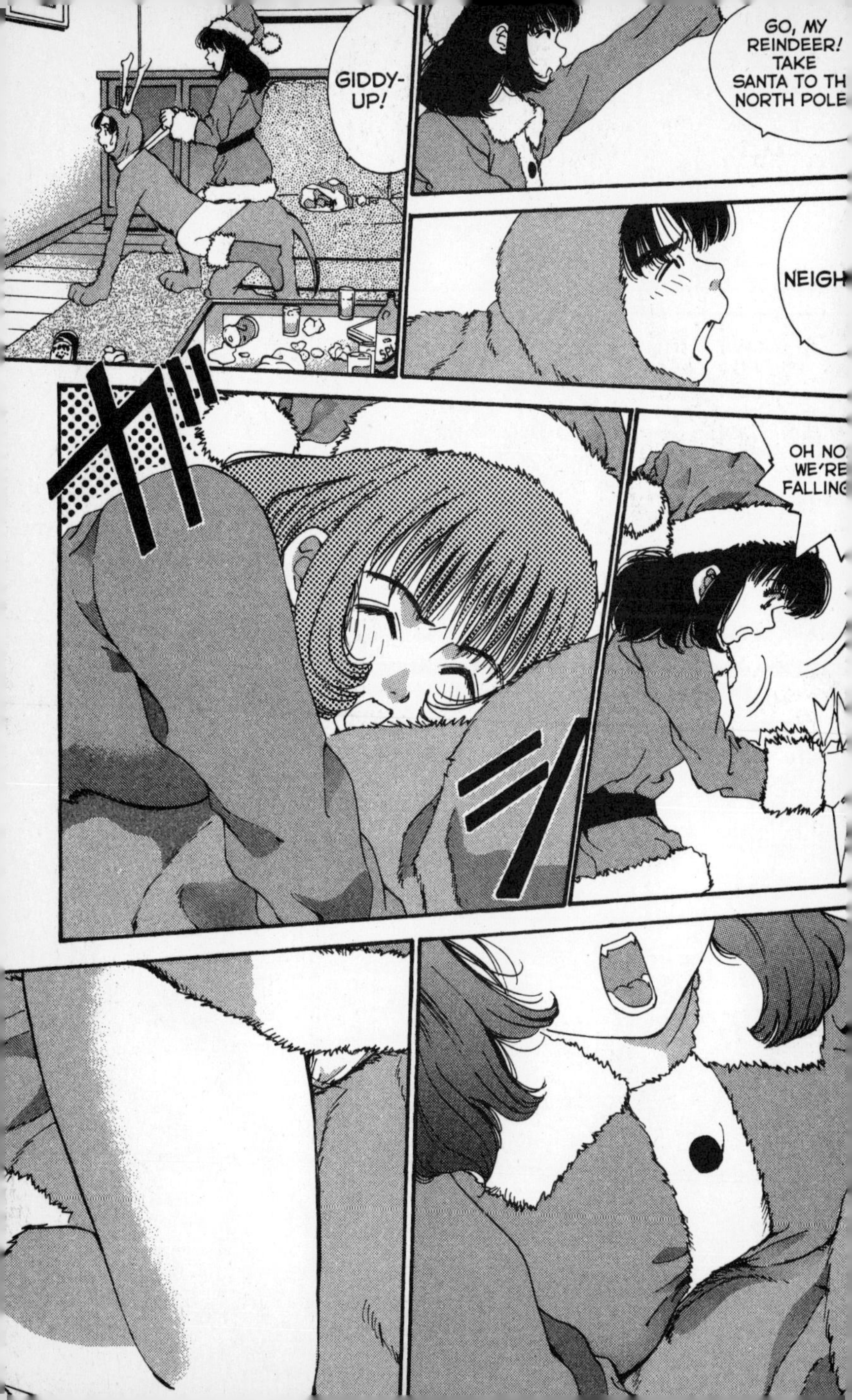
GO, MY REINDEER! TAKE SANTA TO TH NORTH POLE
NEIGH
GIDDY-UP!
OH NO WE'RE FALLING

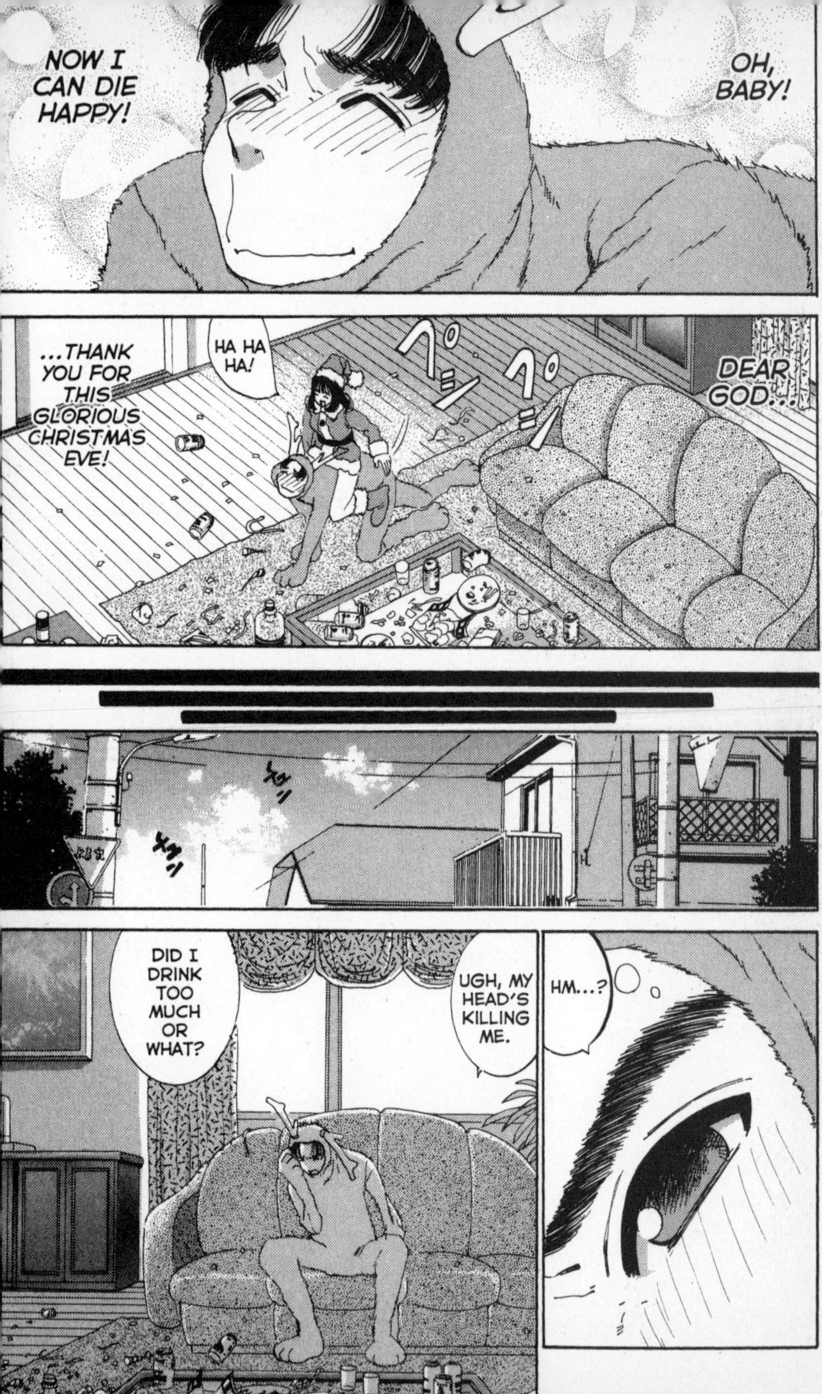
OH, BABY!
NOW I CAN DIE HAPPY!
DEAR GOD...
HA HA HA!
...THANK YOU FOR THIS GLORIOUS CHRISTMAS EVE!
HM...?
UGH, MY HEAD'S KILLING ME.
DID I DRINK TOO MUCH OR WHAT?

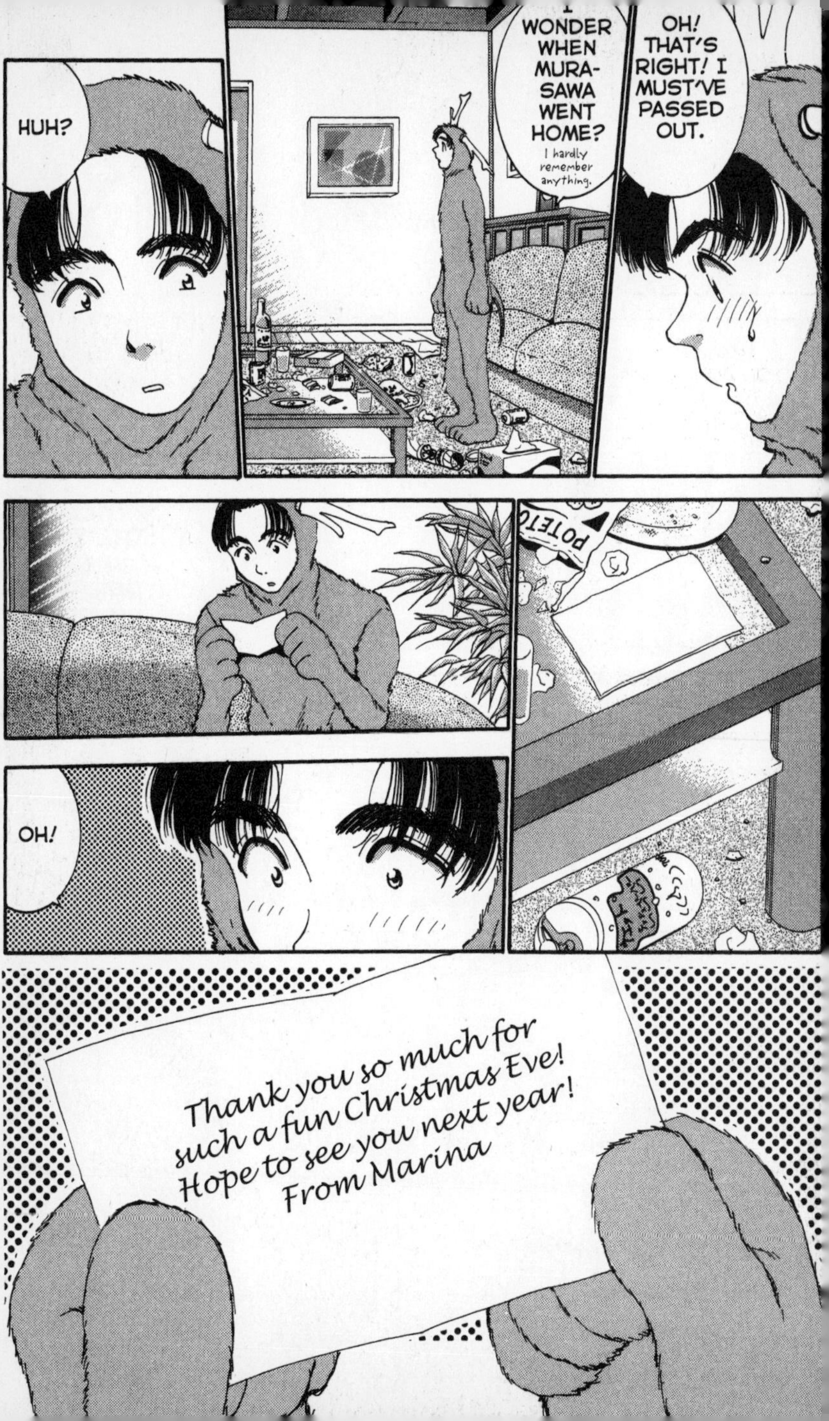
OH! THAT'S RIGHT! I MUST'VE PASSED OUT.
I WONDER WHEN MURA-SAWA WENT HOME?
I hardly remember anything.
HUH?
OH!
Thank you so much for such a fun Christmas Eve! Hope to see you next year! From Marina

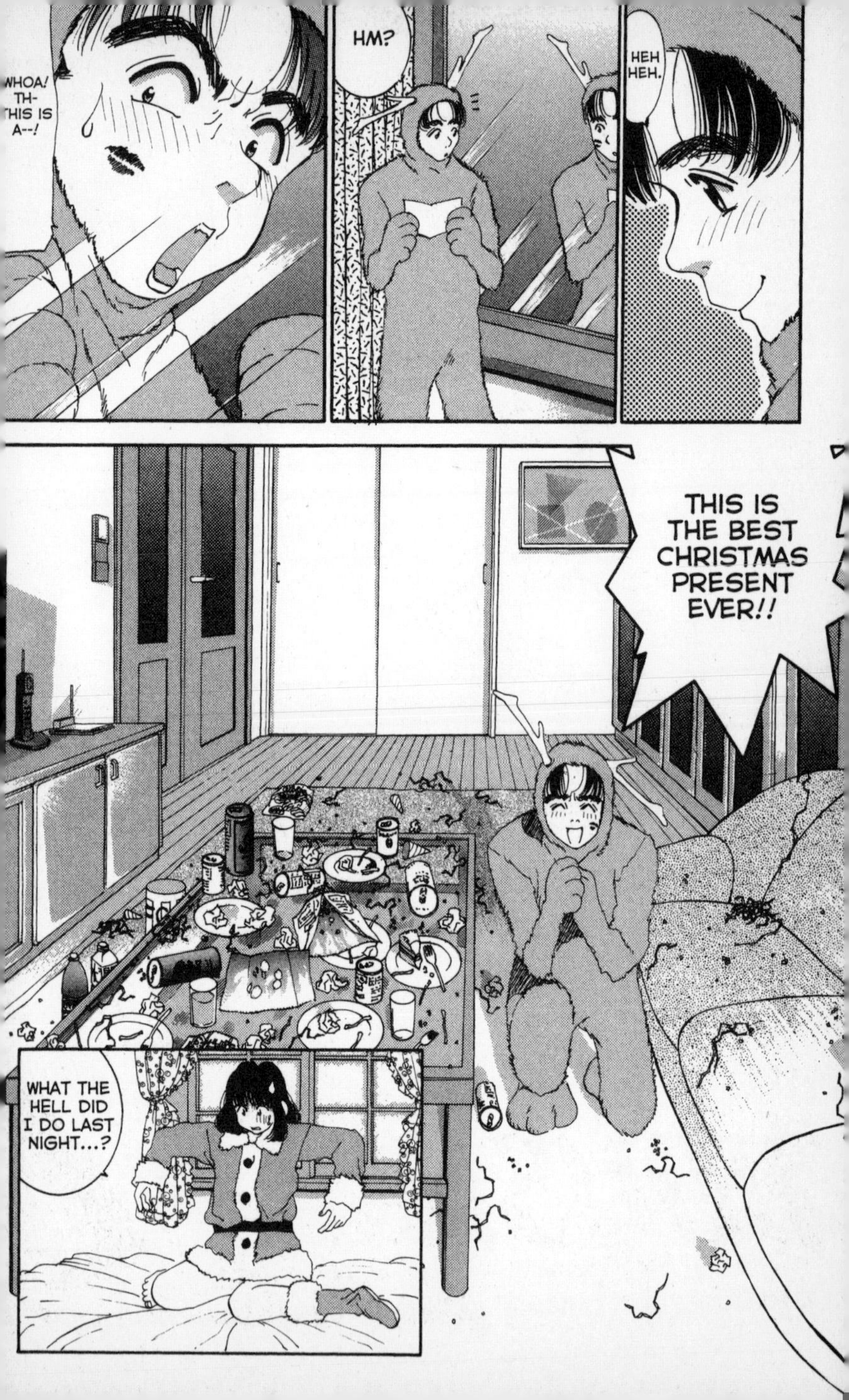
HEH HEH.
HM?
WHOA! TH-THIS IS A--!
THIS IS THE BEST CHRISTMAS PRESENT EVER!!
WHAT THE HELL DID I DO LAST NIGHT...?

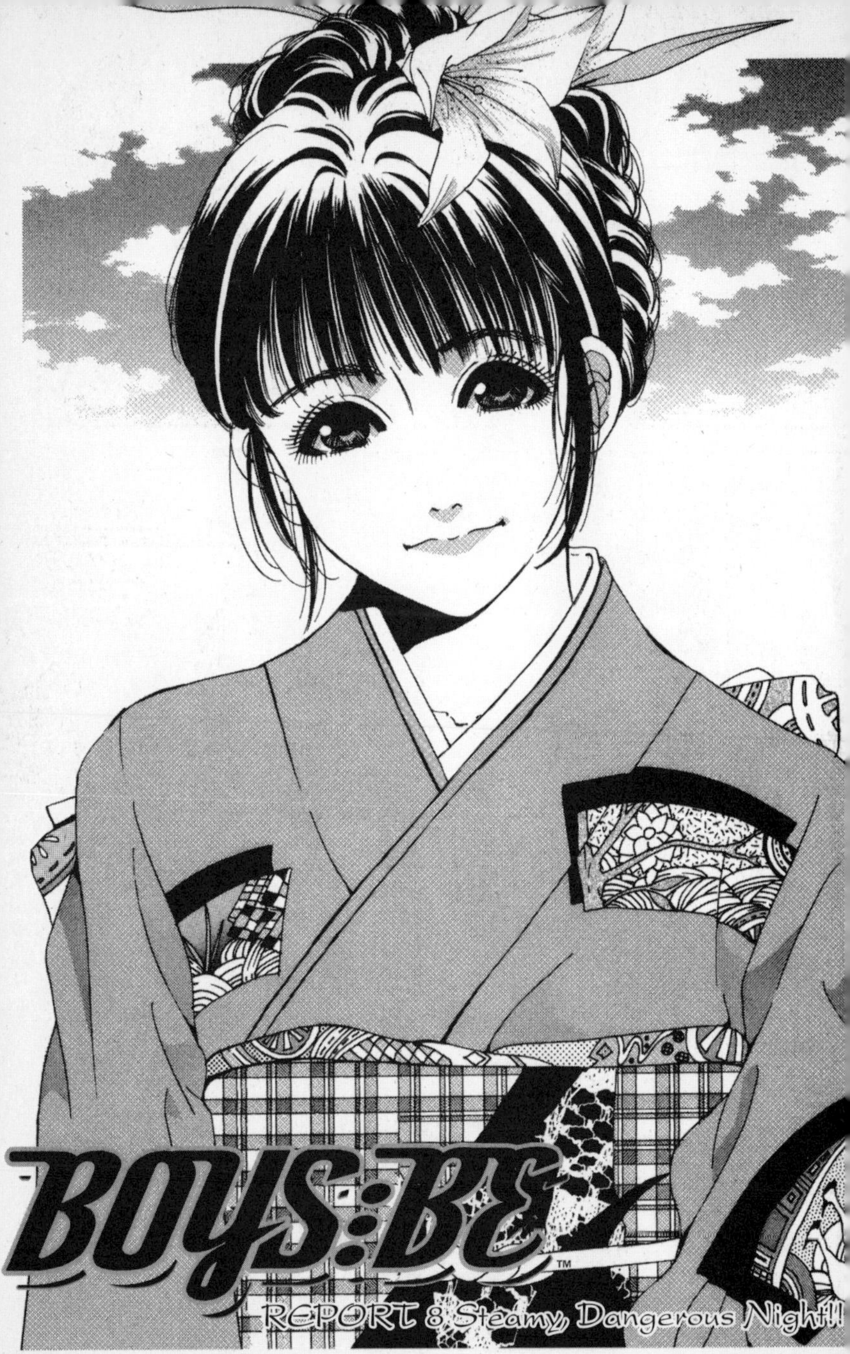
BOYS BE...™
REPORT 8 Steamy, Dangerous Night!!

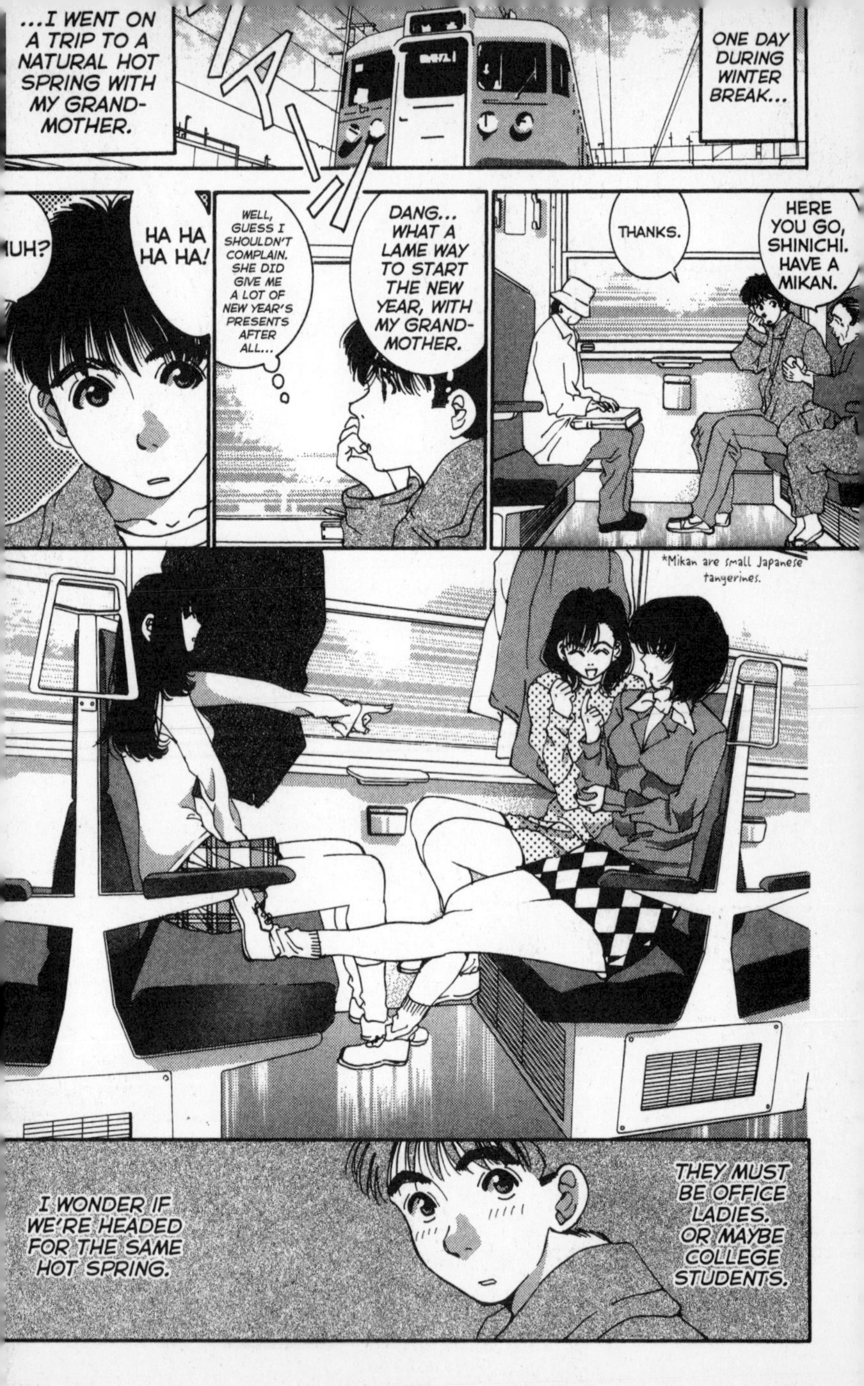
ONE DAY DURING WINTER BREAK...
...I WENT ON A TRIP TO A NATURAL HOT SPRING WITH MY GRAND-MOTHER.
HERE YOU GO, SHINICHI. HAVE A MIKAN.
THANKS.
DANG... WHAT A LAME WAY TO START THE NEW YEAR, WITH MY GRAND-MOTHER.
WELL, GUESS I SHOULDN'T COMPLAIN. SHE DID GIVE ME A LOT OF NEW YEAR'S PRESENTS AFTER ALL...
HA HA HA HA!
HUH?
*Mikan are small Japanese tangerines.
THEY MUST BE OFFICE LADIES. OR MAYBE COLLEGE STUDENTS.
I WONDER IF WE'RE HEADED FOR THE SAME HOT SPRING.

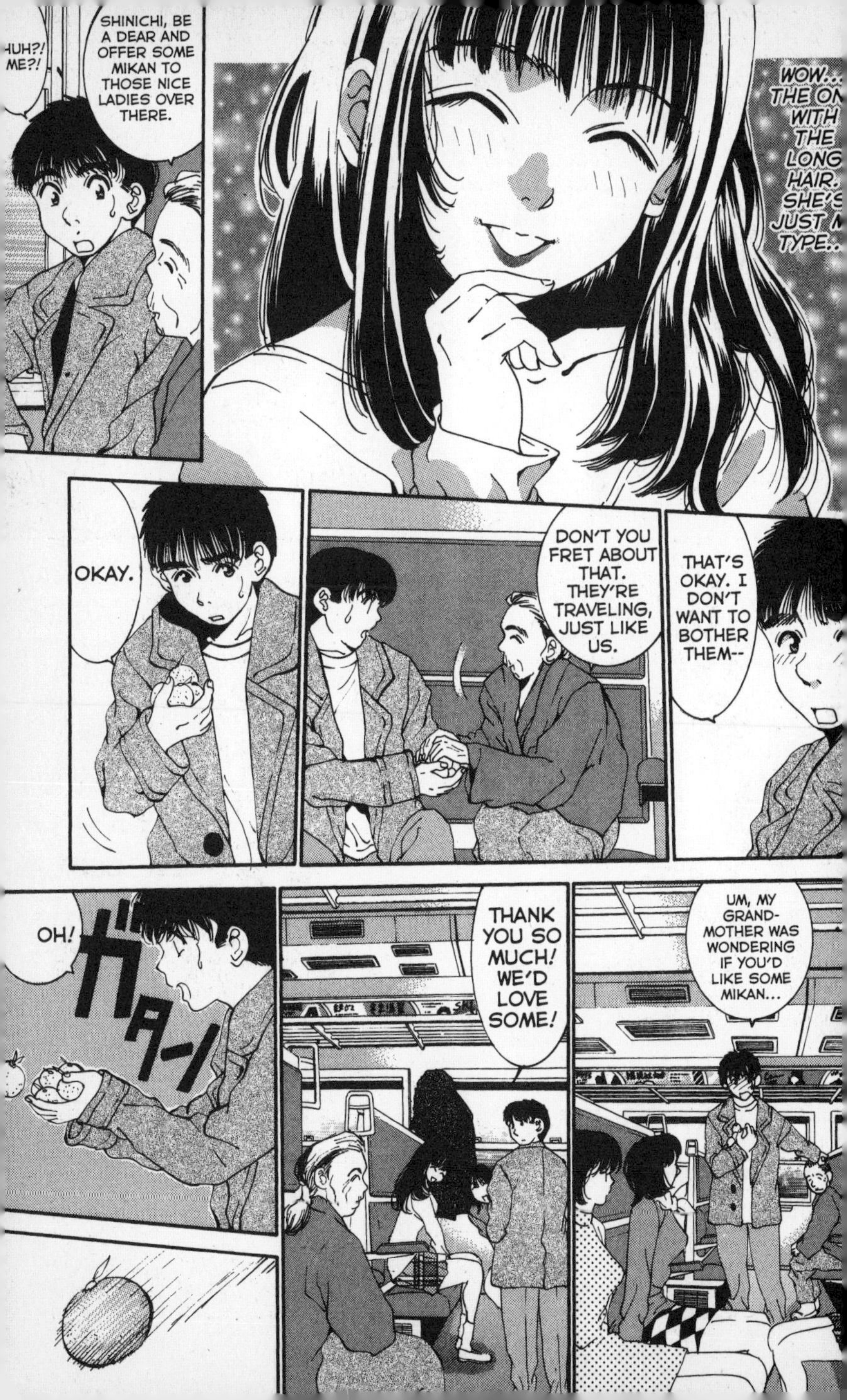
WOW... THE ON WITH THE LONG HAIR. SHE'S JUST M TYPE..
SHINICHI, BE A DEAR AND OFFER SOME MIKAN TO THOSE NICE LADIES OVER THERE.
HUH?! ME?!
THAT'S OKAY. I DON'T WANT TO BOTHER THEM--
DON'T YOU FRET ABOUT THAT. THEY'RE TRAVELING, JUST LIKE US.
OKAY.
UM, MY GRANDMOTHER WAS WONDERING IF YOU'D LIKE SOME MIKAN...
THANK YOU SO MUCH! WE'D LOVE SOME!
OH!
ガターン

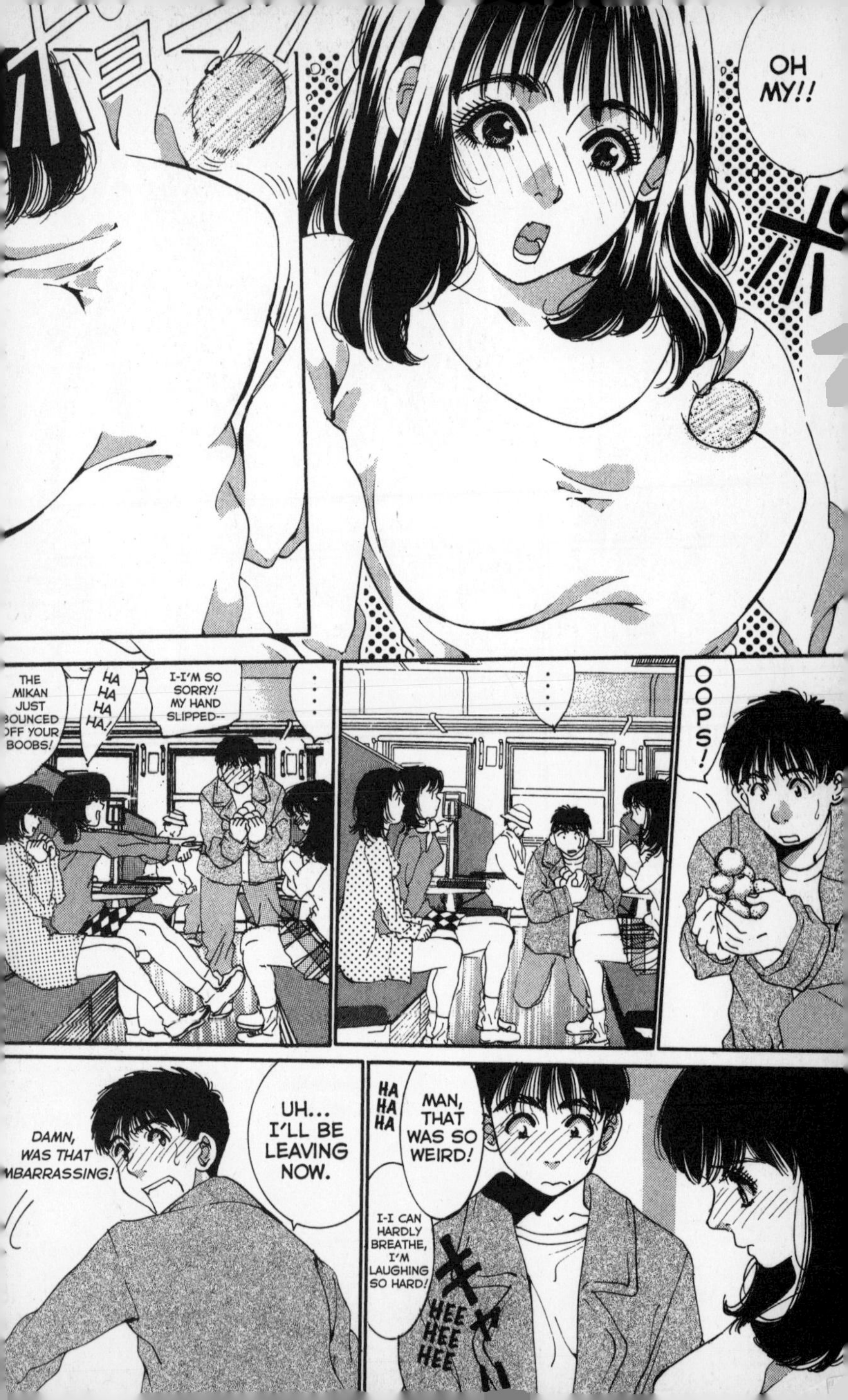
OH MY!!
OOPS!
...
...
I-I'M SO SORRY! MY HAND SLIPPED--
HA HA HA HA!
THE MIKAN JUST BOUNCED OFF YOUR BOOBS!
MAN, THAT WAS SO WEIRD!
HA HA HA HA
I-I CAN HARDLY BREATHE, I'M LAUGHING SO HARD!
HEE HEE HEE HEE
UH... I'LL BE LEAVING NOW.
DAMN, WAS THAT EMBARRASSING!

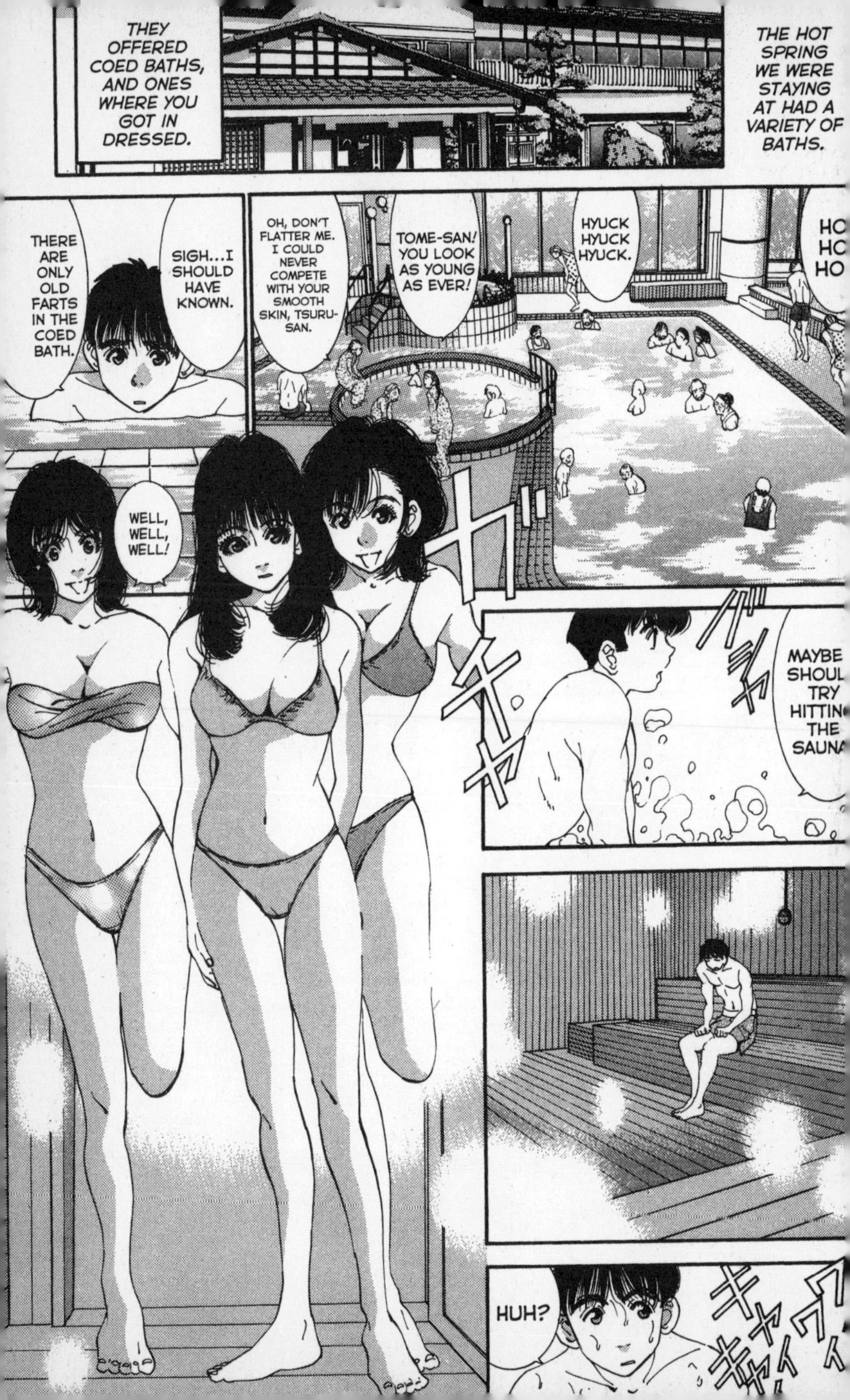
THE HOT SPRING WE WERE STAYING AT HAD A VARIETY OF BATHS.
THEY OFFERED COED BATHS, AND ONES WHERE YOU GOT IN DRESSED.
HO HO HO
HYUCK HYUCK HYUCK.
TOME-SAN! YOU LOOK AS YOUNG AS EVER!
OH, DON'T FLATTER ME. I COULD NEVER COMPETE WITH YOUR SMOOTH SKIN, TSURU-SAN.
SIGH...I SHOULD HAVE KNOWN.
THERE ARE ONLY OLD FARTS IN THE COED BATH.
MAYBE SHOUL TRY HITTIN THE SAUNA
HUH?
WELL, WELL, WELL!

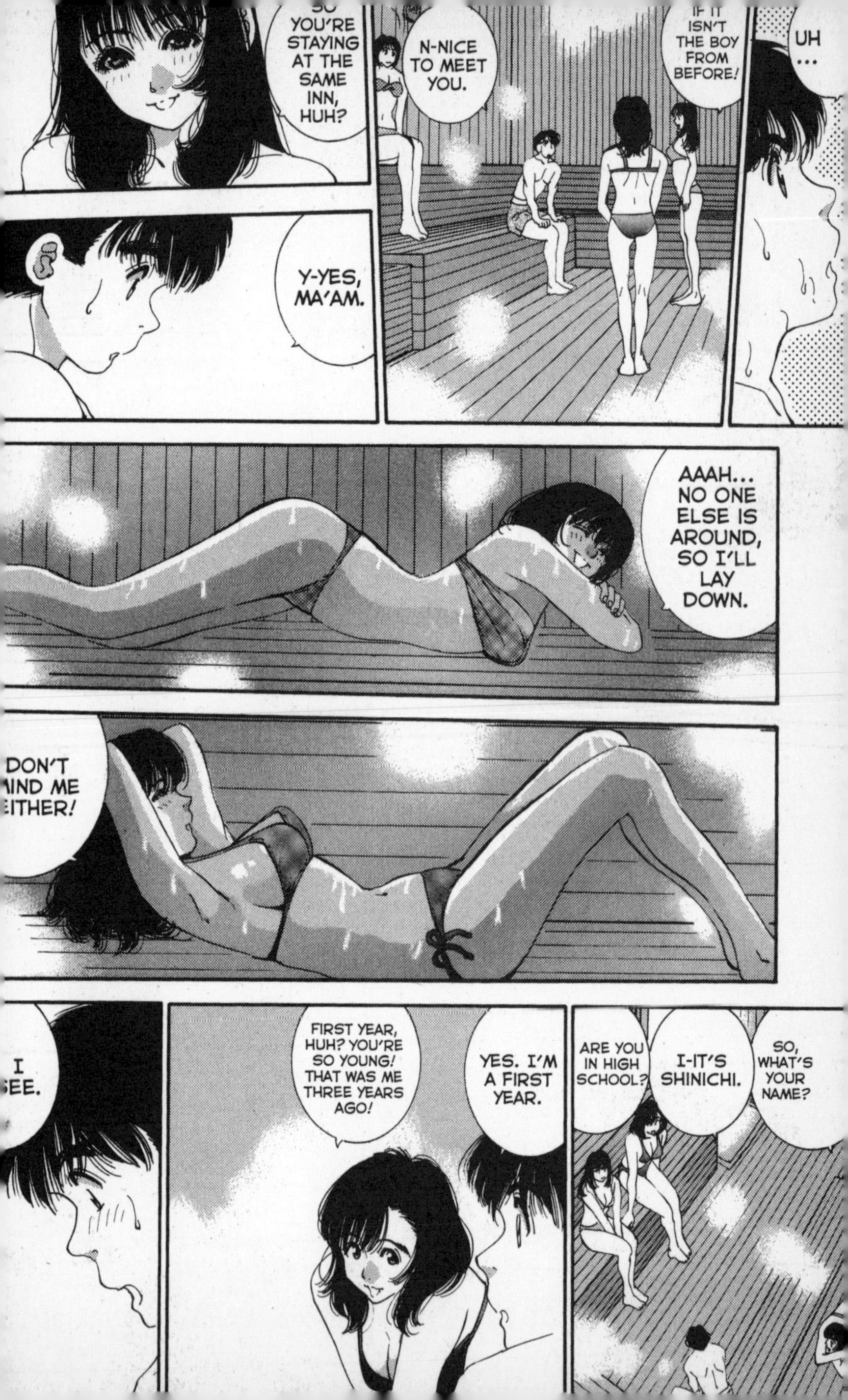
UH ...
IF IT ISN'T THE BOY FROM BEFORE!
N-NICE TO MEET YOU.
SO YOU'RE STAYING AT THE SAME INN, HUH?
Y-YES, MA'AM.
AAAH... NO ONE ELSE IS AROUND, SO I'LL LAY DOWN.
DON'T IND ME ITHER!
SO, WHAT'S YOUR NAME?
I-IT'S SHINICHI.
ARE YOU IN HIGH SCHOOL?
YES. I'M A FIRST YEAR.
FIRST YEAR, HUH? YOU'RE SO YOUNG! THAT WAS ME THREE YEARS AGO!
I EE.

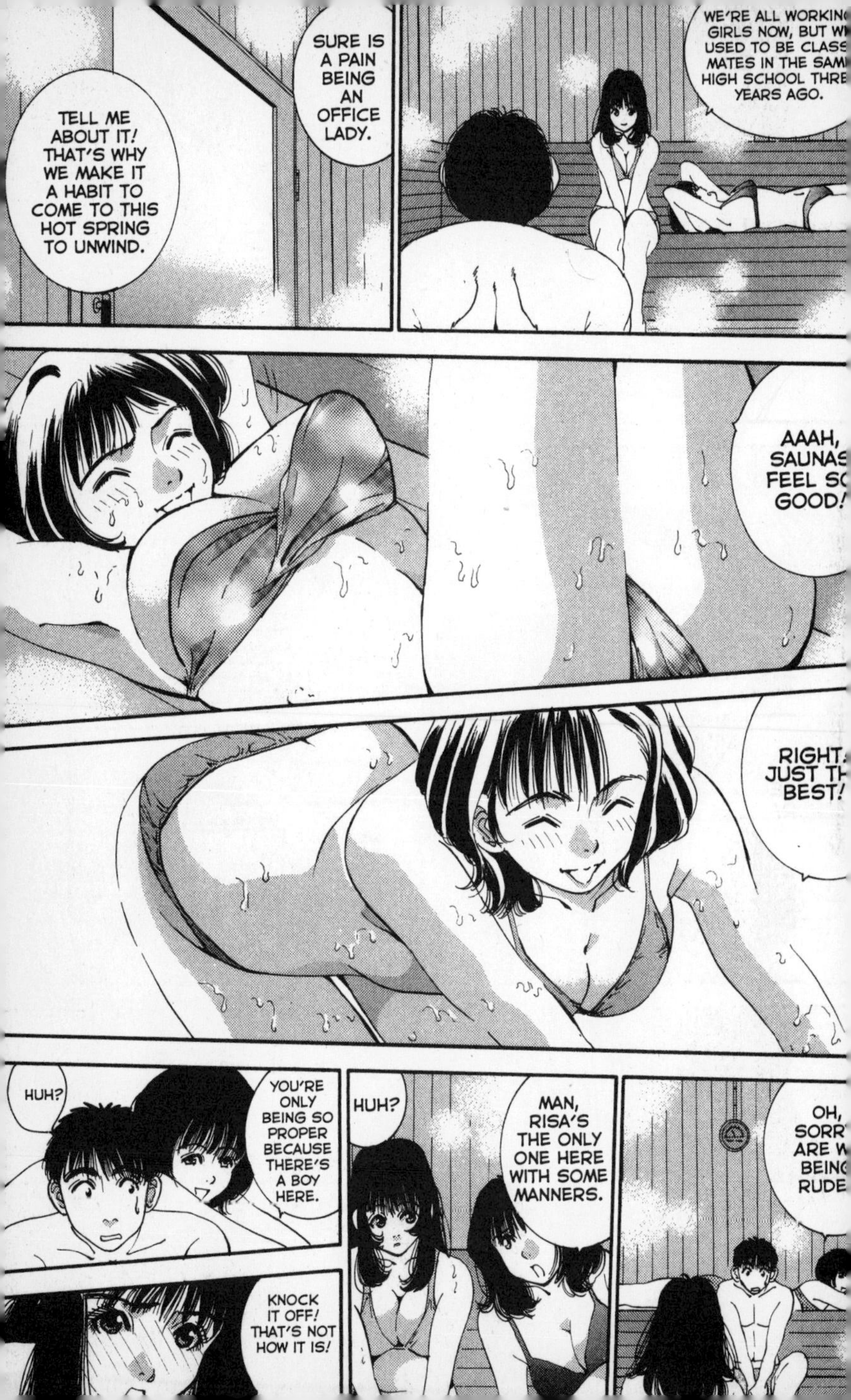
WE'RE ALL WORKIN GIRLS NOW, BUT W USED TO BE CLASS MATES IN THE SAM HIGH SCHOOL THRE YEARS AGO.
SURE IS A PAIN BEING AN OFFICE LADY.
TELL ME ABOUT IT! THAT'S WHY WE MAKE IT A HABIT TO COME TO THIS HOT SPRING TO UNWIND.
AAAH, SAUNAS FEEL S GOOD!
RIGHT. JUST TH BEST!
OH, SORR ARE W BEING RUDE
MAN, RISA'S THE ONLY ONE HERE WITH SOME MANNERS.
HUH?
YOU'RE ONLY BEING SO PROPER BECAUSE THERE'S A BOY HERE.
HUH?
KNOCK IT OFF! THAT'S NOT HOW IT IS!

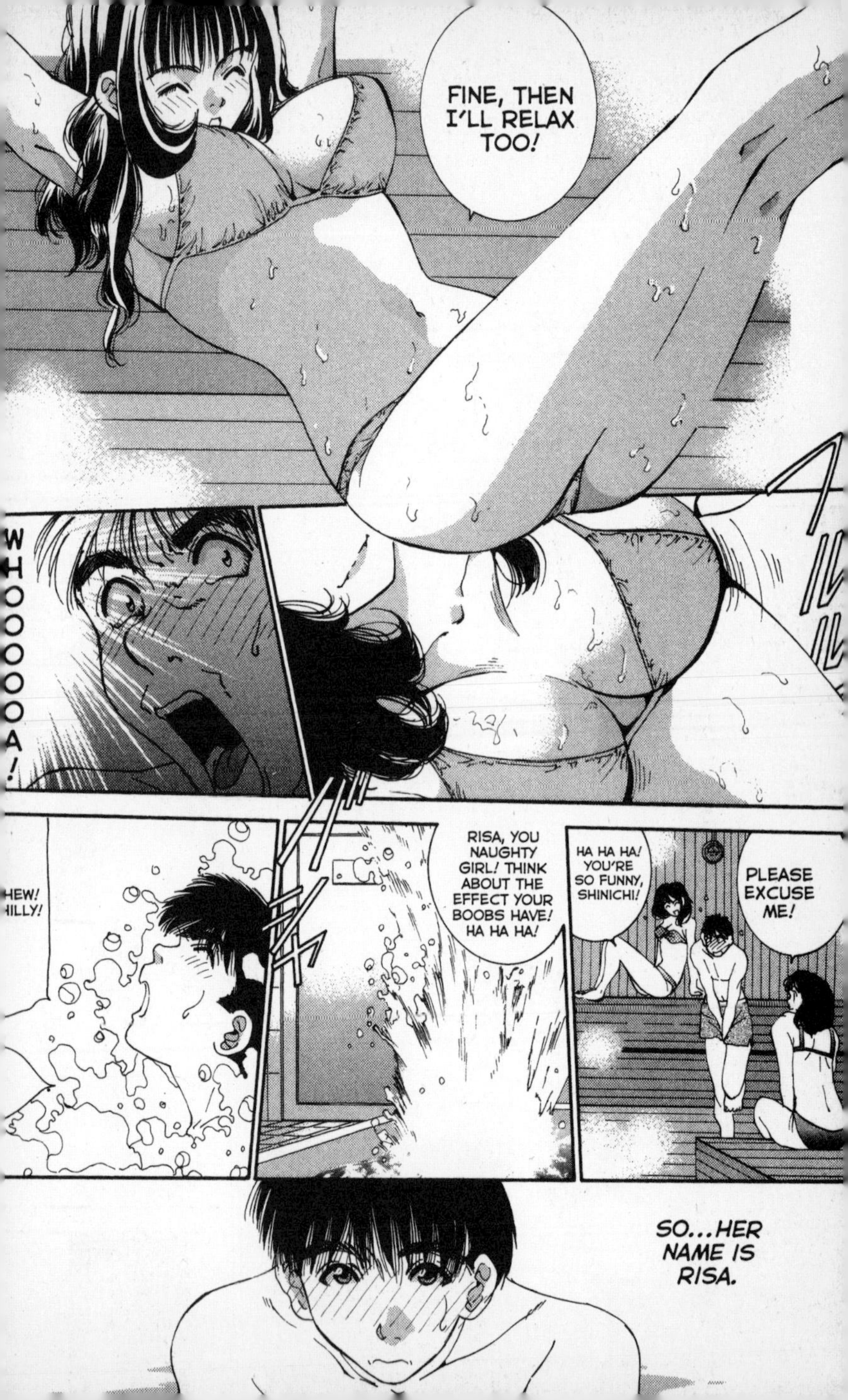
FINE, THEN I'LL RELAX TOO!
WHOOOOOOA!
PLEASE EXCUSE ME!
HA HA HA! YOU'RE SO FUNNY, SHINICHI!
RISA, YOU NAUGHTY GIRL! THINK ABOUT THE EFFECT YOUR BOOBS HAVE! HA HA HA!
HEW! HILLY!
SO...HER NAME IS RISA.

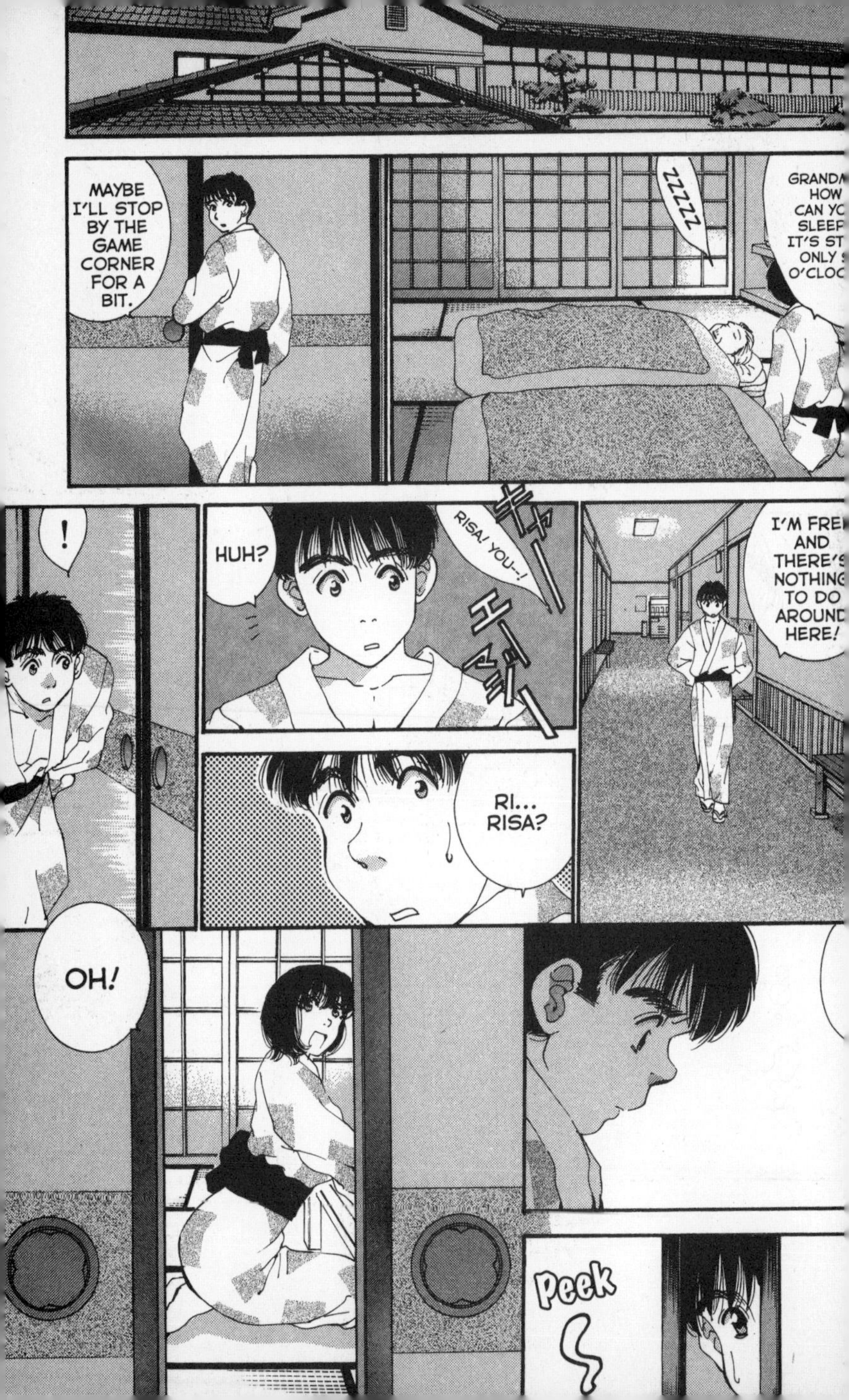
GRANDM
HOW
CAN YO
SLEEP
IT'S ST
ONLY
O'CLOC
ZZZZZ
MAYBE I'LL STOP BY THE GAME CORNER FOR A BIT.
I'M FRE
AND THERE'S NOTHING TO DO AROUND HERE!
RISA! YOU--!
HUH?
RI... RISA?
!
Peek
OH!

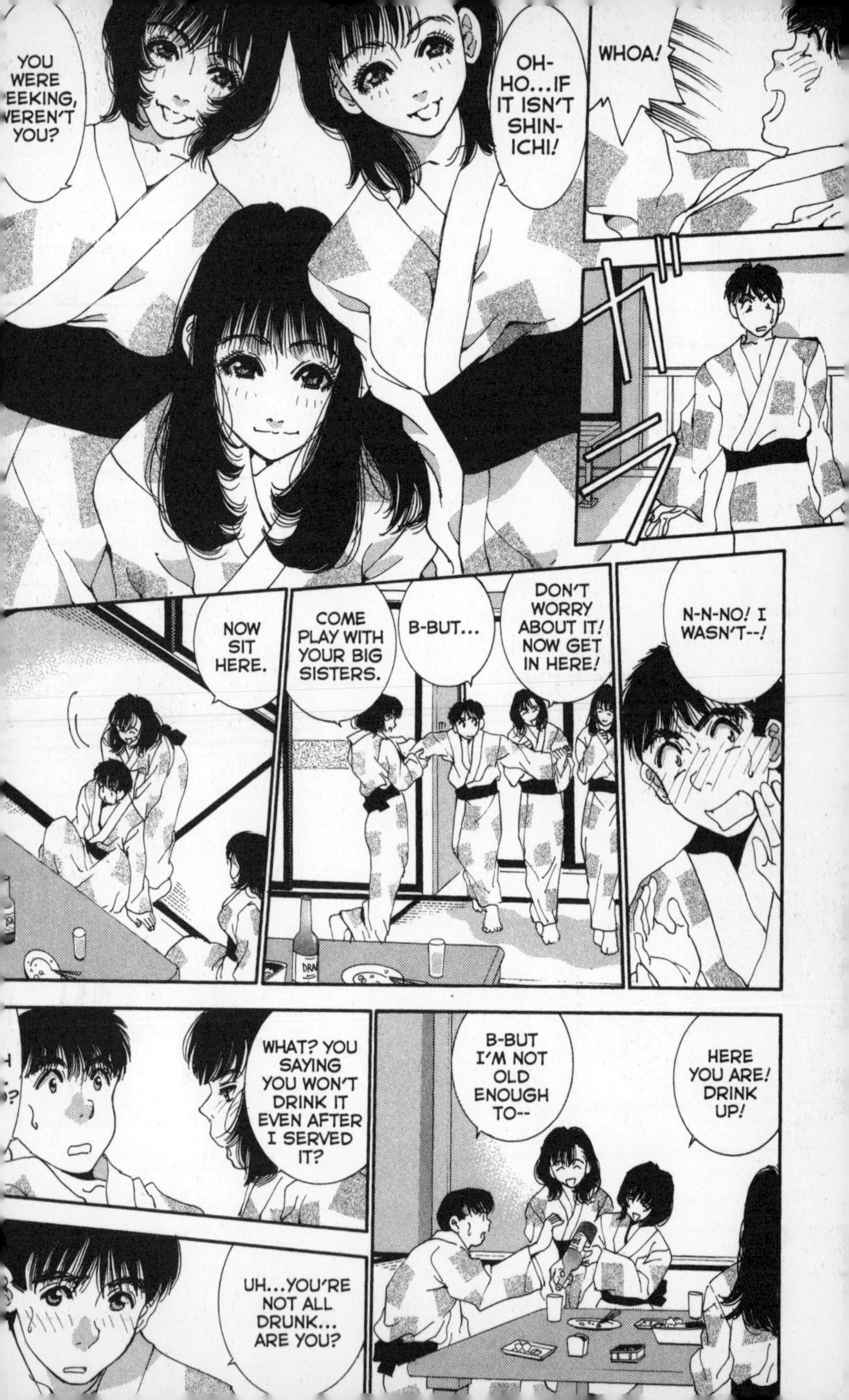
WHOA!
OH-HO...IF IT ISN'T SHIN-ICHI!
YOU WERE EEKING, VEREN'T YOU?
N-N-NO! I WASN'T--!
DON'T WORRY ABOUT IT! NOW GET IN HERE!
B-BUT...
COME PLAY WITH YOUR BIG SISTERS.
NOW SIT HERE.
HERE YOU ARE! DRINK UP!
B-BUT I'M NOT OLD ENOUGH TO--
WHAT? YOU SAYING YOU WON'T DRINK IT EVEN AFTER I SERVED IT?
UH...YOU'RE NOT ALL DRUNK... ARE YOU?

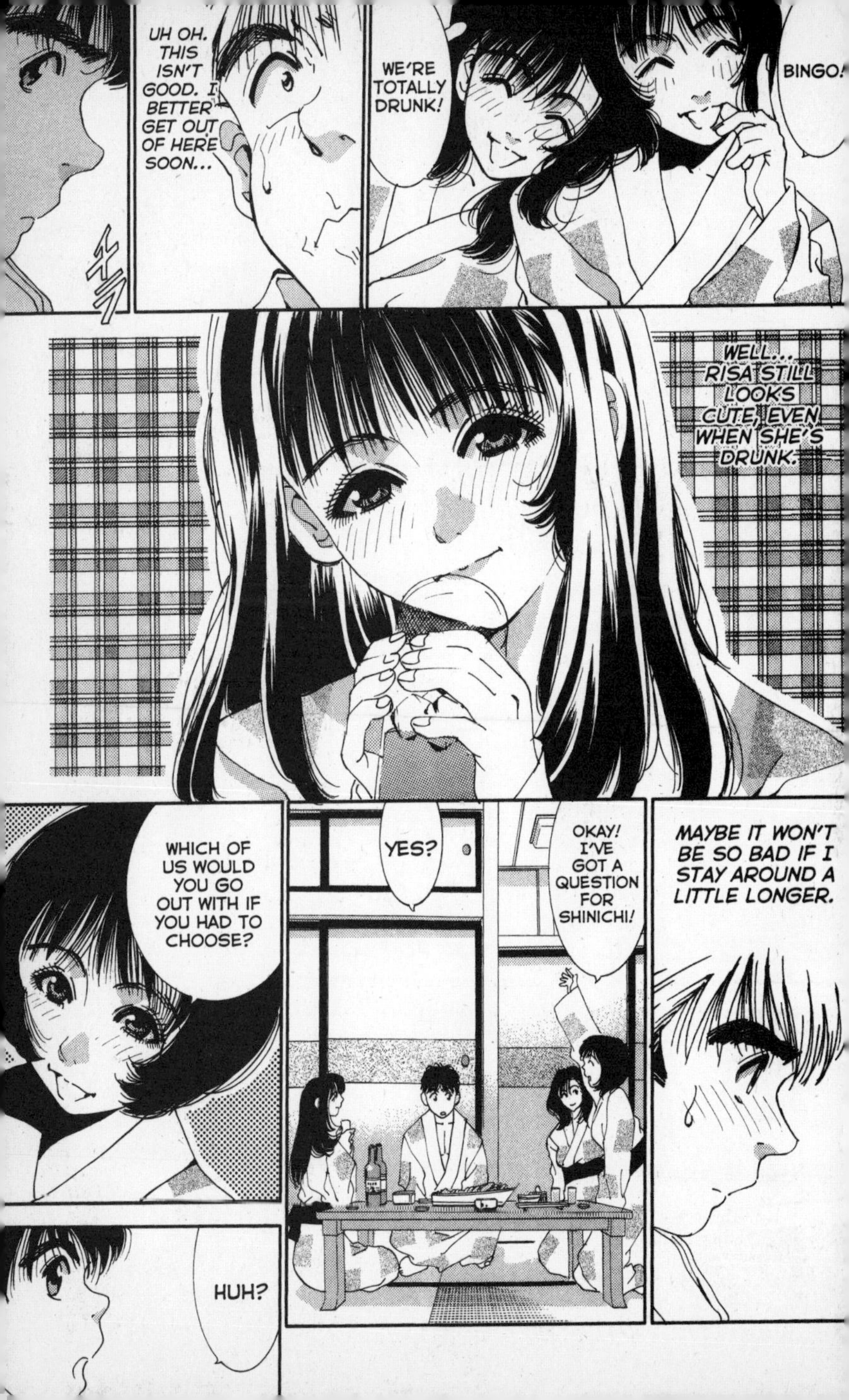

BINGO!
WE'RE TOTALLY DRUNK!
UH OH. THIS ISN'T GOOD. I BETTER GET OUT OF HERE SOON...
WELL... RISA STILL LOOKS CUTE, EVEN WHEN SHE'S DRUNK.
MAYBE IT WON'T BE SO BAD IF I STAY AROUND A LITTLE LONGER.
OKAY! I'VE GOT A QUESTION FOR SHINICHI!
YES?
WHICH OF US WOULD YOU GO OUT WITH IF YOU HAD TO CHOOSE?
HUH?

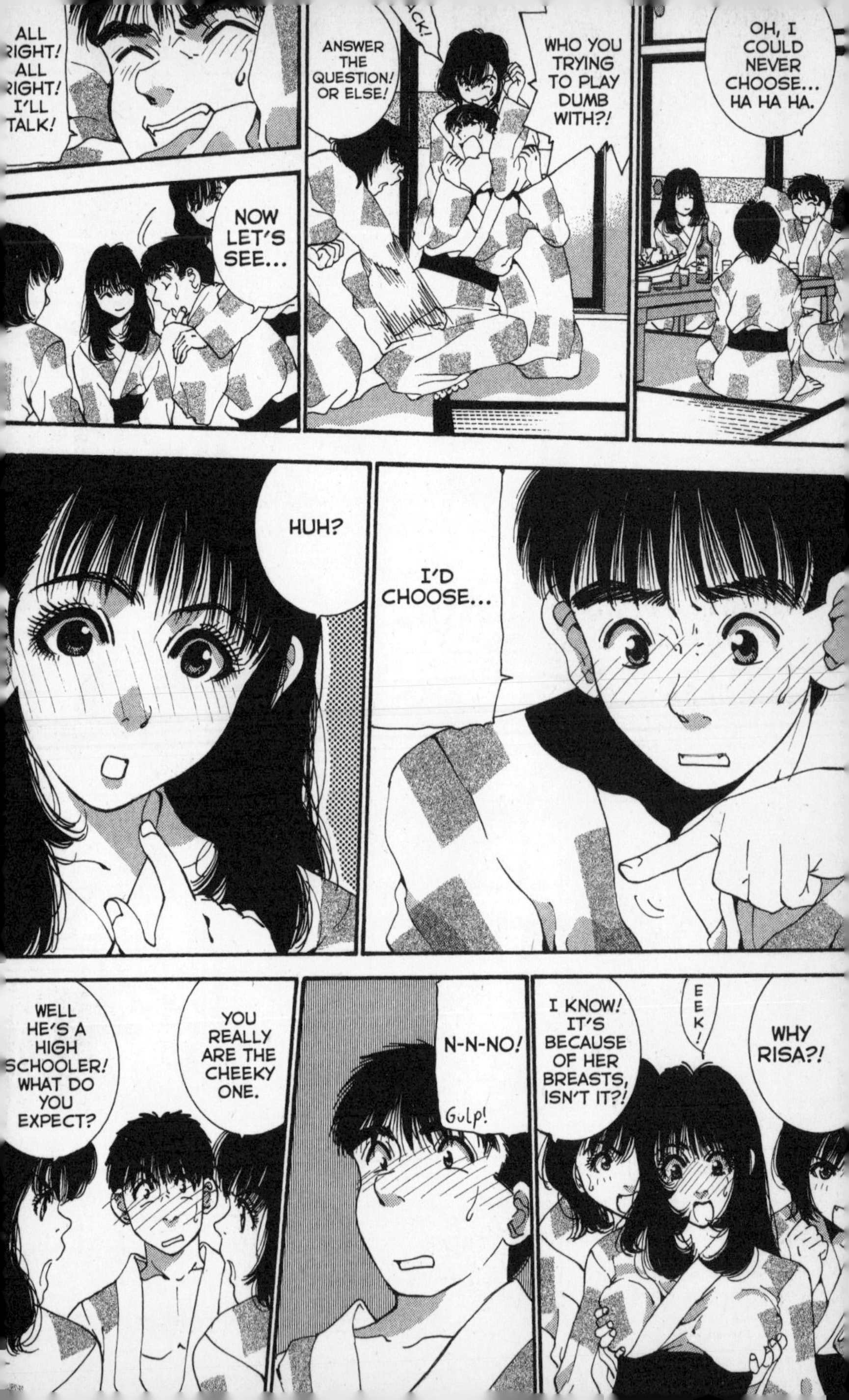
OH, I COULD NEVER CHOOSE... HA HA HA.
WHO YOU TRYING TO PLAY DUMB WITH?!
ANSWER THE QUESTION! OR ELSE!
ALL RIGHT! ALL RIGHT! I'LL TALK!
NOW LET'S SEE...
I'D CHOOSE...
HUH?
WHY RISA?!
EEK!
I KNOW! IT'S BECAUSE OF HER BREASTS, ISN'T IT?!
N-N-NO!
Gulp!
YOU REALLY ARE THE CHEEKY ONE.
WELL HE'S A HIGH SCHOOLER! WHAT DO YOU EXPECT?

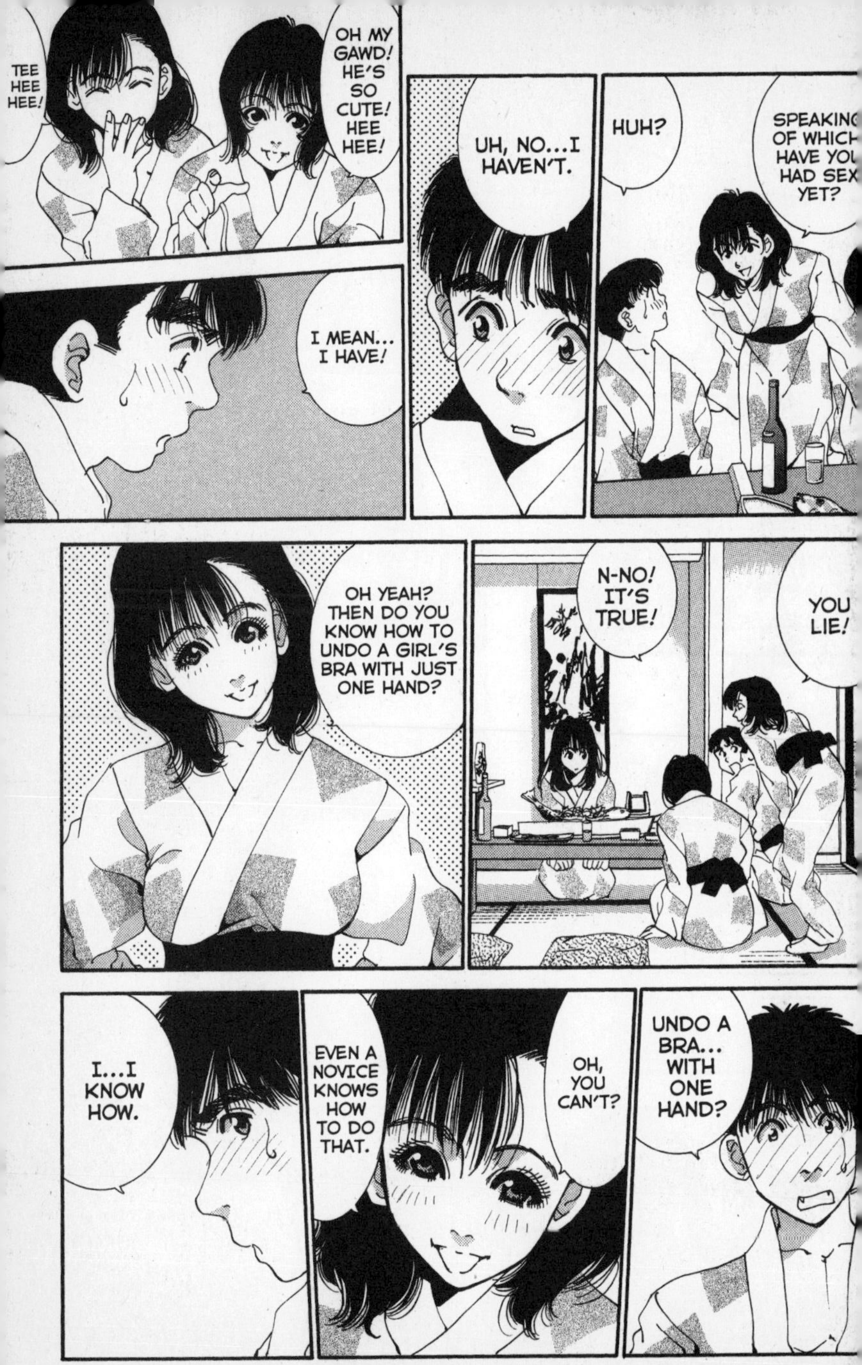
SPEAKING OF WHICH HAVE YOU HAD SEX YET?
HUH?
UH, NO...I HAVEN'T.
OH MY GAWD! HE'S SO CUTE! HEE HEE!
TEE HEE HEE!
I MEAN... I HAVE!
YOU LIE!
N-NO! IT'S TRUE!
OH YEAH? THEN DO YOU KNOW HOW TO UNDO A GIRL'S BRA WITH JUST ONE HAND?
UNDO A BRA... WITH ONE HAND?
OH, YOU CAN'T?
EVEN A NOVICE KNOWS HOW TO DO THAT.
I...I KNOW HOW.

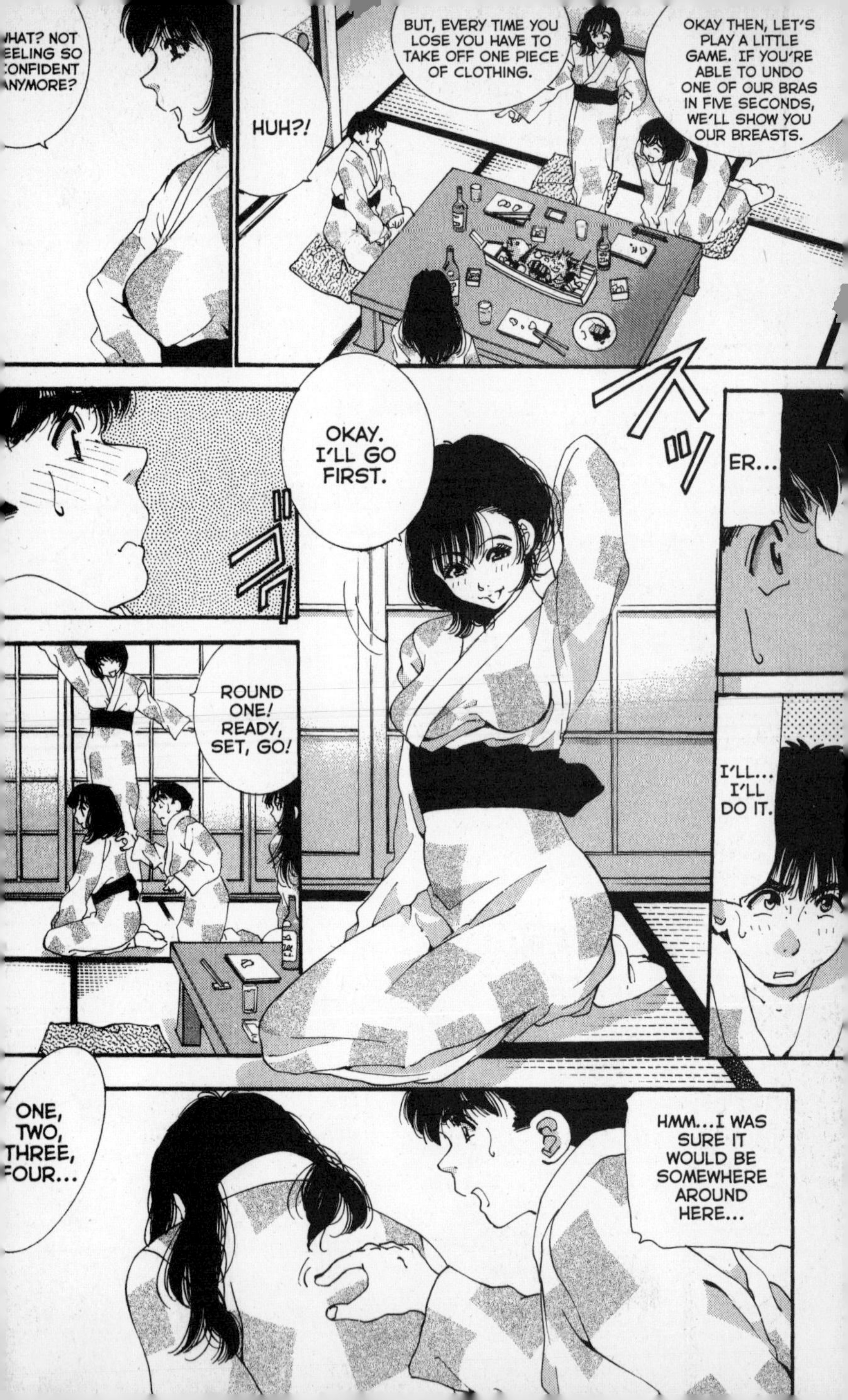
OKAY THEN, LET'S PLAY A LITTLE GAME. IF YOU'RE ABLE TO UNDO ONE OF OUR BRAS IN FIVE SECONDS, WE'LL SHOW YOU OUR BREASTS.
BUT, EVERY TIME YOU LOSE YOU HAVE TO TAKE OFF ONE PIECE OF CLOTHING.
HUH?!
WHAT? NOT FEELING SO CONFIDENT ANYMORE?
ER...
I'LL... I'LL DO IT.
OKAY. I'LL GO FIRST.
ROUND ONE! READY, SET, GO!
HMM...I WAS SURE IT WOULD BE SOMEWHERE AROUND HERE...
ONE, TWO, THREE, FOUR...

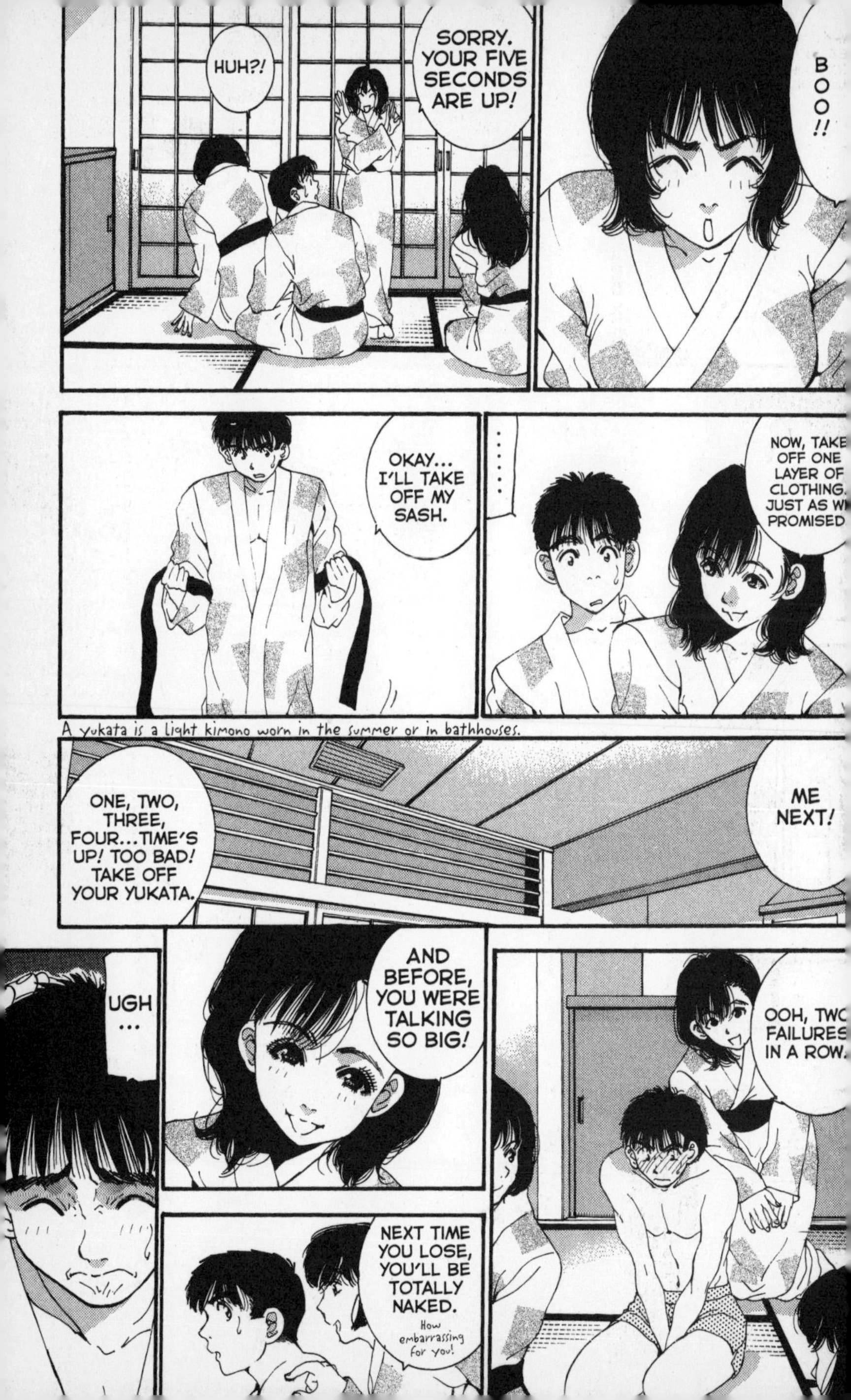
BOO!!
SORRY. YOUR FIVE SECONDS ARE UP!
HUH?!
NOW, TAKE OFF ONE LAYER OF CLOTHING. JUST AS W PROMISED
......
OKAY... I'LL TAKE OFF MY SASH.
A yukata is a light kimono worn in the summer or in bathhouses.
ME NEXT!
ONE, TWO, THREE, FOUR...TIME'S UP! TOO BAD! TAKE OFF YOUR YUKATA.
OOH, TWO FAILURES IN A ROW.
AND BEFORE, YOU WERE TALKING SO BIG!
NEXT TIME YOU LOSE, YOU'LL BE TOTALLY NAKED.
How embarrassing for you!
UGH ...

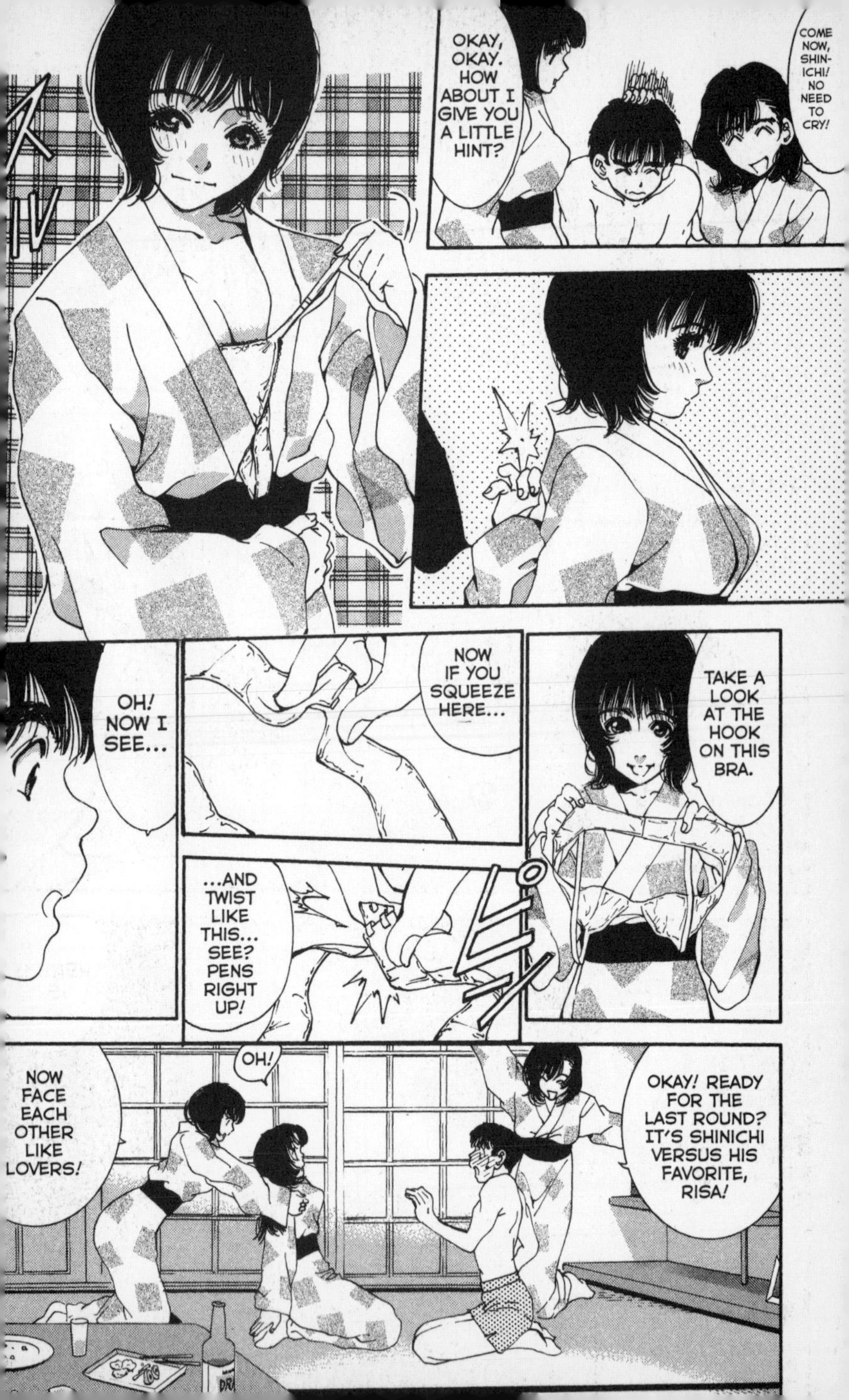
COME NOW, SHINICHI! NO NEED TO CRY!
OKAY, OKAY. HOW ABOUT I GIVE YOU A LITTLE HINT?
TAKE A LOOK AT THE HOOK ON THIS BRA.
NOW IF YOU SQUEEZE HERE...
...AND TWIST LIKE THIS... SEE? PENS RIGHT UP!
OH! NOW I SEE...
OKAY! READY FOR THE LAST ROUND? IT'S SHINICHI VERSUS HIS FAVORITE, RISA!
OH!
NOW FACE EACH OTHER LIKE LOVERS!

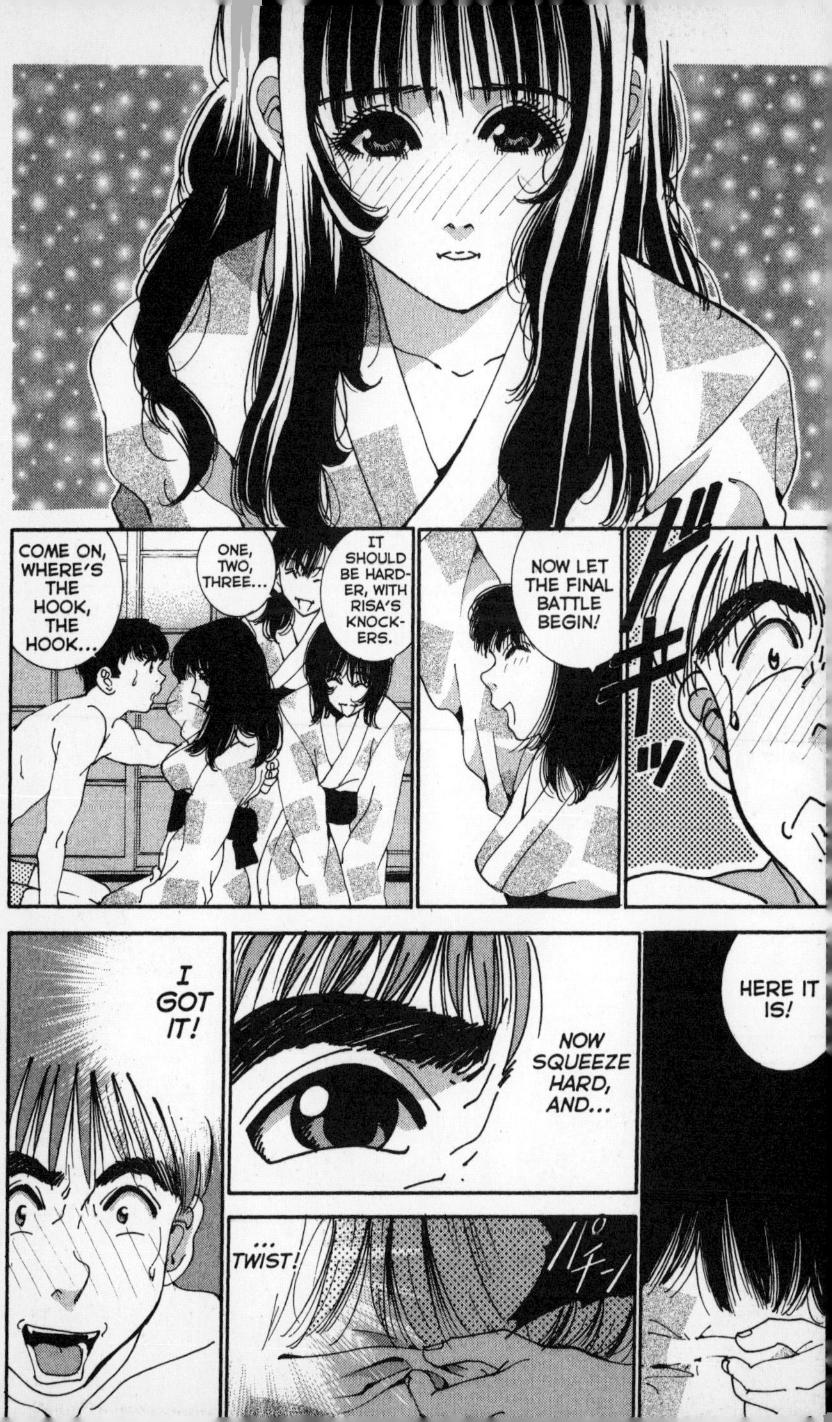
NOW LET THE FINAL BATTLE BEGIN!
IT SHOULD BE HARDER, WITH RISA'S KNOCKERS.
ONE, TWO, THREE...
COME ON, WHERE'S THE HOOK, THE HOOK...
HERE IT IS!
NOW SQUEEZE HARD, AND...
...TWIST!
パチーン
I GOT IT!

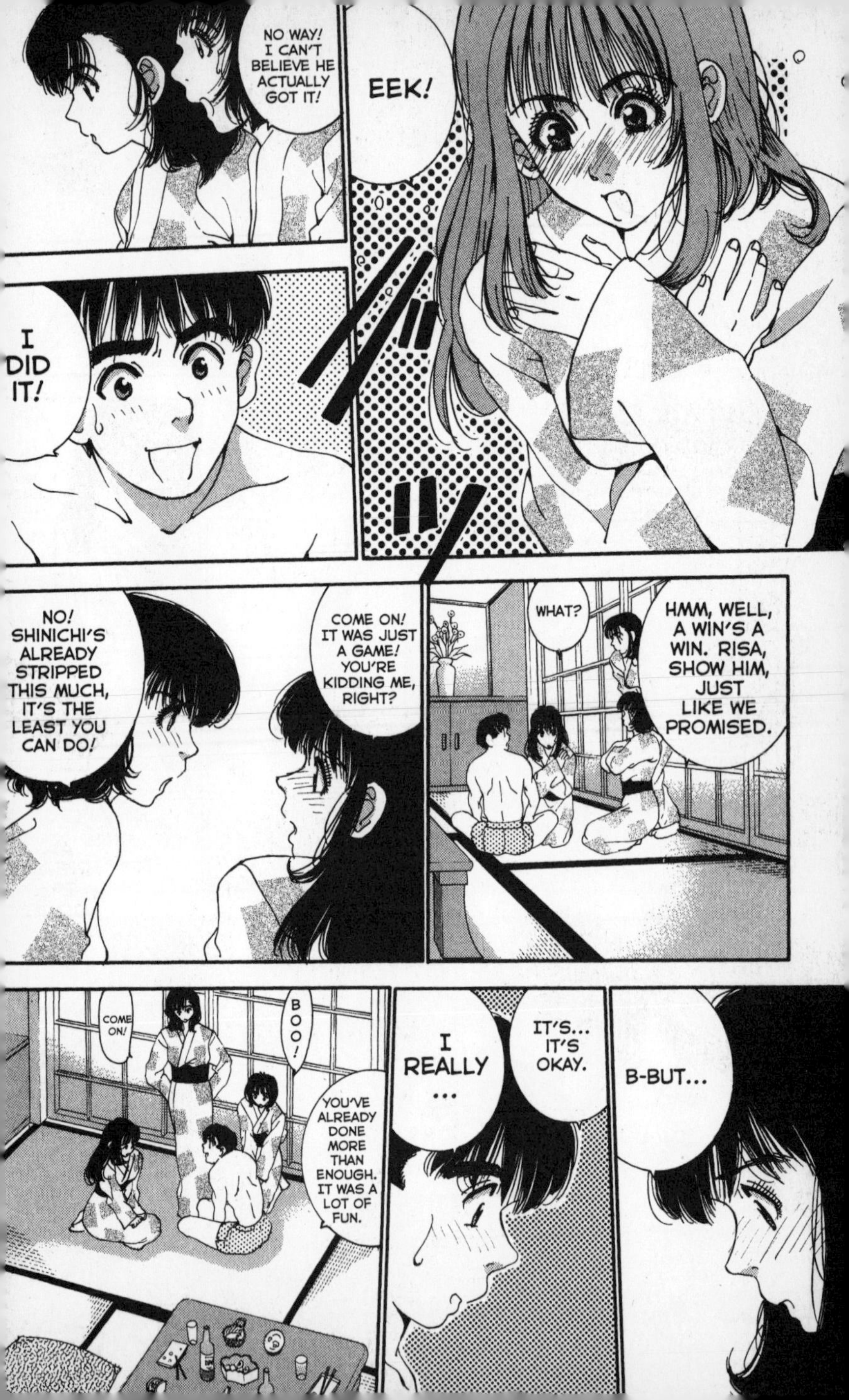
EEK!
NO WAY! I CAN'T BELIEVE HE ACTUALLY GOT IT!
I DID IT!
HMM, WELL, A WIN'S A WIN. RISA, SHOW HIM, JUST LIKE WE PROMISED.
WHAT?
COME ON! IT WAS JUST A GAME! YOU'RE KIDDING ME, RIGHT?
NO! SHINICHI'S ALREADY STRIPPED THIS MUCH, IT'S THE LEAST YOU CAN DO!
B-BUT...
IT'S... IT'S OKAY.
I REALLY ...
BOO!
COME ON!
YOU'VE ALREADY DONE MORE THAN ENOUGH. IT WAS A LOT OF FUN.

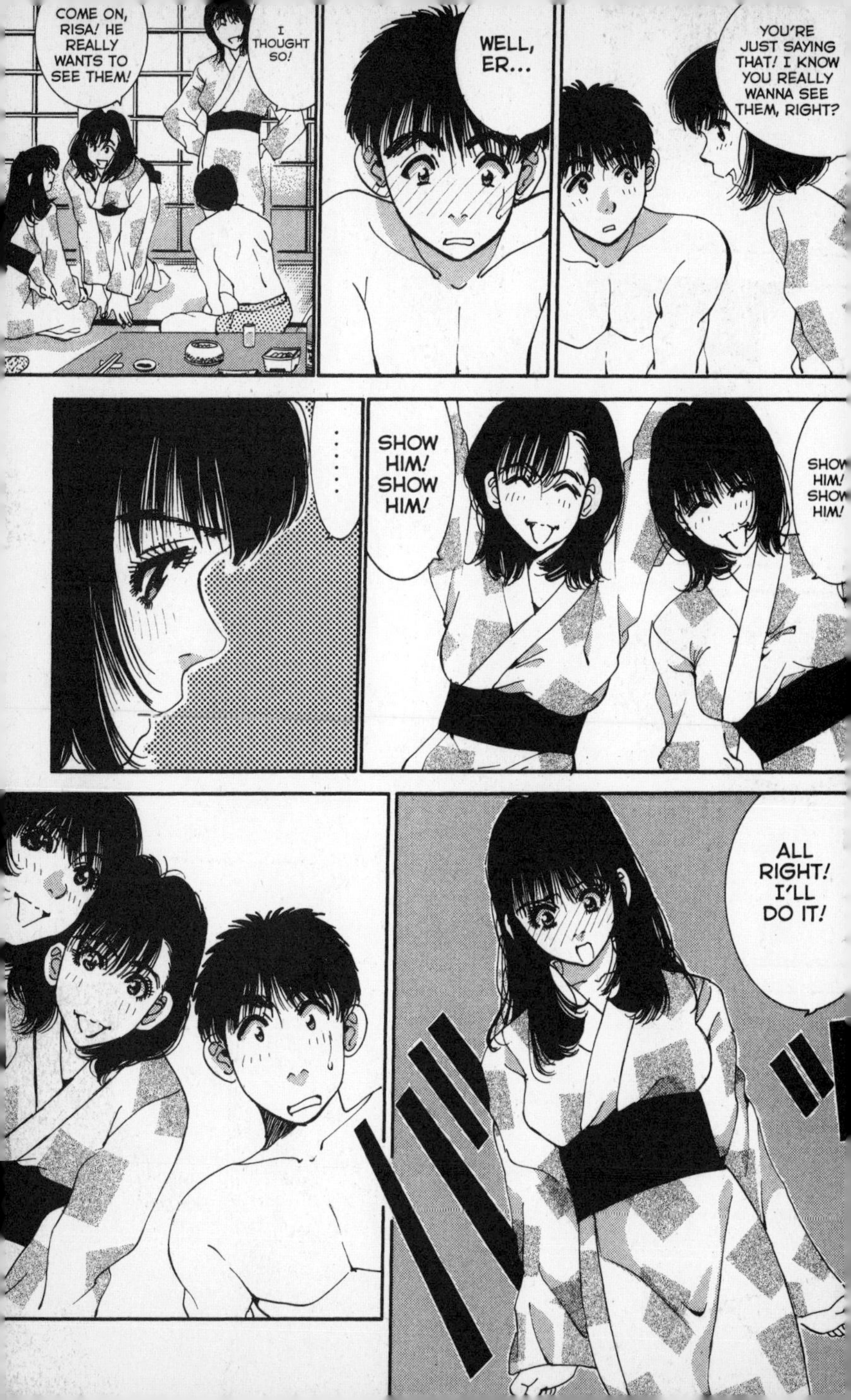
YOU'RE JUST SAYING THAT! I KNOW YOU REALLY WANNA SEE THEM, RIGHT?
WELL, ER...
I THOUGHT SO!
COME ON, RISA! HE REALLY WANTS TO SEE THEM!
SHOW HIM! SHOW HIM!
SHOW HIM! SHOW HIM!
......
ALL RIGHT! I'LL DO IT!

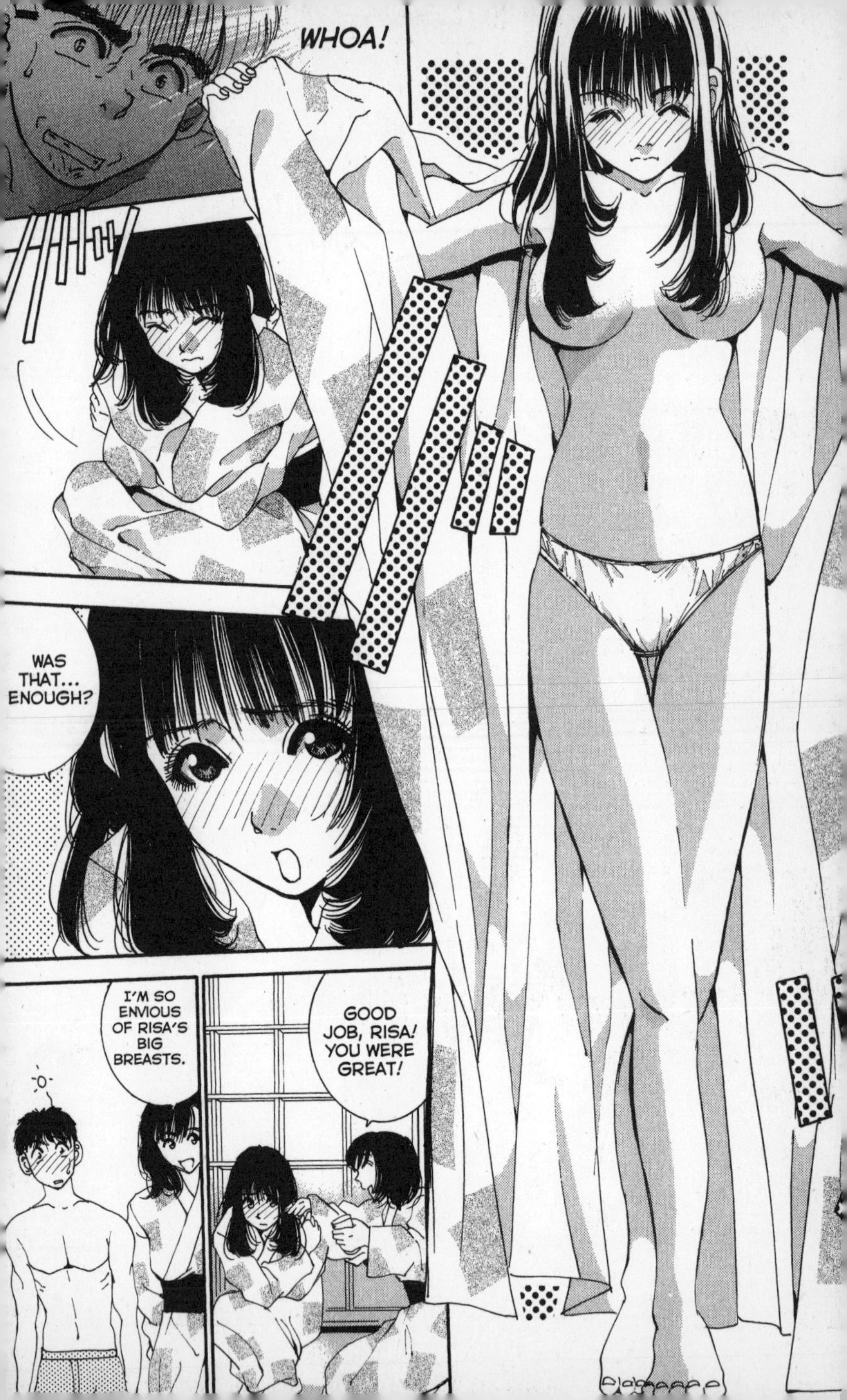
WHOA!
WAS THAT... ENOUGH?
GOOD JOB, RISA! YOU WERE GREAT!
I'M SO ENVIOUS OF RISA'S BIG BREASTS.

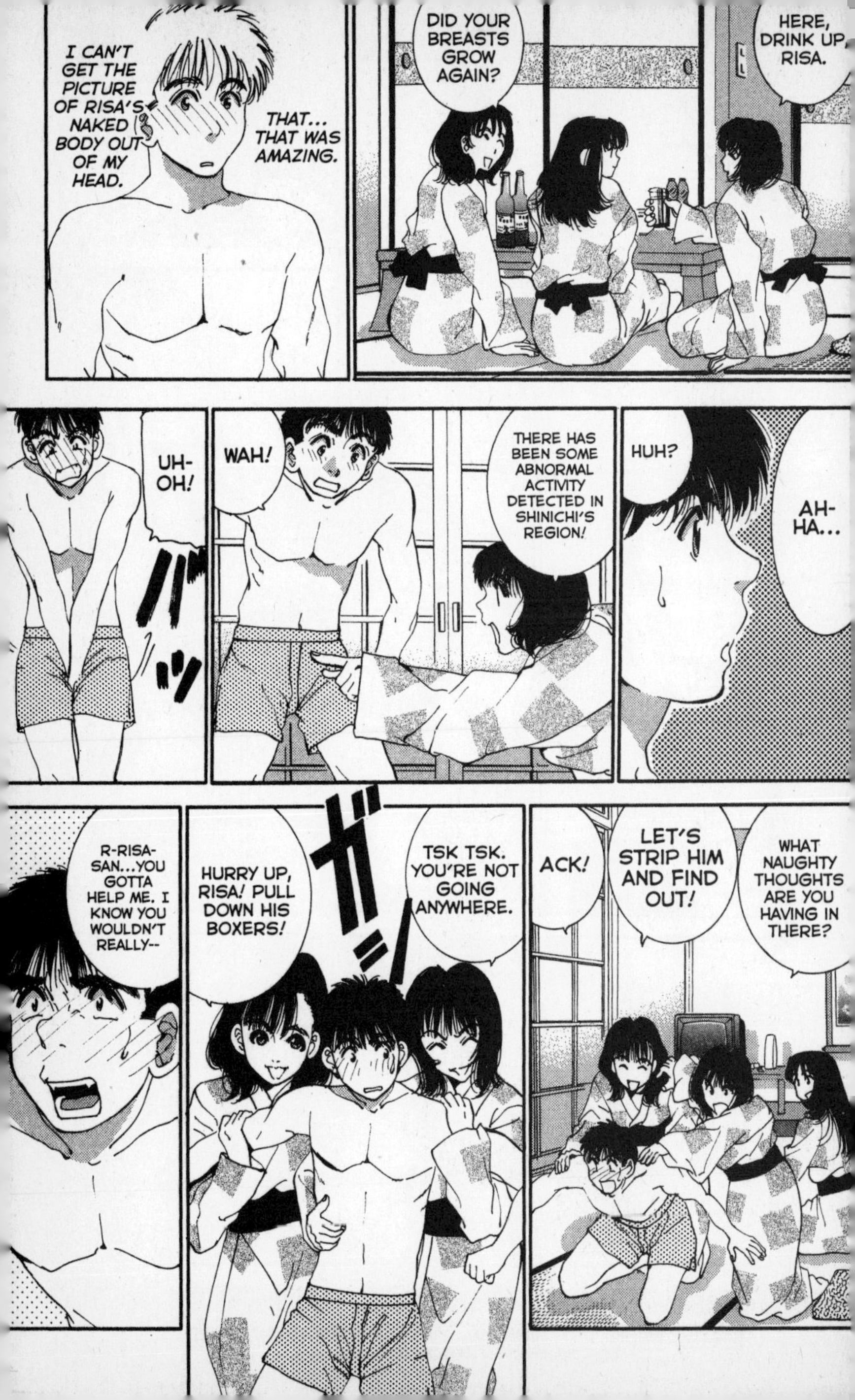
HERE, DRINK UP, RISA.
DID YOUR BREASTS GROW AGAIN?
THAT... THAT WAS AMAZING.
I CAN'T GET THE PICTURE OF RISA'S NAKED BODY OUT OF MY HEAD.
AH-HA...
HUH?
THERE HAS BEEN SOME ABNORMAL ACTIVITY DETECTED IN SHINICHI'S REGION!
WAH!
UH-OH!
バッ
WHAT NAUGHTY THOUGHTS ARE YOU HAVING IN THERE?
LET'S STRIP HIM AND FIND OUT!
ACK!
TSK TSK. YOU'RE NOT GOING ANYWHERE.
ガッ
HURRY UP, RISA! PULL DOWN HIS BOXERS!
R-RISA-SAN...YOU GOTTA HELP ME. I KNOW YOU WOULDN'T REALLY--

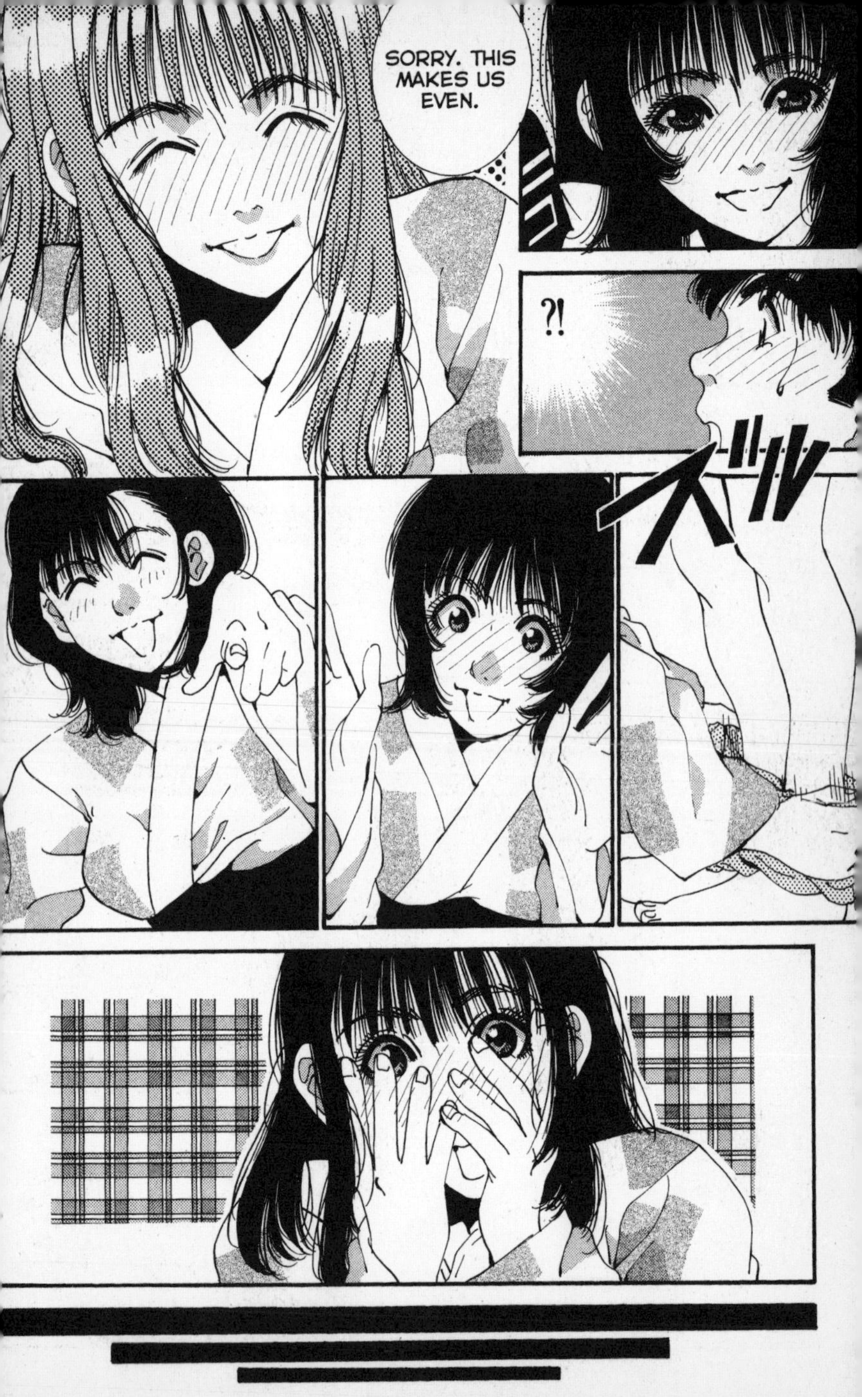
SORRY. THIS MAKES US EVEN.
?!
ズル

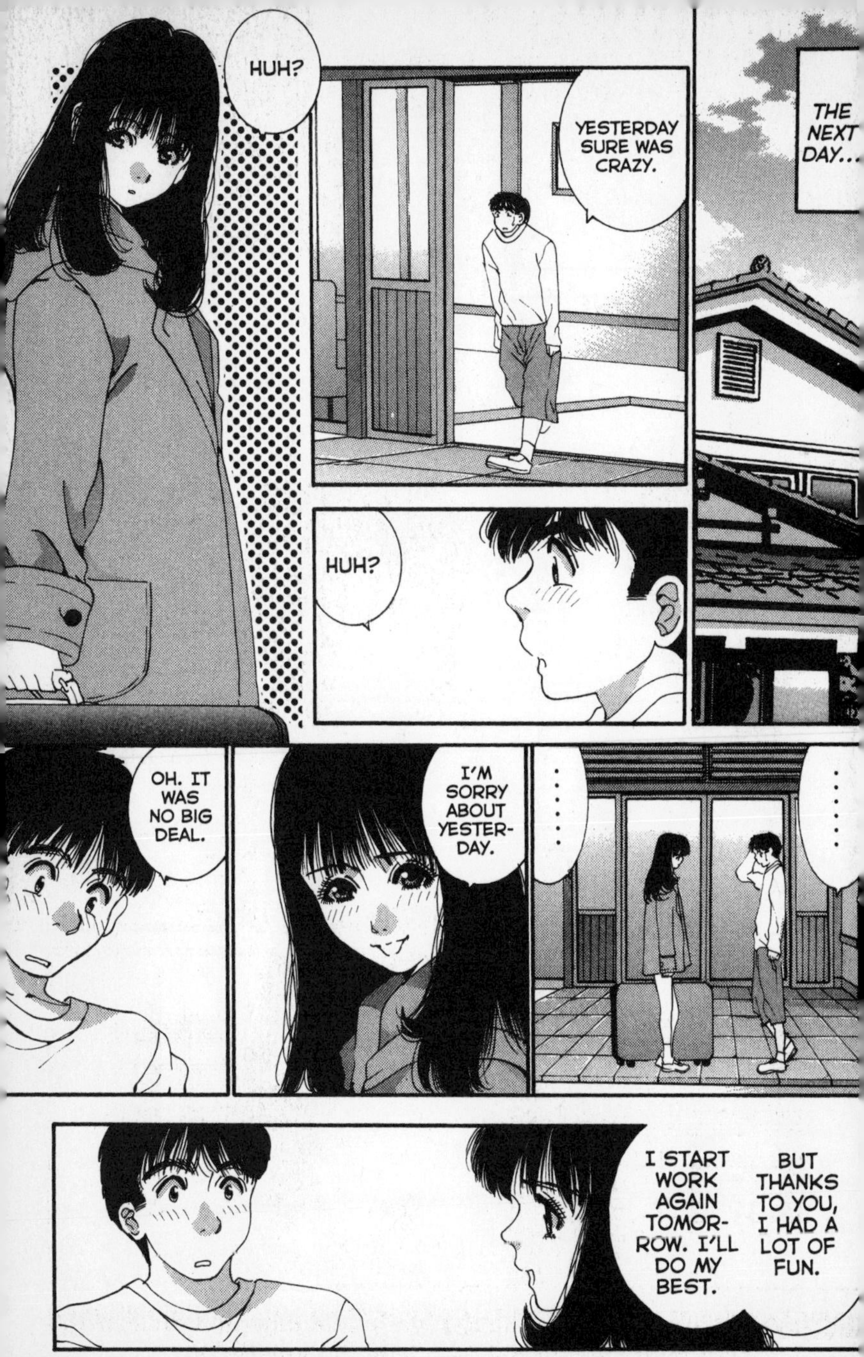
THE NEXT DAY...
YESTERDAY SURE WAS CRAZY.
HUH?
HUH?
......
......
I'M SORRY ABOUT YESTER-DAY.
OH. IT WAS NO BIG DEAL.
BUT THANKS TO YOU, I HAD A LOT OF FUN.
I START WORK AGAIN TOMOR-ROW. I'LL DO MY BEST.

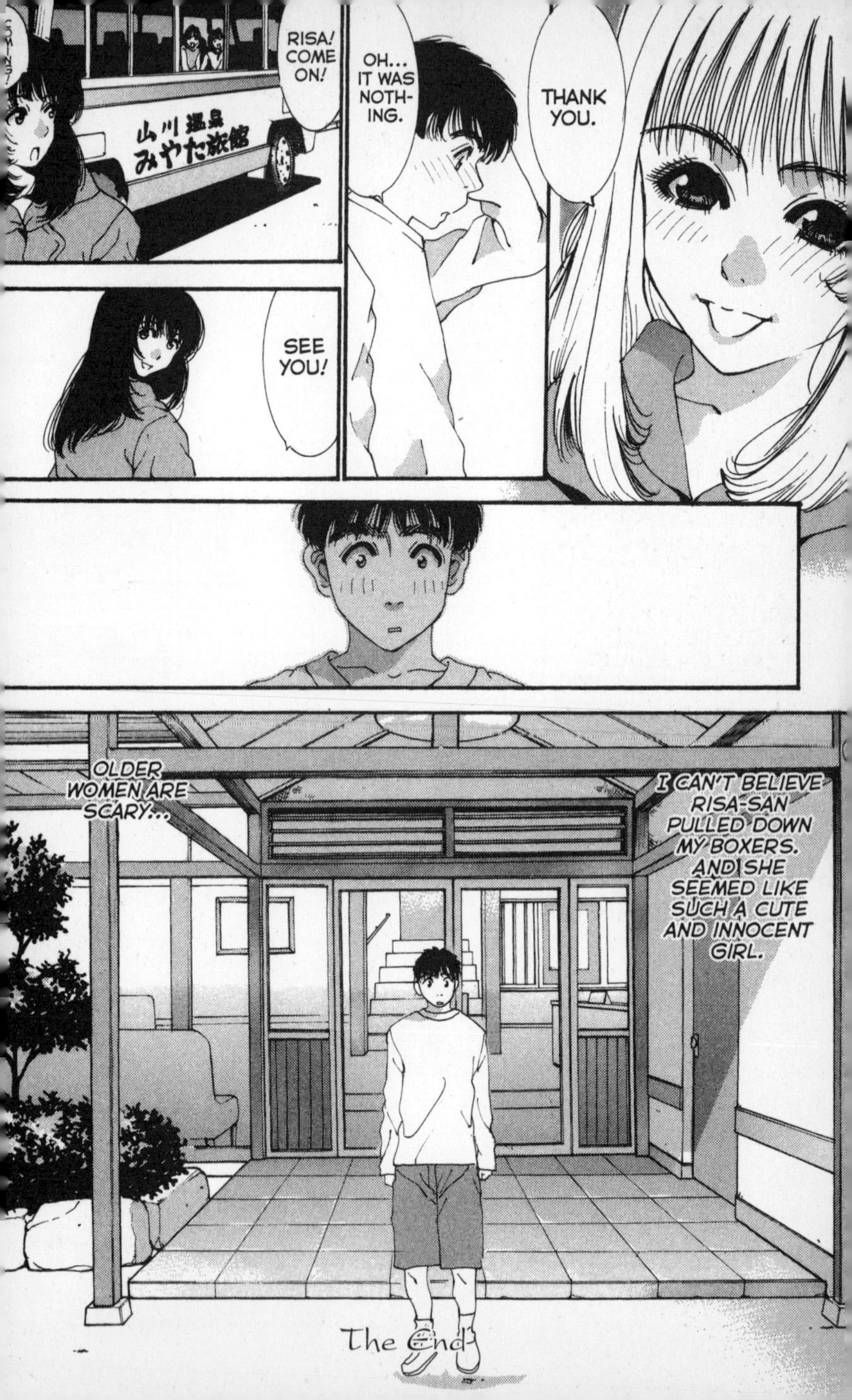
THANK YOU.
OH... IT WAS NOTHING.
RISA! COME ON!
COMING!
山川温泉
みやた旅館
SEE YOU!
I CAN'T BELIEVE RISA-SAN PULLED DOWN MY BOXERS. AND SHE SEEMED LIKE SUCH A CUTE AND INNOCENT GIRL.
OLDER WOMEN ARE SCARY...
The End

THE TRUTH IS, I'VE BEEN HIDING SOMETHING. I'M REALLY A HUGE JACKIE CHAN FAN! WELL, NOT JUST JACKIE CHAN, BUT ALSO BRUCE LEE! I'M REALLY A FAN OF FIST-FIGHTING. IT'S PROBABLY BECAUSE THE WORLD I WAS BROUGHT UP IN WAS THE GOLDEN AGE OF BRUCE LEE AND JACKIE CHAN. NOT TO MENTION THAT ONE OF MY HOBBIES IS PLAYING VIDEO GAMES, AND ALL THE ONES I OWN ARE FIGHTING ONES.

THAT'S WHY I'VE BEEN THINKING THAT I WANT TO DRAW A FIGHTING MANGA SOMETIME...BUT THAT'S STILL UP IN THE AIR.
-TAMAKOSHI

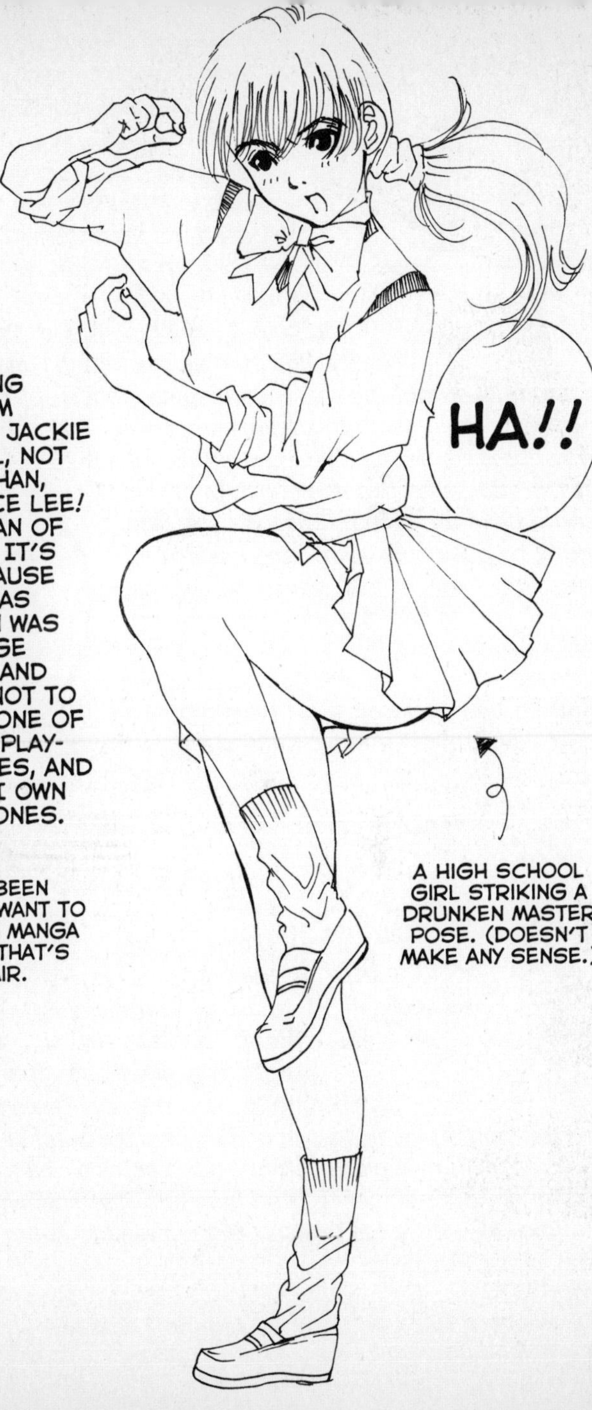
HA!!

A HIGH SCHOOL GIRL STRIKING A DRUNKEN MASTER POSE. (DOESN'T MAKE ANY SENSE.)

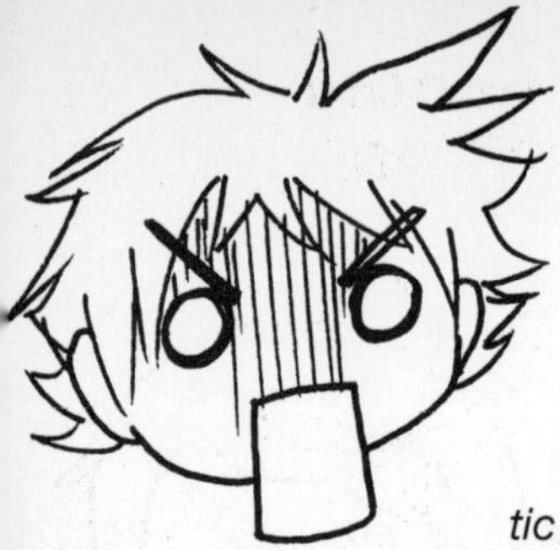

By far, the worst coupling for this volume of **Boys Be** was Report 7. There's absolutely NO way Marina and Shinya would be a compatible pair. After that messy Christmas Eve party, you can bet your bottom dollar that they'll never hook up again (much less look each other in the eye at school). Let's be realistic here. Horny boy. Alone. Drunk girl. Reindeer outfit. That's just a formula for disaster. Guys, if you're ever thinking that a drunk girl's gonna appear before your very eyes like a gift from above, think again. Best to send her on her way home as soon as you can rather than entertain yourself with some cheap panty shots and drunkard's breath, because she's going to be puking up something nasty in no time flat. And I'm sure you don't wanna spend your Christmas day cleaning up the mess.

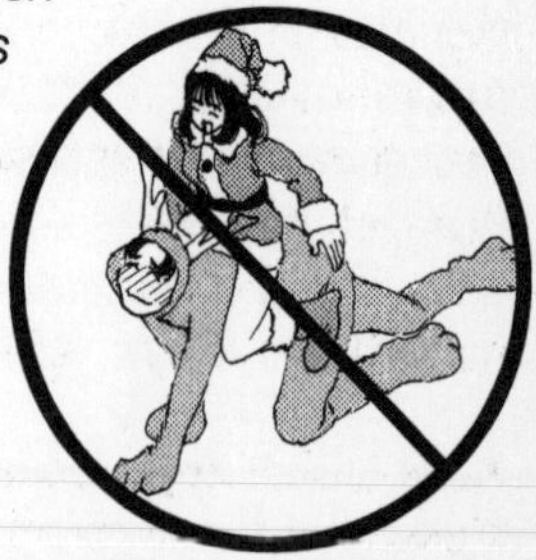

Bottom line: Hold on to at least SOME of your dignity, both you girls and guys.

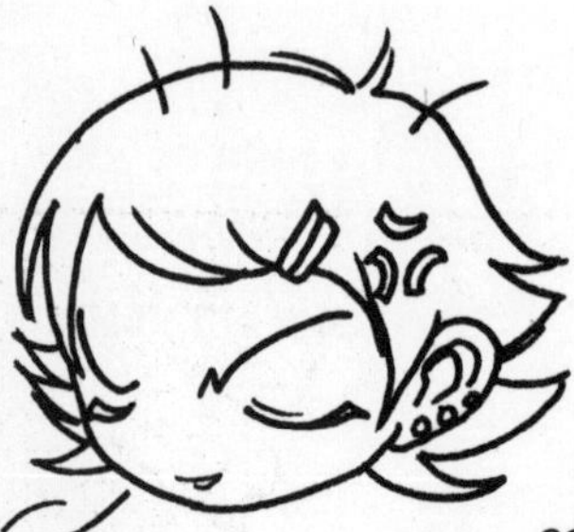

Report 6 was another atomic bomb of mistakes and regret. Would you let a simple-minded waitress, who's only trained to serve tea and some T&A, make you turn against your best dude? Poor, clueless Izumi's found herself caught in a power struggle between two lifelong friends, Yuu and Takeshi, only to have herself fought over like a piece of meat in the butcher shop window. Going out with the girl your friend has a crush on behind his BACK?! Come on, people, we've seen how this little scenario turns out in the movies! Lucky for Takeshi, Yuu decided to submit to the Alpha dog, or fur would fly.

Best advice: Back off from your friend's crushes. You're just gonna get hurt.

Twin Talk: A Guy's Guide to Girls
By Kathy and Chrissy Schilling

Hands down, Masahiro from Report 4 is a dream-guy come true. His innocent nature, amazing sense of generosity and appreciation for a really great gal... sigh...I melted the first time I read it. (^_^) I mean, from the start he's different from the rest of the guys: finding positive, encouraging points about Ogata's model-material height and there's not a glimmer of doubt for her when  *he first gets her invitation to date. Overall, his encouragement rather than teasing of her height -- finalized through his presentation of her desired high-heels -- is not only kind but manly! Not to mention how he apologizes for hurting her feelings. How many times does a guy go that far? Guys, take note!*

Final word: Appreciate a girl (or guy!) for who she is.
If you can't, you're probably into her for the wrong reasons.

GUY of the Month

Next Time in BOYS BE

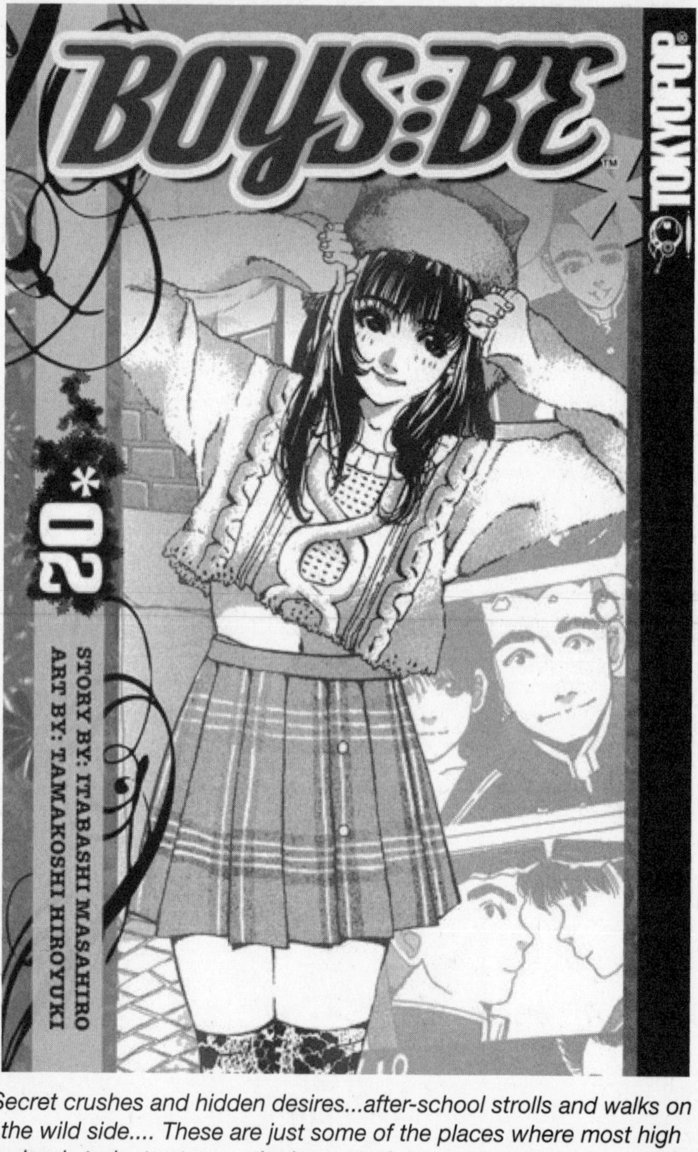
BOYS:BE
TOKYOPOP
*02
STORY BY: ITABASHI MASAHIRO
ART BY: TAMAKOSHI HIROYUKI

Secret crushes and hidden desires...after-school strolls and walks on the wild side.... These are just some of the places where most high school students stop on the journey of discovering love. Valentine's Day is approaching and the competition to give and get chocolates is causing a frenzy! Ordinary guys and the girls of their dreams tip-toe along the fine line between friends and something more!

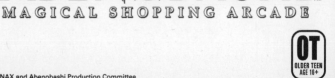

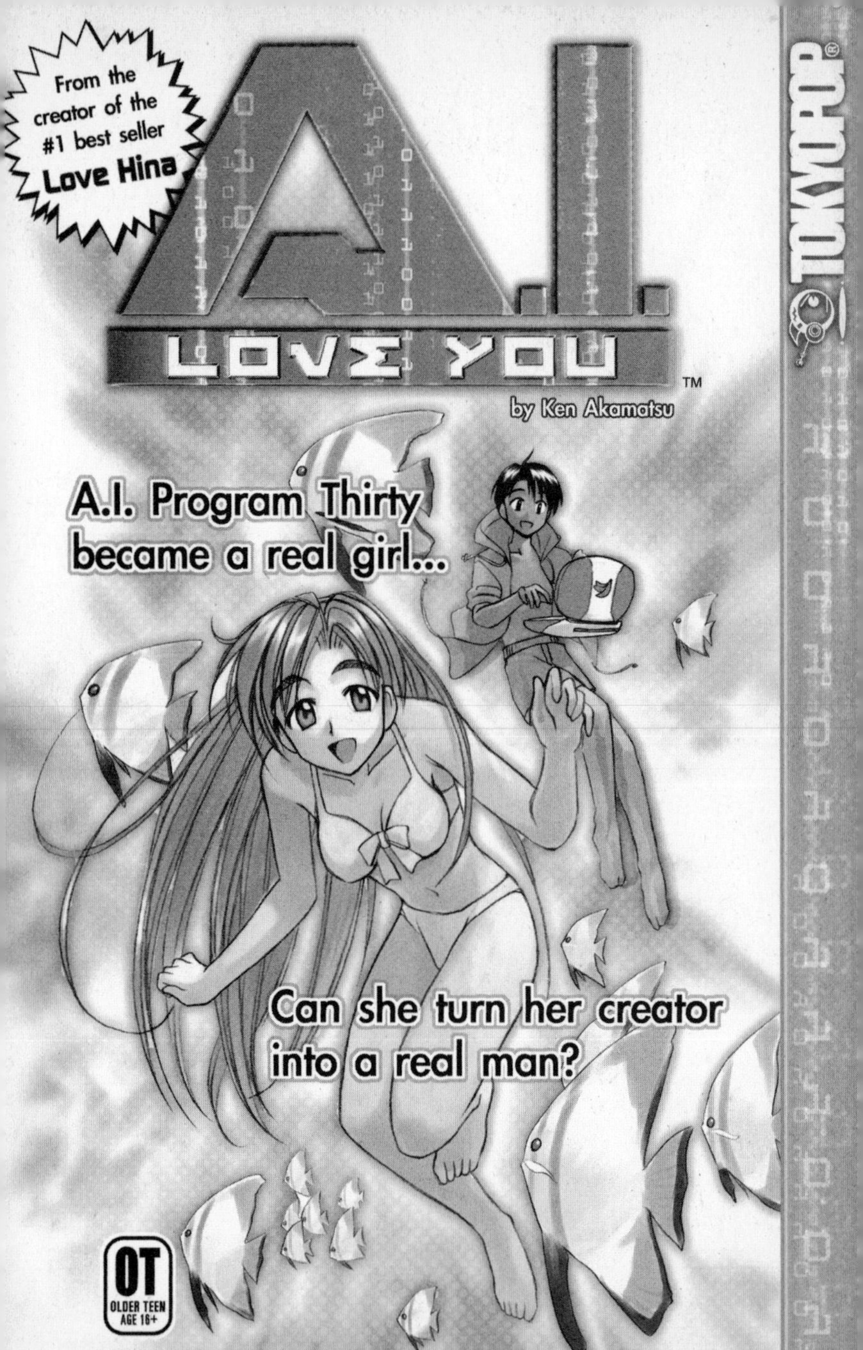
From the creator of the #1 best seller Love Hina
A.I. LOVE YOU™
by Ken Akamatsu
A.I. Program Thirty became a real girl...
Can she turn her creator into a real man?
OT
OLDER TEEN AGE 16+
TOKYOPOP
www.TOKYOPOP.com

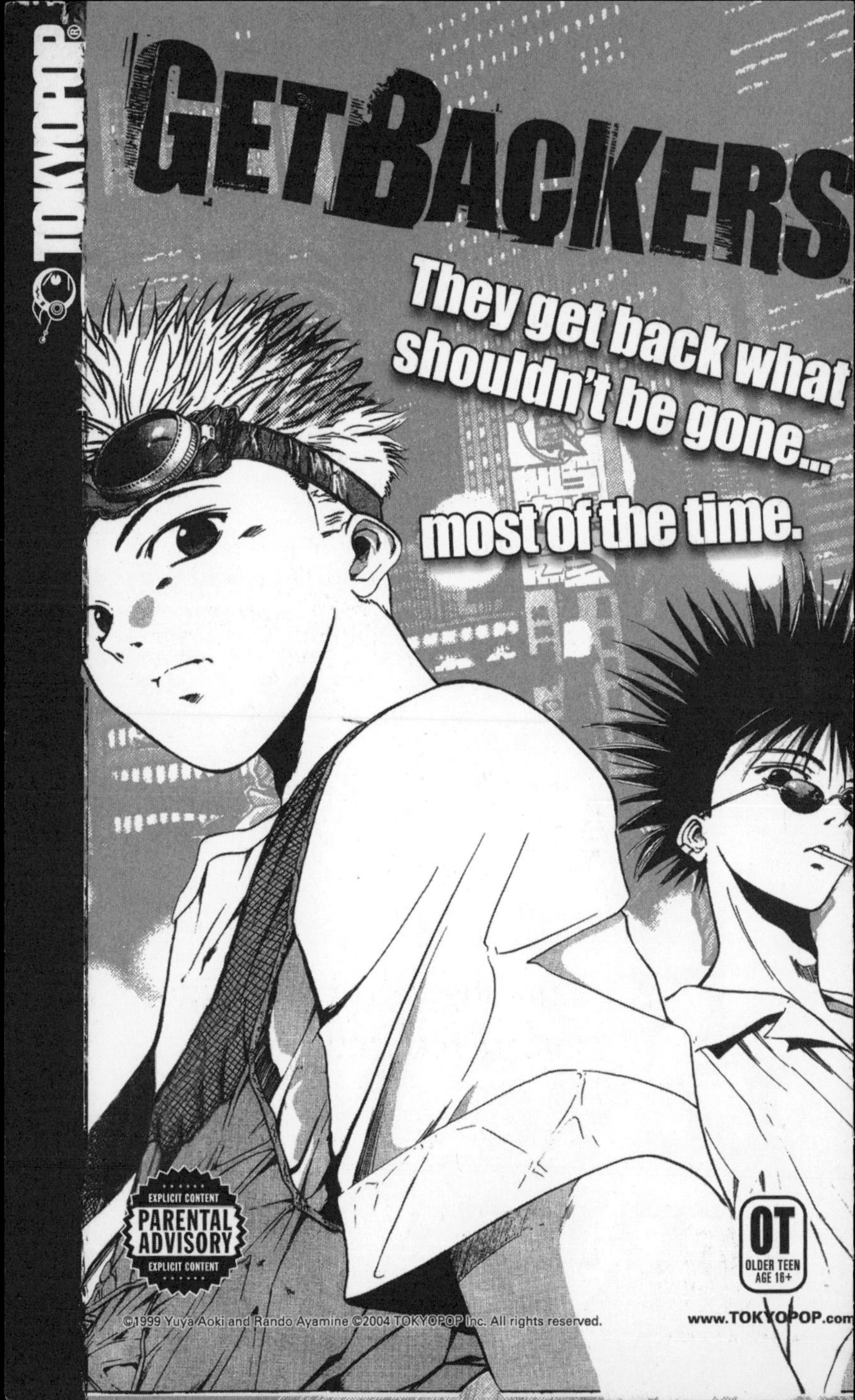
TOKYOPOP®
GETBACKERS™
They get back what shouldn't be gone...
most of the time.
EXPLICIT CONTENT
PARENTAL ADVISORY
EXPLICIT CONTENT
OT
OLDER TEEN AGE 16+
©1999 Yuya Aoki and Rando Ayamine ©2004 TOKYOPOP Inc. All rights reserved.
www.TOKYOPOP.com

LOVE (TRIANGLES) CAN DRIVE A GIRL TO THE EDGE.

TOKYOPOP

Crazy
Love
St----

LEGAL DRUG™

When no ordinary prescription will do...

FROM CLAMP CREATORS OF CHOBITS & TOKYO BABYLON

OT
OLDER TEEN
AGE 16+

ALSO AVAILABLE FROM TOKYOPOP®

PLANET LADDER
PLANETES
PRESIDENT DAD
PRIEST
PRINCESS AI
PSYCHIC ACADEMY
QUEEN'S KNIGHT, THE
RAGNAROK
RAVE MASTER
REALITY CHECK
REBIRTH
REBOUND
REMOTE
RISING STARS OF MANGA
SABER MARIONETTE J
SAILOR MOON
SAINT TAIL
SAIYUKI
SAMURAI DEEPER KYO
SAMURAI GIRL REAL BOUT HIGH SCHOOL
SCRYED
SEIKAI TRILOGY, THE
SGT. FROG
SHAOLIN SISTERS
SHIRAHIME-SYO: SNOW GODDESS TALES
SHUTTERBOX
SKULL MAN, THE
SNOW DROP
SORCERER HUNTERS
STONE
SUIKODEN III
SUKI
THREADS OF TIME
TOKYO BABYLON
TOKYO MEW MEW
TOKYO TRIBES
TRAMPS LIKE US
UNDER THE GLASS MOON
VAMPIRE GAME
VISION OF ESCAFLOWNE, THE
WARRIORS OF TAO
WILD ACT
WISH
WORLD OF HARTZ
X-DAY
ZODIAC P.I.

NOVELS

CLAMP SCHOOL PARANORMAL INVESTIGATORS
SAILOR MOON
SLAYERS

ART BOOKS

ART OF CARDCAPTOR SAKURA
ART OF MAGIC KNIGHT RAYEARTH, THE
PEACH: MIWA UEDA ILLUSTRATIONS

ANIME GUIDES

COWBOY BEBOP
GUNDAM TECHNICAL MANUALS
SAILOR MOON SCOUT GUIDES

TOKYOPOP KIDS

STRAY SHEEP

CINE-MANGA™

ALADDIN
CARDCAPTORS
DUEL MASTERS
FAIRLY ODDPARENTS, THE
FAMILY GUY
FINDING NEMO
G.I. JOE SPY TROOPS
GREATEST STARS OF THE NBA: SHAQUILLE O'NEAL
GREATEST STARS OF THE NBA: TIM DUNCAN
JACKIE CHAN ADVENTURES
JIMMY NEUTRON: BOY GENIUS, THE ADVENTURES OF
KIM POSSIBLE
LILO & STITCH: THE SERIES
LIZZIE MCGUIRE
LIZZIE MCGUIRE MOVIE, THE
MALCOLM IN THE MIDDLE
POWER RANGERS: DINO THUNDER
POWER RANGERS: NINJA STORM
PRINCESS DIARIES 2
RAVE MASTER
SHREK 2
SIMPLE LIFE, THE
SPONGEBOB SQUAREPANTS
SPY KIDS 2
SPY KIDS 3-D: GAME OVER
TEENAGE MUTANT NINJA TURTLES
THAT'S SO RAVEN
TOTALLY SPIES
TRANSFORMERS: ARMADA
TRANSFORMERS: ENERGON

You want it? We got it!
A full range of TOKYOPOP products are available now at:
www.TOKYOPOP.com/shop

07.15.04T

ALSO AVAILABLE FROM 🐱 TOKYOPOP®

MANGA

.HACK//LEGEND OF THE TWILIGHT
@LARGE
ABENOBASHI: MAGICAL SHOPPING ARCADE
A.I. LOVE YOU
AI YORI AOSHI
ANGELIC LAYER
ARM OF KANNON
BABY BIRTH
BATTLE ROYALE
BATTLE VIXENS
BOYS BE...
BRAIN POWERED
BRIGADOON
B'TX
CANDIDATE FOR GODDESS, THE
CARDCAPTOR SAKURA
CARDCAPTOR SAKURA - MASTER OF THE CLOW
CHOBITS
CHRONICLES OF THE CURSED SWORD
CLAMP SCHOOL DETECTIVES
CLOVER
COMIC PARTY
CONFIDENTIAL CONFESSIONS
CORRECTOR YUI
COWBOY BEBOP
COWBOY BEBOP: SHOOTING STAR
CRAZY LOVE STORY
CRESCENT MOON
CROSS
CULDCEPT
CYBORG 009
D•N•ANGEL
DEMON DIARY
DEMON ORORON, THE
DEUS VITAE
DIABOLO
DIGIMON
DIGIMON TAMERS
DIGIMON ZERO TWO
DOLL
DRAGON HUNTER
DRAGON KNIGHTS
DRAGON VOICE
DREAM SAGA
DUKLYON: CLAMP SCHOOL DEFENDERS
EERIE QUEERIE!
ERICA SAKURAZAWA: COLLECTED WORKS
ET CETERA
ETERNITY
EVIL'S RETURN
FAERIES' LANDING
FAKE
FLCL
FLOWER OF THE DEEP SLEEP, THE
FORBIDDEN DANCE
FRUITS BASKET

G GUNDAM
GATEKEEPERS
GETBACKERS
GIRL GOT GAME
GRAVITATION
GTO
GUNDAM SEED ASTRAY
GUNDAM WING
GUNDAM WING: BATTLEFIELD OF PACIFISTS
GUNDAM WING: ENDLESS WALTZ
GUNDAM WING: THE LAST OUTPOST (G-UNIT)
HANDS OFF!
HAPPY MANIA
HARLEM BEAT
HYPER RUNE
I.N.V.U.
IMMORTAL RAIN
INITIAL D
INSTANT TEEN: JUST ADD NUTS
ISLAND
JING: KING OF BANDITS
JING: KING OF BANDITS - TWILIGHT TALES
JULINE
KARE KANO
KILL ME, KISS ME
KINDAICHI CASE FILES, THE
KING OF HELL
KODOCHA: SANA'S STAGE
LAMENT OF THE LAMB
LEGAL DRUG
LEGEND OF CHUN HYANG, THE
LES BIJOUX
LOVE HINA
LOVE OR MONEY
LUPIN III
LUPIN III: WORLD'S MOST WANTED
MAGIC KNIGHT RAYEARTH I
MAGIC KNIGHT RAYEARTH II
MAHOROMATIC: AUTOMATIC MAIDEN
MAN OF MANY FACES
MARMALADE BOY
MARS
MARS: HORSE WITH NO NAME
MINK
MIRACLE GIRLS
MIYUKI-CHAN IN WONDERLAND
MODEL
MOURYOU KIDEN: LEGEND OF THE NYMPHS
NECK AND NECK
ONE
ONE I LOVE, THE
PARADISE KISS
PARASYTE
PASSION FRUIT
PEACH GIRL
PEACH GIRL: CHANGE OF HEART
PET SHOP OF HORRORS
PITA-TEN

07.15.04T

STOP!

This is the back of the book.
You wouldn't want to spoil a great ending!

This book is printed "manga-style," in the authentic Japanese right-to-left format. Since none of the artwork has been flipped or altered, readers get to experience the story just as the creator intended. You've been asking for it, so TOKYOPOP® delivered: authentic, hot-off-the-press, and far more fun!

DIRECTIONS

If this is your first time reading manga-style, here's a quick guide to help you understand how it works.

It's easy... just start in the top right panel and follow the numbers. Have fun, and look for more 100% authentic manga from TOKYOPOP®!